Penguin Books
Piaf

Simone Berteaut was born on 29 May 1918, in
Lyons. She was taken to Paris, when only eleven
days old, by her mother. Jean-Baptiste Berteaut
gave her his name, but Louis Gassion was in
fact her real father, making Simone and Edith
half-sisters. Her grandmother was a full-blooded
Indian and a descendant of the Incas.

Simone Berteaut was educated in the streets
of Paris. At the age of eleven, along with most
of the children who lived in the slums, she
began work in a factory. She did not meet her
half-sister until two years later. It was this
encounter that was completely to change her
life. From that moment on, Simone gave up
everything to sing in the streets with Edith, and
they stayed together for thirty years.

Piaf

SIMONE BERTEAUT

*Translated from the French
by Ghislaine Boulanger*

Penguin Books

Penguin Books Ltd, Harmondsworth,
Middlesex, England
Penguin Books, 625 Madison Avenue,
New York, New York 10022, U.S.A.
Penguin Books Australia Ltd, Ringwood,
Victoria, Australia
Penguin Books Canada Ltd, 2801 John Street,
Markham, Ontario, Canada L3R 1B4
Penguin Books (N.Z.) Ltd, 182–190 Wairau Road,
Auckland 10, New Zealand

First published in England by W. H. Allen & Co. Ltd, 1970
Published in Penguin Books 1973
Reprinted 1974, 1975, 1976, 1977, 1979

Copyright © Opera Mundi, Paris, 1969
English translation © W. H. Allen & Co. Ltd, 1970
All rights reserved

Made and printed in Great Britain by
Hazell Watson & Viney Ltd, Aylesbury, Bucks
Set in Linotype Pilgrim

*For you, Edith, I have written this book
faithfully, without cheating; it contains your
laughter and your tears.*

*Since you died I have been waiting for
you to take my hand, but God, the way
is long!*

*I would like to thank Marcelle Routier
who helped me so much in the writing
of this book.*

CONTENTS

LIST OF ILLUSTRATIONS

ACKNOWLEDGEMENTS

The author and publishers are grateful to the following music publishers for kindly having consented to our using extracts from the songs of Edith Piaf in this book:

Les Editions Paul Beuscher-Arpège, 25 boulevard Beaumarchais, Paris 4e
  'Simple comme bonjour' (*R. Carlès, Louiguy*)
  'Elle fréquentait la rue Pigalle' (*R. Asso, L. Maitrier*)
  'Où sont-ils tous mes copains?' (*M. Monnot, Piaf*)
  'De l'autr' côté d'la rue' (*M. Emer*)
  'Le Brun et le blond' (*H. Contet, M. Monnot*)
  'Elle a des yeux' (*M. Monnot, Piaf*)
  'Mais qu'est-ce qu'j'ai?' (*H. Betty, Piaf*)
  'Petite si jolie' (*M. Achard, M. Monnot*)
  'Demain il fera jour' (*M. Achard, M. Monnot*)
  'Mariage' (*H. Contet, M. Monnot*)
  'Elle est formidable' (*G. Bécaud, R. Vérnardet*)
  'A quoi ça sert l'amour?' (*M. Emer*)
  'Et pourtant' (*M. Emer, P. Brasseur*)
  'C'est merveilleux' (*H. Contet, M. Monnot*)

Les Editions Chappell, 4 rue d'Argenson, Paris 8e
  'Margot coeur gros' (*M. Vendôme, F. Véran*) Copyright Chappell S.A.

Les Editions Salabert, 22 rue Chauchat, Paris 9e
  'Milord' (*M. Monnet, Moustaki*)

Les Editions Raoul Breton, 3 rue Rossini, Paris 9e
  'La Petite Boutique' (*R. Carlès, O. Hodeige*) © 1937–1965 by Ed. Vianelly
  'Bal dans ma rue' (*Michel Emer*) © 1949 by Ed. Edimarton
  'Monsieur Lenoble' (*M. Emer*) © 1948 by France Music Co. N.Y. Ed. Breton
  'L'Hymne à l'amour (*M. Monnot, Piaf*) © 1949 by Ed. Edimarton

Book One

Her life was so sad that it
was almost too beautiful to
be true
— SACHA GUITRY

I

FROM PAVEMENT
TO BROTHEL

Edith Piaf was my sister: we shared the same father, Louis Gassion. He wasn't a bad sort but he was a ladies' man who was never known to turn down an invitation to prove his manhood. He couldn't identify all his kids, because his girl friends were not always too sure who had fathered which child. He claimed some who did not belong to him, but there were others he never knew. He had more than nineteen, but don't try to find them now! In those days no one bothered to contact the marriage authorities before a baby was made, or after it was born.

But I did have another father, and this one was recognized officially. Jean-Baptiste Berteaut gave me his name, even though he was not responsible for my entry into the world.

My mother, married at fifteen, divorced at sixteen, already had three daughters of indeterminate origin when she met my real father. At that time she lived in the same building as he did at cité Falguière. Dad had been mobilized, and I was conceived when he came home on leave. It was not a chance meeting, as my mother and Louis had been going together for some time.

But this relationship did not stop my mother looking for other men; they were scarce in wartime. As soon as Dad had left for the front, she ran into an eighteen-year-old, Jean-Baptiste Berteaut. Fresh from Autun, Jean-Baptiste didn't think twice about getting saddled with a wife, two years his senior, three daughters, and another on the way . . . me.

Thus on his twentieth birthday when poor Jean-Baptiste left for his regiment, he was supporting five children, and before I had reached the age of reason there were nine at home; not all of them belonging to Berteaut, as we called him. Strange as it may seem my mother and he adored each other. But occasionally she would go out on the town with a well-filled pocket-book, and come back with the pocket-book empty but a new bun in the oven.

By mere chance I was born in Lyons, but when I was only eleven days old my mother took me with her to Paris, where she sold flowers in the streets outside the Belleville church in the place de la Mare.

In our home, education was not considered indispensable, and I hardly ever went to school. But I went quite willingly at the beginning of each term to take advantage of the extra warmth and light, and on the first of January to get shoes when they handed them out. Apart from that, however, Mother saw no point in education. 'It's like money,' she would say, 'if you don't have a lot, you're poor.'

At that time school was not compulsory, so I learned my lessons in the streets. They aren't very strong on etiquette there, but I quickly learned a great deal about life.

I often went to see Gassion, my father, in his lodgings at cité Falguière. I enjoyed being with him. I was sure that he loved me, because he thought that I resembled him, with my small-boned, supple body and big dark eyes exactly like his own. He taught me tricks, gave me big glasses full of pure grenadine with lumps of ice, and pocket money to spend. I really liked my father.

He had no use for nicknames, unlike most parents, and he called me Simone. He was always pleased to see me, and anxious to confirm that I had grown. That was probably his way of judging whether my mother was feeding me properly. On that basis, however, you might suppose that I often went hungry, because to this day I am only four feet ten and a half inches tall.

Dad was an acrobat. He did not perform at funfairs, or circuses, or music halls; the pavement was his stage. He understood the street, and knew just which strip of pavement paid off. He did not set up shop just anywhere. He was respected in the business as a true professional. When I said 'I'm Gassion's daughter' it really meant something.

When he found a wide avenue or street, where there was room for passersby to jostle and crane their necks, Dad rolled out his carpet. It was just a little scrap of threadbare cloth, but they knew at once that this was for real, that they were going to be entertained.

He would take a swig of wine before launching into his patter. Edith, who had spent six years with him, from eight years old until she was fourteen, imitated him well, and in a raucous shout exactly like his, 'You're in for a treat now, ladies and gentlemen. This isn't a trick, the artist himself is going to work before your very eyes, no safety net, no sawdust, no shit! It's for real. For a hundred centimes we'll begin.'

At that moment a stooge would throw ten cents on to the rug, and another, twenty.

'I am going to perform before you, for my honour and your pleasure, one of the most unique acrobatic tricks in the world. The great Barnum himself, the circus Emperor, has offered me fabulous sums to join him, but I said to him, "A man from Paris can't be bought." It's true, ladies and gentlemen, I said, "You keep your money and I'll keep my freedom."'

'Come on, try a little harder and the show will begin. Crowned heads of Europe and beyond have been stunned by my act. Even King Edward of England and the Prince of Wales came down from their palace into the street like everyone else to see me. Art makes equals of everyone. Come on, my lords, a bit more money, and I'll begin.'

And Dad gave them their money's worth because he was a good acrobat.

I had just about learned to walk when he started teaching me to tie myself in knots. One day he said to my mother, 'I must teach Simone how to do something, so that she can make a living,' but Mother did not give a damn whether I made a living or not!

I lived completely in the streets. My mother came home late if she came home at all. I was too small to have any notion of what she did. Sometimes she would take me into a bar and dance while I slept on a chair. Once or twice she forgot me and she would have to pick me up from the city orphanage the following morning. The state always took care of me. I remember that, later on when I was five, she became a caretaker somewhere in Ménilmontant.

I used to see my father, but I didn't know Edith who was living in Bernay. I was two and a half years younger than her. I had heard people mention her, but that was all, although I knew that Dad loved her more than me. 'Well, naturally,' he said. 'You have a mother, and she doesn't.'

I suppose I did have one, though I hardly knew it; but for a long time I thought she was as good as any other.

I was born in a hospital, but Edith was born in the street, right there on the pavement.

'Edith wasn't born like the rest of us,' Father told me. 'It was in the middle of the war, after the battle of the Marne. I was in the infantry, part of the "do or die" troops. The poor are always shoved up front where the action is because there are more of them. Edith's mother was called Line Marsa, but her real name was Anita Maillard: she was a singer, born in a circus, a real child of the sawdust. One day I got a letter from her saying, ' "The baby is due soon, ask if you can come home on leave."

'They let me go; it was a real stroke of luck. The flowers in the guns had faded months before. We didn't believe in the glorious war any longer. Berlin was too far away. I made tracks for home. There was no coal, no coffee, no wine, and the black bread was full of straw. I found all the neighbours clucking around Line. "Awful, isn't it, what with the war and her husband at the front."

' "Out of the way, ladies," I said to them. "I'll take care of everything." It was 19 December 1915.

(When Edith told the story of her birth, she used to add, 'Three o'clock in the morning in the middle of winter was hardly the time to slip out of my mother's belly to see if it was any better outside than in.')

'I had hardly had time to say hi, drop my pack, get a bite to eat, and get my head down when Line started shaking me, crying, "Louis, this is it, the pains have started. I'm in agony, the baby's coming."

'We staggered down the street like drunks, Line clasping her stomach with both hands. We stopped under a gas-lamp, and she gasped, "Leave me, run to the cops and ask for an ambulance."

'A few yards away there was a police station on the rue

Ramponneau. I rushed in shouting, "My wife's having a baby out there on the pavement."

' "Good God," replied the grey-moustached police chief. And the cops pulled on their capes and took off as if they were all qualified midwives.

'So my daughter was born under a street lamp in front of 72 rue de Belleville on a policeman's cloak.'

A pretty good début for a singer of songs about real life.

'Her mother wanted to call her Edith in memory of Edith Cavell, an English spy who had been shot by the Germans a few days before on 12 December. "It's very distinguished," she said. "With a Christian name like that she's bound to be noticed." '

An astrologer could not have predicted Edith's life more accurately.

When Dad went back to war, his wife was still in the Hospital Tenon.

At the end of two months, Line, who, as Dad remarked, was a cold fish in spite of being an artist, packed her daughter off to her mother who lived with her family on rue Rébeval. I regret to say that they did not have much in common with your ideal children's picture-book family. The grandmother and her old man were like a couple of sponges soaked in red wine. 'You can pickle yourself in alcohol,' the old girl would say as she put a little in Edith's baby-bottle. Edith was never told what her grandmother's name was; she called her Mena.

Line meanwhile had stopped writing to Private Louis Gassion, chasing lice in the trenches in company with other heroes. She had taken her leave without much fuss, 'Louis, we're through. I have left the little one with my mother. Don't bother to come and see me when you get back.'

This, however, was no reason for Louis to abandon his child. On his last leave, at the end of 1917, he went to see how Edith was doing. She had rickets and looked as though her balloon head were perched on four matches. A little scarecrow. She was so dirty that you would have needed a pair of pincers to pick her up, and Dad wasn't too fussy about things like that normally. 'I must do something,' he said to himself. 'When this bloody war is over I'll be going back to the streets, but the gutter isn't the

best nursery for a little girl.' At that time there were fewer
welfare benefits than there are now. Besides, it would never have
occurred to him to make use of them. Despite his poverty and
his lackadaisical ways, he would never have left his daughter in
a state-run orphanage, like abandoning a puppy to the animal
pound.

And so father Gassion, feeling pretty blue, settled down in a
bar and ordered a glass of absinthe. Usually he only got drunk
on red wine, it was cheaper and better for the health, but that
day he needed something stronger. He decided to write a letter
to his mother who cooked for a cousin of hers. The cousin was
a nice woman who could have been a farmer's wife, but had
chosen instead to run a brothel in Bernay, a town in Normandy.

The grandmother and her cousin replied, 'Don't worry, we'll
come and fetch the child ourselves.'

Instantly the rescue party set out: Louise (the grandmother)
and Marie (the Madame and cousin) went up to Paris to tear
Edith away from her maternal grandmother, who kept insisting
that 'She was having such a lovely time here with us, such a
lovely time.'

When they got the child home, the prostitutes were all delighted. 'Having a child in the house brings good luck,' they
said, and immediately got down to scraping her clean.

Two, three, four times the bath was filled, the dirt leaving
great rings around the tub. How they scrubbed while Edith
cried and tried to fight them off.

Later, Edith spoke of it herself. 'Grandma Louise had bought
new clothes for me, but when she threw my old rags in the
garbage I cried. Then she wanted to take off my shoes, and I
started to bawl, "Those are my Sunday shoes." My toes were
coming through.'

While they were washing her face, they noticed that her eyes
were glued shut and put it down to the dirt. It was not until two
months later that one of the girls noticed that Edith kept bumping into everything, and that she looked at the light and the
sun without flinching. Edith was blind.

Edith remembered that time very well. She used to speak of it
with a kind of terror which she never overcame.

The tarts adored her, and played with her. 'They were very sweet to me, I was their mascot. I saw nothing, but I heard everything. They were good girls. Working in a brothel is very different from street-walking. They're two separate worlds and they despise each other.

'I had learned to walk holding my hands out in front of me to protect myself from bumping into everything. My fingers and hands had become sensitive. I could identify materials by touch, skins as well. I would say, "This is Carmen," or "Here's Rose." But above all I lived in a world of sounds and words, those that I didn't understand I turned over and over in my mind.

'I loved the player piano much more than the regular piano, which was only used on Saturday evenings when the pianist came.

'Since I lived in the dark, in a night-time world, I was very sensitive, and there is one sentence that I shall never forget. It was about dolls. I had never had a doll, and when someone wanted to give me one, Grandmother said, "It's not worth it. She doesn't see anything and she breaks everything."

'But the tarts, sweet girls who saw in me the baby they never had, or dreamed of having, made rag dolls for me. I spent whole days sitting on a little stool with a lapful of dolls I couldn't see, trying to get to know them with my hands.

'My other grandmother had taught me to drink red wine. At Bernay when they gave me water instead, I started to cry. "I don't want water. Mena said it's bad for you, it makes you sick. I don't want to get sick."

'As I sat on my little stool, surrounded by night, I tried to sing. I could listen to myself for hours on end. When they asked me, "Where did you learn that?" I replied, "Rue Ramponneau," and they knew what I meant. Mena used to go to a bar there. She would take me along with her to the local bars and dance halls, and say in her strong accent, "Sing, baby, sing 'L'Hirondelle du Faubourg'."

> On l'appelait l'hirondelle du faubourg
> Ce n'était qu'une pauvre fille d'amour . . .

[They called her the swallow of the slums. She was nothing but a poor tart.]

'That made everyone laugh and they paid for a round.'

Edith well remembered her life in Bernay. She recalled that the women were kind, that there were parties every evening, that everything was gay. It smelt of cigarette smoke and liquor, and champagne corks popped all night. She heard the sounds in the distance, for her grandmother did not feel she belonged in the *salon*. Her ears picked up what they could as she hung around in the hallways.

Some of the customers knew her. To Edith they fell into two categories: those whose knees were covered in fine cloth and who had cultivated voices, and the others who sounded rougher and whose trouser legs prickled.

The 'ladies', as Edith called them, were gentle and smelt good. After she left, she did not see them again until the death of her father, when some of them came to the funeral.

'I didn't know Dad in those days. I had never "heard" him – I can't say "seen" him.

'I was four years old, I think, when they took me to the ocean. I found it full of strange music and new smells. And the sand wasn't like the regular ground where they were always saying, "Don't touch, it's dirty." I filled my hands with it and I let it slide through. It was like water that I could hold on to.

'Then I heard a man's voice I didn't know saying, "They tell me there's a little girl called Edith here."

'I held out my hands to touch him and said, "Who are you?"

' "Guess."

' "It's my daddy," I cried.

'I saw him, for the first time, two years later.

'I've always believed that that journey through the darkness made me more sensitive than other people. Much later, when I wanted really to hear something, really "see" a song, I would shut my eyes. And when I wanted to bring out a sound from my guts, deep down, as if it were coming from very far away, I would shut my eyes.'

I was very young when I first heard them talking about my sister Edith. My mother, chatting with her friends, had said, 'Yes, Simone has a sister. Her name is Edith. She's blind.'

So I had a blind sister, or half-sister at least. She was living in a dump with my father's mother, and I wasn't really interested in her. There were already a number of half-brothers and half-sisters at home, and I didn't see why she should be more interesting than the others. We all had different fathers. So what?

Edith was blind for nearly three years. Shortly after her birth a cataract had developed and no one had even noticed.

Her Grandmother Louise took her to Lisieux and it was there that miraculously she regained her sight. Indeed, to Edith it was a real miracle, one that she always believed in. From then on she prayed regularly to Saint Theresa. For a long time she wore a medallion, and she always had a little picture of the saint by her bed.

It was quite extraordinary, the way the miracle came about. I think it was Dad who told Edith how it happened. But even at seven she remembered something. Edith always had an excellent memory.

Life in Bernay was not like the rue Rébeval. She was now the centre of attention. If you live in a brothel, you see the world, a high-class world full of educated gentlemen. Instead of thinking a little blind girl is a stroke of bad luck, they try to make her better. Even if it costs money.

And whore-houses make a lot of money, even in Bernay. The restoration of Edith's sight could certainly be called a miracle. Edith's grandmother had taken her to be treated in Lisieux. 'There's not much hope that she'll recover,' the doctor said.

All the same, Grandmother took Edith regularly for her treatment. The child didn't say a thing, although they used silver nitrate which must have burned dreadfully. In her darkness she dreamed of light, of sunshine. She tried to remember rue Rébeval in Paris as it was when she could see. But she was very small, and she had never seen well. Light, to her, was something hazy.

In the brothel, as throughout the countryside, they worshipped the little saint of Lisieux. One day Carmen said, 'Why can't St Theresa, with her shower of roses, perform a miracle for our little one?'

The whole company agreed, even the girls who had no real

reason to believe in miracles. Grandmother and the Madame thought it was a good idea, and between customers the girls said a few prayers.

A tart's prayers – and her money – are as good as anybody else's, and the Madame vowed that if the child got her sight back she would donate ten thousand francs to the church – in 1921 that was quite a sum.

The date was fixed: 19 August 1921. The 15th is a holiday, and you can't shut up shop on holidays. The brothel was in a state of turmoil. 'We're all going, girls,' said Madame. 'We'll lock the house up. It'll give you a breath of air.'

The girls swapped clothes – 'Grab my black hat and gimme your smart little dress, it looks quite decent.'

Naturally, Edith and her grandmother were included in the outing. The child was dressed to the nines. The tarts were rigged out like real ladies, with hats and gloves – but no make-up.

In the parlour that morning Madame clapped her hands, like any other day, and made her inspection. She felt their shoes were out of place, too much polish, and the heels were too high. The girls went out so rarely that they only had work shoes.

As they made their way through Bernay, the curtains were tugged this way and that. 'Get your boys home quick, the girls are out!' But it was not like that at all; *these* 'ladies' were on a pilgrimage.

That day Lisieux witnessed an almost unbelievable procession; all the tarts walking one behind the other through the town. You would have thought they were a bunch of convent girls on an outing the way they kept their eyes lowered. They went into the basilica with the child, and all day, or almost all day, they burned candles and said their rosaries. To kill two birds with one stone, as it were, they also asked favours for themselves. They sighed and luxuriated in the holiness of it all. When they left the basilica they felt utterly sanctified – except for their feet. 'My feet are killing me. Honestly, I wish I could take off these damn shoes.'

That night, dead tired but pleased with the work that they had done, the 'ladies' went home and had a wild party without any men at all. They even polished off some champagne. They went to bed feeling that a good job had been well done, and patiently they waited for the miracle. It was fixed for 25 August, the festival of St Louis, her father's name-day. 'St Theresa, let the little one see on St Louis's day,' Grandmother had pleaded.

The miracle is that it actually happened on that very day.

From early morning until noon the girls had risen, one after the other, and slipped into the kitchen in their dressing-gowns, their heavy perfumes mixing with the spicy smell of the sauces. Yawning and with vacant expressions, they peered at Edith. They looked at her eyes. They asked her questions. 'You know that the sun's shining?' And she held her hand out.

'Yes, I can feel it, it's hot.'

By seven o'clock in the evening the whole house was demoralized. The miracle was pretty slow in coming. They no longer dared believe in it.

'It's time she went to bed. Perhaps it'll work tomorrow,' advised Grandmother.

But where was Edith? She was in the parlour with her hands on the keys of the piano, which was no surprise to anyone. She tapped out 'Au clair de la lune' with one finger; she enjoyed doing that.

'Go to bed, Edith,' said Grandmother.

'No, I'm looking at something very pretty.'

That fairly took her breath away. Was this the miracle they had waited for, believed in, and then given up hoping for?

Grandmother was trembling. 'What's pretty, my treasure?'

'That.'

'You can see?'

Yes, she could see. And the first thing that she saw was the keyboard. Everyone fell to her knees, and crossed herself. The brothel was closed. Too bad for the customers!

Edith was seven.

When Father came back, he was very happy. Edith was now like the others, she could see. He had a normal child.

For about a year, Edith went to school. She had a lot to learn, but the good people of Bernay were appalled. When Dad went to Bernay, the curé of the school gave him a lecture.

'You'll have to take the child away. You must understand that her presence here is a scandal. When she couldn't see it was all right for your little girl to be brought up in an establishment of that kind, but now she can see, sir, what an example for her pure little soul. We can't tolerate this.'

And there was Edith, the pure little soul, standing at her father's side.

Those were not good years. Edith often spoke of them with bitterness. On the other hand, Dad thought it was all rather a joke, and he talked about them willingly.

From the age of seven until she was fifteen, he dragged Edith from dance halls to bistros, from alleys to squares, from towns to villages.

'I walked so far with Dad that it's a miracle I have any feet left at all. My legs should be worn down to the knees.

'My job was to take up the collection, to smile and say "daddy" – that encouraged a lot of people to give money.

'In order to get together enough money to pay for an absinthe, he was quite cunning. We would go into a café. He would seek out a woman who wasn't too hard-looking and he'd say to me, "If you sing something for the lady, she might give you some money to buy chocolates."

'I sang and he pushed me towards the women. Then other people would give money too. He took my earnings, saying very paternally, "Give me your money, I'll look after it for you." We had to live.

'He didn't tell me, but I knew that he loved me. And I didn't say anything about it to him either.

'One evening in a mining town, Bruay les Mines, I think, I was singing in a café, and this wooden-faced couple was listening to me very disapprovingly. "She'll strain her vocal chords," the woman said. Even at that time, I belted it out at the top of my voice.

' "Where's your mummy?" she asked.

' "She hasn't got a mother," Dad replied.

'Well, that started off a whole flood of advice and fond attention. At the end of an hour, after having bought drinks for my father and a grenadine for "the little one", they offered to look after me. I could go and stay with them, and learn how to sing properly. They wanted to adopt me and offered to pay Dad a lot of money. He absolutely hit the roof.

' "Are you out of your minds? My daughter's not for sale; perhaps she hasn't got a mother of her own any more, but she has lots of stepmothers."

'That was true, I never wanted for female company. He was always changing women.

'Dad knew when he was on to a good thing. And he had found a very good thing. When he had finished his number, he picked up the rag which was on the carpet, wiped his hands with it, and announced, "And now my little girl is going to come out and take up the collection. And then, to thank you, she's going to do three perilous forward somersaults, and three backwards."

'And so I circulated among the spectators and went back to Dad. Then he became very concerned, he felt my forehead and said, "Ladies and Gentlemen, are you heartless enough to allow this little girl to do these dangerous somersaults with a hundred and three degree fever? She's ill, and your money will allow me to take her to the doctor. But I'm an honourable man, I don't break my word. If there is anyone here who wants to see her do it, she will."

'And then once more he would slowly look around the audience saying, "If you want to see her perform, raise your hand."

'No one dared raise his hand when he looked at the pale, skinny little urchin with her damp, dome-like forehead, and the feverish eyes which seemed to consume her whole face.

'Only once did the plan backfire. A grumpy old man protested, "I paid for it and I want to see it. This is just a put-on." Dad didn't turn a hair. "The child will sing 'J'suis vache' for you."

> *Trois semaines après qu'il était parti*
> *Je couchais avec tous ses amis*
> *Ah j'mériterais des coups de cravaches*
> *J'suis vache*

'I was nine years old.'

That was the first time that Edith sang in the street. It would not be the last. Father had dreamed of turning her into an acrobat, but he sighed, 'This child's got all her talent in her throat, and none in her limbs.'

No, he was not a bad father, he did more than could be expected of him, even if he did it badly. I would rather have been in Edith's place with Dad than with my mother. He would have liked to have had me, but he couldn't take on another child, poor thing. What the hell could he do? Even when she was a kid, Edith was enough of a handful for one man.

2

THE STREET MY TEACHER

It was when I was about six that I heard people talking about
Edith's miracle. Mother either spoke about it with awe or
laughed it off, according to her mood.

I also knew that Edith had been living with whores in a
brothel somewhere. I knew what whores were, I saw them and
talked to them every day, but I had no idea what a brothel was.
My mother explained to me that it was a kind of hotel where
prostitutes were locked up at night. I thought they must be
pretty stupid to let themselves be locked up when they could go
free on the streets, but by the time I was twelve I had better
things to think about than my fifteen-year-old half-sister.

I knew that Edith had been living with Dad and that she had
run away. 'That girl takes after her mother, running off like
that,' Mother said to me. I didn't think it was so wicked, in fact
I envied her.

Dad was still giving me bone-breaking lessons. We met at the
home of another acrobat. His name was Camille Ribon, but we
called him Alverne. Each time I performed a trick, Dad said,
'Your sister can't do that.' And I was quite pleased with myself,
but it was slight praise after all.

Alverne often saw Edith and encouraged her to work. She had
done well to leave, but Dad made her come to his sessions all the
same. He felt they were all part of a daughter's education. He
also taught her French history. When he forgot a date or he got
stuck over some fact or another, he concluded, 'It's such a long
time ago, give or take a hundred years, it doesn't matter.'

As the rue des Pancoaux was next to the rue des Amandiers, I
often went to Alverne's house. 'Simone should come round and
see her sister one evening after work,' Dad said to my mother.

I was twelve and a half, but I already went to work. I worked
at the Wonder factory, assembling headlamps; it was much more

complicated than making batteries, and I earned eighty-four francs a week for working a ten-hour day. I ran a machine called a bezel. The conditions were criminal, but we accepted them without question.

One day Mother said to me, 'You know, your half-sister Edith is at Alverne's today, let's go over. I want to see what she looks like.'

I was pleased to be going to Alverne's. His apartment was scruffy, but we ate well there. That was all I cared about, I didn't think about meeting Edith.

It was a poorly furnished, filthy little room. There were some rings hanging in an empty door-frame. A shapeless creature in a boy's shirt was suspended from them. It would never have occurred to me that this was my sister had I not seen two little white hands poking through the shirt-sleeves.

'Are you Edith?'

'Yes.'

'Well, you're my sister then.'

Edith was fifteen. We started talking, a little guardedly at first. Then she asked me if I knew how to do a certain trick. Since I had had a lot of practice with Dad, I performed several somersaults while she watched. Edith always needed to admire people. In order for her to love someone, she had first to admire them. My somersaults astounded her. She was so happy she was dazed. Here I was, her younger sister, and I knew how to do something better than she. She thought that was great. But in the end it was she who bowled me over. She asked me what I did. 'Nothing very interesting,' I replied. 'I work in a factory and earn eighty-four francs a week.'

I could see that she was better dressed than I. She was wearing a sweater and skirt which fitted her, and which had obviously been bought for her. I was jealous of her, but Edith was never interested in someone unless she could do something for them. 'You can't go on doing that,' she said. 'Why don't you come with me?'

'But what do you do?'

'I sing in the streets.'

Now it was my turn to be astonished.

'Can you make money doing something like that?'

'You're darn right. No one pushes me around, I'm free, I work when I want to. I'll hire you, if you like.'

I couldn't believe it, I thought it was wonderful. I would have followed her to the ends of the earth. As, in fact, I did.

Edith decided to sing in the streets because when she trailed around after Dad she had sung in the bars and public squares. Dad wanted her to be an acrobat because he felt that a kid throwing herself around in public looks more pathetic than one who sings. But Edith really had no athletic talent. When Father wasn't in the streets of Paris, he performed in the barracks, particularly the ones around Versailles, which he liked very much. Obviously this made an impression on Edith, and it gave her what was to become a lifelong taste for soldiers, especially Colonials and Legionnaires.

There was a little bench at Alverne's, and we sat on it while Edith explained. 'Dad taught me the trade. I know the good neighbourhoods. I know what to do.'

'But you aren't with him any more?'

'No. We got fed up with each other; besides, he took all my money. And I must say, I'd had more than enough of my "step-mothers". Especially the last one. She was always slapping me and I'm too old for that. What's more, she threw me out because some boy gave me a kiss. Imagine!'

'When I left Dad, I wanted a more steady life. Up till then I'd snatched a bite whenever I could, but I knew I couldn't stand in the street and start to sing. There has to be two of you, and you look silly if there's no music. People don't take you seriously. You look more like a beggar.'

'So what did you do?'

'I read the "help wanted" column in *L'Ami du Peuple*. I chose it because of the name. It cost fifteen centimes. Well, I got a job in a dairy on the avenue Victor Hugo. It was awful. I got up at four in the morning, delivered the milk, and washed out the store. It's a very classy neighbourhood, but they're rotten tippers. It's no good waiting for a tip from other people's maids, they keep it for themselves, the bitches!'

'I couldn't stop myself from singing while I worked. But no

one liked my voice so they threw me out. Then I worked in another dairy, until I realized that I wasn't cut out for that kind of work.'

'How did you get round to singing?'

'There was this fellow, Raymond, who helped me decide. He liked my voice. He had a girl-friend called Rosalie, and together we formed a trio, Zizi, Zozette, and Zozou. We went round to the public squares and bars for a time. I'm on my own now, doing quite well. I learned to play the banjo too.'

It was a beautiful evening, I remember. When it was time for her to leave, Edith said to my mother, 'She can come and work with me, if you like. Singing in the streets is quite profitable, you'll see.'

My mother didn't give a damn what I did, I could be a tart for all she cared.

So we went off together. We got to the first street, it was the rue Vivienne. We must have made about a hundred francs that evening. When Mother saw that I could earn more this way than at the factory, she was delighted. 'We'll go halves,' Edith said.

We took my mother to one of the neighbourhood dances at the Temple, because she enjoyed them. It was a pretty awful affair, just a band of pimps and hooligans. There were two or three men playing rather half-heartedly on the accordion and banjo. They passed a hat round for the money, and we danced on sawdust. The place smelt of sweat and alcohol. The men there didn't wear collars, but artificial-silk cravats.

When my mother had used up all the money that Edith had given her – fifty francs – we left. All the way home she kept calling me 'Momone darling', and even went so far as to kiss me. Normally she couldn't stand to have me within spitting distance.

That evening I realized for the first time that we slept four to a bed, without sheets or blankets, and that life had more to offer. I had just met Edith, who was free to try something better. I had so much to think about that I couldn't fall asleep.

When I did get to sleep, I woke up with a start. Was I going to miss Edith? I jumped out of bed, pulled on my boots – I slept with all my clothes on – and rushed out.

Edith and I had decided to meet that day at ten o'clock. I was late. If I didn't make it I would miss the most important opportunity of my life. Edith was my one chance of escape.

Just as I arrived I met her coming out of Alverne's. A few seconds later and I would have been too late.

I might have seen her again, but it would not have been the same thing. I would have gone back to the factory, gone on living with and supporting my family – if you could call that collection of drunkards, pimps, and whores a family.

Being loved really meant something to a child from my neighbourhood. When she saw me her whole expression changed. She smiled, a smile such as one does not often see, and for the first time I knew what it was to be truly happy. We hugged each other as if we had been separated for ten years.

I put my hand in hers and we went off to sing in the streets. My job was to collect the money. It went well, and that evening when we went to my home we shared the money with Mother. Several days passed that way. Then Edith said, 'I ran away from Dad so that I could lead my own life, not to be nagged by your mother, or turn my profits over to her. You're not to, either. We must be free to work. Let's live together.'

I was dumb with happiness.

We went to find my mother, and Edith, who had a great deal of nerve, announced, 'I'm hiring your daughter on a full-time basis, she'll be my responsibility. She's going to come and live with me in my room.'

Practical as ever, my mother replied, 'That's fine with me, but you'll have to give me a receipt for her.' Edith was pretty cool. She made out an employment contract, the first she ever signed. It was quite funny because my mother hardly knew how to read, and Edith hardly knew how to write. But she did it all the same.

'I, Edith Giovanna Gassion, born 19 December 1915, in Paris, residing at 105 rue Orfila, an artist by profession, hereby declare that I have engaged Simone Berteaut for an indefinite period and undertake to supply her board and lodgings and a salary of fifteen francs a day. Signed in Paris, 1931.'

My mother kept that scrap of paper in a drawer for a long time. She showed it to everyone.

I was beside myself with joy at the thought that I would never have to return to that hole. Fifteen francs a day was a lot of money, much more than I'd earned in the factory, especially since I earned nothing on Sunday there and with Edith I did.

We left together. Two children without a cent in the world; small human beings, both under five foot and weighing about ninety pounds apiece.

Each day Edith gave my mother fifteen francs in coins, which she counted out, one by one, into Mother's hand. After a while we only went every other day, then every three days, and then we stopped going altogether. That is how, aged twelve and a half, I finally left my mother, who, let it be said, could not have cared less.

Life with Edith followed a certain pattern. She always knew how to organize things, and she had a way with people. She asked whatever she wanted of them, made the most outrageous requests, but I have rarely met anyone who was able to refuse her. It was impossible to say no to Edith.

I sang the first songs in the mornings. I sang badly. In fact, it's only recently that I have realized just how bad my voice is. I had always believed that Edith had stopped me singing out of jealousy. From time to time you get these crazy ideas. In any case, it did not matter very much to me, the most important thing was not singing but being close to Edith.

I sang the opening songs because Edith had trouble with her voice in the morning, and we had to wait for it to come back. Even when she was fifteen, she was completely toneless when she woke up. She had to drink some coffee and take Gargyl – a throat linctus – and we had to earn ten francs in order to buy it. So I used to gather the first ten francs. It took a long time!

Edith's voice returned as soon as she had swallowed the coffee and Gargyl, and we could go wherever we pleased. She could have sung all day and all night. The most extraordinary thing is that even then she had the same voice, the voice that made her famous, the voice that was soon to be worth millions.

She sang so loudly that her voice blotted out all the street sounds, even the car horns. 'You'll see, Momone, I'm going to sing so that my voice will be heard all over Paris; even at the top of the Eiffel Tower windows will open for people to listen to me.'

She was right, people tossed coins at us as though they came from heaven, she caused great traffic jams. So much so that one day a cop said to her, 'Look here, this is my beat, and I can't let you go on like this. Go across the street and sing "Le Chaland" [The Barge] for me. It's my favourite song and no one sings it like you.'

We crossed the street. Edith sang for him and he gave her five francs. She kept the money to show her friends that evening. 'Look, a cop paid to hear me sing . . . Now I've really made it!'

At that time we didn't go into the courtyards. We used them much later, when Edith had started working in a cabaret in the evening, and was tired the following morning. If we were in a courtyard she could sit on a dustbin and even fall asleep on it.

You don't get very good audiences in courtyards, you're forcing them to listen to you. Some of them enjoy it, but not all. The concierges didn't appreciate us, either. Sometimes they tried to get rid of us, and Edith would tell them to fuck off. That infuriated them, the windows would open, but not so that they could throw down coins, and when it turned cold, the windows stayed closed. The women were less generous than their men. For each sentimental daydreamer, whose eyes fill with tears each time he hears a love song – and tears always make people generous – there are plenty of old hags with hearts of stone, who, by the look of them, are not only unmoved by love songs, but have no fond memories to be brought back anyway.

Edith did not pass the hat round, that was my job. 'With eyes like yours it's a cinch,' Edith said to me. 'Don't give up, don't let one of them get away.'

So I stared at them until they put their hand into their pockets.

We moved around a lot. That's how you get to know a city. When we arrived in a new place, we first had to find a policeman and ask him where the police station was so that we could go and sing as far away as possible. In their eyes we were just beggars.

We had been taken into police stations more than once, but they always let us go. It was easy, because we were minors, too young to be convicted. The cops thought we were just playing around. They did not take us seriously, and we made up stories to put them off the scent. We told them that we lived with our mum and dad and they were not very well off, and that we were singing for fun so that we could get enough money together to buy a dress, or some shoes, or go to the movies, or anything we could think of. They swallowed it. The only thing we could not tell them was the truth, as then we would have been sure to find ourselves in a reform school or orphanage.

Two children running around the streets all day can get into all sorts of trouble. But our hobnailed shoes were the guardians of our virtue.

We didn't dress like ruffians, but we weren't far off. I had a beret in which I took the collection. We both had the same hair-style with fringes that we cut ourselves. Edith thought it would be better if we were immediately recognizable as sisters. 'You see, it's easier to make the police believe that you're my sister if you look like me, since we don't have any identification papers.'

I was quite happy. I wanted to look like Edith. I loved her not because she was my sister, half-blood ties are not very strong, but because she was Edith.

We lived at the Hôtel de l'Avenir, at 105 rue Orfila; it's still there. Each time I pass it I stop and look up at the third-floor window, our old room. It was a single room without running water, there was a bed, a table with a wash-basin, a tumble-down closet, a night table which was not too bad, and nothing else. I said to myself, a bit ironically, that this was where our best prospects lay – in the Future.

But when we were coming home late on the Metro, and Edith was half asleep, she would open one eye and say, 'Don't worry. We'll be rich. Very rich. I shall have a white car with a black chauffeur, and we'll dress exactly alike.'

She believed it. She was certain that she would become a star, but to make quite sure she went to church and prayed to St Theresa. 'Give me twenty centimes,' she would say to me. 'I want to buy a candle.'

Edith never kept a cent on her. It was I who kept the money.

But while we were waiting for fame and fortune, we sang in the street. When we had enough money, we went into a restaurant and spent it. Then we went back and sang some more so that we could go to the movies. We never thought about the ten francs we would need the following morning. We ended each day broke, we had to spend everything. Edith never changed.

Some days we would make three hundred francs; that was a lot of money in 1932.

When I met Edith she had already had some lovers. She was broken in at fifteen, and could not even remember the first one. He had not left her anything, no keepsake, nothing at all. Her second lover was a circus performer she met at Alverne's who played the banjo and the mandolin. He sang 'Quand refleuriront les lilas blancs' [When the White Lilacs Bloom Again]. He had taught her three notes of 'Les Gars de la Marine' [Navy Boys] and she always started with them on her banjo. She played badly, but it was like the guitar today, everyone played a little.

Our repertory consisted of 'Le Chaland' [The Barge], 'Le Dénicheur' [The Bird-Nester], and 'Mon beau sapin' [My Lovely Fir Tree]. (In the rich districts we had to find something better, so we sang the whole of Tino Rossi's repertoire for them because 'It had class!') Our theme song was 'Les Mômes de la cloche'.

C'est nous les mômes, les mômes de la cloche
Clochardes qui s'en vont sans un rond en poche.

That was not quite right for the smarter districts, but it was our national anthem. You have to know how to choose your songs according to the district. You really earn your singing diploma in the streets. The public, jostling up against you face to face. You can hear their hearts beating. You learn their likes and dislikes. And if occasionally someone sheds a tear, you know the collection will be good.

In some districts we went barefoot, but in others we had to put on sandals, because the passersby would have been shocked, and if we didn't wear sandals, we earned less. To save the soles, we would tie the straps together and wear them round our necks. We must have been the first beatniks; not very clean and with a banjo instead of a guitar. But our way of life too had its roots in poetry and hope and the desire to be free while you're young.

I don't remember being hungry or cold. My memory would have me believe that there were no winters during those years. There were, of course, but I cannot recall them. It never rained either!

We covered every section of Paris, from Passy to Montreuil. On Saturday it was not a good idea to go into the rich districts because the people were shopping. They were in a hurry, and had better things to do than bother about us.

During the week we did the Champs-Elysées. Passy was good in the morning, when the women were still there. On Saturdays we went into the working-class districts, they gave less at a time, but they gave more often. They also gave because they liked what they heard, not because they wanted to help us out.

We made a good living. We actually had enough money to dress well, but we didn't know how to. We wore skirts and sweaters, nothing more. From time to time we bought new ones, when the others got too dirty to put on again. We never washed anything.

There was always a crowd of men and boys surrounding Edith. She enjoyed it, but she was older than I, and I was still very young, and probably not very attractive. We had fleas, and that must have put people off a bit. The boys used to look us up and down and reject us, no doubt because we were dirty.

A year after I met her, when Edith was sixteen and I was thirteen and a half, we started to go into the barracks, particularly in the middle of winter, since they gave us shelter. As I said, Edith had already developed a taste for soldiers, lock, stock, and barrel. We had to get permission to sing from the Colonel, and that took time. Once or twice we went with a friend called Zoé – I have no idea what became of her – she was a great help. You can't play hard to get with soldiers, they don't appreciate it, and Zoé was an easy catch, she went with any man who asked her, no matter who. If he did not appeal to us, she took him on.

Edith sang, and I did my acrobatic tricks in the canteen. When we had finished, the soldiers made dates to see us in the neighbouring bars. That is how Edith came to know the difference between the Foreign Legion bars, the Colonial ones and the naval ones.

A soldier meant nothing to us, he was just a man in uniform. We owed him nothing, and he made no unreasonable demands on us. But when we were surrounded by soldiers and we could see that they were enjoying themselves because of us, we at least felt we existed. When we stopped going to the barracks, we still went to the bars. When a man looks at you, you feel that you amount to something; that's living. You can let your hair down when men are around and laugh as much as you want, and soldiers aren't hard to get.

3

FOUR IN A BED

One evening in a bistro near the Romainville base we met Louis
Dupont. He had come to get some wine for his mother; he
lived with her in a shabby old house near by. It was a case of
love at first sight with him and Edith, and that very evening he
moved in with us.

He was a small, blond boy of eighteen (Edith was only sixteen), and I did not think he was anything out of the ordinary,
in fact he looked rather insignificant compared to the strapping
soldier Edith had fallen for earlier. This one just sat down at our
table, propped his wine bottle against the wall, and, looking at
Edith, said, 'Do you live around here?'

'No,' she said, 'I'm from Ménilmontant.'

'That's why I've never seen you before.'

'Yup, that's why.'

'Are you going to come back?'

'I don't know. It depends.'

'What does it depend on?'

'Well, if I want to.'

'Do you think you will want to?'

'I don't know.'

'Can I buy you a drink? Waiter, two pernods, please.'

'What about my sister?'

'Make it three,' he ordered.

'What do you do?' asked Louis.

'I sing, I'm an artist.'

'Wow,' he breathed. 'Do you make much?'

'A bit. What do you do?'

'I'm a bricklayer, but at the moment there isn't much brick-
laying to be done, so I'm working as a delivery boy. It's not
bad. With tips I make around a hundred and sixty francs a
week.'

He must have been angry when Edith and I laughed.

'Well, that's not bad. I'm only eighteen.'

'On good days we can make up to three hundred francs. But I don't care what you do. I like you. You don't need money for that.'

They went on exchanging facts about themselves as if their lives depended on it. I'd heard it all before, but it did not end in the usual way. He had to take the wine home to his mother, and while he was away Edith could not stop talking about him.

'Do you think he'll come back?'

'Of course, he's got it bad.'

She smoothed down her hair as though she was in a movie. She slipped out to put on some more lipstick, a horrible bleeding red like raw meat. She tugged at her sweater, which was fairly clean for once. Her eyes were full of anxiety – the way they were when she was in love.

I was going to see and hear these gestures and words repeated so many times during our life together that I would eventually lose faith in them. Each time Edith fell in love, she was sixteen again, and it was her first and last love, the kind that only happens once in a lifetime, the kind that lasts for ever. She believed it, and so did I.

She started pacing up and down. She became jealous, possessive, and suspicious. She always shrieked at her men, expected too much of them and was altogether unbearable. They beat her and she cheated on them. Shouting, violence – that was what love meant to her – and she loved it.

'Momone, when love starts to cool you have to heat it up again or get rid of it. It doesn't keep in cold storage.'

It didn't matter to her whether her love lasted for a year or for a day.

'Love isn't a question of time, it's a question of quality. I couldn't love any more passionately after ten years than I do in one day. It's okay for the middle classes to keep a check on their emotions: they're misers, that's how they get to be rich. Perhaps it's a good way to make money, but it's a lousy way to make love.'

And so, in that Romainville bar, when Edith was sixteen and

had just met little Louis, she was already hot for him. I was only fourteen, and all I could do was follow. So I followed.

'If that Louis doesn't come back, I'll do something really stupid.'

It was nearly one o'clock. To forget him, she drank and looked around for someone else. Both of us sat at our table with our arms folded and our eyes riveted on the door, waiting.

Louis came in, but was it him? No, it must be his brother or another member of his family. When we met him originally he was wearing dishevelled blue overalls. Now he wore a jacket and tie, his hair was parted on the side and slicked down with cooking oil.

'My name's Louis Dupont,' he said, 'they call me little Louis. Let's live together.'

'Oh yes,' replied Edith, in seventh heaven.

It was as cut and dried as that. Of course he made up a host of stories, he said he had heard her sing and that he admired her voice. Actually he hated her to sing; he flew into a temper when she went out, saying it was not a woman's job. He was jealous because other men looked at her when she sang, and above all he was afraid that she would leave him. Like all his successors, little Louis wanted to keep Edith to himself.

But in the bar that evening they gazed into each other's eyes. Edith's face had changed noticeably; her eyes had grown enormous, smouldering and tender at the same time. This was love, and her whole body shook with desire.

We all three went back to the rue Orfila to the Hôtel de l'Avenir. It had not occurred to anyone that I should go and sleep somewhere else. You have to have more money than we had to be able to afford separate rooms. Anyway, we did not see anything wrong in it. There was a well of purity in Edith that nothing was ever able to contaminate. Obviously it's not customary to have three people in bed together, but when you're eighteen and poor, love-making is so wonderful that you do it in silence. Their rhythm rocked me to sleep like a baby.

Edith shacked up with little Louis because he was the first one who thought of asking her, and she flourished on it.

'You know,' she said to me, 'this is it, I'm hooked. That's not bad at seventeen, is it? Do you think he'll propose to me?'

'Would you say yes?'

'I think so.'

But Louis did not dare. His mother needed his pay, and she would never have allowed it. That did not change things for them, though within two months Edith was pregnant. 'I'm going to have a baby. We'll have a kid of our own. Are you pleased?'

I did not know what I was supposed to say. Privately, I thought that it would not make life any easier. But neither of us really knew what it would mean. We did not understand anything. We made no preparations because we had no idea what a new-born baby needed.

For a few days Edith felt very important. 'I'm going to have a baby,' she confided seriously to her friends.

They had mixed feelings about the news. But not Edith. She was living with Louis, and she was going to have his child – that was right, that was the way things should be. Louis was pleased enough, but he had no idea what was in store either.

Perhaps if Edith had become a bricklayer's wife, this would have been the end of the story. A plump little housewife singing while she made dinner … at first. After a while the singing might have stopped. Perhaps she would have started to drink and become an old shrew with too many children.

But nothing changed. Louis did his job, and Edith did hers. He still didn't like her being an artist, and would have preferred it if she had stayed at home. His nagging got on our nerves.

'It's a stupid job. It's not even a job anyway, it's just playing around. You're going to be a mother. Who ever heard of a mother singing in the streets!'

Poor boy! It was just as well for all of us that there were streets. His dream was to live with Edith in two rooms with built-in closets, while he went out every day to a good job – a man with a trade. Unfortunately, the dream did not work out.

When Edith became noticeably pregnant she had to stop being a street singer. It didn't seem right with a fat stomach; we didn't look like artists any longer, we looked like beggars. So we started making pearl funeral wreaths. We signed on in a shop down beside the rue Orfila. We did spray-gun painting, while other women put in the pearls. Edith sang while she worked, and her friends liked it.

'You see, it's marvellous,' Louis Dupont said. 'You're paid every week. It's steady work. You're inside and you can still sing. Doesn't that change everything?'

Actually it did not change much. We still ate canned food in our dingy room, sitting on the bed because there were no chairs. Louis had been home-making. He had taken three forks, three knives, and three spoons from his old lady. Edith did not want plates, though. 'I'll never do dishes,' she declared. And she never did.

'Anyway, I'd rather eat in a restaurant.'

Singing in the street paid well enough for us to eat in restaurants: making wreaths didn't.

'Making wreaths is good business. People are always dying,' Louis observed correctly. He was trying to talk her into doing it permanently, but she was not interested. She wanted the street. She wanted her freedom.

The streets cast an extraordinary spell over you, and singing there is almost like being in heaven. Louis was jealous of it. They fought over it, often ending up in the police station near by at Gambetta. It could not last much longer – he was a little workman and she was already on the way to becoming Edith Piaf. She did not know it, it did not show, but she was.

Poor Louis, he had good reason to be jealous; she cheated on him more and more, but she hung on to him all the same, because she wanted to keep him. I do not know if she still loved him, but she always liked to have a man about the house. It was a steadying influence.

She had an easy pregnancy. If she had not grown big she would not have felt anything. On the date the baby was expected, we went to Tenon. She stayed while I went back to the funeral wreaths.

'When's it due?' the girls asked me.

'Now.'

'Has your sister got everything together for the baby?'

'She hasn't got a thing. What do you need?'

'Well, nappies, a crib, rompers. He won't be like Jesus, you know, he can't run around naked.'

We had not thought of anything like this.

The girls could not get over it. They could not believe that anyone could be so thoughtless, or ignorant.

'You can't wrap him in newspaper. There's no time to lose, you must take everything to your sister now.'

'What do I buy it with?'

We were stumped. Then a big girl called Angela said, 'Don't worry about it, we'll see to it.'

So each of the girls gave some part of the layette – and what a mixture it turned out to be! But it was a real kindness.

Edith was very happy with her baby. She called her Marcelle. She liked the name; it would crop up several times in her life among people she loved – Marcelle, her daughter, and Marcel Cerdan. Louis was another name that mattered – there was Louis our father, Louis the baby's father, Louis Leplée, and Louis Barrier.

Marcelle was a beautiful baby and Louis was delighted. But he did not ask Edith to marry him, which was just as well, because it was all over and Edith would have said no.

Once they had the baby, Louis imagined that he could hold on to Edith now, that he could start laying down the law. But Edith said immediately, 'I'm going back to the street. The baby needs money, I've got to earn some. You can stuff that wreath-making job.'

Now there were four of us in the room, and even worse four people in the bed. There was no heating. Edith kept warm in Louis's arms, and I was lucky to have the baby. I went to bed in an enormous sweater, and put her little body against mine under the sweater.

We did not know that you are supposed to boil the baby's milk, so she drank it unboiled. We thought it was enough simply to wash out the bottle and give it back to her. We let it get warm, and put sugar in it because Edith thought sugar was good for her. 'It gives you strength,' she said.

We wrapped the baby up and took her with us to sing in the streets. She never left us. Edith would not be separated from her child for anything in the world. That was her way of loving her. She would not dream of leaving her all alone in the hotel. So we dragged her everywhere with us, all around Paris. We took the Metro, never the bus, because of the draught.

When the baby was dirty, we put in a longer day in the street and bought her some clothes with the extra proceeds. We never did any laundry. Until she was two and a half years old, Marcelle only wore new clothes. It was a good system. We did not know how to do the washing anyway. Edith sang very well, but she was no housewife.

Thus we lived from day to day, and it wasn't a bad life. In the evenings Louis looked after the baby at the hotel. It was late when we got home, and Louis was often asleep. There were nights when we did not come home at all. Edith always did exactly as she pleased. She had not been tamed by the hard times she had been through.

And something new was happening: Edith was beginning to be aware of the fact that she might have a successful career before her. She did not sing any better, but she had put together a sort of repertoire; there were love songs, old favourites, and the usual street songs, but now she felt that there was something more to being a singer. We used to stop in front of the billboards advertising 'real artists', those who sang in the music halls like Pacra, the A.B.C. Bobino, and Wagram – Marie Dubas, Fréhel, Yvonne Georges, Damia, all the big stars. You could go into the bars and hear them on the jukeboxes. Edith was transfixed by them.

'It's as if I can see them,' she said. 'Don't laugh, when I hear them I can see them too. That's one of the things that's left over from being blind. Sounds have forms, faces, gestures. A voice is like the palm of a hand, no two are alike.'

When we first met I had taught her a lot of things. For example, she did not know that the Champs-Elysées existed. I knew about it because when I was a child, living with my mother on the rue des Pancoaux, I decided that there must be another world outside Ménilmontant. I was seven, and I wanted to go to

the Champs-Elysées, of which I had heard, to see if it was real. So
I set off, and that's how I discovered the Claridge. It was beautiful and clean, like nothing I'd ever seen before. The only other
hotel I knew was the one where Dad lived in Falguière. After I
had seen the Champs-Elysées I knew it was the most impressive
place in the world.

So when I met Edith, and found that she did not know the
City, I took her to all the beautiful parts of Paris. At first we just
went for fun, but later we worked those areas very successfully. I wanted to show Edith there was something else in the
world besides our wretched houses and dirty streets. I wanted
her to understand that we were surrounded by ugliness, but that
there was no need to settle for that kind of life.

When she was alone, she confined herself to Ménilmontant.
That was her petit-bourgeois side, she was afraid of the unknown. I had even visited the Place du Tertre. Line Clevers, the
singer, had singled me out of a crowd of kids who were waiting
at the stage door of the Folies Belleville, and taken me to her
home for a bath. I was very young, about ten, but not one detail
escaped me. We ate outside at one of the little tables in the
square. I thought it was marvellous. I watched all the rich people
on parade, and I tried to behave like a princess. I was beside
myself with delight.

And so I took Edith to the Place du Tertre. It was as we
started to climb towards Montmartre that Edith began to make
progress, to have confidence in herself. There she saw people like
us working hard for peanuts. She arrived, started to sing, and
everyone listened to her. All the other performers were jealous,
for she was making real money. She earned more than they did,
although they were in the same line of business. That made her
think. Singing didn't necessarily mean the street, it could also
mean 'in there' where the stars were.

At times like this, little Louis was completely forgotten. One
evening as we were walking down the rue Pigalle we passed the
Juan les Pins night club and saw Charlie the doorman, whose job
it was to persuade the hesitating passerby that he would have a
better time inside than out. Charlie started talking to us. He
could see that we were a couple of ragamuffins from the left

bank, our appearance gave us away. But Charlie enjoyed chatting with us, we weren't like his regular customers. 'What do you do?' he asked us.

'I sing,' replied Edith.

At that point Lulu, his boss, shot out of the club like a bat out of hell. She looked rather forbidding, in her mannish clothes, and with her hands on her hips. I always felt that she probably carried the masquerade even further by wearing men's underwear as well.

'What are you doing?' she demanded of Charlie.

He replied calmly, 'I'm talking to these two girls. It seems that this one is a singer – she wants to be a star.'

'So you sing, do you? Well, come in and show me how good you are,' she barked.

After having listened to Edith, Lulu said, 'You're okay; you've got a good voice. How about the other one?'

'She's my sister.'

'And what do you propose I do with her?'

'She can dance. She's an acrobat.'

'Tell her to get undressed.'

Once I was stripped, she looked me up and down and said, 'You'll do.'

My sweater, skirt, and slip off, there was nothing else to remove. A puff of wind would have blown me into orbit. She gave me a balloon and some music. When I was facing the audience I hid what had to be hidden with the balloon, and when I turned away, the balloon was in the air. I uncovered everything, but nobody could see that I was completely nude. I thought I looked pretty good because though I had filled out a lot, I was still slim. I was as flat as a board, no breasts, no thighs, nothing.

'You're underdeveloped, like a child,' said Lulu. 'That'll please everyone. All my customers hanker after jail bait. How old are you, anyway?'

'She's fifteen. She's my sister, so I'll be responsible for her.'

I was fourteen and a half actually, but we were familiar with the regulations about the employment of minors, as indeed was every kid who hung around the streets. It was our kind of to-getherness. Singing at Lulu's was Edith's first engagement. She had graduated from the street to the inside. It was not very different, though. Edith sang, everyone enjoyed it, but no more, things had not changed much. We had not grasped the fact that Lulu was not giving us a hand-out, that she was hardly a phil-anthropist throwing away her money in support of the Arts. If she had hired Edith, it was simply because she was worth it.

Little Louis saw no cause for celebration in Edith's new job, however. He was thoroughly miserable.

'That place is a hang-out for prostitutes. I don't want any more to do with you. We're finished,' he announced.

Edith did not agree. She wanted someone to look after the baby at night. But their relationship could not hold together much longer.

We took off with the baby to the Hôtel Au Clair de Lune in the rue André-Antoine. It was close to our work, and Edith liked the neighbourhood – Blanche, Pigalle, Anvers. We did very well without Louis as nursemaid. Little Marcelle was about a year and a half now, and she was not difficult to look after.

We did not take her to Lulu's club. During the day she trailed around the streets with us, and at night we left her to sleep in our bedroom. She did complicate life, though.

We sang in the streets during the day and in the evening we went to Lulu's. Sometimes we were so exhausted that we slept under the benches. The hookers were nice girls: they sat on the benches and hid us with their legs so that Lulu would not see us. We had also made friends with a boy who worked there. When he had cleared away the plates, he would find one that had only been nibbled at, and bring it to us saying, 'Come on, quickly, dinner's ready.' In a flash we were down in the basement eating someone's leftovers.

That was the good side of the club; but there was another. The agreement was that Lulu should pay Edith fifteen francs a day, but she never gave it to us, she always found some reason to fine us. We had been hired to arrive at nine o'clock; if we were five

minutes late we had had it. We were fined for something practically every evening. A fine was five francs, and since there were
two of us, that made ten. In the morning we seldom had more
than a few centimes left. In addition, Lulu was always slapping us – and me in particular. I never understood why. She
must have enjoyed it.

The one way to make money at Lulu's was to play the cork
game. You sat at a customer's table, chatting with him and encouraging him to drink champagne. You kept the corks, and
when the club closed they were all counted and you got your cut
of the profits. To be successful at that game you had to be a
glamour girl. It was difficult to play without thighs and tits. The
girls from Lulu's were really luscious and beautifully turned out.
It was a time when women wore a lot of make-up – jet-black
eyelashes, blood-red lips, and platinum-blonde hair done up in a
way that made you dizzy. No man would want two grubby little
street urchins to share his champagne when there was such
heavy competition.

When we were not asleep we sat in our corner like wallflowers. Once Edith succeeded in persuading someone to drink
an orangeade, and they talked about it for six months! But we
stayed, all the same, because, as Edith said to me, 'I'm not always
going to be a street singer, and at least I have a chance here.
One day someone, an agent or a talent scout, will come along,
notice me, and hire me.'

I can still feel the atmosphere of that club, heavy with smoke
and desperate sadness. We stayed there from nine o'clock in the
evening until the last customer had collapsed over his bottle.
The pianist played anything that came into his head, and the
exhausted girls listened. They were tired because there was
nothing to look forward to. I guess they're all dead by now.

For Edith, the pianist played:

> C'était un musicien qui jouait
> Dans les boîtes de nuit
> Jusqu'aux lueurs de l'aube
> Il berçait les amours d'autrui.

[He was a pianist who played / In night clubs / Until the first rays
of dawn / He fostered other people's love.]

She sang it in a little voice and, as day dawned, the last client was thrown out, the girls were thrown out, the pianist was thrown out, and – last but not least – we were thrown out.

Breathing the pure air of the rue Pigalle, Edith took my hand and said, 'Come on, let's go and sing.'

Women who had slept through the night appeared at their windows and threw us down the few coins that were necessary for coffee, Gargyl, and breakfast, and as soon as we had collected enough money we could go to sleep.

Edith was very strict with me at Lulu's – very, very strict. She was guarding my virginity. Six months later, when I was fifteen, it was gone, but she continued to watch over me.

'You can't touch Momone, she's special, she's my little sister,' Edith would warn.

Even when she went to bed with some fellow she would not leave me behind, but took me along. It did not bother me; nothing could stop me from sleeping, I was so tired.

Since we had got rid of little Louis we did not have a man at home, so there was no need to rent a room during the day, and we changed hotels constantly. For a while we stayed at the Eden beside the Eléphant, a restaurant where a whole meal cost a few sous and every tenth meal was free. It was convenient and economical. You could rent a room for twelve hours, which, of course, was cheaper than twenty-four. We dragged Marcelle around the streets with us. She was a beautiful, easygoing child, who laughed all the time.

There were, as always, a lot of men around Edith. If she could not find someone she liked at Lulu's, she found him elsewhere, so did I. The pimps liked us and became our friends.

The men who came to Pigalle at night were not *la crème de la crème*, but they were the kind who liked us. We were not fussy and nor were they. We were very similar, almost from the same family, the slums, and we made them laugh.

Our boy-friends were thieves, pimps, swindlers, and receivers. Our girl-friends were tarts, the natural partners for these gentlemen. Our neighbourhood was real, it was alive. There was never any fuss. You came in, 'Hi'. You went out, ' 'Bye'. No one ever asked, 'Where do you come from?' or 'What are you up to?'

Edith always hated people to ask her questions, she didn't want to have to account for herself.

We spent our days in the streets. That was the only way that Edith could stand being cooped up at Lulu's all night. When we sang, the baby came along in a little push-chair. She must have been about two when we met a sailor beside the Madeleine. Edith always had a soft spot for sailors. Through them she learned about the world, she called it travelling by proxy. He was handsome and his red pompom cap and blue uniform suited him. He listened to us patiently, waited until we were finished, threw some coins into my beret, and said to us, 'You're cute, you sing well. You should try your luck.'

I was pissed off and I could see that although he was addressing both of us, he meant it all for Edith. He had poise. He probably made a good living in civilian life. He went on, 'But you don't look very neat, or well dressed.' Then he came right out and said it, 'You're dirty.'

Edith took all this with a smile, she thought he was attractive. She was taking stock of him with every inch of her little body, approving his five-foot-ten frame. She replied gamely, 'I don't look like this usually. It's just because I'm working. You should see me in the evening, I look great. This outfit is for the public. If you could see me as I really am, you wouldn't even recognize me.'

This was exactly what the sailor was waiting for. He wanted to take Edith out, but he didn't want her on his arm looking the way she did – we were not exactly chic. So he made a date to see us that evening at the rue Royale.

We went quickly to our daytime hotel. All three of us got washed in one basin. I don't know how we managed it, but by the time we had finished we looked even worse than we had in the morning. Edith had put on a red velvet dress that looked as if it were made out of a discarded theatre curtain, terribly gaudy, with grey cat-type fur around the neck. She had plastered her hair back, made up according to the latest fashion – an almost white face with a blood-red mouth – and she looked like the clown from a shabby miming troop. She had borrowed some shoes with stilt-like heels from Madame Jézéquel, our landlady.

'You see, when I take his arm I mustn't seem so small.'

But since she took size three and Madame Jézéquel took a good eight, the toes had been stuffed with newspaper. All this for the sailor's benefit.

We set off for the Metro with the baby in my arms. When we arrived in front of the Naval Administration building, Edith said to me, 'Go over to Maxim's and ask how much a cup of coffee costs. It's supposed to be a smart place, he'll be pleased to see us there.'

I went over and the barman quoted me a price around five francs. I thought he was teasing me because we were not dressed properly, so I started to bawl him out, but Edith dragged me away.

'Don't make a scene. Come on, it doesn't matter. Let's buy a paper.'

So we bought a paper. Under the arcades near the Ministry we spread it on the ground and sat on it. There we waited patiently for the sailor. He had probably said to his friends, 'I've met two little waifs, come and take a look at them.'

When he arrived and saw us sitting on our newspaper with the baby, he stared in horror. 'It's impossible. You're even worse than you were this morning,' he cried, and with that he left us flat.

Nothing like this had ever happened to us before. We were absolutely miserable. We picked ourselves up and got back on the Metro. We daren't look at each other: we had been so sure that it would be a success. She had made herself look the more beautiful, since she was obviously the favourite.

On our way to meet him she had kept saying, 'He's good-looking, isn't he? Did you see his eyes? He's got lashes like a girl's. Don't you think he's got a terrific build? Won't he be surprised to see me looking like this. He won't be able to get over it.'

That was true, he didn't get over it! I could see all this was tormenting her on our way home. She was heavy-hearted, and so was I. That kind of thing sets you back.

In silence, we ate a can of sardines in our hotel. Then we left to go to Lulu's.

'The guy was a drip. It would never have worked,' Edith remarked later. She never mentioned it again, but I know she never forgot about it. That was not our lucky period.

One morning as we were going into the hotel, Madame Jézéquel caught up with us. I used to wonder when that woman slept, she was always waiting around for the rents.

'I've got some news for you.'

'Bad?'

'You can decide that for yourselves. Your husband came and took the baby away. I couldn't do anything. He had his bike in front of the door, grabbed the child, and rode off. I couldn't say anything, she's his daughter, you know.'

'You did the right thing,' said Edith. 'It was all arranged.' She always found a ready answer to any situation. Even if she didn't fool anyone this time, it made us feel better.

When he took Marcelle, Louis had said, 'I'm taking my daughter back because this isn't the right life for a child. If her mother wants her, tell her she has to come and get her.'

He hoped that this would make Edith come back to him, that she would return to the hotel in the rue Orfila. As far as he was concerned she was his daughter's mother and his wife; she must go back. But that was not the way to handle Edith. Besides, there was nothing to go back to, now their relationship was finished. Edith did nothing. In all honesty, the kid did get in the way when we worked.

So little Louis kept the child. But he couldn't look after her properly : she stayed all alone in his lodgings. She was better off with us because, in spite of everything, she got plenty of fresh air and was in good health.

At first we missed her. We said nothing about it, but there was an emptiness in our lives. Often we had worked for her alone.

From the day that Louis took Marcelle from us, Edith never mentioned him again, not to pass judgement, not to reminisce, he was utterly forgotten.

Then one miserable evening, when we were ready to cry we were so fed up, Louis came to us. Somehow he always found us. He came straight to the point, 'The baby's in the hospital. She's very sick.'

We ran to the Children's Hospital. The child was tossing feverishly on her pillow. Edith whispered, 'I'm sure that she knows who I am. You see, she recognizes me.'

I didn't want to destroy her illusions, but here was a two and a half-year-old baby with meningitis. She was already in a world where she could not recognize anything.

Edith tried to speak to the doctor who was in charge of the hospital, but he did not want to see us.

When we arrived at the hospital the next morning, we went upstairs and the nurse said to Edith, 'Where are you going?'

'I'm going to see Marcelle Dupont.'

'She died at six forty-five this morning.'

Not a word more.

Edith wanted to see Marcelle once more. They sent us down to the morgue. She wanted a lock of hair, but there was nothing to cut it with. The kind man in charge of the morgue lent us a nail-file. It was difficult to cut with; the baby's head was jerked from side to side as we sawed away. I shall never forget that scene.

We had to find some money for the funeral. Little Louis said that he had none. He was not a bad kid; he was so young, perhaps no more than twenty when the baby died. Edith was nineteen. They were only children themselves.

I had to take care of everything. All Edith could do was get drunk on neat Pernod. I thought she was drinking herself to death. I found a room near a night club called Le Tourbillon that we used to go to. Some fellows helped me carry her up there. But we still could not get her to sleep.

The next day things were a little better and we went back to Lulu's. Someone had told Lulu that Edith had lost her baby and she had taken up a collection for us. All the girls gave us money, but we still needed ten francs to bury Marcelle. Edith started walking up and down the street saying, 'So what! I'll make it myself.'

It was the first time. She had never done that before, never. She was walking down the boulevard de la Chapelle when a passerby picked her up. In the room he asked her why she was doing it. Edith told him that she needed another ten francs to bury her baby daughter. The man gave her more than ten francs and left.

It was one of our darkest times, perhaps the worst, but, in all honesty, it didn't last long. A few days later we had forgotten that little Marcelle was dead. We did not think about it again. We never visited the cemetery. We were only kids, after all.

4

PAPA LEPLÉE

Life went on as before – the streets by day and Lulu's by night.
By now we had been at the club for more than a year and there
was still no sight of any agent or talent scout.

Edith, who spent her life waiting for love, wasn't thinking
about it any more. She was waiting to make her name as a
singer, but that wasn't coming either even though she sang as
well as she knew how at Lulu's. We had been to see a publisher
who set words to music. Edith didn't know a note of music. She
had an extraordinary memory though, and if someone played
her the song two or three times, she knew it off by heart. The
pianist who accompanied her played as he wished, and Edith
sang without taking much notice of him. The miracle is that it
sounded okay.

Edith's fan club had grown since she had started at Lulu's, and
she was asked to go to different places, to the Tourbillon, and the
Sirocco whenever she was needed. It wasn't very much, but it
was a start. We were usually happy and Edith was sure that
everything would work out. She would take me by the shoulder
and say, 'Don't worry, it'll be okay. We'll get away from all this
crap.'

But at that moment we were right in the middle of it.

All those flea-bitten night clubs, the mangy bars in squalid
districts, and the drab street: my common sense kept telling me
that this was not a launching pad for the moon.

Even our love life was dull, nothing but one-night stands.
Edith hardly cared. She went with anyone. It was all pretty
shitty.

Edith liked our neighbourhood. She liked the tough, down-
to-earth roughnecks she called 'men'. Not the half-baked little
bastards who gave themselves airs and graces but had nothing to

offer. We made good friends among the pimps, friends who never let us down and never forgot us.

They didn't bother us with their business – they were too professional – but all the same, there were two of them who looked after our interests, Henri Valette and Pierrot. Edith was the one who actually went to bed with them, but I shared in the fun too. They put us on their beat, but not as tarts – the idea would never have occurred to them – they were our protectors. In the neighbourhood it was 'in' to have a tough protector, and ours were the very best.

Edith took them with us to sing in the street. They kept guard at the corner, watching out for cops and played *baron* – that means they threw a five- or ten-franc note into the beret to encourage others to give. There was no risk of losing their money because they got it all back along with our takings. The arrangement didn't last long. It was becoming too much like work for them. They figured that pimps who got up at eight o'clock in the morning to stand around on street corners waiting for money and cops, lacked class.

When we stopped working for them, we didn't stop seeing them. We stayed on in the neighbourhood. It had become our own.

One day, for no particular reason, we decided to go to the Champs-Elysées. We had worked several streets and not made much. Edith said as usual, 'If it goes on like this I'm going to stop, we don't have a dime.'

But we were to have more than one very soon.

It was on the rue Troyon that Louis Leplée entered Edith's life. He was a very well-dressed, elegant gentleman, not our usual type of customer at all, with his silver-white hair and dandified looks. He couldn't stop looking at Edith. Ridiculously, I thought to myself, 'When she stops singing I think he's going to propose to her. He's all ready for the wedding ceremony, he even has his gloves on.'

Then he came up to us and said to Edith, 'If you would like to sing in my club, come and see me tomorrow.' And with that he gave us a ten-franc note.

Edith didn't know what had hit her. He had written his

address, Le Gerny's, rue Pierre Charron, on a scrap torn from a newspaper. Edith gave it to me straightaway, saying, 'For God's sake don't lose it. It may be worth a fortune.'

Every five minutes she would break off in the middle of a song and say to me, 'Have you still got that address?'

When we got home Edith was excited. We had been to look at the outside of his cabaret: it was certainly a cut above Lulu's.

'That man's got a really classy place. He'll look after me. I'm sure to find an agent in a place like that, someone's bound to come along. And it's near the Champs-Elysées. Do you still have the address?'

That scrap of newspaper decided Edith's future.

We celebrated that evening at Pigalle, where we told everyone. We met the singer Fréhel. She went to the same bar as we did, Le Pigalle. We were very impressed by her, her name was advertised in big letters, but this didn't stop her from hanging around with our crowd. She could really get pissed, which was not so elegant, but what a voice! 'Le Gris qu'on roule', 'Mon homme', 'Tel qu'il est il me plaît' were among her better-known songs.

She tried to put us off the job at Gerny's. 'They'll swindle you. There's still a white-slave trade going on. They don't just sign you on out of the blue, especially around the Champs-Elysées, it's impossible. They're up to something. You mustn't go.'

She could not realize that Edith was already one of the greats, a star in the making. She refused to believe it then and it was only much later that she grudgingly admitted it.

As soon as Edith had a little ray of hope, no matter what, we would go to see Fréhel because Edith admired her so much, and each time she would set out to demoralize us. If Edith said, 'I'm going to sing this song,' Fréhel would shriek, 'No, no, don't do it, sing anything but that.'

She also liked us to get drunk with her. When Edith was really rolling she would take her to a café or a club, anywhere where there were people, then deliberately push her forward and say, 'Look, she can sing too. She'll sing for you now. Go on, Edith.'

Then poor Edith, drunk as a lord, would sing in a dreadful, drunken voice. It was painful, and humiliating. Fréhel often bought our sandwiches or drinks for us, but she never gave us good advice, never offered us any help in our work.

Finally, Edith saw through her and we stopped talking to her.

But that evening, the evening of the day when we met Leplée, we were truly happy. We drank to celebrate, not to get drunk. 'I mustn't go to bed late. I must pay attention to all the little things,' Edith had decided.

We said nothing to Lulu. We were afraid that something might go wrong, so we got away as soon as we could.

The following morning we went to sing in the streets as usual after our black coffee and the Gargyl. Nothing had changed. Edith had put on her black skirt for her interview with Leplée; it was the only one she had. She had brushed it off, not with a clothes-brush, we did not own one – we wetted a newspaper and rubbed at the stains. She stuck down her fringe with soap, the rest of her hair went its own way. We had bought a lip-stick for her, a nice dark, garnet red, and then we bought two pairs of navy espadrilles, since we could not go barefoot to Leplée's; we reckoned we were dressed just right.

Legend would have it that we arrived late for our meeting with Louis Leplée, but that is not true. We arrived half an hour early at La Belle Ferronière, where he had told us to meet him. Edith realized that this meeting could be very important. It was a miracle to meet someone who owned a cabaret, who had dough and who treated us properly. It was incredible. All we were terrified about was that he might have forgotten us. We were so scared we couldn't even talk.

It was around four o'clock in the afternoon when Leplée showed Edith into his cabaret, Le Gerny's. He made her sing all her songs without accompaniment, just as he had heard her the first time.

Then he said calmly, 'That's fine. It sounds better in here than it does in the street. What's your name?'

'Gassion, Edith Giovanna.'

'That's not a show-business name.'

He actually said show business! He spoke to her as if she were an established singer. He was well dressed and he smelt good, he had a nice voice and spoke correctly in a way that we weren't used to. Edith wondered if he were serious and devoured him with her enormous eyes. You would have thought she was gazing at God. I knew that expression well, it was the one she used when she was working, when she was listening, when she wanted to understand everything and commit it to memory, to let nothing escape her.

Leplée banged emphatically on the table. 'The name is very important. What's your real name again?'

'Edith Gassion, but when I sing I call myself Huguette Elias.'

He swept these names aside with a wave of his hand. I was fascinated by his clean, almost shining fingernails. Edith and I never thought a man would have his nails manicured. The pimps we knew weren't big enough for that type of refinement.

'Well, *mon petit*, I've got a name for you – *la môme Piaf* [the Little Sparrow].'

We weren't wild about *la môme Piaf*, it didn't sound very artistic. That evening, Edith asked me, 'Do you like *la môme Piaf?*'

'Not much.'

Then she started to think. 'You know, Momone, *la môme Piaf* doesn't sound all that bad. I think Piaf has style. It's cute, it's musical, it's gay, it's like spring, it's like us. That Leplée isn't so dumb after all.'

Edith liked and respected Monsieur Leplée straightaway, and there grew up a genuine affection between them. She called him Papa Leplée, and he responded by treating her like an adopted daughter.

For a good week following their meeting, Edith rehearsed with a pianist. There were rows at first. Edith found it difficult to follow the music: it was up to the piano to follow her.

'I'm the one that's singing, not him, I wish he'd shut up,' she growled.

So she sang the way she wanted to.

There was a lot of publicity to launch her. Everywhere we saw billboards and ads proclaiming, '*LA MOME PIAF* IN CABARET AT GERNY'S.'

'That's me,' said Edith. 'Look, my name! Pinch me, Momone, I can't believe it!'

That was not exactly true, she did believe it. It was all she could talk about, and I was very proud to be her sister.

She was no longer the old Edith. For a week she didn't drink a drop, didn't go to bed with anyone. She was turning herself into a virgin once again. All she could talk about was her luck and her fears. 'You know, I'll be all alone on the bill that night. I'll be the star. Papa Leplée is mad to do it that way. What happens if it doesn't work? It'll be enough to finish him. And what if they don't like me? What if everyone starts booing?'

Le Gerny's dazzled us; as far as we were concerned there was nothing better. We could only compare it with the clubs around Pigalle and Blanche – we didn't know the smart ones. And when Edith, looking at herself in the broken bits of mirror which we shared and fiddling around with her hair, said to me, 'I'm going to Gerny's on the Champs-Elysées,' it took our breath away.

Louis Leplée's cabaret was not really very smart, but it was the in place in Paris at that time. You did not go there to show off, you went to eat and listen to the singers who, if they were not the best-known singers in town, at least were good. And you went for the atmosphere; above all, you went to have a good time.

Louis Leplée said to Edith, 'I'm not Polin's nephew for nothing. You're too young to know, but in the good old days around 1900 he was the king of the Caf' Conc'. It's thanks to him that I have music in my blood. So, you can trust me, *mon petit*. You aren't like the others, and the audience will recognize that.'

She believed him: she knew that he was right. He had not taken any risk with her. He conducted an experiment because he liked singing, real singing: he was tired of dumb lyrics and phony sentiment. Either his street singer would capture the whole of Paris or he would be a laughing-stock.

And capture Paris she did.

Even if Edith's style had not been right for his club, he would have signed her up, because he believed in her the minute he met her.

We had never met a man as kind as Leplée, we didn't know such a person existed. He was the first person to teach Edith her profession. At Lulu's she had performed off the cuff, with no training. Lights, music, the setting of a song, the choice of song, gestures – she knew nothing about all these. She planted herself in the middle of the floor with her hands at her sides, and just sang. He did not dare tell her too much, he was too scared of ruining her natural qualities. All the same, he made her learn some new songs, 'Nini peau d'chien', 'La Valse brune', and 'Je me fais si petite'.

He had thought of everything except a dress. It had never occurred to him that anyone could be as poor as we were, and have practically no wardrobe.

'Do you have a dress for tomorrow evening?' he asked.

Without hesitation, Edith said, 'Yes, a very pretty black one.'

It was a lie, as I knew only too well. Leplée was curious, and not completely convinced.

'What's it like? Long or short?'

'Short.'

'Okay. It mustn't be too fancy.'

'It's really very simple.'

'Wear it tomorrow.'

As we went out Edith said to me, 'We don't have time for the street, but we must have some dough. I really am dumb, I never thought about what to wear. I'll tell you what, we'll ask Henri (our pimp), he can't turn us down.'

Henri didn't have enough on him to buy a dress, but he gave us money to buy needles and wool, so we sat down to knit the dress!

Edith knitted very well and loved it (later each of her men would automatically receive his own hand-knitted sweater). Suddenly she got furious, 'Papa Leplée said all the bigwigs will be there. I'm the star and I'll be wearing a black knitted dress. That'll give them a bit of a turn. After all, I'm a street singer, and we don't parade around with a train in the streets.'

We knitted like mad all night, with needles as thick as posts so that it would go faster, and every hour she tried on our handiwork as far as it had gone.

She had chosen black, not because she particularly liked black, but because she never wore anything else on stage. She always pictured herself in black.

The following evening, the night of the premiere, we arrived nearly two hours early. Edith placed my hand on her chest, saying, 'Feel how my heart's beating. It'll have to get used to it.' That was true, she led it a merry dance right to the end of her life.

The straight skirt had been easy to make, so was the sweater top, but we did have problems with the sleeves. We had to start again, and we ended up with a dress minus one sleeve.

As usual, Edith came up with the solution, 'I'll sing with bare arms like Fréhel, it's more dressy.'

When Leplée arrived, he said, 'Go and get dressed so that I can see what you look like.'

We slipped into the toilet, which we used as a dressing-room, and Leplée came over. But when he saw the dress there was an explosion. He, who was normally so polite, started to shriek, 'You're mad, God dammit, you can't be serious. Bare arms! Who do you think you are, Damia? Fréhel? They have real arms, they can get away with it, but what do you think you look like with your matchsticks?'

He grabbed poor Edith by the arm and started shaking her like a rag in front of the mirror. 'We're ruined. No one should trust girls like you. And that other idiot' (that was me) 'couldn't she tell you how awful you look? It's enough to make one weep!'

Weep! We were the ones who started to cry. Everything had been loused up because we had no money.

Luckily, Maurice Chevalier's wife, Yvonne Vallée, was in the club. When she heard Leplée yelling she came over to find out what it was all about. 'Louis, you're out of your mind. You're terrifying the child. She won't be able to sing at all at this rate.'

'Do you think I'm going to let her sing looking like that?'

'Don't you have any sleeves?' she said to Edith.

'I've only got one. We didn't have enough time to make the other, and I can't sing with one sleeve.'

'Don't you have a scarf?'

In those days it was apparently the fashion for singers to drape themselves in silk scarves, but we didn't know that.

Edith, who never had much colour anyway, was as white as chalk. 'It doesn't matter, everything's ruined. I won't sing.'

'Here's your other sleeve,' Yvonne said to her. And she gave her her own scarf, an enormous square of violet silk.

From then on, Edith always liked violet: it became a holy colour to her, she believed it brought her luck.

Meanwhile, she was green with stage-fright. I was shaking so hard that my teeth were chattering like castanets. People kept putting their heads round the door to tell us who was there, Maurice Chevalier, Yvonne Vallée, Jean Tranchant, Jean Mermoz, Mistinguett, Maud Loti, and Henri Letellier who was owner of the *Journal*, one of the largest daily newspapers of the time.

Edith and I listened to the roll call with mounting apprehension. We were breathless with fright. She, who loathed water, swallowed glass after glass of it. 'I'm so dry, my tongue's stuck to the roof of my mouth.'

Around eleven p.m., as was the custom, Louis Leplée and his band filed into the room, playing and singing 'Les Moines de Saint-Bernardin'. The current attraction was on next: the new girl.

Laure Jarny, the manageress of Gerny's, came to fetch Edith. 'You're on,' she announced.

Edith looked at me. 'Momone, I've got to succeed this evening, I'll only get this one chance.'

Quickly she made the sign of the cross. It was the first time she had ever done it before going on stage, but afterwards she always did it.

Gerny's was not like Lulu's; Monsieur Leplée did not want me to sit with the audience, I didn't belong there. He stuck me in the washroom, but the job of cloakroom attendant didn't appeal to me, and quietly but firmly I fell into step with Edith. That evening I wanted to be out front listening.

It was hot. The women had bare shoulders and backs, or were draped in little nothings of fur – clearly not rabbit – and their jewellery obviously didn't come from Woolworth's either. The men were in evening dress. They were very noisy. The lighting was a tangerine orange, the fashionable colour. When the room was plunged into darkness there were 'ohs' and 'ahs' and giggles from the ladies.

Leplée came forward with a single spotlight fixed on him. He had arranged everything himself. In a few words he told how he had discovered Edith at the corner of the rue Troyon, that she was authentic, and stunning.

She came out and, with a sweep of his hand, Louis Leplée introduced her, 'From the street to the cabaret, I give you *la môme Piaf*.'

There was a murmur and then, as the spotlight picked her out, a hush fell upon the whole place. This was something new; they waited expectantly. Would she make them laugh or cry?

All alone in the harsh light, with wispy hair, white face, and scarlet mouth, her hands hanging limply on the lop-sided, black knitted dress, she looked lost and dejected.

She began to sing:

> *C'est nous les mômes, les mômes de la cloche*
> *Clochardes qui s'en vont sans un rond en poche*
> *C'est nous les paumées, les purées d'paumées*
> *Qui sommes aimées un soir, n'importe où.*

People were still talking as if she didn't exist. But in desperation, her eyes full of tears, Edith went on singing. Inside she was suffering, but she kept singing, thinking to herself, 'I'll be okay, I'll be okay.' Suddenly the plaintive words of Edith's song caught the listeners' attention, they became mesmerized. When the song ended no one said a word. There was a stunned silence. An unbearable, throat-constricting silence. Then the audience broke into wild applause, it sounded like a thunderstorm beating down on a drum. I cried with happiness. Edith Piaf had captivated her first Paris audience.

I heard Leplée's voice saying to me, 'That's it. The kid's made it.' It did not occur to him to send me away. The spectators were surprised, delighted, amazed to hear a youngster singing about unhappiness and poverty, a mere child who could sing about life. It was not so much the words as Edith's haunting voice which spoke to them.

For Edith it had been the hardest moment of her life so far, but in all her days it remained the sweetest. She was drunk with happiness.

When she had finished her act she was invited to sit at Jean

Mermoz's table, and Mermoz addressed her as Mademoiselle. She couldn't get over it. She was never shy usually, but this time she was speechless. The success had completely gone to our heads, we could hear bells ringing.

They say Maurice Chevalier cried out, 'That kid's got what it takes,' but that too is part of the legend. He had already heard Edith singing during a rehearsal. He did not say much, something like, 'Try it, she could catch on. She's a natural.' And there he was right, they had never heard a voice like hers. She did not have to force herself to sound genuine, she was born in the streets. They had never seen a poor, skinny little thing like her on stage before, with shabby clothes and simple gestures. The singers they knew were imposing, like Annette Lajon, Damia, and Fréhel : women who took up the whole stage with their presence.

She had been a success because she had shocked them, as if a bucket of cold water had been thrown in their faces. But she was not yet the great performer she was to become. It would take years of work to make her a real star.

When we left, the sun was rising. It was a beautiful day, a glorious day. Her little black dress looked pitiful away from the bright lights, but Edith walked like a queen. She took my hand, 'Come on, Momone, I need to be in the streets. I owe all this to them. We'll go and sing to thank them. It'll do me good.'

She did not sing in her usual style that morning. It was as though she was singing a hymn, thanking God for the change in her life.

'I can't believe it,' she said to me. 'Yesterday those people were just faces that I saw in the newspaper, now I've just spent the evening with them, sitting at their table. I'll never get over it.

'They were so nice. Really kind, they gave me champagne. I never had anything like it before. It's so good. Rich folks' lemonade! It doesn't taste the same as our sparkling wines. I'll let you taste it one day. And they passed the hat round for me. Mermoz lent them his. He must have masses of women he's so handsome. I wouldn't mind going with him myself, I can tell you.'

She let go of my hand, which she had been holding as we walked along, and said with a sigh, 'He's not for me. Not yet, but one day he will be. You understand, Momone, love is important to me. One day I'll have all the lovers I want, and lots of money too.'

In our room she still talked about Mermoz: it lasted for days and days. 'Look at me. Me! I've seen Jean Mermoz. I've sat at his table. I've drunk champagne with him. And you know what he said to me? "Mademoiselle, may I offer you a drink?" '

I was a good audience. I was only seventeen, and I day-dreamed along with her.

We had come up from nothing. The day before we had lived in fear of the cops. They could have put an end to all our plans. Our men were guttersnipes, who could beat us up as much as they pleased. We had virtually no family or relatives. If we had fallen sick, we could have died unknown on some street corner or in the state hospital. Our family burial vault was the communal grave at Pantin. We knew all that well enough. And then suddenly everything had changed. It was more than a dream come true, because we knew that dreams are only fantasies that you act out in your mind. This was for real. And Edith had talked to Mermoz and the others, she had sung to them, she had drunk with them. If they had heard her on the street the day before, they would not have even given her a second look. It was indeed a dramatic change.

Edith could not stop. 'It's not only Mermoz's looks, it's his voice too, I could listen to him talking for hours. Maurice is a great artist, but beside Mermoz he just disappears. Mermoz over-shadows him. You can find men like Maurice in Ménilmontant and Belleville. He's no better than I am: he can sing, so what? But there can only be one man like Mermoz in the whole of France.'

... And he had touched her hand: he had marvellous teeth. He had put a thousand francs in the bottom of his cap. He had bought her flowers, as he had bought them for the other women who were there.

'No man ever bought flowers for me before.'

Would she never stop? The guys and Fréhel and the other

girls began to tease her. They called her Madame Mermoz and Princess Piaf. But Edith paid no attention to them. With each telling, the story got wilder – she was going to be a movie star, she would be going to America, she was turning down contracts left, right, and centre.

Fréhel was a wet blanket, as usual. 'Calm down, Edith. Santa Claus only comes once a year, and not to everyone even then. Until someone starts writing songs for you alone you're a nobody and your repertoire's a joke, just a collection of old songs.'

She had not said it out of kindness, but the advice served just as well; Edith picked up hints about her career very quickly.

She wanted to do everything all at once, but it was not as easy as all that. Edith did not have enough of a name to interest the music publishers. They saw no reason to take a chance on her with a new song so we had to plough through all the old stuff. There was never anything for us. But we began to sneak into the publishers' offices, to sit in the corner and listen to the singers who did have names trying out the new songs.

'Seeing them, listening to them, I'm really learning,' Edith confided to me.

We were so small and though we were a bit better dressed, we were no smarter than before. No one took any notice of us. Then, one day, Edith met Annette Lajon, who was a well-known singer at that time.

It was at the office of Maurice Decruck, the music publisher, who liked Edith a lot. We were there as usual when this big blonde lady swept in. She took up quite a lot of room, she was pretty, well-dressed, and very sure of herself. She started to sing 'L'Etranger':

> *Il avait un air très doux*
> *Des yeux rêveurs un peu fous*
> *Aux lueurs étranges ...*
> *Comme tous les gars du Nord*
> *Dans les cheveux un peu d'or*
> *Un sourire d'ange*
> *J'ai rêvé de l'étranger*
> *Et le coeur tout dérangé*

Par les cigarettes
Par l'alcool et le cafard
Son souvenir chaque soir
M'a tourné la tête . . .

'Momone, I absolutely must have that song. It was made for me. Listen to the words. It's about Mermoz and the affair I want to have with him. I could put my whole heart into singing it.'

During the whole of her career, Edith sang love songs, and each one was about the man who was passing through her life at that moment.

We stayed in our corner for the whole rehearsal. Annette Lajon was not pleased. She came over to Edith and said, 'Who are you?'

'Edith Gassion.'

'Don't you know that rehearsals are supposed to be private?'

'Oh, but Madame, it's so marvellous to listen to you. You sing so beautifully.'

Edith seemed sincere and Annette Lajon left us alone. When she had gone, Edith said to Maurice Decruck, 'I want "L'Etranger".'

'But that's impossible, my dear, Annette has taken it and she must be the only one to sing it. You can have it later.'

In the street, Edith burst out laughing. 'Did you see how I took her in with my compliments? I'll sing her song this evening.'

'How are you going to learn it?'

'I already know it.'

And it was true. We did not have the music, but the pianist at Gerny's, Jean Uremer, was very quick on the uptake. Edith hummed the song for him several times until he got the melody right. That evening she made a great hit with it. Leplée was delighted and we were as excited as kids.

Four days later, we were in the toilet, when I saw in the mirror that Annette Lajon had suddenly come in. I shouted to warn Edith. She turned round and got a tremendous box on the ears. It was only fair.

'If you didn't have talent, I would have done that in public, in the night club.'

Edith didn't say a word, there was nothing to say.

A few weeks later Annette Lajon won the Grand Prix de Disque with 'L'Etranger'.

'She didn't steal it,' said Edith. 'But I'll keep the song in my repertoire all the same.' She did, too; Edith always got her own way.

There were always important people at Leplée's. Politicians, industrialists, artists, international figures, the best. Edith thought she was an artist, but to them she was simply a phenomenon. And because she was, she was invited to a real dinner party at Jean de Rovera's house one evening. We had no idea who he was. Maurice Chevalier said to Edith, 'You must go, he's the manager of a big paper called *Comoedia*. I asked him to invite you. You'll enjoy yourself, you'll see. I'll be there too, *mon petit*.'

'I'd like to go very much,' replied Edith. 'But I won't go without my sister.'

'Fine. You'll find that they're very smart people. There'll even be a minister there.'

That didn't alarm us a bit, we had them at Gerny's too and we knew how to handle ourselves when they were around. All the same, to see them in their homes was rather different. We were excited and unsuspicious. Edith put on her black dress, it was finished now, we had knitted the other sleeve. It was still the only dress she had. I was wearing black too. Edith had heard somewhere that black was dressy.

And there we sat in the middle of all those people wearing evening dress. The women had jewellery that sparkled as much as the crystal and silver on the table. I could never have imagined a scene like this, neither could Edith.

Behind every chair stood a flunkey. Neither of us believed this ever happened except in the movies. We were ill at ease: it's embarrassing to have someone watch your every move. We were not sitting beside each other. They had put me a long way from the centre of attention. I was nobody, her sister, just a freeloader. The two men on either side of me addressed not a single word to me. Not once did they say, 'Would you like the salt? the bread?' or 'Are you all right?' Nothing. They talked to their other neighbours and they listened to Edith. She was the interesting one.

They had invited her because she was so 'natural'.

In fact these smart people were just making fun of Edith. From the start of the meal they had urged her to talk and they laughed at her. At first Edith thought that she was perhaps wittier than she realized, or that it did not take very much to amuse them, which in fact it didn't.

'She's so funny,' they said. 'She's priceless.' Someone asked her 'What do you call this?' and I thought she would reply 'Up yours!' But she could not realize that they had invited her merely to laugh at her. Since I was not included in their circle, I had quickly seen what was going on, and I felt embarrassed for her.

Maliciously, they had ordered a dinner consisting of things that were difficult to eat. Fish, for example, which we had never learned about. You can have no idea how difficult it is to eat fish if you have never been taught how to.

Then they brought out finger bowls, which again we had never seen before. Everyone watched us: they were waiting to see what Edith would do. So was I. 'She'll know,' I said to myself.

Edith did not want to lose face, and since no one had done anything with the damn bowls, she wanted to show them she knew what they were for. So she picked hers up and drank. It was logical, a bowl is made to drink from. That was just what they were waiting for. They let out a shriek of laughter I shall never forget, as they rinsed their fingers, and the meal continued.

Even the servants in their white gloves were part of the general hilarity, they were in on the joke.

'I want some bread,' said Edith.

'Give some bread to Mademoiselle Piaf.'

'I want something to drink, please,' said Edith.

'Water for Mademoiselle Piaf. Oh, of course, you'd rather have wine, wouldn't you?'

In the end Edith asked for nothing: she had got the message.

They took away her plate before she had finished. Then they served us quails. No one touched them with their fingers: bones were removed with forks and tips of knives. It's easy enough when you've learned how. When I saw Edith's pinched white face, I knew that she was going to do something. She was thinking, 'I can't sit here like an idiot looking at all these bastards eating.' So she tore off the drumstick with her fist and faced them all squarely. 'I'm going to eat with my fingers, it's easier.'

No one laughed.

When she had finished she wiped her hands on her napkin and stood up. 'We've had fun, but I'm afraid I can't stay, I have work to do. Are you coming, Momone? Monsieur Leplée is waiting for us.'

I could have wept for joy. You should have seen their faces. They sat there like a lot of stuffed dummies, as Edith robbed them of their evening's entertainment.

When we got down to the street, Edith began to cry from the humiliation. When we arrived at Gerny's she told Leplée everything. Big tears ran down her cheeks. I was sick at heart to see her so distressed.

'You see, Papa, I don't amount to anything. I don't know anything. You should have left me where you found me, on the pavement.'

'But it is they who were in the wrong, the ill-mannered fools, not you,' Papa Leplée explained, stroking her hair. 'Isn't that so, Jacques?'

Jacques was Jacques Bourgeat, a friend of Leplée's. He seemed old to us then, although he was not yet forty. He was a kind man, a sympathetic word and a smile were all we knew of him.

He said, 'Better still, *mon petit*, you've just proved that you're a great lady. When you know what you lack it isn't difficult to make up for it, and you will.'

On our way home that night, Edith said to me, 'Don't look now, but we're being followed. Don't worry, we'll take him for a walk.'

We started off, but our pursuer stuck close to us. Suddenly we were fed up. We had had enough annoyance that evening.

'Let's wait and find out what he wants. We aren't scared of one man, are we?'

We faced our shadower. He was tall, well dressed: a hat was pulled down over his eyes and he had bundled himself up in a scarf.

It was Jacques Bourgeat. When we recognized him Edith laughed as if she would never stop. 'I thought you were a dirty old man following us home.'

'You spoke so bravely this evening, I wanted to talk to you, to see if I could help you a little.'

She had found a friend, a real one. He was not the kind of man we were used to, not the type you find hanging around our bistros. True, old Jacques was a bit of a ladies' man, a bit of a bottom-pincher, but he wasn't interested in the bottoms of girls like us. There wasn't much to pinch, anyway.

He was a writer and an historian, and so tolerant that Edith said to him, 'You aren't good, Jacquot, you're stupid. You don't see the bad things in the world even when they're right under your nose.'

'I don't like ugly things, so I don't look at them. I look at you because you're beautiful inside.'

Jacques Bourgeat, our Jacquot, took Edith under his wing. He wrote a poem for her, which is in his book 'Paroles sans histoire' [Words without Story]:

> La vie te fut dure;
> Va, ne pleure pas,
> Ton ami est là.
> La vie t'a blessée,
> Petite poupée;
> Va, reviens à moi,
> Je suis près de toi.
> La vie cette gueuse,
> Te fit malheureuse;
> Va, console-toi
> Je souffre avec toi.

[Life has been hard to you / Come on, don't cry / Your friend is here / Life has wounded you / Little doll / Come back to me / I am close to you / This beggar of a life / Has made you unhappy / Come, don't be sad / I suffer with you.]

'That's beautiful,' said Edith. 'Is it really for me?'

He would often stay with us until dawn, and Edith listened passionately to everything he told her. But there were times when she stopped seeing him for a while; there was so much she did not understand, so many words she did not know, and she got tired of asking, 'What does that mean?' Jacques guessed what the trouble was, and patiently he began to teach her her own language. But first of all he wrote this song for her, 'Chand' d'habits':

> Chand'd'habits, parmi les défroques
> Que je te vendis, ce matin,
> N'as-tu pas, tel un orphelin
> Trouvé un pauvre coeur en loques?

Edith's career was going up like a firework display. She gave her first public performance at the cirque Médrano on 17 February 1936, at a benefit gala for the widow of Antonet, the famous clown. Since the programme was in alphabetical order Edith's name came between Charles Pélissier and Henri Pilcer. 'Look, my name's as big as Maurice Chevalier, Mistinguett, Préjean, Fernandel, Marie Dubas ... It's like a dream come true.'

And in the circus ring she looked so small in our knitted dress, with the single spotlight playing on her. She was as pale as a clown, with her feet planted firmly in the sawdust, and her head up.

After the gala she cut her first record at Polydor; it was 'L'Etranger'. We laughed about it, but not spitefully, because we realized that actually old Lajon had been quite decent to us.

Then Cannetti booked her for Radio-Cité. At the end of the broadcast the switchboard was flooded with calls from people clamouring to hear more of the Little Sparrow and asking who she was; and they signed her up for another six weeks.

That evening, Papa Leplée said to Edith, 'Would you like to go to Cannes?'

'On the Côte d'Azur?'

'Yes, you're going to perform for the Petits Lits blancs ball at the Pont d'argent.'

'Oh, Papa, is that really true?'

We usually only bought newspapers to stuff in our shoes, but these days, since we had been at Leplée's, we had been reading some of the articles, because Edith was occasionally mentioned. So we knew about the Petits Lits blancs, and we knew that it was not somewhere we could have been invited under normal circumstances.

When we reached the street, Edith's feet were hardly touching the ground, she was so elated. We did not know that we would need parachutes soon.

Work was going well. She was learning her trade and working hard. So as not to lose touch, but also because she enjoyed it, she would occasionally go back and sing in a street or two.

She had a very good friend in Papa Leplée, whom she loved with all her sparrow's heart, and in Jacques Bourgeat, who was teaching her so much, and who remained a friend throughout her life. In the next twenty-five years or so Edith was to write him more than two hundred letters, something she did for no other man.

But as far as her love life was concerned, she was really over-doing it. It was the height of the soldier, sailor, and toff period. It was like a madness.

None of the pick-ups ever came to hear her sing; they would not have been allowed in. They waited for her outside, and I must say that they numbered patience among their virtues. They cooled their heels in La Belle Ferronière, which was very close to Gerny's. Never had so many denizens of Pigalle descended on the Champs-Elysées at one time. Some hung around all night waiting for Edith to come and retrieve them. I don't want to exaggerate, there perhaps weren't fifty of them, but when you counted those who were waiting for Edith, and the others who had come to help them pass the time, there was quite a crowd.

They drank and Edith paid. She was always very generous.

Leplée would often go and chat with Edith's men across the street. He was perhaps a little too interested in the sailors, the down-and-outs, the little guttersnipes, some of whom were really very pretty. Leplée was generous, too; between him and Edith that crowd had a great time.

Louis Leplée had not needed Edith to introduce him to the low life. But Edith had brought the whole gang right up to his doorstep, and that is why she found herself in jail.

For seven months Edith had been happy in her way, and if other people disapproved, well, that was tough! Then, on 6 April 1936, everything fell apart. Louis Leplée was murdered.

> *Il a roulé sous la banquette*
> *Avec un p'tit trou dans la tête*
> *Browning, browning . . .*
> *Oh! ça n'a pas claqué bien fort,*
> *Mais tout de même, il en est mort*
> *Browning, browning . . .*
> *On appuie là, et qu'est-ce qui sort*
> *Par le p'tit trou? – Madame la Mort.*

Edith sang 'Browning' several years later, but she always felt sick inside as she repeated the words. It was her Papa Leplée who had been shot in the dark.

The curtain was ready to go up on that drama, but nothing was different at Gerny's.

'You know, *mon petit*,' Leplée remarked, 'everything's coming along very well. In three weeks you'll be at Cannes at the Pont d'argent. But you must understand that you haven't completely made it yet.'

'I know, Papa, I've a lot to learn.'

'And you must work.'

'I know, but why say all this to me this evening? Do you feel all right? You don't look too well to me.'

'I know. I had a dream last night, a nightmare, and I can't get it out of my mind. My mother was there beside me and she said, "My poor Louis, get ready, we'll soon be together again. I'm waiting for you." '

'Oh, go on, dreams don't mean anything,' Edith replied.

But I could see she was scared. I felt like running away and hiding; death gives me the creeps.

'It's not like me to believe in dreams, *mon petit*, but all the same . . .'

The three of us stood there for some minutes. No one said a word, no one moved.

'I don't want to leave you now, Edith, you still need me. Everything's happening too fast for you, you could lose your grip, you still need help. Basically you're still naïve, an innocent. In this world everyone's out for what they can make: they fight tooth and nail, and they fight dirty. In the meantime, be good this evening. You've got a recording session at nine a.m. to-morrow, and you have a date at Pleyel in the evening. So go straight to bed, no running around. Promise?'

'Yes, Papa.'

'Do you swear it?'

'Yes, Papa. Here take my hand.' She gave him her hand and spat on the ground.

When we got outside, Edith said to me, 'It isn't late.'

I understood what she meant only too well. Without thinking I said, 'It'd be better if we went to bed, you have a lot of work to do tomorrow.'

'I can take care of my own work,' she said disdainfully. 'If you're tired, go home. I'm going to have a drink, I won't be able to sleep without it. Papa and his dream have upset me; I've got to get it out of my mind. Do you believe in dreams?'

I did not have much of an opinion either way. Later on I did, though!

'Okay, but not more than one.'

'I promise.'

Edith was being very generous with her promises that night.

What a night it was! One of our pals was leaving for his regiment and we wanted to give him a royal send-off. Edith kept her promise – not more than one glass ... in each bar! But the number of bistros and clubs we went to made up for any lack she might have felt. It was a long time since we had had such fun. She needed it because 'her' Papa Leplée's strange mood earlier that evening had depressed her.

'It's my last night of freedom,' the conscript bawled like an idiot. 'You must all help me make the most of it.'

He had nothing to complain about; we gave him plenty of support, we even carried him to the station. How we managed to hoist him on to his train, drunk as he was, I shall never know.

When we got back to our rooms by Place Pigalle, we looked at the time. Eight o'clock. Edith ordered a very strong triple coffee, and downed it saying, 'Momone, I can't do it. We'll have to ask them to make it a bit later. I can't sing. I must get a couple of hours' sleep. I'm going to call Leplée, come with me.' She had a bad hangover, the worst for a long time.

When she was in that state, she could not bear to be alone. I felt rather unsteady myself, everything was hazy and swirling around me.

'Hello, Papa.'

'Yes?'

She looked at me, 'What am I going to say?' She plunged in head first. 'I can't come. I've just got home. I'll explain everything to you. Could we make the date for noon?'

'Come here immediately, do you hear? Immediately!'

'Okay, I'm on my way.' She hung up.

'Momone, we have to go now. He's angry. Do you think my voice sounded all right?'

In the taxi we began to sober up.

'Momone, that didn't sound like Papa's voice on the telephone. What's going on?'

A crowd had gathered in front of Leplée's house at 83 avenue de la Grande-Armée. Cops were running all over the place and more police cars kept pulling up. We didn't understand what was happening; we broke out in a cold sweat of fear.

At the entrance to the building a policeman asked us where we were going.

'To Monsieur Leplée's.'

A plain-clothes detective, with his hat pulled down over his ears, said to Edith, 'Are you *la môme Piaf*? Well, go on up, then, they're waiting for you.'

I stayed on the pavement. I should have left immediately, but I could not. All around me people seemed to be talking nonsense.

'They've murdered someone.'

'It's Louis Leplée, the cabaret-owner.'

'In that world,' said one gossip-monger, 'you have to expect this kind of thing.'

The concierge was strutting about importantly. 'There were

four of them, all young men. They got him with one bullet. They gagged Madame Secci, his maid. I didn't discover them, but a friend of mine did.'

That obviously annoyed her. She wanted to be the first in on the act.

'. . . It was the neighbour opposite. She was going out to do some errands around eight o'clock. What a sight she saw! Poor old Madame Secci had been tied up. The neighbour called me and I helped her to free Madame Secci. "They've killed my boss," she cried. What a shock!'

I didn't give a damn for her shock. I wanted to know just what was going on, and why Edith had not come back to me.

The concierge rambled on, '. . . She told us that Leplée was still alive when she got there. He was asleep, but he usually was at that time because he got home late. Then someone knocked on the door: it was a special knock, like an old friend would give. She opened up because Leplée entertained young men at all hours of the day and night. They pointed the revolver straight at her face, she said. What could she do? They tied her up and gagged her. She couldn't hear everything they said, they were speaking too low. But she did hear them say to Leplée, "This is it, you've fooled us once too often." A man asleep in his bed, can you imagine? What a way to be woken up.'

Edith finally came out, flanked by two ghastly-looking women with muscles like men. I smelt cops. They were followed by two inspectors.

Poor Edith was holding her felt beret in one hand, while with the other she wiped her eyes with a handkerchief. Tears were running down her cheeks, her face was tired and ravaged. The two women were holding her arms. They forced her to stop so that the photographers could do their job – and so that they could get themselves in the picture as well. Edith did not move, nor did I. Only her look met mine. Her smile, which was no more than a grimace, said, 'Don't do anything, Momone. Wait for me and be good.'

I watched her getting into the black maria with the two inspectors. There was nothing more I needed to know. The concierge chattered on, added a few frills and then started the story again, revelling in the notoriety. She could stuff her story for all I cared. Edith, Edith, Edith! ...

I went back to our hotel and waited – but not for long. The cops came to arrest me.

They fired questions at me, and their conversation, though lacking in courtesy, was not lacking in interest.

'You the friend of the Gassion girl, the singer?'

'Yes, sir.'

'Live here with her, did you?'

'Yes, sir, but I worked too.'

'Show me your work permit.'

'We didn't need a permit, Edith and me. I helped her; I was her dresser.'

'Did you ever collect money in the street?'

'Yes, sir.'

'You hung around public thoroughfares. You were a beggar and you're a minor. Come on, get your stuff together, you're under arrest. Do you know what a vagrancy charge is?'

There was no need to reply.

It was 1936. I was put in a cell with the prostitutes, and waited for a medical examination for forty-eight hours. Then, because I was a minor, they sent me to the Bon Pasteur, a reform school at the Charenton bridge. I was to remain there for two and a half months.

They asked me about Louis Leplée, but they could see that I knew nothing. Even if Edith and I had known something, if we had had the tiniest notion who was mixed up in the crime, we would have kept it to ourselves. We were very young, but not too young to realize that the streets are not like law courts – there's no defence there, and people have long memories, very long. In any case, we were not the kind to turn police informer; nor would it have brought Louis Leplée back to life.

I had no idea what was happening to Edith. I got news of her in an unromantic and, because of the location, painful way. They used newspaper instead of toilet paper in the toilets at the reform school. One day I saw a photo of Edith. I stole all the pieces which mentioned the case. NIGHT-CLUB SINGER

IMPLICATED IN LEPLÉE AFFAIR. They were really going to town.

I stashed the bits of newspaper all over me. The story was not complete, some pieces were missing, but all the same I learned that Edith was being kept under constant surveillance, and that they had stretched her again and again on their rack.

What was she feeling like? I was sick for her: I cried all night in my blanket, stinking of the other girls' sweat. The constant questioning could not be in her favour. I picked up the gist of what was happening, but not the details. When I rejoined her two and a half months later, she told me everything, nothing was forgotten.

'Oh, Momone, when the bastards pushed me into Papa Leplée's room, and I saw him stretched out across the bed, with his silk pyjamas, and his head on one side, I started to cry so hard that I choked. He looked beautiful, too pale, but otherwise he could have been asleep. They made me go round to the other side, it wasn't beautiful at all. There was a big hole full of blood where his eye should have been. The manageress, Laure Jarny, was hunched up in an armchair in the bedroom sobbing into her handkerchief, she kept saying, "My poor Edith, poor little thing." And I kept crying, "It can't be true, Papa Leplée, it can't be true."

'A cop said to me, "Okay, you've seen him, now come with us."

'They took me to police headquarters, and the quai des Orfèvres. Superintendent Guillaume was in charge of the case, a thin man with a big grey moustache. When you looked at him you almost felt you would like him for a father, he had this reassuring I-understand-everything manner.

' "You don't look stupid, my dear. So don't waste our time. You only have to tell the truth," he said.

' "I don't know anything. I was out on the town with some friends," I answered.'

He sent Edith back to some inspectors, young ones since they were usually tougher than the old ones. And they started to cross-question her. She was not making a statement, but being questioned. It is better that way, anything is permitted.

The police theory was that Edith had known an ex-soldier called Henri Valette. When she went to work with Leplée, they said she had broken up with him and, to get his own back, he had killed Leplée. It was a simple theory, but the cops aren't up to anything more complicated. Edith was in luck, though, Leplée's maid did not recognize Valette from a photo.

They had lost round one, so they passed on to the next. This was the version that I had read in the paper under the headline, THE LITTLE SPARROW HAD TWO LOVERS. According to them, Edith was sleeping with Jeannot the sailor at the same time she was going with Georges the Algerian. This was true. Unfortunately for Edith, she had introduced Georges the Algerian to Louis Leplée. We had often seen him at Gerny's or at the Belle Ferronière, where he waited for Edith with Jeannot and scarfaced Pierrot. These four guys fitted the description of the wanted men very well.

Edith knew them all.

The police asked the same questions for hours on end.

'Was Georges your lover?'

'Yes.'

'Was he a special friend of Leplée's?'

'They were friends.'

'Don't monkey around with us. He was his special friend, wasn't he?'

'I never saw them alone together.'

'If you go on like this we'll get angry, and you won't like that at all. Georges came to fetch you with two friends, two young boys and a sailor.'

'Yes.'

'Were you with Georges at seven this morning?'

'No. I was with some other friends.'

'Georges came to join you later, didn't he?'

'No.'

'You're lying.'

'It went on and on, it was never-ending, Momone. My head was bursting. They ate sandwiches, drank beer, and smoked. I could not go on.

'Then old Guillaume came to fetch me again. He took my

hand like a good daddy, and I found myself back in the same place in his office.

' "Tell us the truth. We know everything about you, you can't hide anything from us."

'Luckily he didn't know half of it!'

Edith was released all the same. They told her to stay around for further questioning.

A few months later the case was finally solved. By then Edith no longer cared.

5

BIRTH OF AN IDOL

I was at least warm at the detention centre. I had a roof over my head and food to eat. And I had company, even if the 'audience' wasn't quite like Gerny's. To have sunk so low, however, was humiliating. There was no news of Edith. It was probably the best thing, because I would surely have been misinformed; accuracy did not play a big part in the Leplée case, but I felt abandoned. I was wrong.

Our old boy-friends, the pimps and their pals, had been very kind. After two and a half months a character called The Limp came to get me out, with the help of our Henri. It wasn't easy, but he had found my mother and made her agree to say she would take me back. The Limp must have been quite a charmer because, as far as my mother was concerned, from the moment that I stopped bringing home the bread, I was welcome to stay where I was. I always felt that the boys must have threatened her with a beating if she did not co-operate.

I went before the court around three o'clock one afternoon. My mother was there, looking almost honest. I was astonished to see her. Needless to say, my two protectors were waiting outside.

It all went off very well, an impeccable example of court 'procedure'. The social worker said that my mother's apartment was clean, that she never drank and that she was a sensible woman. There were extra details thrown in for good measure – I learnt that I had some birds and a cat at home that I adored – I who had neither animals, nor clothes, nor love! The boys had taken care of all these touching details. I have no idea how they did it, but it was a stroke of genius. Ten more minutes and I would have believed it myself. In proper judicial tones the magistrate said to me, 'We have resolved to send you back to your mother.' I went straight to my mother's house, in order to keep up the pretence, but I left again for Chez Marius in the rue des Vertus, where, according to Henri, Edith was singing.

When Edith saw me her face broke into that marvellous smile, like the one she had given me long ago, it seemed, outside Alverne's.

'There you are at last,' she said. 'You've taken long enough. Now we can start all over again.'

We were in terrible straits; we were completely broke. Edith could count her friends on the fingers of one hand – Jacques Bourgeat, Juel the accordionist and J. Canetti of Radio-Cité, who was a terrific help.

One of the first things that Edith said to me was, 'You know, I don't feel let down. I went to Papa Leplée's funeral at Saint-Honoré-d'Eylau. I put a wreath on his grave with a message "In memory, from his Little Sparrow". Jacquot paid for it. You should have seen the expression on their faces. I wore my black dress, the one we knitted. The other women had on every kind of black fur, and everybody treated me as though I had no business being there. But I did, Momone. Few of them had as much right as me.

'That evening I was stupid enough to drop by Gerny's. It was closed, but a few had come to say goodbye to Laure Jarny; there were the employees, the flower girl, the maître d', and, of course, some of the singers. One of them said to me, "My poor Piaf, it's a pity you've lost your protector. He was the only one who believed in you; now you'll have to go back to the streets." I could have happily clobbered him.'

(I withhold his name, because he is famous today and he is still singing.)

'I thought I knew about life, but I had no idea how awful people can be. I shall never forget, I've learnt my lesson.' But she did forget, and for the rest of her life she went on befriending people she should have avoided; people who were not worth the trouble, who cheated and deceived her; hangers-on who trailed behind her, latching on to her money like fleas on to a dog.

We went on talking half the night, hardly drinking a thing. Edith told me everything that had happened while I was away. It was not a pretty story. Some nights she hung around the bars,

some nights she went home. For weeks on end she had cried like
a child, lying on her bed with her head under her pillow.

If her 'friends' had given up on Edith, the newspapers had
not, neither had the police. They watched her discreetly after
their own fashion, prowling around her like jackals.

'Each time I opened a paper I started to shake,' Edith told me.
'They talked about the Leplée affair, and since I was the only
woman they could get their teeth into, they tore me apart.
When they couldn't get any more copy out of me, they started
inventing it. I didn't exactly come out smelling like a rose. They
implied that I was an accomplice; better still, I had driven the
others to commit the crime. I was sick with disgust.'

Edith thought she was lucky to keep working. The managers
of clubs of all kinds buzzed around like flies. They didn't offer
her much money, but she could not afford to be fussy, she
reeked of the scandal, and they exploited the publicity.

Edith had been engaged by a night club in the Place Pigalle
called O'Dett. This is how she described it.

'You've no idea what it was like. A graveyard in midwinter's
more welcoming than that crowd glued to their tables. There
wasn't a sound, they were being "polite", but their politeness
was like a kick in the guts.

'I bowed and left the stage the same way I'd come on, but in
my mind I could hear them drooling over the sensational stories
in the newspapers. "There's no smoke without fire ..." "She
procured for him." "You have to expect this kind of thing from
someone off the streets." It's hard to sing without ever being
applauded, but I had to eat.

'Still, O'Dett was pleased. I was his main attraction. But I
knew they weren't coming to hear the street singer, they just
wanted to peer into the gutter.

'One evening I think that they must have left their good
manners in the cloakroom. The first song was met with silence
as usual, then someone whistled.

'A decent-looking man with white hair got up and gave them
a piece of his mind. "One doesn't whistle in cabarets, one leaves
that kind of behaviour to kids loafing on street corners."

' "Don't you read the papers?" someone called out.

' "Yes, but I leave the police to make the final decision. They let her go. And she's here as a singer. If you don't like what she's doing, shut up or go home." '

And as he started to applaud Edith, others followed suit.

Despite this, Edith did not renew her contract, she just did not have the courage.

'That's when I started to fall apart. Canetti had been really sweet, he booked a tour for me in the suburban cinemas as an additional attraction, and I sure was an attraction. The first theatre I sang in was the Pathé at the Porte d'Orléans. They all turned out to see the girl who was the centre of the Leplée affair. I couldn't even hear my first song myself, they were making such a din. But I always finished my routine.

'Can you imagine how I felt when I got out of those places? I wanted to cry. I used to get terribly drunk. I felt like the lowest of the low.'

'And the men?'

'Nothing much. They come and go. I can't stand being alone. I don't even want to tell you about it. But now you're back, Momone, we can start all over, it'll work.'

But she did not believe it. She wanted to drop everything and go back to working in a factory or singing in the street. I didn't want that for her. It was a filthy life, and we had just been getting used to something better. People who wash every day smell so good: they talk like people in books; and we now knew what it felt like to have a carpet under our feet. There was definitely a better life somewhere, and we knew where.

One day I dragged Edith along to a church, and we prayed for something good to happen; and something did happen. Were our prayers answered, or was it the two Cinzanos we drank that gave us courage?

We drew up a whole new set of plans in a local bistro. We had remembered the magical word – 'agent'. Quick, we must get the telephone directory and look for Fernand Lumbroso's number; he was Marianne Oswald's agent (she was a singer who was very highly thought of by the élite of the day). The miracle was that we remembered his name. With a telephone token in one fist and Edith's tiny little hand in the other, I found myself in the telephone booth under the stairs of the bistro, near the wash-room as usual.

We exchanged a few words and made an appointment to see the agent immediately. Off we set for Lumbroso's place, regardless of the way we looked, although we had made a slight concession by pasting our hair down with a bit of soap we found in the toilet.

Believe it or not a contract was signed straightaway; fifteen days in a cinema in Brest. Edith was to go on in the interval and sing four songs for twenty francs a day. Twenty francs sounds marvellous when you don't have one. But one glance at this important gentleman, and I was convinced that some of those francs would be needed to repay him for our first-class return tickets. I was wrong, we travelled second-class!

Brest was as dull as the second-class train ride. And I thought to myself that the next time we signed a contract with Lumbroso, it would be more expensive; then, perhaps, he would send us to Nice. Meanwhile we were on tour, our first. At least the people didn't give a damn about the Leplée scandal down there. Brest is really a lost town, grey and wet. It was unbelievably depressing.

Edith was sharing the bill with the movie 'Lucretia Borgia', starring Edwige Feuillère. There weren't many people in the cinema during the week. On the first evening Edith made friends with some sailors in a café – there's no shortage of sailors in Brest. On the second day, we installed our sailors in the audience. There were even a couple of officers among them. Edith sang for the sailors alone. I had a place in her act. I was, as they say in show business, her stooge. I was dressed like Edith in an identical black skirt and sweater, with a white collar and little red bows; we had the same hair-style and were practically the same height. My job was to introduce Edith. I would stand on stage so that everyone applauded me, then I announced, 'Love songs and old favourites will be sung for you by the Little Sparrow.' And as I pointed towards the wings, the audience saw my double coming on stage. They enjoyed that.

My job was finished, but I didn't leave the wings. Edith always needed to have someone she loved near by when she sang.

When I think back I realize what a great act Edith had. She sang the hard-luck stories that Fréhel used to grind out, like 'Correqu'et réguyer' and 'Le Grand Totor'; she also sang 'La Fille et le chien', 'Entre Saint Ouen et Clignancourt'. Apart from the songs Leplée had taught her, her repertoire consisted mainly of comical songs.

The manager of the theatre was by no means thrilled with us, however; he never stopped complaining. Certainly Edith did not take her work as seriously as she had with Leplée. She was careless, she arrived late, and the performance did not meet with the approval of the regular customers. And anyway, our sailors were keeping some of the regular customers away. The navy men were rowdy, rude to the other people, and left immediately after the interval. It made Edith laugh, but not the manager.

The evening that we left, as he was paying her, he asked, 'So are you proud of yourself? Are you satisfied with your performance?'

'Yes,' replied Edith.

'Well, don't ever come back to my cinema.' And then he told her what he thought of her; it was neither polite nor encouraging. Later he was to offer Edith outrageous fees. He went quite mad, even came to Paris to see her, but all Edith said was, 'No, I won't come, you don't look like a man who keeps his word.'

When we got back to Paris, Lumbroso was not very pleased to see us. The manager had made a complaint so we started on our round of local cinemas again.

On the very first evening, we found that the Leplée affair was still not forgotten. When Edith went on stage with her accompanist, the audience unleashed a string of abuse, 'Throw her and her pimp out,' they yelled. This period of our lives did not last as long as it seemed, but it left us drained and defeated. Edith would hold her hands out to me, imploring, 'It can't be true, Momone. It's a bad dream, I'm going to wake up soon.'

Thanks to Leplée she knew a lot of good people who could have helped her; like Canetti, Jacques Bourgeat, Raymond Asso (whom we had met by chance), and many others. But she would rather die gasping in the gutter than ask for favours. They knew our situation, then why didn't they rush to the rescue? That was what she believed and hoped they would do, but it didn't get us anywhere. They probably didn't know how poor we were.

'Luck is like money; it goes away faster than it comes,' Edith would say to me with a grim smile.

She accepted any job that came along, singing in seedy little bars – you have to make a living somehow.

The first reasonable-looking man Edith met about this time was Roméo Carlès. We went to the Globe, an artist's hang-out on the boulevard de Strasbourg, every evening. The two-bit agents came along there hoping to find, among all the down and outs an artist who was worth exhuming for a short spell, someone with a name that was no longer famous but was still recognizable, like Edith's. The Globe was a sort of show business labour exchange. Roméo Carlès, the song-writer, bought us a drink. He didn't know Edith, but was touched by her downcast expression. 'What do you do?' he asked her.

'I sing and I've come here to see if anyone's got a job for me.'

Roméo did not paint a very cheerful picture. 'You won't land a good contract here. You're too small, and you're badly dressed; and you should fill out a few of those curves.'

'I know, but while I'm waiting,' Edith replied, 'I thought I'd look around.'

'Would you like to sing my songs?'

'You bet.' She knew Roméo Carlès by name, but that was all.

'Well, come and listen to me one of these evenings. I'm at the Coucou and the Perchoir.' And that evening Edith was happy. She started daydreaming right away. She was delighted that some songs had been offered to her without any mention of the Leplée affair. What she did not know was that Roméo always had his head in the clouds, the name the Little Sparrow didn't ring any bells with him.

The next day she decided, 'Let's go and listen to Roméo.'

I was nervous because Edith was a bit high at the time and when she was like that she often behaved stupidly. We set off for the Perchoir, a club for song-writers in vogue on the rue

Montmartre. When we got there Roméo Carlès was on the stage. In her loudest voice Edith shouted, 'I've come to see my Roméo. Hey, Roméo, it's your Juliet!'

The Perchoir had a fairly chic clientele. As Edith roared with laughter they got angry; they were already at the throw-her-out stage. But Roméo took it all very well, he shouted something back, and everyone laughed, some people thought it was all staged, just part of the act.

'We won't get any songs now,' I thought to myself. 'That's screwed it.' But not at all! Before singing 'La petite boutique', he called to Edith, 'This one's for you, my Juliet, so be good and listen hard.'

Edith may have been drunk earlier, but once her career was at stake she quickly sobered up. Playtime was over.

> *Je sais dans un quartier désert*
> *Un coin qui se donne des airs*
> *De promesses aristocratiques*
> *J'y découvris l'autre saison*
> *Encastrée entre deux maisons*
> *Une minuscule boutique.*

During the interval, she rushed backstage and said to Roméo, 'Is that true? Are you really giving me "La petite boutique"?'

'You don't deserve it.'

'Oh, yes I do. Listen, this is how I'll sing it.' And she started to sing snatches of it. (Edith kept the song in her repertoire for a long time.) Roméo was delighted.

'What will you pay me?' he teased her.

'A kiss.'

And that, quite literally, is how it started between them.

They stayed together for about six months. Edith was something of a bonus for Roméo, since he was already going with Jeanne Sourza, a comic singer with a lot of talent.

Edith liked her Roméo; he was not much to look at, but he was kind and very intelligent. He was amused by Edith's waif-like quality. He was the first man during those miserable months to have faith in her, and at that time faith was more important than love.

'You see, Momone, I can't be through if a man like Roméo Carlès gives me one of his songs.'

He did better than that, he wrote one especially for her. He got the inspiration for 'Simple comme bonjour' from both of us, Edith and me.

> *C'est une histoire si banale,*
> *Vraiment si peu originale*
> *Que je ne sais comment en vérité*
> *J'vais vous l'expliquer . . .*
>
> *La blonde et la brune*
> *S'entendaient depuis toujours.*
> *La mort en a pris une*
> *C'est simple comme bonjour . . .*

To raise her spirits, Lumbroso, who was a good man at heart, dared to get her an engagement in Brussels. 'You're leaving right away, this evening, so behave yourself properly. Be on time. Don't get drunk. If you do we're finished, you and I. I won't do another thing for you. I won't care this much for your future.' And he snapped his fingers – as if he were squashing a flea between his thumb and forefinger.

Edith promised Lumbroso everything he asked.

'At least,' she said to him, 'in that neck of the woods they won't be asking me about Leplée all the time.'

'Perhaps not. But Belgium isn't the end of the world.'

She left that evening; I had to stay behind, as I was still a minor without a passport. In order to get one you have to have your parents' authorization. When she got to Brussels, Edith wrote me, 'Give your mother everything we have so that you can get a passport, and come over here quick.'

Everything that we had – it wasn't much. Three coloured cushions, and some blue saucepans that we had bought one day when Edith decided that we could save money if we cooked at home. She didn't go very far with that particular economy! There was also an alcohol-burning stove, but I kept that for ourselves. Thanks to the cushions and saucepans, my old lady agreed to take me to the commissariat to give her authorization.

It took ages and by the time I had the passport, Edith had returned. I was livid, all that trouble for nothing.

'Don't get upset, Momone, we'll be going back.'

Edith had met a new man called Jean M— in Brussels; he was Belgian, a musician in the club where she worked near the place de Brouckère. I could see she was in love with him. Her face lit up – she was radiant, 'I've met this fabulous guy, handsome and blond. You know, the real Nordic type with blue eyes.' (I was sure of that, she never could resist blue eyes.) 'The kind of blue you never see around here. It's because of their sky up there.'

And so it went on. I already knew what was coming but I listened anyway. I was a good audience.

'I must get another contract. It shouldn't be difficult. Everyone enjoyed me in Brussels. I didn't do anything stupid.'

And she got her second contract.

'Come on,' she said, 'let's go. You must travel to foreign countries. You'll see; Brussels is great, it's abroad. Everything's different. You don't look at things the same way there, or the people.'

She had told me so much about her Jean M— that I could almost see him. But during the train journey, Edith began to recant, 'You know, he hasn't got quite such a good build as I told you. Well, what I mean is that physically...' The nearer we got to Brussels the more she played him down. And at the station, I saw standing on the platform an ugly-looking, fat, bald creature; it was unbelievable. Fortunately Edith had prepared me for the shock. She looked at me, 'He's not too bad, is he? He's very kind. You'll see. He's come to fetch us.'

We had a sort of Belgian meal with lots of fried food and lots of beer. And then Jean said to Edith, 'I'll see you tonight at the club.'

This displeased and deflated Edith. 'Let's go to his place and surprise him,' she said when he had gone. So we set out, looking a bit shabby with our battered old suitcases. The address was false. Edith looked at me. There was a hard glint in her eyes which I knew well. 'Who the hell does he think I am? He's going to pay for this. Think, Momone, I've got to find out where he lives.'

In the night club that evening I made some casual inquiries and found out his address. He was shacked up with a woman. They weren't married, but they had been together so long that she was considered his wife. He had certainly taken Edith for a ride. When she had digested that bit of news, she was comically angry. 'I know I wanted to believe he's handsome when he's as ugly as sin; that I loved him when actually I don't give a damn; but I don't want him to take me for an old tart who'll believe anything. Come on, we'll go and serenade him.'

We reached his place and started to sing under his window which he opened straightaway; he had recognized the voice. He gave a wobbly smile and threw down a few coins. He was not very generous, but he wanted us to leave. We left. And with our 'earnings' we stood ourselves a few drinks. Once more we installed ourselves in front of Jean's house and this time we were in much better spirits. Edith had been singing love songs during the first round, but that was not good enough now. We sang 'Le Catéchisme', a very dirty song about giving candles to nuns, but not for holy purposes!

We then went up to Jean's door, but he wouldn't open it.

Besides being a member of the orchestra in the club where she sang, Jean was also her accompanist. When they got together the next night, Edith was completely drunk. She was still determined to get even with him. When she came on stage, she had to negotiate some steps, with the musicians on each side of the staircase. She came downstairs literally on her knees. As the stage was above the dance floor, Edith's behaviour could hardly go unnoticed. She clung to Jean, who was playing the piano, crying, 'Jean, I love you. I can't live without you. You're so handsome, I can't ever forget you.' But it didn't work; he remained impassive; he ignored her. So we went off to the market and bought some camemberts. Back at the club we crossed the dance floor, tangoing along with the dancers, and offered the camemberts to Jean.

'Here you are, Jean,' Edith shouted. 'This is my parting gift.' All the Belgians laughed till they died. They should have paid us for the show, but they didn't.

So that love affair ended with camembert! When we got

home Lumbroso, who knew what had happened, was not over-joyed to see us. 'You idiotic drunken women, I've had as much of you as I can stand. Don't ever come back, there'll never be another date for you, never.'

He would live to regret that statement. But he had had to put up with a lot from us. We were broke again, but Edith was optimistic.

In those days we learned what misery really means. A few months isn't much in a lifetime, but they are long and hard when things go badly. We even had to sell the few decent clothes we had bought during our days with Leplée.

I had discovered a new trick to make a bit of money – photography. I would saunter down the street between Clichy and Barbès, pick up some man and go for a drink with him. We would talk, exchange life stories. At that point I would get out a picture of one of my little 'brothers', a year-old baby holding a teddy bear. Then, at the right moment, I would say, 'Actually he's my child, not my brother at all. His father abandoned me. I don't even have enough money to buy his food . . .,' or 'I have to pay for his medicine . . .,' or 'I've left him with the concierge, and I need money to get him back.'

It never failed; the victim would hand over some dough, and in exchange we'd make a date for the next day – a date I wouldn't keep. I didn't go to bed with them; it would have served no purpose. I'm not saying that I did not kiss them, sometimes I had to; so I always chose the ones who weren't too bad-looking.

Edith accepted this way of life – she could not do otherwise – but it was dreary and seemed to offer no hope of improvement.

6

THE FIRST BOSS:
RAYMOND ASSO

Our fortunes were at their lowest ebb when Edith saw Raymond Asso. She met him, by chance, in La Nouvelle Athènes, an artists' café. They had known each other back in the good old days when Edith was singing at Gerny's and he was scouting round music publishers for new material for Marie Dubas. He was her secretary. At the same time he was submitting his own songs to publishers.

He was a strange man, around thirty, and a former Foreign Legionnaire. He had been in the Algerian army, too, which made for a mixed background. For Edith there was no more impressive uniform than the big cape, the boots, the pants, and the tarboosh cape; it was the stuff her dreams were made of. Mine too! 'They're so romantic,' we would say to each other, and we welcomed them with open arms. We used to fancy ourselves making love to them wrapped in the folds of their capes.

When Raymond talked to Edith about his life with the Algerian troops she listened with pounding heart and stars in her eyes. The details enthralled her, right down to the seventy-two regulation pleats in their red pants. The desert, the sand, the sun, were hot and colourful, and blazed so vividly in her imagination that she felt as if she had been there.

Normally, with all this going for him, Edith would have fallen right into the ex-Legionnaire's arms. But not this time: it didn't even occur to her. There was something dry and stand-offish about Raymond which deterred her. Their first meeting went something like this:

'Hi, Edith, how're things?'
'Okay.'
'Not too good?'
'Not really.'
'Why?'

Then they started to talk seriously and made dates to see each other again. She had confidence in him; he looked reliable, as though he knew everything there was to know. A real man. He was slim, almost thin, with black hair. He was not handsome, he rarely laughed, but he had something.

When they were together they talked show business. Edith asked masses of questions, especially about Marie Dubas. She practically worshipped her, and wanted to know everything about her: how she worked, how she chose her songs, how she lived, everything.

This curiosity and admiration for Marie had started long before she knew Raymond, back in the days when we were singing in the street. One day when we had a few francs to spare, Edith said to me, 'We're going to the A.B.C. to hear Marie Dubas.'

We bought two places in the gallery. 'What a woman,' murmured Edith, leaning forward, her little white hand clutching my arm.

In two successive songs Marie made the audience cry and then laugh. She could do anything she wanted with them. She wasn't particularly good-looking; but her dark, burning eyes were unforgettable. When she sang you forgot about the way she looked, but you never forgot her voice. She wore one of those deceptively simple dresses. As for her movements – you should have seen her imitating a woman in the Metro. And when she sang 'La Prière de la Charlotte', her hands and arms were so eloquent of the misery that it tore your heart out.

Edith, her eyes full of tears, prayed and cried along with her. I cried for both of them. 'Do it again,' Edith kept shouting. 'Go on, do it again.'

At the end she said, 'I'm going to her dressing-room; come on, Momone.'

We had a lot of nerve, going along in our baggy skirts, old sweaters, and sandals, but Marie was kind to us; it was as if we were old friends.

'Do you like music?' she asked Edith.

'I'm a singer,' Edith replied.

'Where?'

'In the streets.'

But Marie Dubas – the great Marie Dubas – did not laugh. She looked at Edith so kindly that it warmed our hearts and said, 'You'll come back and see me some time.'

She was not asking us, she knew it. When we left the A.B.C. Edith said, 'Did you hear how she spoke to me? That was Marie Dubas. You know, when she stops singing no one will be able to take her place.'

Part of Edith's interest in Raymond lay in her devotion to Marie. She was sure that he knew how one became a Marie Dubas. When they first met, Raymond did not do so very much for her, it was almost as if he were afraid of committing himself. He gave Edith some cursory advice, of the I-would-do-it-this-way ... but-do-what-you-want kind. He realized that she was not open to just any sort of suggestion.

'You do okay, you have enough to eat,' he said, 'but you need someone to manage you, you've got a lot to learn.' It was a tentative sort of offer, but Edith did not understand, or did not want to. She realized that she would have to give herself over to him completely, and there were certain aspects of that relationship that did not interest her. So she replied, 'Yes, I know, I need an agent. I've been looking for one for a long time, but never found him.'

'You need more than that,' replied Raymond. 'You've fallen from quite a height. Now they're going to expect more from you than before. You don't come from the street any more, you come from Gerny's. There's a difference.'

Edith was like an animal that had been broken but not tamed. She probably did not have the patience to go through the hoop a second time. Everything that Raymond said to her was true, but she didn't want to hear it; it was too depressing.

One evening Raymond came into the Nouvelle Athènes with the closed, hard expression he wore on bad days. 'Look, I've got a contract for you. You're going to accept it and you'll be wrong.'

'Don't put yourself out on my account,' Edith said to him. Asso began to needle me, saying I wasn't on his side. In fact I didn't like him very much, his know-all manner irritated me.

'What's it for?'

'A month in Nice.'

'The Côte d'Azur,' said Edith. 'I can't turn that down. Where exactly?'

'At the Boîte à Vitesses.'

'Is it a good place?'

'Fair.'

'There's no need to look as though you're going to someone's funeral, we ought to be celebrating,' Edith exclaimed.

'If you wanted to wait I could find something better,' replied Asso.

'I can't, and anyway, I don't want to. I'd like to put some space between Paris, the Leplée affair, and me. I was left in peace in Brussels; it'll be the same down there, it's *la province*.'

That was an illusion: the provinces are never far behind Paris. Down there the Leplée affair was still the subject of dirty-minded gossip, and Edith's name spelt scandal. Naturally, that was why she had been offered the contract.

I was only just eighteen; how could I understand that Raymond was being a real gentleman? It was not until several years later that I realized what our departure for Nice must have meant to him. He probably did not want to admit it, but he was crazy about Edith. He was as proud as a cock sitting on his perch, waiting for the hen to fly up and join him; he certainly wasn't going to get down and flirt with her. He played little games with himself about our departure. 'If she goes, I'll give her up. If she stays, I'll take care of her.' That was the way Raymond put it.

He thought that it was all over, that Edith was escaping him, particularly when she said, 'Did you find anything for Momone in this club?'

'No.'

'Too bad. We'll make out somehow.'

You should have seen his face. Raymond didn't like me any more than I liked him, and he hoped that this trip would separate Edith and me. Probably he had thought of joining her later. Raymond was jealous of the influence I had over Edith; indeed, he was jealous of everything. I was a considerable threat, for I criticized him, I disagreed with him if I felt like it, and I obviously didn't care about him.

Before we left, he took me aside to give me a lecture. 'Listen. You have a lot of influence over Edith. You must stop her running around, sleeping with everyone she comes across, and drinking so much.'

'Do it yourself, if you're so keen,' I replied. 'She's happy the way she is, and so am I.'

'You know what you are?' he spat out through clenched teeth. 'You're her evil spirit.'

I roared with laughter when he said that, and it infuriated him. When I thought about it again later – me, Edith's evil spirit – it made me giggle. But I was wrong to take it so lightly, Edith was impressionable. Later he succeeded in bringing Edith round to his opinion of me.

Although he was against our departure, he nevertheless took care of everything. He bought us two new suitcases, and second-class tickets. 'That'll give you some prestige,' he added (at that time there were three classes on the French railways).

Knowing how unreliable we were, he accompanied us to the station and saw us on to the train. You would have thought he was a devoted father seeing off his children. He gave us all sorts of advice, 'Don't eat in the compartment, go to the dining-car, it's more becoming.' Then he went off towards the little bookstall to buy us 'something to read'. They sold all kinds of trash, but Raymond knew how to choose. He came back looking pleased as punch. 'Here, I'm sure you'll like this,' he said holding out a book. I looked at the title, 'Une Petite Fille comme ça', by Lucie Delarue-Mardrus. Edith read only the worst kinds of rubbish, 'Deceived on the day of her wedding!', 'Sacrificial Love!', 'Virgin and Mother!', 'Seduction at Twenty!', etc.

She had no intention of reading the little girl book, so I took it. I opened it up, and from the first page to the last I was enthralled. I believed in this story. For a long time Edith and I had believed that all fiction was fact.

It seemed that the train would never leave, but at last it started up. Raymond held Edith's hand as long as possible and

Edith let him. I thought to myself, 'You've really got it bad, *mon vieux*.' He even smiled at me.

Poor Raymond, he was an innocent.

The Edith–Raymond saga is a serial film. The script had already been written, but Edith didn't realize it – although she never lacked a sense of drama. The first episode had just come to an end on the platform at the Gare de Lyon.

At the first stop, we moved into the third class, where the carriages were full of soldiers; but first we bought two litres of red wine each.

There were no military in our compartment so Edith said, 'We'll change again.'

But we didn't. A rather handsome man was sitting beside her. He looked far too well dressed to be in the third class and Edith began to eat him up with her eyes. She slid towards him, and when he took her hand, she quite naturally let her head rest on his shoulder. The power that she had over men was unbelievable. I watched them, and I could see love written all over their faces, the kind you only see in the movies. The trip had started well.

I had plenty of time to read 'Une Petite Fille comme ça'. 'Read it and tell me about it later,' Edith had said.

I watched them as I read. They went well together, like people in a novel. At one point the man went out into the corridor for a smoke, so we quickly took a swig from our bottles, which we had almost forgotten.

'I don't know where he's going,' said Edith to me. 'He said the Midi, not far from Nice. I'll make sure, though, because I'm never going to leave him. I'm mad about him, Momone.'

Before we arrived at Marseilles we caught a glimpse of the sun. I was half asleep, but it was beautiful all the same. Then we plunged into the dirty shade of the Gare Saint Charles at Marseilles.

'I'm going out to stretch my legs,' our companion said to Edith. 'Wait for me.'

'Kiss me.'

He kissed her. It was nothing new; they had been doing it all night. When he got out two policemen came up to him. Without any fuss they slipped on the handcuffs, and it was all over. He turned back and smiled at Edith for the last time.

She was as white as death, her mouth open as though she was about to cry out. I handed her the bottle and she took a long gulp. We did not say anything. There was nothing to say. The train started up again.

'What did you think of him, Momone?' she asked, finally.

'He was nice, but I think he might have become a burden.'

We did not mention it again.

Edith never attempted to spare Raymond's feelings and the first thing she told him about when we got home was the train episode. I could see from his tight expression that he did not appreciate her candour. Nevertheless Raymond wrote a song about it, and it became one of her greatest successes, 'Paris-Méditerranée':

> Un train dans la nuit vous emporte,
> Derrière soi, des amours mortes,
> Et dans mon cœur, un vague ennui...
> Alors sa main a pris la mienne,
> Et j'avais peur que le jour vienne.
> J'étais si bien contre lui.
>
> Lorsque je me suis éveillée
> Dans une gare ensoleillée,
> L'inconnu sautait sur le quai.
> Alors des hommes l'entourèrent
> Le soleil redoublait ma peine,
> Et faisait miroiter ses chaînes.
>
> C'était peut-être un assassin...
> Il y a des gens bizarres
> Dans les trains et dans les gares.

Our arrival in Nice was less romantic. As we left the station, the first thing we saw was a sandwichman. 'Momone, he's got my name written on his back,' Edith shouted. 'Let's catch up with him and buy him a drink.'

We rushed after the poor fellow, and as we caught up with him we read, WAS THE LITTLE SPARROW THE MUR-

DERESS? WAS IT HER? FIND OUT THIS EVENING BY COMING TO THE BOÎTE À VITESSES.

Edith was furious. 'Oh no. They're not going to start that all over again. Murderess. The shits, the bastards. Will I never get away from it?'

I saw things somewhat differently. 'They're bastards, okay, but after all it is publicity. At first people will come to see you because you're notorious, but you'll sing, they'll listen, and if they come back it will be for you alone.'

It was the kind of logic that Edith caught on to fast. She thought for a moment. 'I'll go along with that, but the woman who runs the club has to do it properly. I want lots of sandwich-men, not just one poor old beggar. If we're going to use the scandal, we'll do it on a grand scale. That's what I'll tell this madame.' And she did tell her. Edith already had an instinct for what was right, she knew all the tricks of her trade. She made mistakes in her personal life, but never in her work. Even if it meant swallowing WAS SHE THE MURDERESS? She justified herself quickly. She had been booked for a month by the Boîte à Vitesses; she stayed three. It was badly paid, a hundred francs a day for her and her accompanist, René Cloarec.

We had fifty francs left after we had paid René, which was not very much. We had never eaten so much spaghetti in our lives.

'Momone,' Edith decided, 'you're going to have to work. If you don't you can't stay here. You're going to dance.'

'If you give me another fifteen francs a day, my sister will do her dance number for you,' she announced to the startled manageress. 'She works in the best clubs in Montmartre. I made her give it up and come with me because she needed some sun. See how pale she is. You'll have to take her on if you want me to stay.'

Edith had the most fantastic nerve. I don't know if the woman believed her, but she agreed to the proposal.

In our bedroom, Edith arranged my act. She cut up an old black satin dress, stuck on a green bow and looked at me, 'That's okay. That's one act. You'll have to do classical dancing, because you're wearing satin.' Then she bought a child's overall, and made me wear a red bow. 'With your flat shoes, that'll be the second act. (I wore flat shoes, because she couldn't tolerate my being two inches taller than she was.) 'You can do your acrobatic number in the overall. Call yourself Cabbage Top.'

Being an acrobat was one thing and I had not forgotten the lessons I had had from Dad, but classical ballet! I wasn't even in time with the music. So I did anything that came to mind.

Edith had unearthed a little hotel near the passage Emile-Négrin. We thought it was very smart, but unfortunately the management did not feel the same way about us. One day we came home and the door of our room was open; we could see a cleaning woman pushing a pile of rubbish with a broom – empty sardine cans, a bit of camembert, empty bottles, bits of paper.

We looked at each other. 'Was all that stuff in our room?' Edith asked innocently.

In the bedroom the woman was muttering, 'The little sluts. I've never seen anything like it.'

We had thought we were keeping things tidy by just stuffing everything under the bed.

The American fleet often anchored off Villefranche, and the sailors turned up in Nice. Then we really went to town; Edith adored American sailors. 'They aren't complicated. And since I can't understand a word they're saying, they don't bore me.'

They were blond, pink, and well scrubbed. Edith made them laugh. She would say to them, 'You are good boys,' in an accent they loved. She also knew 'yes', 'no', 'good-bye', 'good morning', and 'kiss me'; and that was sufficient for what they required. When she went off to do her act at the Boîte à Vitesses, she locked them in the room. I say 'them', because there were sometimes three waiting for her at once. One morning at five o'clock a 'prisoner' broke down the door of his room because his ship was about to sail and Edith had forgotten him. She was out drinking with the others.

Edith celebrated her twenty-first birthday in Nice. She didn't have a birthday cake with candles, because at that time we didn't know it was the done thing. We celebrated with a good bottle of wine. We had been living together for six and a half years.

Our tour in Nice over, we took the train again, third-class, not because of soldiers and sailors this time but strictly for reasons of economy. We did not meet any interesting men, there were no shoulders for Edith's head. We held hands with each other because we were so fed up.

Edith had no illusions about our stay in Nice. We had drunk a lot and had a good time, but we were no further on. We had merely used up a bit more of our youth. Nothing was waiting for Edith in Paris, no contract, not even the hope of one. After three months' absence the Little Sparrow's name was forgotten in the big city and well she knew it.

When we arrived at the Gare de Lyon it was dark and dirty, but all the same it smelt good; it was home. It was our home, it was Paris, as she sang later:

> *Oh! mon Paname!*
> *Que tu es loin d'ici*
> *Et que la Seine était jolie*
> *Sous le soleil du mois de juin.*

Edith telephoned Raymond Asso from the station. 'Raymond, you told me you wanted to look after me, didn't you? Well, I'm ready now.'

'Take a taxi and come over.'

She hung up. I could not get over it, 'Why did you call him, of all people?'

'Can you think of anyone else? He once said to me, "If you ever need me, call." That's what I did.'

'You never told me.'

We argued a bit more, but I was too tired. Anyway, it might as well be him as another. We certainly needed someone to look after us.

We set off for the Hôtel Piccadilly in Pigalle. Raymond was waiting for us. He lived there with a woman called Madeleine. They had been together so long that it seemed as if they were married.

Looking more forbidding than ever, he said, 'I've got a room for you.' But there were tears in his eyes, he was so happy to see us. The second episode of the Piaf–Asso saga was about to begin. And indeed Edith's real career was about to begin too.

Leplée had discovered Edith, but it was Asso who first made her great. It was not easy, but he did a marvellous job. Raymond was an exceptional man.

He laid his cards on the table straightaway. 'I'm going to help you, I know show business, and I know the people in it. I guarantee that if you listen to me you'll never be hard up again, but you'll have to work hard, and do as I say. You're finished with pimps and drinking. If you say yes, I won't let you go, ever. If you say no, you can go and knock on someone else's door, I'm not going to let you make a fool of me.' It took Edith's breath away; no one had ever spoken to her like that. Those words, that voice; it was frightening. She said, 'Yes.' Very meekly.

In all honesty, I wanted her to say 'No'. But if she had said no just because of me, then I really would have been her evil spirit.

Edith did not think of Raymond in the same way she thought of other men, the ones she went to bed with. He was the one who could give her good songs, find her contracts, look after her. She believed everything he said. She had confidence in him. Yet that was not enough. No man who said good night to her and then trotted off to his own bed could have any authority over her. Then one day things suddenly changed. She came into our room with an enormous smile on her face. She was laughing so much that she could hardly talk.

'Momone, I know I'm mad, but I'm in love. Guess who with?'

It was impossible to guess with Edith.

'With Raymond Asso,' she shouted triumphantly.

That really hit me.

She explained how it happened. 'I was coming upstairs, he was going down. I looked at him, and I understood everything; why we shout at each other, why he gets on my nerves. I love him. I must be out of my mind not to have understood. It's the first time that it ever happened to me this way, usually I think about it before anything else.

'But what do you see in him?'

'Come on, Momone, you have to be blind not to see how handsome he is. He has sensational eyes, so blue! There's only one other man in the world with eyes like that.'

It was always their eyes that got her. Blue eyes were the barometer and the criterion. When Edith said of her current man, 'Do you think his eyes are really blue? They're grey, and not even a very attractive grey,' the suitor in question might as well pack his bags. He was through. I was familiar with Edith's lectures on the subject of eyes. 'Momone, blue is attractive. It's like light. And eyes can't deceive you, it's true, you know; words and actions can lie, but never eyes.'

Well, Raymond had the necessary eyes, so he was ready for service. I didn't think he was very good-looking, rather undistinguished in fact. He reminded me of a tree in winter, all black and dry, with branches that were all right for crows to settle on, but not for sparrows.

'Don't argue, Momone, something clicked.'

When 'something clicked' with Edith there was no more to be done but wait for the next move.

Raymond was frank with me. 'You see, Simone, now that everything's working out between Edith and me, we'll do a good job.'

'You mean you still haven't finished?'

In his superior way, he called my bluff. 'Listen, I know your kind. I'm not an innocent; if you want us to be friends you'll have to stop trying to mess things up. For once you're not in the driver's seat, understand?'

'Yes, sir, Sergeant-Major, sir.'

That made him laugh, but not me.

For the first few days, everything went along swimmingly. Edith was driving me mad with her hysterical chatter, 'Momone, he's so great. What a man. And he knows so much. I really trust him. Raymond's more than my manager, he's the man I needed all along. Don't you think life is strange? He was there, right beside me, and I didn't even see him. How lucky I was to meet him.'

She was so happy she had forgotten all about Madeleine's existence, but I hadn't. I was sure she would make trouble.

There is no such thing as a wife who surrenders her husband without a hassle. Even if she's no longer interested in him herself, she rarely wants to hand him over to another woman on a plate. At first things went quite well. We were fairly friendly with Madeleine, who was a nice girl. Edith did not advertise the affair. When she was alone with Raymond, it was for work. She would say to Madeleine and me, 'While you're both out doing the shopping, I'm going to work with Raymond.'

These working sessions of course took place in our room.

I dragged out the shopping as long as I could. 'Momone, I'm counting on you,' Edith would say. 'I need at least two hours.'

Taking that amount of time isn't easy when you only have a loaf of bread, a can of sardines, and a bottle of wine to buy – and no watch. I looked at all the clocks we passed; I went into all the shops, comparing prices. Madeleine was astonished, 'I had no idea you were so economical; Edith is such a spendthrift.' 'Yes,' I replied, 'but I manage the money side.'

'Don't you think that Edith and Raymond work together a lot?'

Putting on my most innocent expression – and it was innocent – I said, 'Well, they have such a lot to do.'

Madeleine was not taken in though. She was waiting for it to blow over, and I was waiting with her. I used to think it was funny, but in a way we were both being cuckolded.

Once the first 'I love you, I adore you' was over, Raymond put Edith to work. There, too, we had some surprises in store for him. He hardly knew us and he couldn't believe that anyone could be as ignorant as we were.

There were some strange sessions in our room. Edith lay sprawled out on the bed, Raymond sat astride a chair, a pipe in his mouth, his head a little to one side, taking little puffs making a pah ... pah ... pah sound. From the street came the sound of horns, from far off the sound of music. It was the carnival at Pigalle.

'Edith, it's carnival time at Pigalle,' I said. 'Are we going?'

Edith looked happy, she raised her head smiling, 'That's a good idea.'

'No,' declared Raymond. 'You're through with all that.'

I felt like biting him. 'You can't lay down the law all the time,' I shouted. It was like a terrible hunger; I was only eighteen and longing for the fun, the lights, the music.

'Yes I can.'

Raymond pointed me out to Edith with the stem of his pipe. 'Listen to her, your Simone. Carnival. And what then? Are you going to learn to sing on your way to the fair? You have other things to do. You don't even know how to read.'

Within a few minutes Raymond had won. It infuriated me, but I knew he was right. Edith indeed knew nothing, she could barely read. She decoded a page so slowly that reading bored her. As for writing, she wrote only to me and to Jacques. She was not self-conscious with him and, as for me, I hardly knew any more than she did.

At first, in order to sign her name without making mistakes, Raymond had to write it out and she would then copy it until she knew it by heart. He composed the phrases, and she signed 'With all good wishes from Edith Piaf', 'In friendship . . .'

There was one thing that Edith could not bear, and that was the dictionary. 'The Larousse is a big cheat. You look for a word, you find it, they send you back to another word and you haven't got anywhere. And as for the grammar, it's too complicated. I know the present, the past, and the future. That's all you need to live.'

She shook the book under my nose, 'But look here, the conditional, the pluperfect, the imperfect. What do you need all those for? I give up.'

Edith was much too intelligent not to realize that she was missing a lot of things, and that drove her to work even harder. Raymond enlisted my help. When Edith yawned or started off after red herrings, or said 'I'm fed up' he would reply drily, 'Simone's understood. *She* knows what it means. If you're as bright as she is you'll have to prove it.'

That made Edith mad; whatever I could do, she could do. But Raymond had to change the bait from time to time; she did not swallow the same one for long. On the day that Edith replied angrily, 'I don't give a shit what Simone's doing,' Raymond hit back with, 'How about Marie Dubas?'

'What the hell's she got to do with it?'

'You think it's enough just to go up on stage and open your mouth. I'll tell you what the hell Marie Dubas has to do with it. If someone mentions Baudelaire to her, she doesn't ask for his telephone number so that she can ask him to write her a song. If a man kisses her hand, she doesn't start shrieking obscenities at him. If she's served fish, she doesn't put all the bones in her mouth, neither does she spit them out on to her plate because she doesn't know what to do with them. If she's introduced to a cabinet minister, she doesn't say "How's tricks?"'

To all of which Edith retorted, 'I come from the streets, everyone knows that. So if they don't like me, they can leave me alone.'

'And that's just what they'll do. There's no shame in being from the lower classes; but there *is* shame in wanting to stay gauche and ignorant. Marie Dubas knows how to behave herself in life, at table, and with other people. She's gracious. There's a required minimum and you haven't even reached that yet. I'm sick of you, of your moods, of your stupidity!'

Edith was choking with rage. I thought she was going to tear the whole room apart. Then suddenly, she quietened down. There was a tense silence, and Edith became very humble. I felt sorry for her, she looked so little and so lost.

'I am learning, Raymond, but don't leave me,' she pleaded. 'I love you, you know I love you.'

Raymond took her in his arms, calling her '*ma petite fille*', and gently stroking her hair. After the bitterness, he poured on the sweetness. 'If you let me help you, if you listen to me, *mon petit*, you'll be the greatest ever.'

Raymond was a wizard; he knew exactly what to do. Calling Edith '*ma petite fille*' wasn't much, perhaps it was ordinary, but she had never heard it before. The kindest people she had known, Louis Leplée and Jacques Bourgeat, used to say '*mon petit*'. It was fatherly and protective, but with Raymond it was '*Didou, Didi. Mon Edith ...*' We were not used to that kind of talk, and such words meant something to girls like us.

So Edith melted. 'He's so intelligent. He knows so much and he explains things so well. It really is something to be treated like that. I love him very much, you know. I really do love him. He can make me do anything he wants.'

That was not entirely true; they continued to have their ups and downs. Edith got tired. It's not much of a life at twenty-one to hear someone nagging all the time, 'Don't do that.' 'Hold your fork like this, don't put your knife on the table.' 'Don't fill your glass so full.' 'Don't make a noise when you're eating.' 'Don't talk.' 'Eat with your mouth closed.' It is not easy to keep your mouth closed when you're eating, unless you learned to do it as a child. When Edith had grasped one thing, Raymond would launch an attack on something else. 'You have no idea how to dress.' This was true; Edith had terrible taste. She adored frills, pleats, little ribbons, and lots of lipstick. She thought nothing of wearing yellow, purple, and green all at the same time. She thought it looked gay. There was nothing I could do about it. When we went out together, I would let her walk along looking as though she was decked out for a fancy-dress party; I wore simple little dresses which clung a bit, so that the men would look at me. I always hoped that, thanks to my clothes, I might attract the cutest guy, but it was always Edith who ended up with the best-looking ones.

On the day Raymond criticized Edith's lack of dress sense there was quite a scene.

'Don't interfere with things you don't know anything about. My clothes are none of your business.'

'You look good on a stage in your little black dress.'

'It's the principle that counts. Off stage I can do what I want.'

'Off stage you have to carry on the same style that you do on stage. It's part of your personality.'

To develop Edith's personality he made her talk for hours on end. She would tell him stories and she loved to chat. She always knew what to say to hold a man's interest. Instinctively she told him what he wanted to hear, and she was never wrong.

Raymond was entitled to the same treatment as the others, only for him she gave it a poetic twist. She was the poor little girl from the back streets, a little lost, but so appealing. She took care over the details: her family, the men she had had; the miserable evenings she had spent alone; everything that had happened. True or false, Raymond did not care. She helped him to fashion and fill in the details of her 'personality'.

Listening to her he realized that Edith could not sing other people's songs, that he would have to find a repertoire to suit her. She needed something straightforward with no frills. He got to work and wrote songs for her himself, making notes on a laundry list with a blunt little stub of pencil. He did not always need a whole story like the one on the train about which he wrote 'Paris-Méditerranée'. It didn't take much to get him going. One day I said to him, 'You know Edith used to hang around the rue Pigalle...'

'Shut up a minute.' He started to write, and left us. The next day he read us 'Elle fréquentait la rue Pigalle':

> *Elle semblait tout' noir' de péchés,*
> *Avec un pauvr' visage tout pâle,*
> *Pourtant y' avait dans l'fond d'ses yeux*
> *Comme qu'èque chos' de miraculeux,*
> *Qui semblait mettr' un peu d' ciel bleu,*
> *Dans celui tout sal' de Pigalle.*

It was Raymond who created the type of ballad which came to be identified with Edith.

It was great when we all three sat together discussing the songs; I loved it. When we worked like that Madeleine would often come round too, and bring us coffee. Where work was concerned we were one big happy family.

When the words were completed, Marguerite Monnot supplied the music. Raymond Asso was an absolute genius to have persuaded Marguerite Monnot to work with us. The first time we saw Raymond and Marguerite together, Edith and I wondered what those two could have in common. Asso was tough in his way, and nervous. Marguerite had a sweet, oval face and fair hair and was always up in the clouds, with a gentle little smile on her lips. While Raymond agonized over a sentence, Marguerite would dream. 'I'm going to introduce you to Marguerite Monnot,' Raymond had said to Edith. 'She's the one who wrote the music to "L'Etranger".'

That was a good enough recommendation. 'L'Etranger' was

one song we would never forget. We were all three together in the room waiting for Marguerite, who was always either early or late. When she came in she said, 'Well, my dears, this is a nice place you've got here.'

Raymond laughed, 'It's a hotel, you know.'

'Yes? Well, it's nice anyway.'

She cannot have looked at it very closely; the Piccadilly was a bit shabby. The rugs were more thread than design; but that didn't make any difference, Marguerite refused to notice anything unpleasant.

Edith was impressed: she stared at her as if she could see her very soul. She slipped her hand into Marguerite's, saying, 'I'm sure that you're a great person.'

'Oh!' Marguerite exclaimed. She sounded as surprised as a lady who just realizes she's been raped.

Edith nicknamed her Guite straightaway, and they became fast friends.

The first time that Edith went to Guite's home, there was a moment so charged with emotion that I wanted to burst into tears. 'Touch my piano,' Marguerite said to her. 'Put your hands on it.' Edith put her hands on the keys and closed her eyes. 'Guite, this was my dream when I was five years old and I was blind, and I could only hear.'

'So listen now.'

Marguerite had beautiful pianist's hands. She placed her fingers on Edith's. 'Come on, play with me.'

Edith's face broke into a radiant smile. She looked like a child who was too happy to speak and could only laugh. That was how Edith learned to play. She adored it. She said she understood music better when she could play herself.

Raymond and Marguerite were as different as chalk and cheese, but they worked wonderfully together on a song: it was a true marriage of minds. And together they put Edith on the map.

The work sessions went like this: Edith read the words as if she were already singing them, Marguerite dreamed, Raymond waited – he could not be sure of the song until the music was finished.

When the reading was over, Marguerite listened to it once more, then said, 'I think I see it now.' And she would sit before her piano and play, transporting herself to a world of her own – a world which she never really left.

Guite and Edith were friends right up to Marguerite's death in 1961. A quiet death; she had not looked ill, and we didn't know she was; she rarely talked about herself. She slipped into death as gently as she had passed through life.

Marguerite was as important to Edith's career as Raymond was. She taught her what a song was; she made her understand that music is more than a tune; that, depending on the way you interpret it, it can mean as many different things as the words – and with as many nuances.

'The best gift that Raymond gave me was Guite,' Edith would say. 'A remarkable and good woman. She doesn't live on this earth at all, but somewhere else, in a blue world full of beautiful, clean things. When I think of angels, I think they must be like Guite.'

But that did not stop her from bawling her angel out sometimes. 'Your feet aren't on the ground, Marguerite.' (That was bad, Edith loved using nicknames – Guite, Momone, Riri, etc. – when she called you by your proper name, she was being mean.) 'You're impossible. There's no greater music writer than you. But you don't show yourself. You don't care about publicity. You sign any contract that comes along. We should give you a lawyer to take care of your affairs.'

And Guite would reply sweetly, 'It isn't important. Listen to this, it'll calm you down.' Then she would start to improvise, sometimes going on for hours on end.

When she was three and a half Marguerite Monnot had earned her first fee playing Mozart in the Salle des Agriculteurs. She should have made her career as a concert pianist; she had studied with Nadia Boulanger and Cortot, and they didn't teach song-writing!

Marguerite composed her first song by mistake. Tristan Bernard, one of the great comics between the two world wars, had brought her a poem called 'Ah! les jolis mots d'amour'.

'Could you put a few notes to it?' he inquired.

'I don't know how.'

'Try.'

The resulting song was charming. It was sung in a film with Claude Dauphin. Afterwards, with the same ease, she had done 'L'Etranger' – that became her trademark – then 'Mon Légionnaire'. After that Marguerite was consistently successful. Not only did she write almost all Edith's music, but she also composed the music for the show *Irma la Douce*; the lyrics, by Colette Renard, were a mixture of poetry and slang which travelled very successfully to other countries, particularly America.

Marguerite only had to put her hands on her piano and the music just flowed from her fingers. She only truly came alive when she was composing. It is easy, in recalling those times, to skim over the bad patches, but in fact the relationship between the three of us (four if you include Marguerite) had its ups and downs, to say the least. There were fights violent enough to shatter the windows. Edith gave up several times. Being constantly told 'you look like a tart', 'you eat like a pig', 'a kid of six can read better than you', is enough to drive anybody round the bend.

Edith and I had never been kept on a leash. Even in the Leplée days we had lived in the street, and we were free. We did not know what it meant to have a master, and we certainly had no intention of finding out. When she had had as much as she could take, Edith would say to me, 'I'm sick to death of your Raymond. Come on, let's go out.'

I was not the one to dissuade her. We were suffocating in the courtyard of the Piccadilly, we needed some air. So we escaped at night, when Raymond was spending time with Madeleine in order to keep up appearances. That in itself was enough to throw Edith into a rage: 'Either he's mine or he's hers. He's got to make up his mind if he wants it to last.'

Edith always came alive between eleven at night and six in the morning; and the man who wanted to hold on to her had to match her hours, and not only in bed.

'Life isn't the same at night as it is during the day,' she said. 'The night is warm and full of lights. The people are different, they're more easy-going. I always feel I'm meeting old friends at night, even if I've never set eyes on them before. And they look different too, everyone is better-looking.'

She wandered from café to night club to bistro. We caught up with our old friends and drank with them. The next day she would have a hangover and not want to work, which infuriated Raymond.

One morning they had a tremendous fight. She was in bed, half-asleep; I was beside her. Edith yawned so widely you could see her tonsils. 'Raymond, give me a break. I don't want to see you this morning,' she called out.

'Well, you're going to hear me,' he answered.

'Don't shout, my head's killing me.'

'Simone, snap out of it and make her some coffee.'

'Fuck off,' I answered.

'I've had enough of this,' he shouted. 'It's got to stop. Edith, you're going to get out of bed or I'll leave you, do you hear me?'

He shook her, but she promptly fell asleep again. He went quite berserk, and even hit her. In the end she realized he was not going to give up; he was determined to win this fight. His chin set, a hard gleam in his eye, he paced up and down the room – the size of which didn't allow him very much scope.

I didn't say a thing. I got up, made the coffee, and Raymond let forth a torrent of abuse, 'You live like a whore without making a penny. You've got to give up these pimps and their girls, your band of good-for-nothing friends who hang around you for what little you have. You let yourself wallow in the shit. You've got to let them go, it's vital if you're going to succeed in your career. When you've got a spot at the A.B.C., can you see them trailing after you? The reporters will have the time of their lives.'

'My friends came to Gerny's.'

'And did it help you become a success?'

Suddenly she realized what he had just said, 'Me, go to the A.B.C.? You're kidding.'

'No. It's what I'm working for and it's what we'll get.'

Edith seemed stunned by the thought of the A.B.C. We looked at each other – Edith singing in a big concert hall! We could not believe it, but Raymond was not joking.

'Raymond, I can't do that to my friends. They've always been so good to us. They've never given up on us. Without Henri I wouldn't even have had a dress for the opening at Gerny's.'

'You don't have to worry about that now. Let me do it. They must learn to respect you.'

Edith didn't even understand the word; in the streets there is no 'respect'.

Raymond had the courage to go and dig up Edith's pals, the ones she hung out with all the time. What a bunch : petty pimps and layabouts more or less on relief, but Edith and I had belonged to them, they had been our 'protectors'. It had not lasted, but they still retained the rights to us.

How did Raymond scare them off ? Since he would not tell us, Edith preferred not to ask him. All she said to me was, 'Raymond is a man. You really have to be someone to be able to do that.'

He was an ex-legionnaire, after all, and he proved it by getting rid of the hangers-on; they had all gone, all our boy-friends, Lulu de Montmartre, fat old Fréhel : he had cleared them all out.

If anyone dared lay a hand on him, he had a magic sentence; his blue eyes would narrow and he'd mutter, 'I hate the feel of human flesh.' Those words really knocked the wind out of me, and they must have had the same effect on others.

Edith may not have been passionately in love with Raymond but she had confidence in him. He was indispensable to her and she could not give him up. Her instinct told her he was the only one who could lift her from the gutter. Asso was Edith's first contact with a man who thought of other things besides drinking, playing, and screwing. I felt that he was not content to stop short at getting rid of the hangers-on, he had someone else in mind. I was frightened for myself and for Madeleine. I knew my Edith. If she gave up something, then she expected something in return. And after all, what was she to do during the evenings and nights if she could no longer run all over town; obviously Raymond must live with her.

Then Madeleine was really furious – but in Edith's eyes, it was

Madeleine who was in the wrong, and Edith had been waiting for this opportunity. Their friendship was over. Edith was unperturbed.

'Raymond, tell your wife you've had enough of her,' Edith had demanded.

'Be a little patient, Edith.'

'You've sent my boy-friends away so that I'm all alone. You chose me, so give up Madeleine. If you don't, *I'll* start giving things up, and you'll be the first to go.'

Raymond loved Edith profoundly. His love for her was threefold, as a husband, as a creator, and as a father. He also knew that nothing could keep Edith from getting to the top. There had been no triumph yet, but he could sense it coming and he did not intend to forfeit his share of it.

He had an old score to settle with me. I got in his way; therefore I must go. I was an inconvenience, and some men don't like sleeping three in a bed; we had only one room and there was no option. During the day I could go for a walk, but at night I needed a bed, too. We had fights, even about his songs. Since I supplied him with ideas, like the one about the rue Pigalle, I felt free to criticize, 'I don't like the way that sounds. I'd put this word in instead.'

He wasn't too pleased about that. He would look me up and down and he always had some comment to make about my appearance. To get my own back on him when he said to me, 'Look at yourself, you're setting a bad example for Edith,' I would run him down in front of her. I didn't miss a thing, and Edith listened to me; it was easy, I made her laugh, he didn't.

I realized that this set-up could not last, that the situation was untenable, but I was stubborn, and so was he.

Raymond was mean, but he was also more intelligent than I. He planned the blow for some time, preparing it with meticulous care. He began by making up his mind to leave Madeleine, and live with Edith. Naturally he could not do that if they stayed at the Piccadilly where they might bump into Madeleine on the stairs. So he chose the Hôtel Alsina on the avenue Junot to move into with Edith. The difference between it and the Piccadilly was like night and day. The room had a bath and a telephone, there were carpets and a decent lobby. He was certainly one rung up the ladder. The A.B.C. contract was in the air, you could smell it; and it had better be a good one because the Hôtel Alsina didn't cost peanuts, Raymond was not made of money, and Edith at that time was working very little. And he had decided to get rid of me in one final sweep. Edith was out and he waited for me in our room. He looked at me sideways with his little blue eyes. I knew that he had something up his sleeve, but I wasn't scared. Inside I was boiling over, but I was sure that I had an answer for everything. Raymond and I spoke 'man to man'!

He smoked a while in silence, then said, 'Momone'.

That was when I knew he was in deadly earnest. He never called me that; I was Simone, and no more. He was nervous, he cracked his fingers. He had dry hands, but they were quite fine, an artist's hands.

'*Ma petite* Momone, you've always felt that I don't like you, haven't you? But you're wrong. I've always got on well with you.'

'Cut the shit.'

'As you wish.'

'I don't give a damn what you think. Tell me what you want.'

'Very well. It'll be easier, anyway. You know that I'm doing everything I can for Edith. I've staked a lot on her. I believe in her. And . . . I don't think you're good for her.'

'I'm the evil spirit. You've said that before. It's not a bad idea, but you have to prove it.'

'You set her a bad example. You run around, you get drunk, and you take her with you. I've got two contracts for her here, one at the Sirocco, the other in a night club near the Champs-Elysées. She's also going to the A.B.C. Therefore she has to change her way of life. You're her past. With you around she's reminded of it all the time. She must forget it. If you stay, she won't succeed. It's not a question of not seeing her ever again, but . . .'

'You've got a hell of a nerve!'

'You mustn't live with her any more. She and I are going to

live in another hotel on the avenue Junot. I haven't taken a room
for you.'

'Is this what Edith wants?'

'Yes.'

'Is that why she went out? She knew you were going to hand
me all this shit.'

'Yes.'

'Then I've nothing more to say.'

I packed my four dresses and left. I did not want him to see
me cry. I was too young to understand that he was playing
games, that he was lying to me. He had counted on my pride
and he was not mistaken. Much later, when I was talking to
Edith about it, I learned that when she got home she had asked
where I was and he replied, 'She went off with some man.'

Edith was outraged. She couldn't stand people leaving her.
She often did it to others, but she did not like it when the tables
were turned. She believed I had walked out on her.

I climbed up the rue Pigalle, our street, all alone. The sound of
my footsteps, my loneliness, and my sadness drove me from
Pigalle to Ménilmontant and I arrived at my mother's without
even knowing why. I found two almost loving arms to hold me
close. For the first time in my life, and the only time, I was not at
my mother's but at Mummy's. In those few moments I forgot
the past – my mother's coldness, her hardness, her greed, her in-
difference, everything. She hugged me to her; at last I was the
little child I had always dreamed of being. This show of tender-
ness revived my will to live.

I had no illusions; I knew that the kindness would be short-
lived.

So I went back to the life I'd led before I met Edith. I worked
on an assembly line at the Félix Potin works, putting chocolates
in boxes. On Saturday I went to the swimming pool, on Sundays
to the movies.

I was alone and lost, unresisting. I had lived with Edith for so
many years, sharing her life, her loves; now Edith and I were
through, I was sure of it, and I needed her love so much. My need
for love was assuaged by someone whom I met at the swimming
pool one Saturday. I felt that the chlorinated water was washing

Pigalle, the pimps, the whores, and the soldiers out of me. I smelled cleaner, and I almost was. At least this newcomer believed in me, in my innocence, and it was so good to have someone who respected me so much; he did not dare touch me. He called me 'Mademoiselle', as Mermoz had called Edith. I was not used to it. So I became his wife before we had time to get engaged. I could no longer bear being alone. I needed someone to echo my thirst for love, to feel a human being close to me. I got married, without saying a word to anyone else, without a wedding breakfast, without the famous wedding cake, without ceremony. One Saturday we stood with perhaps twenty other couples waiting our turn at the Registrar's and we were duly married.

I was mad. I didn't know that it was impossible to give up Edith. That day-to-day existence, the factory routine, were not for me. Then one day I took my courage in both hands and called her. 'It can't be you, Momone. Come on over, I've got a lovely place here. I have a bathroom all to myself.'

'No, I'd rather see you somewhere else.'

We made a date to meet at a smart café called the Wepler near Clichy. When she came in, I could see that things were going well, by her smile, her eyes, her clothes. She was in high spirits. She was sparkling as if she was cheating on one of her men, which in a sense was true; by seeing me she was cheating on Raymond.

She wanted me to tell her everything, but my marriage was so personal, so clean, that I kept it to myself. Edith did not even notice, she had too many things to tell me about – her new songs, her plans, Raymond's advice.

It is strange that I bore him no grudge. I knew he was a useful stepping-stone for Edith, perhaps the key to her success. Edith and I had taken up where we left off. We saw each other several times. One day she arrived, her face taut with anger. 'Momone, I have something to tell you. I can't go on like this. Do you remember our legionnaire?'

I was a bit vague. 'Tell me about him.'

'You remember the time we spent with the legionnaire, Riri, from the porte des Lilas?'

Another Henri. It came back to me as if it had happened yesterday, although it must have been a full four or five years ago, when we used to sing in the streets and the barracks. We had to pay special attention in the barracks because the soldiers would try to slip out without paying. Edith used to stick me at the entrance to the canteen with an empty fruit can in my hand; I had to force them to pay up.

On one particular night, the soldiers were all sitting down, when a legionnaire walked in wearing the white képi and red cummerbund, the whole works. He looked down at me from his considerable vantage point and said, 'I'm not giving you anything.'

Edith was beside me. Always very regal on these occasions, she ordered me to let him go. Then the legionnaire said to Edith, 'I'll see you at the exit.'

He was no better-looking than anyone else, but he had blue eyes. All three of us left together. It is not far from Lilas to the rue Orfila. And we went straightaway to the Hôtel de l'Avenir.

Riri went back to the barracks at seven in the morning, he'd had enough to last him for four days. Edith had a date with him that same evening at six. Since she liked him, we arrived at the barracks on time, and asked for him at the guard post.

'What do you want with him?'

'I'm his sister,' said Edith, 'I've come to see him.'

'And her?' asked the orderly, looking at me. 'Is she his sister too?'

'Naturally,' said Edith, 'since she's my sister.'

'He's in the detention block. Come back another time.'

'He can't be, I have to speak to him. I have a message from our mother, she's sick.'

She pressured the soldier so much that the corporal called the sergeant.

'You'll have to see the adjutant,' he said.

'With luck this won't stop until we get to the General,' Edith whispered to me.

'It's not the regular practice,' said the adjutant, 'but because it's in a good cause I'll send for him.' He brought Riri, the

legionnaire, down to us. He was flanked by soldiers in full
regalia – rifles, helmet, battle dress, spats.

The bastard didn't even glance at us, it was as if he had never
set eyes on us before. Edith was not to be put off. She threw
herself into his arms, whispering, 'You're my brother.'

'You don't look like my sister,' he muttered. The whole post
began to laugh; they weren't so dumb. Riri made a date with her
while the sergeant commanded him, 'Kiss your sisters. Go on,
better than that, you idiot.'

At the end of his four-day confinement, they saw each other
again. It lasted no more than a week; his regiment left for somewhere, and Edith forgot Riri.

That was Edith's legionnaire story. I had no idea why she was
digging it up again.

'Listen, Momone, while we were enjoying ourselves with Riri
at the porte des Lilas, Raymond, whom I'd never heard of, was
writing a song, "my" story. He called it "Mon Légionnaire".
Isn't that fantastic? What a coincidence!'

> J'sais pas son nom, je n'sais rien d'lui,
> Il m'a aimée toute la nuit,
>   Mon légionnaire!
> Et me laissant à mon destin,
> Il est parti dans le matin
>   Plein de lumière!
> Il était minc', il était beau,
> Il sentait bon le sable chaud,
>   Mon légionnaire!
> Y'avait du soleil sur son front,
> Qui mettait dans ses cheveux blonds,
>   De la lumière!

'And do you know who first sang it? Marie Dubas! Raymond
gave it to her. Isn't that awful?'

I tried to explain to Edith that Raymond could not be blamed,
that before he met her he had been free to give his songs to
whomever he pleased, but she would not hear of it.

'The Foreign Legion belongs to me and no one else. He could
have kept it for me. It was my song, "my" story.'

When she was excited she was always unreasonable. I knew Edith so well that I realized she must have plagued Raymond with accusations of treachery for days and nights – especially nights!

She banged her little fist on the table. 'I don't care, I'm going to sing it. Do you hear. I'll make them forget Marie Dubas.'

Today, nobody remembers that Marie first sang it. The legionnaire story has an ending. We saw Riri again, straight after the war I think, in a big music hall called the Étoile. Edith was with Yves Montand. One night a man asked if he could see Edith in her dressing-room. He told them: 'It's Riri, her legionnaire. She'll understand.'

He came in, a bald guy in civvies with the beginnings of a paunch. He was unbelievably unattractive. What a laugh!

'Memories are like certain meals – great while you're eating them, but afterwards you pay the price for having enjoyed them. Still my legionnaire memory's great,' she concluded gamely.

It was easy for me to follow her life with Raymond through our meetings. She told me everything. What bound Edith and Raymond together was not a golden wedding ring, but song. Edith rapidly paid Raymond back everything he had given her; it was thanks to her that he became famous.

Like the others, Raymond lasted no more than eighteen months, yet for a long time after they had split up, people still referred to the Piaf–Asso team.

In Paris the A.B.C. was *the* music hall. It was run by Mitty Goldin, an impresario who could make you or break you if your business was show business. He had come from central Europe to Paris with no luggage except his Hungarian cunning. Now he could boast of having launched many of the big names. Everyone sang at the A.B.C. at some time, but few of them made their début there. They would not have dared. Even the supporting acts had to be tried out elsewhere. There was no lack of training grounds, the Concert Pacra, Bobino, the Gaîté Montparnasse, Wagram, the Alhambra, the Moulin-Rouge, and so on, and that was not counting the local music halls around town; and in the suburbs there were the big cinemas, the Rex, the Gaumont-

Palace, the Paramount. Mitty didn't pay well, but being booked at the A.B.C. was a crowning achievement.

At that time you made your name on stage, records came later; just the opposite of what happens now. The technique of singing wasn't the same either. You didn't use a microphone, you used your voice and your guts. Try to whisper, with feeling, 'I love you' to a room of two thousand people. It was something Edith could do supremely well.

So I got a terrific jolt when Edith announced one day, 'Momone, this is it. I'm going to the A.B.C. And guess which spot I've got?'

'Beginning of the second half.'

Watching me closely, she proudly proclaimed, 'Top billing.'

Top of the bill first time round! I simply couldn't believe it.

'It wasn't easy. You don't know what Raymond had to put up with; the first time he mentioned me Mitty Goldin joked, "Leave the kid in the streets, she's not for us."

' "I promise you she's changed," Raymond insisted. "You won't recognize her. She's not the same girl who sang in the local flicks. I've written her repertoire. In a year you'll be tearing your hair out because you didn't discover her yourself."

' "Well, today I'm saying no."

'You know how Raymond is when he gets an idea into his head. He went back again the next day.

'It wasn't hard to imagine him, sitting on a dirty old bench outside Mitty's office, smoking his pipe. Mitty would come out and ask him, "What are you waiting for, Raymond? Do you have a new song for me?"

' "No, I've come for the contract for the Little Sparrow."

' "Well, you can go back where you came from."

' "I'll be back tomorrow."

' "Tomorrow, the day after, makes no difference; the answer'll still be no."

'For weeks Mitty Goldin wouldn't change his tune. The old bastard made Raymond wait for hours on purpose. I don't know how long it lasted, but in the end Mitty got bored. "Okay, Raymond, she can do the opening number," he conceded.

' "No, you've got to give her star billing."

'And tough old Mitty finally gave in.

'Let's celebrate, Momone. Come on, everyone have a drink on me.' Luckily it was a small bar, there were not many people there. Then Edith decided, 'Now we've had fun, we're going up to the Sacré Coeur to light a candle for St Theresa.'

We pranced along, weaving a little from side to side. It was fortunate that we were at the rue Lepic, near la Butte, and that it ran uphill, there was less chance of our toppling over than if we had been going down.

When we got to the Sacré Coeur, Edith lit a candle for the Virgin Mary, too – something for everyone. She had to share her happiness, she was thanking everyone in Heaven. As we left, Edith took my arm and squeezed it hard. We were both so small, and the whole of Paris with its flickering lights was spread at our feet; it was as if the world had turned upside down, and the sky with its stars was below us. Edith sobered up. Suddenly she sounded serious, 'Momone, the A.B.C. is the very top. I'll have climbed so high I'll be dizzy.'

As I looked at her, I was afraid that she would outgrow me. 'Don't leave me behind,' I pleaded.

'Don't be stupid. But listen, my life's going to be serious from now on.'

What a grand affair the A.B.C. was! We were no longer at the stage of knitting the dress. A new era had begun, one that brought success with it, and millions of francs, and tours, and glory. Edith called me at my concierge's at all hours; 'Come over quickly. I've got news for you, I have to tell you about it now.'

I would rush over.

'Momone, this is it, I've met the Marquise and the Marquis. They entertained me in their office and were very friendly.'

We'd been waiting for this for a while. Monsieur and Madame Breton (of the Breton Publishers) were the king and queen of the business; no career could be made without their assent. They discovered Charles Trenet and pushed him; he had not been much of a success at first, not everyone had liked him. Their catalogue was the musical world's telephone directory.

Edith and I used to hang about their entrance, thinking that perhaps one of them would notice us, but we were too shabby and too small. I had never forgotten Madame Breton; she was a slim little brunette, very lively; with sharp eyes, and a lot of style. She looked like a real Marquise, covered in jewellery, and her bracelets tinkled as she walked.

Edith went on with her story:

'Raymond and I went into their office, it's like someone's living room; I said to myself, "This time things have really changed." Their entrance is near the rue Rossini, it's all black, but it looks good all the same.

' "So you're going to be at the A.B.C.," the Marquise said to me. "Are you pleased?"

' "It's marvellous, the best thing that ever happened."

' "There's only one trouble; you're sharing the bill with Charles Trenet, on the billboard your name *la môme Piaf* will appear beside his. That name isn't good enough, it just won't do."

'She said it gently but drily. I couldn't get over it, it was like being with Leplée all over again, I was going to have to change my name once more. Then, "I have an idea. *La môme Piaf*'s a night-club name, it's already out of date. What about Edith Piaf?"

' "Fine," said Raymond.

'We drank champagne, and she poured some over my head saying, "In the name of song, I baptize you Edith Piaf."

'Here, Momone, touch my hair here, it'll bring good luck. I've brought you the cork, keep it.'

That cork went everywhere with me until I lost it.

'What do *you* think of Edith Piaf?'

So long as she was happy I liked the name well enough, but I was sorry to lose the Little Sparrow. It was part of the past, like a brick that had crumbled with age and fallen from the wall.

So Raymond ceased to be in charge of the choice of dresses, hair-styles, and make-up; the Marquise had taken over the job.

Before the premiere at the A.B.C. she took her to the great designer Jacques Heim. Edith couldn't get over it. 'If only you could see it, Momone. The store, the saleswomen, the clothes, it's too beautiful to be true. When I'm rich you'll have nice clothes too. Do you remember how we used to drool over the dresses in the windows at Tout-Main and Tout-Fait on the Champs-Elysées on our way back from Gerny's? The Marquise says that I can't go everywhere in my stage clothes; I have to get myself up for cocktail parties and receptions and things. How about that?'

The Marquise had chosen a violet dress and violet-lined cape for Edith, and she looked very pretty. There was no question about it, Madame Breton had taste. She had also taken Edith to a beauty salon called Anna Pegova. But there was quite a struggle there. 'Those creams and things, I'm not saying they aren't any good, they're soft and they smell good,' Edith fumed, 'but I'm not having anything to do with their make-up. By the time you've escaped from their clutches you look worse than you did when you went in. Anyway, I *know* my face, it's a friend; I can't stand to see that painted clown grinning out at me from the mirror.'

Three weeks before the premiere Edith could not sleep, could not eat, could not drink.

'I can't stand Raymond,' she cried. 'He's driving me up the wall! Now he wants me to take singing lessons, but I won't. I'd lose everything I have.' And she kept her word; although she was willing to learn everything there was about the business, she never wavered on that point.

'He's getting on my nerves with his advice, he's giving me a headache with his "do this", "don't do that", "say it like this", "sing, don't shout". He's confused me so much that I don't understand anything he says to me any more.

'I'm going to take lessons, but in my own way, and all on my own. Marie Dubas will be at the A.B.C. just before me; I'm going there to listen to her. And you're coming with me.'

I still worked in a factory and I had a husband; it wasn't easy. Easy! To be Edith's sister! When she had decided to do something she never thought about other people. I was too proud to tell her about my private life, she would not have understood; she would have made fun of me. So I arranged my life so that for two weeks, once a day and twice when there were matinees, we went to hear Marie Dubas.

'What a lesson! Look at her, listen to her. Watch her, Momone. When she comes on stage she's made her impact before
she opens her mouth. Raymond explains it well, but it's not the
same thing. When I see her I can understand why she does
everything. It's all becoming clear.'

It would not have been right for Edith to copy Marie – and
Edith never imitated anyone – but through Marie she learned
how to discipline her performance. She used Marie like the little
stone they use to test jewels when you take them to the pawn-
broker. She admired her right up to the end. She would often go
to Marie's dressing-room, and sitting down in a corner, listen to
her criticizing herself; that was a useful lesson, too. Almost before she left the stage, even after a big success, Marie would
start in, 'No, in the last couplet of "Pedro", when I echo Pedro
... Pedro, it's the heat, the sunshine, the castanets, but, at the
same time, there's a plea. I didn't make it appealing enough. And
don't you think that in "La prière de la Charlotte" I overdo it a
bit? It should be very simple. Charlotte isn't doing that for a
man, she's doing it for someone in heaven. Someone who doesn't
need all the dramatics.' Edith got her artistic standards from
Marie Dubas's example.

The premiere was only days away. Edith's and Raymond's
nerves were on edge. He had finally written a legionnaire song
especially for her.

'This is all mine,' she exulted. 'I don't have to beg songs any
more. I don't have to sing other people's, I sing my very own.'
There was a note of triumph in her voice as she sang:

> *Ah! la la, la la, belle histoire,*
> *Là-haut sur les murs du bastion,*
> *Et dans le soleil plein de gloire,*
> *Et dans le vent, claque un fanion:*
> *C'est le fanion de la Légion!*

> *Ah! la la, la la, belle histoire,*
> *Ils restent trois dans le bastion,*
> *Le torse nu, couverts de gloire,*
> *Sanglants, meurtris et en haillons,*

Sans eau, ni vin, ni munitions;
Mais ne peuvent crier: Victoire!
On leur a volé leur fanion,
Le beau fanion de la Légion!

Ah! la la, la la, belle histoire,
Les trois qui sont dans le bastion,
Sur leur poitrine toute noire,
Avec du sang, cré nom de nom!
Ont dessiné le beau fanion!

Ils gueulent: 'Présents de la Légion!'

I count myself lucky to have lived through the adventure of
the A.B.C. I really saw Edith grow before my eyes. Watching her
was like being at the movies when they show you a frumpy old
caterpillar turning into a butterfly. First you see little bits of
wings, all stuck down, then they move a little, but you don't
realize what they are; then they get larger, and longer, and less
crumpled-looking, and whee . . . it's ready to fly away, silky and
velvety and glorious.

Every day something changed in Edith. I'm not talking about
the woman, that part never changed. She was often unfaithful to
Raymond with men who meant nothing to her. No, it was the
artist, testing her wings until she was ready to try them out
under the spotlights of the A.B.C.

Three days before the premiere Edith said to me, 'We're going
to rehearse all night. I have to run through the whole act with
my dress, the lights, everything. You must come.'

'What about Raymond?'

'If you stay in the back of the theatre he won't see you.' I was
happy, but the isolation was a bitter pill all the same.

'It's important, Momone. You must tell me everything you
see. There are masses of things that you won't understand, that
Raymond has taught me; I'll explain them to you: first, there's
the order of the songs. You can't sing them one after the other in
any old order. It's like a pearl necklace, the position of each
pearl tells you what it's worth, how beautiful it is. There are

lights, and you'll see that they change with each song. Papa Leplée's single spot trained directly on me was amateur. There are blues and reds and mixtures, no plain whites. Too much light squashes me.

'They have a trick they call the false curtain. At the end of the fifth song they draw the curtain as if the act were finished. The audience applauds and asks for an encore; even if they're not very enthusiastic it doesn't matter, rather than let the other singers have a second of your time, you ceremoniously open up the curtain again and sing. After that there are more false curtains, more clapping, more encores.

'Because of the lights I'll have stage make-up on, so use your eyes. I don't trust Raymond. I have my own ideas about how I should look; he'd make me look like Marlene Dietrich if he could. He's not stupid, or blind; he's just a man, and men never see straight when it comes to the women they sleep with.

'I want to keep the look of the streets about me; pale with big eyes and a mouth, no more. Raymond and I don't agree about dress, either. He wanted me to add something red, like a scarf. I said, "You're out of your mind. Do you want me to do a little dance too, like Mistinguett?" '

It took her more than an hour to give me all the dope.

The next evening, hidden all alone in my corner, I saw Edith on a real stage.

The curtain was full of light, the velvet seemed alive. People were moving about behind it. The stage hands called to each other.

'Hey, Jules, put out the lights. Lower the ramp a bit more.'

'How's that, Monsieur Asso?'

Raymond came on to the stage in front of the curtain. It was strange to see him again after nine months – time enough to make a baby. His pipe was in his mouth, his face, expressionless as ever, was gleaming with sweat. He was wearing a turtle-neck sweater. I thought he looked quite handsome that evening. He shielded his eyes with his hand, 'Lower the third and the fifth on the balcony. Tone down one and two out front. We don't want to squash her, we want to mould her.'

That bastard really knew his business.

From his seat in the third row, Mitty called out, 'Are we ready to start?'

Raymond jumped into the audience, shouting, 'Let's go.'

And the orchestra started to play. That did something to me, eighteen musicians all playing for Edith, just for her. It was like being in church, I had tears in my eyes. The dark, empty auditorium, smelling of dust and stale tobacco, was like an enchanted cave. The curtain went up and Edith came on stage. The light picked her up and followed her like the wing of a guardian angel. The conductor never took his eyes off her, and she started to sing. She had told me to watch closely, but I couldn't. I leaned against the back of a chair with my head in my hands, and I wept during the whole of the first song. It was too much for me. But afterwards I opened my eyes and my ears and took in everything, like a tape recorder going tick, tick, tick, everything sinking into my mind. What a night. When she had finished, my hands were itching to clap, but one never does, in a rehearsal; it brings bad luck.

The curtain went down; there was silence, then Mitty shouted, 'Great, very good, Edith!' Raymond went to fetch her. He got out his notebook, and Edith stood before him, like a small obedient child, her big eyes lifted to him as if to a master. He loved playing the part of the boss.

'You take too short a break on the third. We don't have enough time to catch up with you, you start off too fast. I went up to the gallery; you don't look at them often enough. It's them you're singing for, you know, they're the ones who'll make you a success. When you bow, look directly at them, try to give the impression that you're looking straight into their eyes.

'On the sixth, "Les Fanions", the spot doesn't come on fast enough, men. There's a gap. She's finished singing before you pick her up. You must start off together, that's the secret of success.'

That evening I realized how much work Raymond had done. Perhaps I had not left for nothing, after all.

Mitty shouted, 'Okay, kids, that's it for this evening. See you tomorrow.'

And the theatre became sad and cold once more.

The next day I was early for our meeting. I had not slept at all. For some time we had been meeting in a bar in Montmartre called Chez Jean Cyrano. Jean was an attractive singer, and he had achieved a modest success. He had a gentle, poetic way with him; but that was not why we met at his place, it was because he had blue eyes! 'Jean's eyes are like a patch of sky,' Edith said, 'the blue fills them completely and spills over. Not like Raymond's.'

It was not difficult to guess that Edith had a crush on Jean Cyrano. It lasted several weeks, while we drank in the blue eyes.

'Well, Momone, what did you think of yesterday evening?' were Edith's first words.

'It was marvellous.'

We hugged each other. 'Haven't you anything else to say?'

Edith was like that, compliments soothed her, they gave her pleasure, but she wanted criticism, she needed it, she invited it.

'As far as the songs go, you can trust Raymond, he's absolutely right.' (How difficult it was for me to say this, but it was the truth.) 'Your hair's all right, but watch your mouth when you make up. You slap on your lipstick any old how; you don't outline your lips, you smear it all over them.'

Edith always made up without looking in a mirror.

'Momone, my style is to wear no paint at all. I'd rather face the public with no make-up, naked like a lover. What about my dress?'

They had made her a little black dress in a kind of bumpy fabric which was then very much in fashion. It had a simple skirt and top with long sleeves and a little white collar.

'I don't like the collar.'

'I wore one at Leplée's.'

'That wasn't the same thing. On a knitted dress, your little false lace collar looked dressy, but on stage with all those fancy lights, I'd rather see your face naked, as you said. So that the only white things showing would be your face and hands.'

'I'm glad you said that. I thought the same thing. I wonder if I can make Raymond swallow it, though. At the moment he thinks he's God the Father.' (On the evening of the premiere, she wore her dress without the collar. That was my victory!)

As she left she handed me a box. 'That's for you for tomorrow evening, the premiere. It's a coat. You aren't going to abandon me.' The following evening, wrapped in my new garnet coat with its fox-fur collar, I felt quite confident, until I saw the auditorium packed, and all the Parisian smart set there. I was too scared to speak. What would happen if they didn't like Edith? She was gambling with her career. She had about thirty minutes to win them over. A bad reception at the A.B.C. would mean starting all over again.

My eyes were burning through the curtain which would go up on her. She came on to the stage looking as sure of herself as if she were in the streets, but I could feel her fear.

I felt a ripple running through the audience. Here was this tiny little woman, standing a little crookedly before them, looking almost impoverished in her short dress (at that time singers wore long dresses), with her sad expression, her white face shining like a light, and yet her voice seemed to echo all their sorrow, all their joy, all their love; it touched each of them directly. For the poor people, it reflected their lives; for the others, it was something that they did not know, that they had passed on the corner of the street not wanting to see.

From the first song on they applauded her. Around me, above me, within me, I could feel the hushed silence while Edith's voice swept through the auditorium like a strong wind. And at the end they begged for more. Although I was a long way off, I could see that Edith was trembling as she bowed. She looked so fragile, you would have thought she was going to collapse. Afterwards she had other successes, enormous ones, but never one like this. It was this one which was to carry her, like a meteor towards victory.

Sitting in the audience, I felt a lump in my throat. 'She'll never be the same again,' I said to myself. 'Now there'll be a barrier between us. This success is a Maginot line separating us.' I wanted to shout to all the people who were applauding her, 'I'm with her.' I was drunk with pride. There I was in my seat, where I belonged, with the rest of the world, and she was up there on the stage, in the limelight where *she* belonged. The distance that separated us scared me, but at the same time all the madness, the delirium around me, made me tremble with happiness.

That evening at the A.B.C. was when she finally turned her back on the squalor of our past lives. But we had lived it together, and I wanted to hold on to it; nearly eight years of communal living bound us together. Later that evening I knew she would be drinking and laughing with other people. I was too young and too prickly to understand that glamour was of no importance, especially to Edith.

I did not go to her dressing-room afterwards. She had said to me, 'Momone, you will come over and kiss me, won't you?' But I couldn't do it. I knew what would happen. Raymond would have picked me up by the collar of my beautiful new coat, as he liked to do, to show everyone that he was strong and come out with some choice idiocy. This was his moment. The A.B.C. triumph was his and he was happy. He enjoyed being the boss, the man who had created this glowing new star, and I was not going to spoil his fun. Poor Raymond, he was preening himself that evening; but it did not matter, I knew he was finished.

Edith was not ungrateful. She liked Raymond, but now he had served his purpose. She kept her friends for life, but not her lovers. She never forgot what she owed him. He had all her gratitude, but that feeling doesn't keep love alive. Each time that he needed her she was there. When he was old and ill, she did not forget him. But their love was over, it had burnt itself out. And for Edith it could never start up again, she needed something new. 'Love is always best at the beginning,' was her axiom.

The next day all the newspapers acclaimed her. I bought them all; it broke me! One critic wrote, 'Yesterday evening, on the stage of the A.B.C., we witnessed the birth of a great singer.' That crystallized Edith's début. That evening finally put the wheels of Edith's destiny in motion. There would be no more bad breaks in her professional life, no more falls, and no more false starts.

7

PAUL MEURISSE:
'LE BEL INDIFFÉRENT'

Outside her career, Edith's life was not a model of order. Everything was messed up – friendships, passions, passing fancies, and, above all, love affairs. She had hardly finished one before she began another. She had strict principles about the break-up of an affair.

'Any woman who lets a man walk over her is a dumb idiot and deserves no better,' was her philosophy. 'There's no lack of men, the streets are full of them. It's before the break-up that you start looking for a replacement, not after. Afterwards you're the one that's being had, but if it's before it's him. That's quite a different kettle of fish.'

She adopted this attitude with a clear conscience. No man could make her change. She cheated him first, then she left him. Sometimes she told them; other times she just laughed behind their backs. And if someone thought that he had been unfaithful first, he was a deluded fool; she had very likely beaten him to it by months. But if the new lover was not ready to move in with her, she said nothing and kept on the old one. She always needed a man in the house.

'A home's no good without a man around, Momone. It's worse than a day without sunshine. You can do without sun, there's always electricity, but a house without a man's shirt lying around, where you don't walk over a pair of shoes or a tie, where you don't see a still-warm jacket thrown over a chair – that's a widow's house; that's depressing.'

At the Hôtel Alsina Raymond lived out the last days of his affair with Edith in all innocence. After his success at the A.B.C. he was sure of his future with her. He believed he was indispensable to her.

Edith was happy. There was enough money, everyone wanted her. Her career was as steady as a rock. All she needed to make her happiness perfect was a new man, and she had just found one.

'Momone, I've met this terrific man. Not at all like the others.'

'Great,' I thought, 'here we go again.' I said, 'What does he do?'

'He sings in a night club.'

'What's his name?'

'Paul Meurisse.'

'Never heard of him.'

'You haven't? That's amazing, you don't keep up with the times.'

It was on the tip of my tongue to say, 'Whose fault is that?' But I kept quiet; I wanted to hear her story.

'I've been singing at the night club on the rue Arsène-Houssaye, and every night before my act I've had a drink at the Caravelle. I was sitting there one evening when I spotted this good-looking type all dressed up like a fashion-plate Englishman at the bar. Very, very handsome. Dark shining hair, glossy as a raven's wing. Black eyes! Yes, he has dark eyes; you have to make changes sometimes. He looks as distinguished as an English nobleman. Perhaps a little too like a model really, but that can be changed. I flashed him a look – you know my candid look, very simple and appealing like a kid with no money but lots of heart. Not a move, not even a twitch of the eyebrow, not a smile.

' "Something wrong with him," I thought, so I gave up. But the next day he was there again. I asked about him and discovered that he sang every evening at the Amiral.

'Listen, Momone, I don't want anyone to know what you're doing, but hang around and find out what you can about him. I'd love to know where he comes from.'

By the next day I knew everything. He was twenty-six, and was born at Dunkirk. His father was a bank manager. He had studied law at Aix-en-Provence, worked as a clerk in a law office, and made his début as a music-hall singer in Marseilles. Then he came to Paris as an insurance inspector – he certainly looked the part. He wanted to be a singer, so he entered and won the prize at the amateur contest at the Alhambra. Mitty Goldin took him on as office boy, and each evening he sang in different clubs.

I unloaded all this data on to Edith. She said, 'What I like about him is his terribly serious expression. And he speaks so well. He spoke to me yesterday. You know how intuitive I am. Well, I went all alone to the Caravelle to hear him sing. I didn't like it. He won't make his career as a singer. He's so stiff, his face is almost frozen, his jacket fits too well, and he wears it buttoned all the way. He sang:

> *Ah! viens, viens ma Nénette*
> *Faire un tour sur les chevaux ... de bois.*
> *Ca fait tourner la tête*
> *Et ça vous donne la gueule ... de bois.*

'The audience for that type of thing is limited, he won't pack the house with it. But that didn't stop me from thinking how handsome he is. What a man! I went to his dressing-room.

'As he knotted his tie he asked me, did I like his act.

' "Not very much," I said.

' "Oh."

' "Does that upset you?"

' "Not at all. I can't please everyone."

' "Don't you want to please me?"

' "That's different. But I wasn't thinking of seducing you with my songs."

' "But you are thinking of seducing me?"

' "My dearest, I dream of it."

'And then he bent over and kissed my hand. It was very stylish and theatrical. But I was cross, I couldn't stop myself from saying, "Are you angry with me, Paul?"

' "Not at all, why?"

' "You didn't kiss my hand at all; I couldn't feel anything."

'He burst out laughing. "But it's just a gesture. Only a farm-hand would really kiss a woman's hand. You must skim it with your lips, no more."

'I felt like a dolt, I had to make up for it somehow. I looked him straight in the eye and said, "That's not what I meant, you could have ..."

'I would never have believed that kissing someone's hand could be so complicated. And then in his dry way he asked me to go to bed with him.

' "Edith," he said, "I think the sooner it happens the better. I don't see why we have to make a fuss about it, nor why women have to say no before they say yes. Will you have a drink at my house one evening? I'll come and fetch you at the end of your act. You're adorable, Edith." Then he did kiss my hands, both of them, properly.'

'What next?'

'It's happened. He's my lover, and he's so different from the others. You have no idea how well brought up he is. He holds my coat. He's always behind me. He lets me go first. I'm not used to it, it's like having a servant.'

'What are you going to do about Raymond?'

'I'm waiting. I don't know if it's going to work with Paul yet.'

I was sure it would last. Paul had astounded Edith; never had she been so amazed by a man. She had often admired them, that was necessary if she were to love them, but she had always been able to tell how a man would behave, how he would react. But she had no idea what Paul would do or say. He was like some exotic creature; if he had eaten orchids for breakfast she would have thought it quite normal.

I was dying to meet him. I have never forgotten the date when I finally did; it was in September 1939.

Edith and I knew little about current affairs, politics was above our heads. In 1938, at the time of the Munich Pact, I had, with the weight of my twenty years, tried to tell her that the news-papers were talking about war. 'Don't worry,' she had replied, 'you won't be expected to make history. If you aren't someone who can get out of a situation easily you pay for it, that's the way life is. It's not worth getting into a sweat about something you can't change.'

She never changed her mind on this subject. Where we came from, it is true, world affairs made little impact. Day-to-day con-versations were neither complicated nor far-reaching. Every day you had to find enough money for your loaf of bread and bottle of wine, and once you had that you didn't care one way or the other about talk of war and the end of the world. In our world, you did not even pay attention to strikes, they could not give you anything good or bad. We were not workers, we were in a class without a name. When we were kids the only person who mentioned politics was our father, and that not much.

But in September 1939 things happened. I have reasons of my own not to forget that date; my husband was called up. The evening before, I had gone with him to the army induction centre at Vincennes. It was like a treadmill. You went in, you were processed, you came out. Inside there were non-coms and officers in uniforms, infantrymen with all their kit, and others who looked as if they were ready for a fancy-dress party in a mixture of military jackets, police helmets with civilian clothes, uniform trousers with regular jackets, yellow shoes with patterned socks, boots with or without puttees.

And there, in the middle of all the noise of men stamping their feet, coughing, spitting, smoking, ignoring their officers' orders, I left my husband. We kissed. We were young, and we did not understand what was happening to us. I had a picture of him in my handbag, he had mine in his wallet. I never saw him again. He was among the first to be killed. I never talk about him now. He didn't have much luck, but then perhaps nor did I.

The morning after his departure I was ready to have some fun, though, when the concierge called to me from the courtyard, 'Mademoiselle Simone, your sister's on the phone.'

I went downstairs quickly. Edith, how marvellous! But at the other end of the wire, Edith was as cold as ice. No 'good-day', nothing.

'Simone, would you explain why you have abandoned me?'

I was speechless.

'Come home immediately.' Those words took me back several years, to a time when if I had misbehaved Edith would order me home like a wayward child.

'But where?'

'To the Hôtel Alsina, idiot, where I live.'

Nothing suited me better. When you're out singing 'Les Mômes de la cloche', the war doesn't touch you very much, but it's a different matter when you're working in a factory. You sink pretty low there, even before the war has really got going, and you can whistle for your food. But now, instead of being alone and miserable, I was going back to be with Edith again. I would never have believed it. I had my life and she had hers, and it had seemed that they were at opposite ends of the pole.

'What about Raymond?' I queried.

'Don't worry about him, he's been mobilized. Well, are you coming or aren't you? Bring your clothes, take a taxi, and leave your key with the concierge.'

As usual Edith thought of everything, except to ask me if I was free. As far as she was concerned I belonged to her and my private life didn't exist. Raymond had left, she was alone, and it was clearly my duty to be at her side.

As I left my street (aptly named rue de la Séparation) I didn't know whether I was coming or going, but my heart was full. I was going to be with Edith, to take up my life with her again. In the taxi I realized that the life we had lived together was as habit-forming as a drug.

I had no time to sort out my ideas, before I found myself sitting on the bidet in Edith's bathroom at the Hôtel Alsina, watching her and listening to her. It was a terrific change. It was the first time that I had actually seen a complete bathroom, and this one belonged to Edith, therefore to both of us. I realized immediately that these sessions in the bathroom would be a part of our lives.

'Are you happy, Momone?'

'Oh yes, yes.'

'Good, so pass me the hairpins.'

We were off.

She made all the important decisions of her life in the bathroom. We were always alone there, no man would have dared interrupt us. We chattered like magpies for hours on end. We discussed everything, her career, her plans, new men, new resolutions made, new oaths taken. Edith gave me her opinions on everything. As we saw more people and things, as her horizon broadened, so the subjects for conversation grew more plentiful.

Her boy-friends could never know her fully. She only talked to them about love. They had no right to anything else, their function was simply to love her.

She let them think that she paid no attention to her looks, that she didn't care. That was part of her personality, part of her public image. 'I'm just a simple little girl. A child of the people, natural, a flower blooming in the pavement! I'm not even pretty!'

But she didn't believe a word of it, it was part of her legend and she knew how to keep it alive. Everyone wrote that she was a woman without much of a mind – which was true if you did not want to look for it – that her beauty lay in her talent, her greatest strength. So Edith went along with them, but when we were together she would make up for it.

'Look at me. My eyes are a very unusual colour, they're violet. And my mouth is mobile, it's attractive. Perhaps my forehead is a bit high, but I'd rather have it that way than too low; at least it doesn't make me look stupid. It's not serious, a few curls here and it looks less big.'

She would roar with laughter and crack her face mask, and as it crumbled all over the place she would shout, 'Look, my façade's cracking. Too bad, I'll try another.'

Edith was a dream customer for the makers of beauty products; anyone as gullible as her would be difficult to imagine.

'Look at the ad in this paper,' she would exclaim. ' "Seduce every man you meet with Dr X's strawberry cream." "Stay young for ever with the Thing's embryonic cell treatment." ". . . Takes away your wrinkles like an eraser." Do you believe it?'

She bought everything she saw or read about. The first day she would shriek, 'Look, how wonderful this stuff is – I don't recognize myself,' but by the second or third day she would start to make faces. 'This stuff's no good. Let's try something else.'

Actually, she did not need anything at all, she had been blessed with a beautiful white, soft, clear skin. On the rare occasions that she washed herself, she used odds and ends of soap, or foul-smelling household soap that should have been used only to scour out an oven.

I always admired her ears, too; they were like a baby's, beauti-

fully shaped and transparent like porcelain. But her most out-
standing feature was her hands. They were slim, small, soft, and
wonderfully warm. When she took your hand in hers, the
warmth mounted to your heart and spread all through you.

So there I was, happily passing Edith her hairpins, rollers, and
pots of cream, and listening to her talk. I had a feeling of con-
tentment and total security. Yet the world in which we lived
was about as safe as Vesuvius in eruption.

When we went out of the bathroom I saw a Chinese sitting on
a chair, and a fellow in a silk dressing-gown lying on the bed
reading the paper. 'Oh, no, not two of them,' I said to myself.
'One yellow, one white. Now we'll be sleeping four to a bed.'
I hadn't had time to speculate any further, when she said, 'This
is Paul Meurisse, he lives with us. And this is Tchang, my cook.'

Paul got up, looking annoyed. 'If you had warned me, Edith,
I'd have put on a jacket.'

I couldn't understand the cook, as I couldn't see a kitchen. But
Tchang got up, picked up the grocery bag at his feet, and went
into the bathroom. It was quite simple, he put a board over the
bath and cooked on a portable stove. Steak and chips was his
speciality.

'What do you think about that?' Edith asked. 'That's something, isn't it, a Chinese cook, and we're saving money as well.'
I had my doubts about that; Edith had never been a thrifty
housewife.

The more I saw of her Paul, the more I realized how impossible it would be for the three of us to doss down together
and I wondered where I would end up.

'I took a room for you beside this one, Momone. Come on,
let's unpack your suitcase.'

Paul bent down and picked up the case. 'I'll carry it for you.
May I call you Simone? Edith has told me so much about you.'

Out of the corner of my eye I watched Edith splitting her
sides with mirth. Did men like this really exist? I'd never seen
one before.

My suitcase was soon unpacked, it was practically empty.
'Good,' said Edith, 'I guessed as much. You can help yourself
to whatever you want of mine.'

That was easy, we were almost the same height; we came out of the same package.

'What do you think of Paul?'

'Amazing! That bit with the suitcase – he was so polite it was funny! And honestly, I thought it was only in movies that men lazed around their bedrooms in silk dressing-gowns; he looks as if he's quite used to it.'

That evening we went out to 'dine', as he called it. He held our chairs, and waited until we were seated, then placed our napkins in our laps. We were speechless with admiration.

I had been so sure that Asso had crammed everything into our heads and there would be no more to learn, yet here was something new; it made me uncomfortable. I was scared of making a gaffe when I ate, but he was cool as a cucumber. He probably had centuries of culture behind him. Yet I didn't find him much fun. I had often wanted to go to bed with some of Edith's men, she had good taste, but I couldn't understand this one. I was wrong, though, for Paul supplied the one thing Edith lacked – class.

When the waiter came over, Edith said, 'I'll have the ...' but Paul silenced her with a frown, and said, 'Madame will have ...' and he reeled off the whole meal for us, ending up with, 'Send the wine waiter over.'

She was on top of the world; what a life she was going to lead with this man.

Raymond did not know she was unfaithful. To Edith a soldier at war was far away; out of sight, out of mind. But soldiers do get leave, and I felt that before long Raymond would appear on the scene.

'Edith, what are you going to do with Asso?' I ventured once.

'I'll keep him on as a song-writer, for the rest he can go hang.'

'And what if he doesn't agree?'

'Don't ask stupid questions, no man has ever stayed with me when I didn't want him any more.'

It was easily said, and it was true, but the partings did not always take place without friction. I'd already seen some of the scenes.

As I had expected, Raymond turned up on his first leave. He didn't knock; after all, this was his home. He was pretty shaken when he opened the door to see me there, apparently quite at home.

'You're back, are you?'

'As you see.'

'Did she take you back?'

'Of course.'

'Where is she?'

'I don't know.' I did know, of course; Edith was with Paul in the room next door.

'Listen, Raymond, why don't you take a bath? You should relax, after all that fighting.'

'Are you making fun of me? Do you know where she is?'

'No. I'll go and see if she's hanging around outside.'

'I can see it hasn't taken her long to get back to her good old ways. It's time I came back.'

'You thinking of coming back? Well, I've got some advice for you; don't hurry.'

I wanted to make him lose his temper so that Edith would hear him yelling, and I succeeded. He started to shout, and she came in. Instead of hello, she said, 'D'you think you're in your own home, carrying on like this? If you've come to get your things, just take them and get out; they aren't heavy.'

'What do you mean, Didou?'

'There's no Didou, nor Didi, nor Edith. You're through, I've had enough. What are you doing, Simone, standing there listening to me? Go next door and mind your own business.'

Raymond didn't miss a trick, 'What's next door?'

'A room. Simone's room. What's it to you?'

'A lot. So she has a room of her own now, does she? You don't sleep together any more.'

'That's no concern of yours, I don't ask you who you sleep with. You ran off and left me.'

'I was called up.'

'So stay called. Beat it; there's no place for you here.'

I withdrew, leaving them shouting at the top of their voices.

In the room next door I found Paul sitting on the unmade bed in his dressing-gown, doing his nails.

'Is that Raymond Asso in there?' he asked.

'Sounds like it.'

A real fight was developing next door and, just as I was thinking of calling the police, Paul put on his jacket and left. That made one less, at least.

The scene lasted about an hour. In the end they calmed down and I could hear Edith crying. He must have hit her, it was the only way to silence her, and Raymond never hesitated to do it when necessary.

In her little girl's voice she was saying, 'You know, Raymond, you had the best of me. You'll always be the one I'll remember in my heart.'

'All the same, *ma petite fille*, you shouldn't have done that to me while I was away.'

I felt sorry for Raymond. To come home on leave and find your 'wife' shacked up with someone else isn't the best of welcomes.

I was beginning to fall asleep when my door opened. Raymond entered: 'I hope you're pleased with yourself. You've got your own way now.'

I expected a slap to punctuate the remark, but he just went out again, slamming the door.

Edith saw him again later and they remained good friends, but Raymond was never the same. He was no more than a lyric-writer whose songs Edith might consider.

Raymond was not always kind to me, but I respected him and I was sorry for him when I saw him leaving again, his shoulders hunched in his soldier's uniform. Perhaps it was because we were so alike. With Paul I always felt I was living with Louis XIV – a great big production number.

That evening, like any other, Edith went off to sing. When we got back Paul was not there. 'Raymond shouldn't have come here,' Edith fumed. 'But if Paul wants to play games with me, he's going to find himself out on his arse. If he's chosen the moment that I kick Raymond out to be jealous, I'll give the conceited bastard hell, much as I adore him.'

She had hardly finished when Paul opened the door. He looked as if he were arriving at Maxim's, with just the right polite and guarded smile.

'My dear Edith, forgive me for being a little late but I needed some peace in which to think. I've decided you mustn't live in Montmartre, it lacks class. You leave yourself open to unfortunate meetings which don't suit me. You have a name to support; you should live at the Étoile.'

I take my hat off to anyone who can make an entry like that after the tantrum she had just thrown. Paul really did have class. Edith was overcome with astonishment.

'It's charming and picturesque to have a Chinese cook in a hotel, but he would be more suitable in an apartment, and so would you.'

An apartment of her own. How wonderful! She had never had one, in fact it had never even occurred to her. She turned to me: 'What do you think about it, Momone?'

'I think Paul's right. It would do something for you.'

Our dream had been to have two rooms with a kitchen one day. At the Étoile we would be hob-nobbing with the cream of Parisian society.

So in due course we moved into a furnished apartment on the ground floor of 14 rue Anatole-le-la-Forge. It was a very smart neighbourhood near the Place de l'Étoile and next door to a bar called the Bidou, which quickly became our home from home.

Paul had a real sense of drama and occasion. When we arrived with all our stuff, he held the keys out to Edith. 'Open the door,' he said, 'this is your home.'

She threw herself at him, 'Oh, Paul, you are a darling.'

But the effect was spoiled because Paul did everything coldly, like a Protestant priest, and Edith's joy was quickly snuffed out. She was beginning to realize that being distinguished all the time is a bore.

Housekeeping with Paul was not what we were used to. He arrived with his leather suitcases, and put everything away himself. When there was a man in the house, we were used to looking after him lovingly, unpacking and storing his things. These were the only times that Edith tidied anything up. She adored dressing up her men, too, even when she hadn't enough money to pay the bills. Some discovered this weakness all too soon, and exploited it all too easily, for Edith took pleasure in just giving.

With Paul it was all very different, however. He had everything made to measure, suits, shirts, shoes. He chose his own socks and underwear. His handkerchiefs, pyjamas, scarves, and ties were pure silk. He was the one with the taste and this annoyed Edith.

'I'd like to buy him a suit, shirts, ties,' she would complain. 'Perhaps we don't have the same tastes, but I have as much as he does. He may have education, but he doesn't have tact. Couldn't he put on one of my ties just once?'

Of course Edith's choices were pretty extraordinary. The ties she picked looked as though they were designed for murals rather than to be worn. Paul would have been outraged. When he had unpacked all his stuff, we were speechless. He had so many pairs of pyjamas he must have changed at least twice a week.

We looked at all his lovely things, but we didn't dare touch them. They were laid out like a luxury boutique.

'It's the first time I've lived with a man who doesn't smell like one – Paul smells only of toilet water, lavender, and good leather,' pronounced Edith. 'He shaves twice a day – Dad only shaved when he was really filthy – and then he dabs on an English after-shave lotion. It's nice and fresh when you kiss him, but do you think it's normal?' She laughed. 'After all, he isn't a girl.'

Paul's beautiful, elegant manners fascinated both of us, but as a daily diet it was becoming indigestible. After Raymond's lessons, we now had to swallow Paul's endless advice. 'Where are you going, Edith? You're not going out looking like that? Aren't you ashamed? You're covered in stains. Edith Piaf can't go out in dirty clothes.'

His cleanliness threw Edith and me into dismay. He even made us wash our hands before meals, the way he did. We hardly knew what a toothbrush was, but Paul insisted that we use them twice a day, particularly Edith, who was in the habit of treating herself to pickled herrings and onions in the dead of night.

P.—7

When Paul said, 'Darling, come on, let's go to bed,' he was impeccable in his pyjamas and silk dressing-gown, smelling of toilet water. Edith invariably wore a nightdress which she could have fitted into three times. She bought them whenever the mood took her, and paid no attention to either cost or size. By day she usually wore old shoes and an ancient woollen coat. Often Paul would look behind Edith's ears to see if they were clean. 'Have you washed?' he would ask, as if you had to wash just to go to bed!

All this hygiene wouldn't have suited me, but Edith didn't mind because she loved him, and when Edith loved a man he could ask anything of her. At first, that is; later on things would change.

This preoccupation with cleanliness made Edith nervous, 'Do you think washing yourself all the time is a sickness?' she would ask. The remark reflected Edith's upbringing. When we were kids, people believed that dirt and fleas were a protection against illness, like some sort of vaccine.

We were under the delusion, too, that Raymond had taught us everything about table manners, but when one day Paul said to Edith, 'Darling, I should like you to eat differently, like the English do,' we looked at each other dumbfounded.

'This is how I hold the knife,' he demonstrated. 'One uses it to push the food on to one's fork.'

'Well, I'm neither left-handed nor an acrobat, and I eat with my right hand,' retorted Edith, and poor Paul just had to laugh and give up.

It was only later Edith learned that talent makes up for a lot of things, that there is always a place for it, that you can be intelligent without schooling.

I slept in the back of the apartment. Edith slept in the bedroom with Paul, in a beautiful bed hung with blue satin. It was normal, but I was not completely used to sleeping alone.

However, life was pretty uneventful. In the mornings, whether or not there was a man around, I woke her up with all due ceremony. I liked to watch her asleep; she looked like a baby. I would slide a finger into her hand (her fist was always clenched), and she would squeeze my finger and murmur, 'Is that you, Momone?'

When she sat up, propped on her pillows, and cautiously began to take note of life, she would inquire, 'Is it a nice day? Open the curtains. Not too fast.'

She hated daylight. She would say, 'My sun shines inside me when night falls. That's the only time I begin to see clearly.'

She took no notice of the man in bed with her; he could go on sleeping or wake up, she didn't care. I sat on the bed, and we were off on our endless chat.

Then she would throw back the bedclothes, uncovering her grumpy bedfellow, and, in her grotesque nightdress, dash into the bathroom, always with me in tow.

Edith laughed while she turned on the taps. The noise of running water is a happy sound. Like a disobedient child who is afraid of being found out, she wet the flannel and the soap, and threw the towels in a heap on the floor, so that Paul would not be cross with her.

When she felt like 'spoiling the master' – she had enjoyed herself the night before, and had not been too drunk to forget it – she would say, 'Make Paul's breakfast.' But more often than not he fended for himself.

It was not the kind of awakening that lovers dream of. I suppose Paul wanted to be King Arthur with his Guinevere, and when he had had enough of our threesome he'd say, 'I'm sick of this, let her go into the kitchen.'

If Edith was in a good mood she shrugged her shoulders or tapped her forehead as if to say, 'He's cracked, don't pay any attention, Momone.'

Sometimes when Edith and I would recall our adventures in bygone days she would needle Paul. 'Why aren't you laughing? Don't you think it's funny?' she would demand.

'Not particularly.'

'I wonder what it takes to make you laugh?'

'Certainly something more stimulating than an account of the various men you've been to bed with. Your past doesn't interest me, there are too many people in it.'

'Why don't you call me a whore while you're at it?'

She could adopt any tack she wished – no one could have been more provoking – but Paul always remained impervious.

'The trouble with him is he's an iceberg. I must be completely out of my mind to fall for anyone so stiff-necked. I'll make him forget his upbringing. He'll beat me yet, you'll see. I want him to beat me.'

Edith adored fights, scenes, crises. Things had to happen around her and within her; that was her life-style. She sang about parties, holidays, love, jealousy, separation, not about housewives and wallflowers; she sang about her own tumultuous life; it came from within.

Next door to us was the Bidou Bar, and to get there we would go down on all fours past our window so Paul couldn't see us. When we came back at unearthly hours, drunk, or with others who were, Paul merely clenched his teeth in silence. He had a way of keeping silent that enraged Edith. She would throw everything that came to hand at him. Cold as a refrigerator, Paul would say to me, 'Simone, there are still some more plates in the kitchen; why don't you go and fetch them?'

Then, in all his dignity, he would go and recline on the bed with a book, turning the radio full blast to his favourite classical music station, which must have pleased the neighbours. His radio was his friend, he really loved it, and he would listen to classical music for hours.

It was still the period of the 'phony war'. Apart from the air-raid precautions, the cretins who dropped a few bombs on us and the communiques from 'somewhere in France', nothing much occurred. And, as the military had to be amused when on leave and the general morale kept up, the clubs, music halls, theatres, and cinemas were always crowded.

The spring had been lovely, and the summer looked promising. Edith, who never cared about the weather, said to me, 'Thank God I've got Paul, this spring is unsettling, the days are too long.'

To relieve Edith's boredom one day I had the marvellous idea of going on a tour of all the bistros on the rue de Belleville.

We set off. We went into each bar on one side of the street, and there were plenty. On the way back we were so pissed by the time we had arrived at the Place des Fêtes that we were on all fours. The concierges in the neighbourhood still remember that night.

When we got back, Edith was determined to make Paul share her mood. She poured herself a glass of wine.

'Edith, that's enough. Go and sleep it off somewhere else, I don't want a drunken woman in my bed.'

'You're a shit-faced, cold-blooded dummy. You make me sick,' she flung back at him.

Without replying, Paul went to the bedroom and shut himself in with his beloved radio.

'It's like that, is it, you bastard?' screamed Edith, white with rage and the effects of the alcohol.

She was drunk enough to challenge the Eiffel Tower. Flinging open the bedroom door, she threw herself at Paul and picking up the radio, she hurled it to the floor and stamped it to smithereens.

Paul stood up, picked up the debris, and looked at Edith swaying in front of him. He took her by the shoulders and said, 'I'm very disappointed in you. You've just done something very unkind.' And with that he left.

Next day Edith bought Paul a new radio. A few months later it would have been almost impossible to replace it.

Edith was contrite but still not happy. 'You see, Momone, it didn't happen, he didn't hit me. And this time I really deserved it.'

Edith had really wanted Paul to beat her. She would have another eight months to wait for that satisfaction.

Edith would certainly have left Paul had she not met Jean Cocteau about this time.

One evening we were having dinner at the Marquise's house. Cocteau was sitting beside Edith, and I'm sure that Madame Breton had previously said the same thing to Jean as she said to Edith, 'Darling, I want you to meet a truly unique person.'

She hadn't deceived either of them. Each was quite out of the ordinary. Jean Cocteau was a marvellous man.

He took Edith's hand. 'I'm so happy to meet you. You are the poet of the streets; we were made to understand each other.'

With an introduction like that, Edith melted. At table they sat side by side, and Madame Breton was beaming. I thought to myself, 'Edith is really someone.' The streets had become a thing of the past. There she was, quite at ease, laughing and chatting with no less a person than Jean Cocteau himself.

He was a poet, playwright, writer, and artist. He understood music, singing, and dance. He juggled with words like a conjuror pulling things from his hat. She knew little, but he knew everything. I could not take my eyes off their hands. Cocteau's were as beautiful as Edith's, and both of them made gestures which served for words, gestures which flew away like birds, delightful to watch.

As he left, Jean said to her, 'I live on the rue de Beaujolais, at the Palais-Royal; you must come to see me. We'll have a long talk. *Petite Piaf*, you're a very great person.'

Edith could not get over it. 'Did you hear how he spoke to me?' she said to me. 'I'm going to see him again. He's not like the other men I know. I can learn so much from him.'

Recently Gilbert Bécaud and Louis Amade wrote a song called 'Quand il est mort le poète' [When the Poet Dies]. Each time I hear it, I think of Jean, with his craze for drawing stars everywhere, on paper napkins, on programmes, on books. He deposited stars on everything. They flowered all along his way. 'I needed a real poet in my life, and now I have one,' mused Edith.

One day she said to Paul, 'I want to read Jean Cocteau's books. Buy them for me.'

I don't know if he did it on purpose, but he came back with a book called 'Le Potomak'. We could not understand a word of it. 'It's unbelievable,' cried Edith. 'When I listen to this man I understand everything he says, when I read him I can't understand a word. I'm going to ask him why.'

'You can't do that,' said Paul. 'It's ridiculous.'

But she did, and Jean, with his usual kindness, explained to her that it was natural she should not be able to understand 'Le Potomak'. Then he gave her *Les Enfants terribles* which we both enjoyed.

Jean Cocteau wrote the most beautiful things about Edith in an article:

Look at this little woman, whose hands are like lizards darting amongst the ruins. Look at her Bonaparte-like forehead, her blind eyes that have recovered their sight. What will her voice be like? How will she express herself? How will she be able to bring all the sorrow of the night out of that narrow little chest. And yet she sings, or more like a nightingale in April, she brings forth her love song. Have you ever heard a nightingale? He toils, he hesitates, he rasps, he chokes, he begins and falters; then suddenly he finds the note. He sings and his voice overpowers you.

Edith thought this so beautiful she cut it out and read it to everyone. When a man like Jean Cocteau could write about her she felt she had indeed arrived.

We had got into the habit of meeting Jean at the Palais-Royal. Under Cocteau's house on the rue de Beaujolais, there was a cellar like a private club where artists, authors, and painters could meet. We were among our own kind. This was the first of the cellar clubs, four years before the ones in Saint-Germain-des-Prés. It had one great advantage, too, you didn't have to move during the air raids.

They were long, those nights during the black-outs, when melancholy Paris seemed to be wearing blue glasses like a blind man. How sad those little blue lights were. The brightly lit city of the past seemed so far away.

But in our cellar we forgot about it, we were among friends. Jean came down from his apartment in a warm dressing-gown, accompanied by his friend Jean Marais, whom we called Jeannot, a good-looking boy who adored Jean. Sometimes Christian Bérard, the interior decorator, whom we called Bébé, would come with them; he had a sweet, round, pink baby face, and a beautiful beard which hung down to his velvet jacket; he made sketches for his scenic designs wherever he was. And Yvonne de Bray came too, with her lively, intelligent, dark eyes, perhaps the greatest actress of the day. These were Jean's friends and Edith was very proud to be one of them.

Edith and Jean were on the same wavelength immediately. Edith did not deceive Jean, she told him everything that passed through her mind. She confided that Paul was the great love of the moment; she still loved him. 'But Paul's driving me out of my mind, yet I feel lost without him; why is that?' she asked.

'My darling,' Jean replied, 'we can never understand the people we love when we're with them. We can't take them as they are, we expect them to live up to our dreams and expectations, but they rarely do, they rarely share those dreams with us.'

Edith did not philosophize about love, all she wanted was a man to love her. It was quite simple. As we were going home in the taxi Edith said to me, 'Jean is an extraordinary person. He's not just intelligent, he's good. When he talks to me and explains Paul, I say to myself, "He's right. I must make an effort." '

When we got back she immediately demanded of Paul, 'Do you love me?'

'Of course,' Paul answered, sounding like a gentleman who had just been asked a rather embarrassing question.

'You can't say anything else, can you? You say "I love you" in the same tone of voice you would say "Dinner is served". If you're sick of me, you should tell me. I can't understand men like you. I'm fed up with your tight, white smile.'

So the battle began again.

The following evening, after talking to Jean, she made more good resolutions but, when she got home and encountered the same iceberg, hostilities were resumed.

One night Edith burst into tears as she was sitting between Jean and Yvonne de Bray. Somehow Edith became very emotional when Yvonne was there – they would empty a whole shelf of wine bottles between them.

'You can't imagine what it's like. I tell him I love him, and he just lies on his bed in his dressing-gown, reading his paper. I tell him I don't want to see him any more, that I adore him, to fuck off, he still goes on reading the paper. It's unbelievable. I break everything, I throw everything I can find at him, words and anything within reach; but he still reads the paper. It's driving me crazy.'

'Darling, calm down. I'll make it all better. Just be patient.'

A few days later Jean called her, 'Edith, come over to my apartment, I've something to read you.'

We hurried over to the rue de Beaujolais. Jeannot, Yvonne de

Bray and Bébé Bérard were all there. Jean Cocteau read us *Le Bel Indifférent*, a one-act play which he had just written, based on Edith's trials as she had recounted them to him.

'The scene is a poorly furnished hotel room, lit by illuminated street signs shining through the window. A divan, a gramophone, telephone, little bathroom. Posters on the wall.

'As the curtain goes up the actress is alone in a little black dress. She is looking out of the window; she runs to the door to check the lift. Then she sits down near the telephone. She puts on one of her records ("Je t'ai dans la peau"), then takes it off. She goes back to the telephone and dials a number.'

The woman's role was based on Edith: a successful singer, jealous of everything that surrounds her lover. It was so true to life that I could hear Edith herself saying, 'Once, in the beginning, I was jealous of your sleep. I would ask myself, "Where does he go when he's asleep? What does he see?" And if you smiled or stretched I would start to hate the people in your dreams. I often woke you up just so that you would leave them. You enjoyed your dreams, and you were furious when I woke you. But I couldn't bear the smug look on your face.'

'Do you like it?' Cocteau queried.

'It's fantastic, Jean.'

'It's for you, Edith. I'm giving it to you, and you're going to act it with Paul.'

'I can't do that, I don't know how. I'm just a singer. And act it with Paul! Oh no, Jean, I couldn't.'

Edith was like that, she believed she could do everything, and yet at the same time she was scared of failing. She had no self-confidence apart from her career.

Jeannot laughed. 'It's easy,' he said. 'Paul doesn't say anything, and you play the whole scene the way you play it with him every day.'

That seemed simple. But it wasn't as simple as that, as we soon realized at the first rehearsal.

Naturally Paul agreed to act in it. A play by Jean Cocteau, and directed by Jean and Raymond Rouleau, was not to be sniffed at, and to give significance to a silent role was a challenge he was pleased to accept.

One talked too much; the other said nothing. The difficulty was that the one who knew how to talk on stage remained silent, while the one who knew how to sing was talking.

During the first rehearsal Edith broke down. Fortunately Paul was not there; Jeannot was standing in for him. She forgot her words. She, who could express everything with a gesture or in a word when she was singing, was unable to move, her hands life-less. It was a catastrophe. She was completely lost.

'Jean, the theatre isn't for me. It's killing me, I would love to have done it, but I can't, I'll never be able to.'

Yvonne de Bray, who was curled up in a corner, said very quietly, 'Edith, you're going to do it, I'll teach you.' She did a good job. I think even I could have been an actress with her as a coach.

It was extraordinary to see Yvonne taking the role apart, sentence by sentence, bit by bit, like the little wheels inside a watch, so that once all the pieces had been put back in place the watch ticked as steadily as a heart.

At the end of the play the hero gets up, puts on his overcoat, and takes his hat. Edith clings to him begging, 'No, Emile, don't leave me.' He disengages himself, pushes her away, slaps her, and goes out, the while Edith stays on stage, her hand on her cheek sayin, 'Eh! Emile ... Oh! Emile ...'

During the rehearsals, Jean protested kindly and politely, 'No, Paul, that's not right. She exasperates you. Her love is too much for you, you can't bear it, so you hit her a real hard wallop. Like a man, not like an aristocrat throwing his glove in a marquis's face to challenge him to a duel. Now come on.'

Paul tapped Edith elegantly on the cheek once more, but she had had enough. 'It's not his fault, he just doesn't know how to do it. I'll show him,' and with all her strength she hit Paul full in the face with the front and back of her hand.

If he could have strangled her I think he would have, but she very calmly and professionally explained to him, 'The front of my hand takes out your cockiness, the back makes it hurt. Get it?'

'Yes,' said Paul through clenched teeth, trying to look un-perturbed.

'Perfect,' said Jean. 'Let's continue.'

Paul, afraid to give way to his rage, once more gave Edith his little well brought up smack and Edith laughed, and so did everyone else.

But on the night of the premiere at the Bouffes-Parisiens she made Paul so angry that he gave her a hearty slap which he really meant.

In the dressing-room afterwards, he asked off-handedly, 'Is that what you wanted? Are you happy?'

She shrugged her shoulders. 'It was theatrical.'

The play ran for a long time, it was the hit of the 1940 season, in a double bill with another of Jean Cocteau's plays, *Les Monstres Sacrés*, starring Yvonne de Bray, with décor by Christian Bérard.

Edith was very proud of her acting; it had given her more confidence on stage. It proved to be more than an interesting experience for Paul. *Le Bel Indifférent* brought him parts in other plays and even in films. 'In an unsympathetic part, Paul Meurisse proves his exceptional acting talents. Not content to play second fiddle to Edith Piaf, he brings a well-defined character to his role,' wrote one critic.

This stage of their war ended with a personal victory for Edith. She had been asked to participate in a benefit concert for the Red Cross and some of the greatest names in show business appeared on the bill. The concert started at midnight and ended around five in the morning. It was the only time that Edith was on the same programme as Marie Dubas, who sang 'La Madelon'. Maurice Chevalier sang his current hit:

> *Et tout ça, ça fait*
> *D'excellents français,*
> *D'excellents soldats...*

I forgot who started singing 'We're going to hang out our washing on the Siegfried line', which was a favourite with the English army. There were lots of men from the Royal Air Force in the theatre; they were very popular with us and R.A.F. blue was all the rage. Naturally, Edith had a little suit in R.A.F. blue.

I think Johnny Hess sang the 'Lambeth Walk', which everyone was dancing to at the time.

As always, Edith had prepared a surprise, and this one really struck home. She sang 'Où sont-ils tous mes copains?' :

> *Où sont-ils mes p'tits copains*
> *Qui sont partis un matin*
> *Faire la guerre?*
> *Où sont-ils ces petits gars*
> *Qui disaient: On en r'viendra*
> *Faut pas s'en faire.*
> *Tous les gars d'Ménilmontant*
> *Ils ont répondu: Présents.*
> *Ils sont partis en chantant*
> *Faire la guerre*
> *Où sont-ils?*
> *Où sont-ils?*

As she sang the final *où sont-ils?* [where are they?], the whole backdrop of the stage was lit with red, white and blue lights. It was like a huge flag unfurling on the stage, and then Edith appeared wrapped in the tricolour. It was her own idea. The audience stood up shouting 'Encore', and singing the chorus. Paul and I were in the wings; we were so moved that we did not dare look at each other.

No one wanted to leave. That evening at Bobino we believed that victory was close, we could feel it. It would not have taken much to start us singing the 'Marseillaise'.

When we left it was warm; the sky was still sparkling with stars. We were lightheaded, although we had not had a thing to drink; we were drunk on hope.

Day was dawning pink on the horizon as we reached home. 'This is the first time that I've felt happy at sunrise,' said Edith.

Paul uncorked a bottle of champagne. We drank a toast to ourselves and to all our hopes. Paul was relaxed and smiling. We were happy to be together, things were going well. Automatically Paul turned on his beautiful new radio. He raised his glass and said, 'To today, 10 May.'

Then we heard the sombre voice of the newscaster, 'At six

o'clock this morning German troops were reported pushing across the Belgian frontier. The Panzer divisions are now advancing rapidly through Belgium.'

That was it. The good times were over.

The following weeks flew past. Paul never turned the radio off. Edith and I didn't understand very much of what was going on; all we kept hearing were new names like Paul Reynaud, Daladier, Weygand; and then Pétain.

Paris was downcast. We became familiar with air-raid warnings; they gave us the shivers, but Edith refused to go into the cellar; she was afraid of being buried alive. So we went off to the Bidou Bar. It was against the law, but they let us in all the same. We turned out the lights because of the black-out, and we waited. Paul went with us, he never left us alone.

We watched cars with strange cargoes pass by. First there were the Belgian refugees with mattresses on the roofs of their vehicles. We thought they were taking their beds with them, but it turned out that the mattresses were for protection against strafing from passing planes. After them came the people from the north and east, sweating with fright and telling appalling stories about the Boches. The word went round that Paris was not safe. It was hard to believe, but people started to leave all the same, and one by one the neighbourhoods emptied. First the smart ones – ours soon became a desert – then the others. The government was evacuated to Bordeaux.

On the walls of the city posters declared that Paris would be defended stone by stone, but panic overtook those who remained, and they fled. Then a new poster appeared: 'Paris is an open city.'

On the radio they urged people to stay at home. It was impossible, we had lost our confidence, fear had replaced common sense. Pétain quavered, 'Men and women of France ...'

We didn't understand what was happening. We clung to Paul. We were not leaving.

My God, Paris was sad on the morning of 13 June 1940. From behind our closed blinds, we watched people stacking their most precious possessions into their cars. The old concierge who lived opposite left on foot with her suitcase in one hand, her canary in a cage in the other. I don't know where she was going, for there was no car for her, and there was no Metro.

In the back room we listened to the radio, it was left on day and night. They spoke about bombings, the pockets of resistance on the Loire, our heroic soldiers. Poor devils, what were they fighting for? Alas, we could not have told them!

Huddled together the three of us could think of only one thing – escape.

'Leave,' Edith had said, 'but where can we go? We don't even have a car. Our feet would be worn to the bone before we had gone any distance, and it'll be the same everywhere.'

She was right, of course. Usually Edith was only preoccupied with her career and her love life, but when she had a stake in something outside, she always saw the issues very clearly. She had not lost her sense of humour, either. When Paul said dramatically, 'We are watching history in the making,' she replied 'Well, hell, if this is history I'd rather read about it than make it.'

I do not remember why Paul had not been called up. I think he was turned down because of his heart. The Germans were on their way, it was only a question of hours. We did not know what they would do with apparently able-bodied men. Yet Paul stayed with us. It was very sad. He could not fight like the others, but, like the others, he could feel the terror, the fever of war. He had the satisfaction, however, of knowing he was acting honourably.

He was doing his duty by staying to protect us. He was not a coward and we were sure that he would have defended us to the death.

The streets were empty. There were thick black and red clouds in the sky. They were burning the fuel reserves in Rouen and other places to slow down the German advance. The sticky fog that hung over Paris made the dead, deserted city even more forbidding. At night the ghostly silence was sometimes broken by a soft footfall, like a graveyard keeper. It was reassuring to know that we were not all alone. All the lights were out; we were waiting. Time had ceased to exist.

Suddenly, in the morning, they drove into Paris like a circus parade, singing, blond and suntanned, bursting with health in their black uniforms.

Edith and I went cautiously to the Champs-Elysées to observe them. All the cafés and stores were closed down with iron bars across the windows. Standing in the sunshine, looking at them, we asked ourselves why we had been so scared. Clinging to my arm, Edith said, 'You see, it's all over. There'll be no more fighting.'

Day by day we watched the people return to our district. The Bidou Bar opened up once more. But we never again saw the old concierge from across the way.

One month later they worked out a deal with the owner of Fouquet's on the Champs-Elysées. Collaboration had begun.

Like all artists, Edith had had to present herself at the *Propagandastaffel*, which was set up on the Champs-Elysées. It was obligatory, there could be no work without it.

And thus life began again, but it was not the same.

Maurice Chevalier was among the first to come back to Paris. Coming out of the Gare de Lyon, he refused a car and took the Metro like everyone else.

Edith had never had so many contracts for so many different benefits. There were concerts for the prisoners and for the Red Cross. People queued for everything, for bread, for cinemas, for theatres, and for music halls.

I don't know if it was the shock of the Occupation, but Edith was very highly strung and excitable at that time. Paul was no longer the Paul we had glimpsed during the defeat; he had again become the spick-and-span gentleman. And Edith again referred to him as 'the mannequin' or 'the iceberg'. He was more withdrawn than ever, more tied to the radio than before. He listened to the English stations.

Paul loved Edith, but their ways of expressing their love did not correspond. She invented the most unbelievable things to make him lose his composure. She teased him in every way you can think of. She made 'secret' dates with acquaintances in cafés, making sure Paul found out about them. He would follow her and stand outside the café for hours in the freezing cold. Once she even went to a brothel, and when she came out she found

Paul waiting for her with a taxi. He took her arm, 'You're coming home right away.'

'No,' screamed Edith.

'You're going to get into this taxi immediately.'

'No,' bawled Edith at the top of her voice.

I don't know if he succeeded in getting her in there by force, but the following day she was covered in bruises.

To get his own back, Paul found himself a girl, a pretty little singer with a modest reputation. She had been running after Paul all the time he'd been with Edith. Edith would refer to her as Paul's 'elderly friend'. Anyone over twenty-five was elderly to us.

Edith of course knew that Paul was seeing this girl. One day she telephoned her. 'I wonder if we could meet?' she inquired.

'Oh no, I'm afraid I'm sick in bed,' the girl replied suspiciously.

'Come on, Momone,' Edith called as she put down the telephone, 'we're going over there right away.'

Marguerite Monnot was with us, so we took her along too. 'Where are we going?' she demanded.

'We're going to give Paul's little piece a good time.'

'I didn't realize you liked her enough to do that.' Completely up in the clouds, and as naïve and kind-hearted as ever, Marguerite had quite misunderstood our mission.

The girl had not lied, she was indeed in bed. We gave her such a thrashing it should have put her off Paul for life. I held her down while Edith hit her. Marguerite watched us, absolutely horrified.

That was the only time we were able to anger Paul. Perhaps he was unfaithful to Edith again, but if so no one knew about it.

I could well understand that from time to time he needed a change, particularly since I always trailed along with Edith. From the beginning Edith would level with a guy, 'You take me, you take her too, it's a package deal. Momone's the best there is and, besides, if I leave her alone, she'll do something stupid.'

I called her Auntie Zizi when she wasn't being too hard on me. Since Marcelle's death I had become her kid in a way. But she was over-protective, so I ran off again.

This time it was so that Edith and Paul could be alone. Even before the Occupation the Marquise and Marguerite had both dropped hints in my direction – 'Two's company, three's a crowd,' 'Sometimes a couple needs a little honeymoon,' and so on.

Perhaps things will get better if I go, I reasoned. If I had talked to Edith about it, she would have said, 'I forbid you to go. Don't worry about it,' but I was determined to make my getaway.

Walking through a transformed Paris, I thought about my other escapades. They usually ended at a carnival. Carnivals are fun, but now it did not bear thinking about, there was no music to speak of except the Jerry-made crap.

So this time I didn't feel up to carnivals. Paris was so sad. I didn't care about men either, and I didn't even feel like getting drunk. So I went to find my father.

He lived in a hotel on the rue Rébeval. Edith paid for his room and clothes. His suits didn't come from the smartest tailor in Paris, but he was clean. He was beginning to look a bit worn, poor old thing, and he was very happy to see me.

'What've you done with your sister? Edith doesn't come to see me very often. I know she has a lot of work to do, but all the same...'

He was more than a little proud of Edith, and he did not hesitate to use her name to bring in a few extra centimes. 'I'm Edith Piaf's father,' he would say, and someone would buy him a drink after he had shown them the gold watch Edith had given him.

The people would laugh and ask him to tell them stories about Edith's childhood. Dad was not ashamed to embroider them a bit; as always he gave his audience their money's worth.

I had decided to stay away two weeks, but at the end of the first week I went home and Edith and I had our usual scene.

'You've had it this time. You can leave for good. I'm through with you, you're a stupid bitch. Where have you been?'

'I spent a week with Dad.'

At the mention of Dad, her mood changed.

'You don't say. It's a good thing you came home, it's about time.'

'What about Paul?'

'I'm sick of him.'

I realized from the way she spoke that it was really over. My absence had not helped anything.

After *Le Bel Indifférent* closed in Paris, they took it on tour. Touring was not much fun at that time. If you have never travelled through occupied France you cannot understand how miserable and frightening the railway stations were at night, with the incessant German warnings over the loudspeakers: '*Achtung! Achtung! Verboten!* ...' Everything was *verboten*, laughter, lights, wine.

We couldn't always get a seat on the train, and often we had to sit on our cases in the corridors. Edith looked small and sad, huddled on her suitcase under Paul's coat. If Paul had not been there, we would no doubt have found some fellows to keep us warm, but Paul watched us like a hawk.

What exasperated us was that when Paul got out of the train he looked as if he had been packed in cellophane, while we looked as if we'd spent the night in a rowdy night club.

We loved crossing the demarcation line. Once we had got through the controls, we took a deep breath. Here was France at last!

Had it not been for *Le Bel Indifférent* Paul and Edith would have separated already. In any case, as far as Edith was concerned, it was all over.

'I mustn't be ungrateful, Momone. Paul has had his uses. Without him I would still be living at the hotel, and I wouldn't even have a secretary!'

We had had the secretary for several months. Paul had explained to Edith that she could not do without one, that they were useful and made a good impression. That is how Madame Andrée Bigeard came into our lives.

'She could answer the telephone instead of you,' Paul had said. You could hardly say that a secretary was indispensable; answering the telephone wasn't a very demanding job. It wasn't as if it rang the whole time, we were not in the great Piaf period yet. To Edith a secretary was one more friend, nothing more. We did not really know what she ought to be doing.

It was practical to have her start work in the morning, as that way we had more time to sleep in peace. Edith sent her out to do the shopping and buy the papers so she could cut out the press notices. That was another idea of Paul's. When the reviews became old, Bigeard had asked her, 'What should I do with them?' Edith replied, 'File them.'

Poor Paul, the secretary was all that remained of him as far as we were concerned.

Edith was unhappy at that time because there was no one around who could write songs to order for her, and she could not live without having a song-writer handy. She needed someone to understand her ideas and desires and translate them into a form that she could use. Raymond was in the army, he did not have time to do much, and Roméo Carlès had not worked out; his poetry did not suit Edith's type of song.

At the very beginning of 1940, there had been the Michel Emer episode. He had come into Edith's life literally through the window. She had been in very bad spirits that morning, nervously preparing for the opening at the Bobino the next day, when the doorbell rang.

'Don't answer it, I won't see anyone,' Edith shouted to me.

I let it ring once more, twice. It was not an impatient ring, quite a timid one, in fact. I went into the front room, a sort of dining-cum-living room, when someone tapped on the window. I looked out and saw a boy, looking like a clown in his soldier's uniform, and making signs at me. It was Michel Emer. He wore thick glasses, like Marcel Achard, and behind their enormous lenses his eyes shone like two fish at the bottom of an aquarium. When he smiled, his teeth were big and white. He looked like an overgrown schoolboy.

Edith had met him in 1939 in the corridors of Radio Cité. He was kind, and seemed intelligent, but the songs he wrote were not for her; they were pretty, with blue skies, little flowers, and birds, but they lacked guts.

I opened the window, surprised to see him again.

'I'd like to see Edith.'

'You can't. She's getting ready for her opening at Bobino.'

'Tell her that it's Michel Emer and that I've got a song for her.'
I went to tell Edith.

'Send him away, Momone, I've no use for his songs.'

I went back to tell him. He stood like an obedient child on the sidewalk. Some men look more imposing in uniform, but he had no presence at all, he looked thoroughly downtrodden.

'She has too much work, Michel. Come back tomorrow or tonight.'

'I can't. I'm at the military hospital at Val-de-Grâce, I have to be back before six. Please, I'm sure I've composed a really great song. Tell her the title is "L'Accordéoniste".'

I hadn't the heart to turn him away. 'Come on in and play it.'

I opened the window and he jumped into the room. He sat down at the piano and began to sing 'L'Accordéoniste'.

After the first few bars, Edith rushed in.

> La fill' de joie est belle,
> Au coin d'la rue, là-bas.
> Elle a un' clientèle
> Qui lui remplit son bas ...
>
> Ell' écout' la java,
> Mais ell' ne la dans' pas,
> Ell' ne regarde même pas la piste.
> Et ses yeux amoureux,
> Suivent le jeu nerveux
> Et les doigts secs et longs de l'artiste ...
>
> Arrêtez! Arrêtez la musique!

As Michel finished, he gazed at us anxiously from behind his blinkers. He was sweating big drops.

'Did you write that, little soldier?' asked Edith.

'Yes, Madame Edith.'

'You might have told me you had talent. Take off your jacket and tie and get comfortable, we're going to work. Start again and give me the words. I want to sing it at the Bobino tomorrow.'

He had come at noon; she let him go at five in the morning. We had kept him going with sausage, camembert, and red wine.

For a sick person, he was in good shape. A little the worse for drink, he mumbled, 'Edith, I have to go before the military tribunal for desertion in time of war. I can't get out of it, but I don't give a damn; I've never been so happy.'

'Don't worry about it,' said Edith grandly, 'I can fix it; I know a few generals.'

She didn't know a solitary one, but if Michel had been in real danger, I am certain that she could have got on to the Minister of War. Edith had the most monumental nerve.

We didn't know how he made out, but the following evening he was at Bobino to hear Edith sing his song. At first it did not go down as planned. The last line shocked the audience, they couldn't believe it was over. But 'L'Accordéoniste' made up for that doubtful reception in no uncertain way. The 78 record sold 850,000 copies; an extraordinary number at that time. Edith sang it for twenty years, from 1940 to 1960.

'Swear to me that you'll bring me others,' Edith had pleaded with Michel. He swore. But when we saw him again, much later, he was a very different boy. I could see straightaway that something was wrong. He looked like a hunted man.

'Edith, it's all over. You won't be able to sing my songs any more. I'm a Jew, I have to wear a yellow star. That's how it starts, but later on . . .'

There was no later on, Edith came through. She paid his way into unoccupied France, and we did not see him again until after the Liberation, when he wrote some beautiful songs for her, like 'Monsieur Lenoble', 'Qu'as tu fait de John?', 'La Fête continue', 'Télégramme', 'Le disqueusé', 'De l'autr' côté d'la rue';

> *Dans un' chambr' au sixième*
> *Au fond du corridor*
> *Il murmura: 'je t'aime'*
> *Moi j'ai dit: 'Je t'adore'.*

> *D' l'autr' côté d' la rue*
> *Y'a un' fille, un' pauvr' fille*
> *Qui n'connaît rien d' l'amour*
> *De ses joies éperdues*
> *D' l'autr' côté d' la rue . . .*

Edith loved Michel's particular brand of songs, and she always called him the 'little soldier'.

'What I like about Michel is that he writes the words and music, and the tunes are easy to remember; it's as if you've already heard them before in the streets.'

But back in 1941, Edith was looking for a song-writer. She plagued Marguerite on the telephone. 'It's your business, Guite, find me someone.'

'Someone for what?' asked Guite.

'A song-writer. I don't need a lover, I've got all I can handle in that department.'

'I'm looking, Edith, I'm looking,' fluttered poor Guite.

Edith hung up, 'I'm mad to ask her. I bet she's already forgotten what I called about.'

About an hour later, Guite called back. 'Have you found someone?' shouted Edith.

'That's just it, darling,' said Guite. 'I wanted to ask you what you wanted me to find you.'

Edith did meet Jacques Larue at that time, he was charming, and later on he wrote her some lovely songs, 'Le Bal de chance', 'Marie la Française'; but when she skipped a date with him and sent me instead, she slowed up the development of that relationship considerably.

A movie, *Montmartre sur Seine*, finally brought her what she was looking for: a new song-writer, and a new lover.

The *Le Bel Indifférent* couple Piaf–Meurisse had attracted the attention of a director called Georges Lacombe. The play had run for three months in Paris, and toured all over France; the public knew Paul and Edith, why not cash in on it? So Lacombe approached Edith with a screenplay called *Montmartre sur Seine*.

Edith had already made one movie in 1937, when she sang 'La Garçonne' alongside Marie Bell. No one had been exactly knocked out by her performance, but *Montmartre sur Seine* was different. She was going to do more than sing one song and get it over with; she would have a real part, the lead.

The idea of making a movie seemed to please Paul. I don't

know if Edith's presence added anything to his pleasure. However, since they were working together, Paul stayed on at the house, where he continued to lead his own life. This short reprieve before his departure was not unpleasant; by now Paul had lost interest in both of us.

Edith enjoyed making movies. The only thing she had against it was that she had to be out of bed early in the morning, when the studio car came to fetch us.

On the first day, in the studio canteen, Georges Lacombe introduced Edith to a tall, handsome, well-dressed man, with a little silver streak in his hair and the spark of the *voyou* in his eye. He was Henri Contet, the publicity man for the film.

'I'm putting her in your charge,' Georges said to Contet.

And that was that. If Paul did not pack his bags immediately, it was only because Henri was unable to move in with us.

One glance told me that Contet was right for us. Edith did not waste much time. That evening, during our bathroom session, she asked me, 'Do you like Henri?'

'He's very nice. I think we'll be seeing a lot of him.'

'Right! He's a journalist on the *Paris-Soir* and he writes for a movie magazine called *Cinémondial*. We've never had a journalist, it'll make a change. And anyway, he'll be useful.'

On 8 August 1941, Henri Contet wrote about Edith:

There can be no doubt, that serious, silent little woman down there under the grey stone arch is Edith Piaf. I have caught her unawares because I am early for our date. Piaf is not alone. A man is facing her and I notice his cruel, unyielding expression immediately; it is a face completely without pity, forgiveness or humour. I think I recognize Paul Meurisse.

... Although she is not crying, she reminds me of an unhappy child, waiting, hoping for fairytale happiness, a simple and straightforward love affair, like the ones in popular novels. I should like to write a song for this Little Sparrow.

> *Celui que j'aimerai*
> *Aura les tempes grises.*
> *De l'or à son poignet*
> *Et de belles chemises...*

... She has not said anything yet, but I know what she is going to say. I can see it because suddenly her eyes, her forehead, her outstretched hands are praying. It is the oldest prayer in the world, a hopeless, heart-rending plea, 'Look after me. I still love you. You're all I have. Please stay.'

... What is Piaf's heart made of? Surely anyone else who had been through everything she has been through would be dead by now.

... Edith Piaf has hung down her head a little more, it is too heavy. I can see her hollow cheeks, her eyes that do not want to see anything more.

... What can I do? Console her? How? I think of all the songs she has sung, weeping real tears, putting her whole heart and all the strength she can find in herself and in her lungs and in her life into them.

... Does she know how to be strong? Her shoulders seem so frail. In spite of myself a new song is forming in my head:

> Elle veut savoir si la Seine
> Peut endormir toute sa peine;
> Et lorsqu'elle a sauté,
> N'a plus rien regretté.

... I hear the sound of a stream, like a river gurgling down its course with hoarse little sobs; Edith Piaf is crying.

I have never seen a man able to resist Edith. There was no reason why Henri should not take her in his arms, and he didn't hesitate.

Several times a day I praised Henri and that made her happy. I did not have to pretend, I really believed it. We were headed for happiness. Edith was like a commoner who had just become engaged to the Prince.

She had a very sentimental side to her, going back to the time when she sang in the street. She used to look at the flower stalls near the Metro and say, 'Do you think that one day a man will buy me flowers from a stall like that?' Since then she had been given enough flowers to go into business on her own. She was satisfied, it was the proof of her success, but ...

'You'll never make me believe that those big bouquets are bought with love; they're bought with money. You must have faith to buy a little bunch of violets, to dip your hand in your pocket and give them without feeling ridiculous. That's a real act of love.'

Henri performed this act quite naturally, and Edith was beside herself with joy; she had at last found a man after her own heart.

The official separation from Paul took place without trouble. In the end both he and Edith were making use of each other, and that kind of relationship entails no heartbreak when it ends.

They waited until the film was finished. They were not sorry to be leaving each other. Paul packed his cases with great care, and kissed Edith good-bye. 'I hope you'll be very happy with Henri,' he remarked, with obvious sincerity.

He was not blind. When he left he was so dignified, I felt like curtsying to him as one would to a marquis.

8

PARIS UNDER THE JACKBOOT

After Paul's departure we changed apartments. We didn't go far, in fact, we moved even closer to the Bidou Bar. We could have drilled a connecting door through the wall, which would have made getting home easier some evenings.

When she changed men Edith liked to change her surroundings as well. Things got off to a roaring start between Henri and Edith; they were of the same breed. He wrote a pile of articles about her, and she understood that publicity was a necessary part of her profession. 'A name's like a lover; if you don't see it for a while, if it's away too long, you forget about it.'

Handsome Henri satisfied her as a lover. Unlike Paul, he didn't turn up his nose at the Bidou Bar, and I didn't bother him, either – a *ménage à trois* didn't disconcert him; indeed he liked me a lot, and we became good friends. But Edith little suspected that he would also turn out to be the song-writer she needed so badly.

One evening we were in the Bidou Bar when he said to Edith, like a schoolboy shyly confessing he wrote poetry, 'I don't know if you'll be interested, but when I was twenty I used to write songs. There was one that Jacques Simonot put to music, "Traversée". Lucienne Boyer sang it: it didn't go down very well, though, it wasn't her type.'

'All the better, you obviously don't write the saccharine kind. Have you done any more?'

'I was so disgusted that I stopped. But since I've known you I've started again.'

Naturally, Edith threw her arms around him. Henri Contet was to write a great many songs for her and, in fact, he was responsible for some of the best, and they stayed in Edith's repertoire. Among them were 'Y'a pas d' printemps', which he wrote leaning on the corner of a table in twenty-five minutes because Edith had told him that it was impossible; 'Coup de grisou',

'Monsieur Saint Pierre', 'Histoire de coeur', 'Mariage', 'Le Brun et le blond', 'Padam ... Padam', 'Bravo pour le clown' :

> *Je suis roi et je règne,*
> *Bravo! Bravo!*
> *J'ai des rires qui saignent,*
> *Bravo! Bravo!*

Henri had made it. But like his predecessors he had disagreements with Edith. Edith wanted him all to herself, but he was at that time shacked up with another singer. Edith was not in the habit of sharing her men, but she forgave Henri everything, because he knew how to make her laugh. He was Edith's lover, but because of this other girl he was never truly one of her men. It was a pity; if he had been, we would certainly have avoided the madness of our life between 1941 and 1944.

We were bang in the middle of the Occupation. The restrictions, police raids, black market, hostages, posters, ID cards stamped with 'the crow on pedals' (as we called Hitler's eagle and swastika), drove us all mad. We felt that nothing was permanent, that we were merely living from day to day. So we made hay while the sun shone. We had never drunk so much; we had to get pissed to forget about our miseries. The Occupation stuck in our throats. Laughter was only a cover-up, it left a bitter taste in our mouths.

Edith's name began to be worth money. There was no shortage of contracts. Her fee was a thousand francs, which wasn't bad. It should have been more, but at that time she had no agent. Still, she was not poor. Sometimes she had two engagements on the same day, but money ran through her fingers like sand. Her expenses were heavy. The Bidou Bar did not do too badly, and the black market drained off a lot of dough. Tchang, the Chinese cook, filled the fridge up at night and by morning it was empty. He had perfected a technique – 'Missy doesn't like butter (or roast beef, or lamb), so Tchang will take it away' – And he took it home so that it would not be thrown away on our 'friends'. Good old Tchang had a wife and five kids to feed.

Edith's friends lasted an evening, perhaps several nights. Each had his own way of getting money out of her. One would look sad until she forked out; others would whisper in Edith's ear, 'My old father's Jewish. He has to get into the free zone, but I don't have a sou.'

'How much do you need?' Edith would reply.

The rate was between ten and fifty thousand francs, sometimes fifty or a hundred to get as far away as Spain. Edith couldn't always provide the whole sum, but she always gave something.

Many P.O.W. camps in Germany looked on her as a god-mother. Edith sent them packages. Her heart and purse were always open for the camps. 'I've loved soldiers so long, and they've given me so much pleasure, I can't ignore them now.'

Others, instead of peddling tales of woe, palmed off piles of stuff, useful and otherwise, on to us. Edith was not vain, but she was proud of her name, and they exploited it. They buttered up their 'Madame Piaf', and the ex-child of the streets was flattered and seduced by their homage.

'With a name like yours, Madame Piaf, you should have a pair of white foxes.'

Living in our new apartment on rue Anatole-de-la-Forge was like living in a revolving door. People came in and went out. They slept everywhere, in our beds, on the floor, in the arm-chairs. It happened all too easily. When we left the Bidou Bar with a group of friends everyone was rolling drunk, and since there was a curfew and no Metro, Edith would say, 'Sleep here, everyone, we'll have one more drink and a snack, then we'll all go to bed.'

We were defenceless. It's a pity that Henri was not master of the house; he would have been perfect. The lines on his face, like a map of Paris, showed his intelligence and maturity; they added class to the toughness that Edith liked so much.

'You know what kind of guy he is,' she would say. 'When he puts his hand under your skirt he does it so well that you can't get angry. You even like it.'

She was not exaggerating. Edith and I could never go upstairs in front of Henri without him gently caressing our buttocks, almost out of politeness.

Henri led Edith a terrible dance. He wanted to come and live with us, but his regular girl held on to him. There would be rows, and occasionally he would announce, 'Girls, this time it's definite. Get everything ready, I'm moving in next month.'

Then we would buy him underwear, socks, handkerchiefs, shirts, pyjamas – the full treatment – and since we had no clothes ration for him everything was very expensive.

'In a week we'll have our own man at home. Everything will be different,' Edith beamed.

But Henri never came. Edith flew into a fury and threw everything out, her hopes flying away with the linen.

The next month it would hopefully be put back again, and on the appointed day Henri would appear. But he arrived with no suitcase. All hope was abandoned. What a good actor he was! His face twisted with sorrow, his eyes full of tears, he would say, 'Edith, forgive me.' She would cry and cling to me, 'Let's give him another few days.'

'I'll move in with you next month,' he promised regularly, and Edith wanted to believe him so much that after every disappointment her hopes soon revived.

In the end we realized he would never come. Henri loved singers, but he also loved his comfort, and his girl was a singer-housewife. She kept her man more than just clean; his shirts were well ironed, there were knife-edge pleats in his trousers, his shoes shone. Henri had nothing to complain about; he was as well groomed as Paul.

Without a man at home, there was nothing to keep Edith in check. She found it even harder to swallow Henri's story when 'good friends' like Léo Marjane came by to build up her morale. Léo was in vogue at one time with hits like 'J'ai donné mon âme au diable', 'Mon ange', 'Seule ce soir', and 'Mon amant de la St Jean'. To be one up on us she would drive herself over in a horse-drawn carriage, wearing breeches and boots which she tapped with her riding crop.

'Hello, Edith, I was coming your way so I thought I'd drop in to see if you'd finally set up house with your hairdresser.' (That was Henri Contet.)

When Léo Marjane left, Edith would say, 'Hairdresser! She should be so lucky!'

During the day everything went along fairly smoothly. Henri

would tell her the latest gossip about their friends, Jean Tranchant, Johnny Hess, Georges Ulmer, Léo Marjane, Roberta Andrex, André Claveau, Maurice Chevalier, Georgius, Lucienne Dellile, Line Clevers, Marie Bizet, Lucienne Boyer, and many others. Edith adored it; she was a natural gossip herself, and very critical, with a caustic, razor-sharp wit. There was a singer called Yolanda who had a few white threads in her hair. 'The only pure thing about her are those white hairs, and even they're artificial,' Edith once remarked.

Edith worked hard with Henri and Guite, who was always around the house. Her accompanists at the time were Daniel White, a young man of about twenty-seven, and Walberg, who was a bit older. She drove them all like slaves, but no one ever complained about it. That little slip of a woman was a tyrant when she got down to work. In the midst of her crazy household, she alone was clear-headed. I used to ask myself what she could be made of; where she found all her strength.

The work sessions often began in the afternoon, around five or six o'clock, and ended at dawn. If she was performing somewhere, the rehearsals got under way at one o'clock in the morning.

If it was Raymond who taught her the tricks of the trade, it was Henri who showed her how to make use of them, how indeed to become the Great Piaf. Asso was an authoritarian, an unyielding master, but Contet never ordered her around or rebuked her. He tried to understand, he knew how to listen and he helped Edith find what she was looking for. With him she began unconsciously to take on the role of the 'Boss' herself, to become the person who, in her turn, would mould others.

She tried out hundreds of songs, for she had a very precise idea of what she was looking for. 'A song is a story, but the audience must be able to believe in it. I'm the lover, my song must be sad, it must be a cry from the heart, it's my life. I can be happy, but not for long; it doesn't go with my looks. The words must be simple, my audience shouldn't have to think, but they should have a gut response to my voice. There should be poetry too, the kind to make them dream.'

When Edith had chosen her song, she started to play around

with it. She learned the words and music at the same time, they were never separated. 'They must both go down together inside me. A song isn't a tune on one side and words on the other, they are a unity.'

When someone tried to give her advice that she didn't agree with, she replied, 'My music school is the street, my intelligence is instinct.'

Then, when she felt she knew 'her' song, she gave the author and composer hell; their martyrdom had really begun.

In the middle of a rehearsal Edith would stop dead. 'Stop,' she shouted, 'Shut up. It's no good, Henri, change this word for me, it doesn't sound right coming from me. I can't say it, it's too complicated.'

At the same time she would attack Guite, who was daydreaming until her time came. 'Guite, wake up and listen. You see this, tra la la la la laa, it's not right. It's too long, it's weak, it's soft as marshmallow. I don't sound as if I'm crying, I sound as if I'm melting away like an old candle. I need a real cry here. Look, something like tra la la la *la*. Sharper at the end, shorter. It has to have a clean break because the girl can't go on. Do you understand?'

They understood, all right, and they had to fix it, to find the right word or note, for hours on end.

(One of the best sessions of this kind took place for 'C'est merveilleux', the words by Henri Contet, the music by Marguerite Monnot:

> *Quand on est tous les deux*
> *Le bonheur nous surveille.*
> *C'est merveilleux ...*
> *Quand on est amoureux*
> *Les beaux jours se réveillent*
> *C'est merveilleux ...*
>
> *La vie est peinte en bleu*
> *A grands coups de soleil*
> *Puisque je t'aime*
> *Et que tu m'aimes*
> *C'est merveilleux!*

Henri had not made the words sufficiently popular for Edith's taste and Marguerite's music was too celestial. Guite adored violins; anything that had to do with happiness was immediately given the full orchestral treatment and she became the infant prodigy again. The haggling went on for days!)

After the fevered birth-pang period was finally over, Edith would try out 'her' song all the time, in the bathroom and in bed. She would wake Henri or anyone else and sing them her latest version over the telephone when she felt like it.

As she was learning the song, the gestures came to her; she did not have to contrive them, she waited for them to be born quite naturally out of the words. 'The gestures can distract both the eye and the ear, when you look too hard you hear less well. I don't want them to look at me so much as I want them to hear me.'

A journalist once asked her, 'Do you work out your gestures in front of a mirror?'

She never laughed so hard. 'Can you imagine me studying my movements in front of a mirror? I'm not a clown. The correct timing isn't put in for the audience's amusement.'

The actual production of a song took place on stage and she would improve it when she was face to face with her audience. If she found that she was thinking of something else while she was singing, she took that particular song out of her repertoire. 'When I know it off by heart it becomes mechanical, and then it doesn't have any meaning.'

During those topsy-turvy days Edith found and perfected her work habits. She sometimes fiddled with them, but she never varied the method. And that is how, aided by her fierce will, she became the great lady of song.

Papa Leplée, Raymond, Jean Cocteau, Yvonne de Bray had all encouraged her, taught her something; now she was reaping the rewards.

The results of all this strenuous work induced Jean Cocteau to write, 'Madame Piaf is a genius. She is inimitable. There has never been an Edith Piaf before, there will never be another. Like Yvette Guilbert or Yvonne Georges, like Rachel or Réjane, she is a solitary star burning in the still night sky of France.'

When she had worked well Edith was happy, she was in good spirits. She cooed at Henri like a dove – until the moment came for him to leave when she wanted to keep him, to sink into the night in his arms. 'My Edith, I must go home,' he would plead.

'Stay just a little bit longer,' begged Edith, 'just this once.'

But Henri knew how to pull out gracefully. 'Edith dearest, the curfew . . . it's not safe for me to be out at night.'

'Go quickly, then, my love. I've kept you too long; I hope nothing happens to you.'

And Henri would disappear into the sinister night of the Occupation. He wasn't running much of a risk, as a journalist he had a night pass. I had seen it, but Edith knew nothing about it.

Henri and she had worked out a system of telephone calls. When he got home he called us, let the bell ring twice and then hung up. We called back, it rang three times and we hung up. That way we knew that he had arrived safely. We also knew that he would not be back before the following day.

She did not believe in sparing her rival's feelings. She would call Henri at home in the middle of the night. If his woman answered, she would say, 'I have to speak to Henri, it's about work.' Then she would talk about her work or their love, depending on her mood. When she hung up, she would say to me, 'Do you think *she* heard what I was saying?'

Out of this deception one of Edith's and Henri's best songs was born, 'C'est un monsieur très distingué'.

'Hello, Henri, I've had an idea for a song. Come on over, I can't do it all alone.'

'I can't possibly come, Edith. What about the curfew? Explain it, I'm listening.'

'Well, I suddenly thought of this sentence, "C'est un monsieur très distingué" [He's a very distinguished gentleman], but I don't know what comes next. The "she" (that's me) in the song could be a poor kid, and he impresses her because of his good manners; but he uses her too, do you see?'

'Yes, we'll see about it tomorrow.'

'No. Don't let it get cold. I can feel I have more ideas coming. I can go out at night, I've got a pass. I'll take a taxi and pick you up. They don't stop taxis.'

. . .

In the taxi she was beside herself. 'I've done it, Momone, I've done it. What a fuss that woman of his will make.'

Naturally they didn't make much headway with the song that night.

Two days later Henri brought her a book.

'You're amazing, Henri.'

'Even more than you think. I've brought you a book to help you write our song. It's called *Back Street*. You'll recognize the story.'

They came within a hairsbreadth of breaking up over this book. Edith read it in one night stone sober – she couldn't read when she was drunk, she still had very poor eyesight, and when she drank it got worse.

In the bathroom the next day she told me the story of *Back Street*. It was about a woman who spent all her life hanging around waiting for the man she loved.

'Obviously he doesn't care a damn about me if he gave me that book to read. Am I supposed to be the poor, dumb girl in the book? Madame Back Street? And as if that's not enough he used it to work out the details of my song "C'est un Monsieur très distingué". It's the same story. He's trying to make fun of me. I'll sing the song because it's good, but for the rest he can go screw himself. He's overcharged me for my one night of love. And I served him breakfast in bed, too! Just you wait, I'm not going to let him get away with this.'

Henri came by with a bunch of violets. He bent to kiss her, but she avoided him.

'Sit down. Why did you give me that book to read? Am I supposed to be like that poor idiot wasting my life waiting for you? So the master wants me to stay home; to cry about him; to knit and to concoct little dishes that he won't be there to eat; to sit back and imagine his happiness from afar. Well, you're damn well wrong. You're going to see how I play the part of a back-street girl, a poor dope who's let herself be hoodwinked by a punk like you. You'd like to imagine that I go around like a sacrificial lamb. Sacrificed! To whom? To some ideal of yours? Me! Edith Piaf! Obviously you don't know me. I don't have to wait for you to come along, I've got plenty of men. And the list's going to get longer, there'll be as many names on it as there are in the telephone directory. I swear that I'm going to make such an ass of you that your ears will stretch through the ceiling into your neighbour's upstairs.'

If Cocteau had been there he would have been able to write a new play with material like that.

Unfortunately, I knew that Edith would keep her word. Revenge was within arm's reach and he came in the form of one Yvon Jean-Claude. He had already deputized on a few occasions, for Edith could not go to sleep without feeling a man's body against hers.

Yvon Jean-Claude was a tall, dark, young singer. For the staging of 'C'était une histoire d'amour' Edith had had an idea that called for a man's voice. She had heard Yves and liked him. So every evening he planted himself behind the backdrop, and when Edith sang, 'C'était une histoire d'amour', Yvon would echo,

> *C'était une histoire d'amour*
> *C'était par un beau jour de fête.*

It was not such a big deal for him, and in the evening he came home with us. She paid him but he slept in our house. He was entitled to eat with us, to go to the Bidou Bar, and sometimes to Edith's bed.

On the evening after the *Back Street* incident, Edith said, 'Momone, you'll see. Henri's going to suffer as much as me. He'll learn what hell jealousy is. He's going to be sick, believe me.'

Unless he was blind and deaf, Henri must have known that Yvon was sleeping with Edith.

One afternoon he opened the door of Edith's room, said, 'Oh, excuse me,' and shut it again. I felt myself turning green. 'This is it,' I thought. 'The catastrophe, and no way out of it.'

But Henri just went to wait in the living-room, and when Edith joined him he looked quite natural. He laughed and joked, and then left as usual. The next day he did not come round, nor did he telephone. Edith did not want to show it, but she was beside herself with anxiety; she kept looking imploringly at the telephone.

'What do you think he'll do? Will he give his tart up?'

Had I been in Henri's place, I would have given Edith up.

The next day Henri came back with a song, 'Le Brun et le blond':

> *Dans ma p'tite ville, y'a deux garçons,*
> *Y'en a un brun, y'en a un blond*
> *Qui m'aiment tous deux à leur manière*
> *Le brun a l'air triste et sérieux*
> *Et le blond rit de tous ses yeux*
> *Je crois bien qu'c'est l'brun que j'préfère*
> *Oui, mais le blond n'a qu'à s' ram'ner*
> *Avec son air de rigoler,*
> *C'est pour lui qu'j'ai envie d'êtr' belle*
> *J' crois bien qu'c'est l'blond que j'préfère*

The song ended with the death of the blond boy, the one who was always laughing; he killed himself. You did not have to be too much on the ball to see that the blond boy was Henri (he had light brown hair with quite of lot of white in it).

Henri left the song with us and went out, saying, 'Good-bye, *mes petites.*'

Edith did not miss a trick. She read 'Le Brun et le blond' to Yvon. I saw his eyes fill with tears.

'What's the matter with the idiot?' Edith asked.

Yvon rushed out of the room, crying like a kid. He kept repeating the line from the song, 'C'est le blond que je préfère' [I prefer the blond one]. 'It's Henri that she loves. I mean nothing to her.'

I could have consoled him, but he really wasn't my type.

Henri always dropped his bombs when things seemed to be cooling off, never in the heat of the moment. The next day he came round, lit a cigarette, cupping the match in both hands like a man lighting up in the wind (the gesture suited him and he knew it), looked around the room, as though he was summing everything up, then threw down the match.

'You want me to come and live here. Look around. You say you're the mistress of the house. It's not a house, it's a brothel. You're like the madame who goes on screwing the customers for fun.' This led to an awful scene.

They fought for a long time, then Henri burst out laughing, 'It's unbelievable, but you might just succeed; perhaps you will make me jealous of you.'

Edith had really run riot lately. We were living through a never-ending procession of lovers. It was not much fun for me. We would go out together on a jaunt, pick up a couple of strangers, and have a drink with them. Edith always chose the best-looking one. 'Listen, Momone,' she would plead, 'if you don't sleep with the other one, he'll follow me and my guy around, and we won't be able to shake him off.'

I didn't always feel like it and then she would wheedle me, 'Momone, *please*. What can it mean to you? Screwing him would be the same to you as drinking a glass of wine.'

There was, of course, a slight difference. But when she begged, 'Do it for me, Momone, please,' I couldn't turn her down.

At last Edith decided to bring Henri to his knees; she took up with an actor named Hémond. She decided that she was in love with Hémond, and for twenty-four hours it was even true.

But Hémond barely lasted two weeks. Edith's protestations of her love for him drove Henri wild. He called her mad, a drunk, a whore, a hysteric, and a nymphomaniac; he had quite a vocabulary. I did not always understand him, but I knew what he meant.

An hour after he stormed out, Edith was desperate; she had totally forgotten her love for Hémond and she was weeping for her Henri. She cried with her head in her pillow, tearing the sheets with her teeth. A real crisis was upon us.

'Telephone him, Momone, tell him I have a song I want to work on right away.'

I called; Edith picked up the receiver and immediately shouted, 'Hang up, Momone, that's his woman.'

The next day, her eyes red from crying, she said, 'Go and see him, Momone. I can't live without him.'

I had heard that before, but I telephoned Henri. He told me to come to his office at the *Paris-Soir*. It was all very impressive; he seemed terribly serious, continually giving orders, the telephone ringing non-stop; I didn't miss a crumb of his performance.

'If you wanted me to come here and watch you, you should have told me before, I have all the time in the world.'

He laughed, 'You're a couple of little devils, both of you, and pretty good liars. Come on, let's have a drink.'

'No, come home, Edith's waiting for you.'

As I went in with him that day I could feel what Henri was thinking. I saw the house through his eyes, the whole bloody mess. It was around three in the afternoon. People were sleeping everywhere, including poor Yvon Jean-Claude, and his sister, Annie Jean-Claude, who was married to the screen-writer Dorffman; old Mme Bigeard was wandering around, doing God knows what in all the disarray; Tchang was cooking – he had learned how to cook beans and chicken now; some guy I didn't know was playing the piano, another was drinking. It was enough to make you throw up.

Edith was in bed, and as Henri went in she cried, 'Henri, you're the one I love.'

When a man heard those words spoken in that haunting voice, his insides melted.

So they were off again – but on a different tack now. Edith had a new need, she wanted him to leave her something of himself – a baby!

Edith never talked about the dead Marcelle. Once only she had said to me, 'It's 31 January, St Marcelle's day; my little girl would be ten today. If your mother had taken her in when we took her over there perhaps she'd still be alive.' That was an illusion. I knew what sort of a nurse my mother would have been.

Edith was very calm and serious as she said to Henri, 'My love, I know that you'll never come to live here, that's all over, but I want to keep something of you, something that will never leave me. I'd like to have your child.'

Henri was very moved by this declaration. He could only repeat over and over again like an idiot, 'You want my child.'

But it wasn't all that easy; if it had been, she would have already borne him quite a few. When Marcelle was born they had told Edith it was a miracle, and that it would be difficult for her to have any more children. Now that we had money we went to see the best gynaecologist. He told her that it was a simple thing, she needed a little operation. She would be in the hospital for forty-eight hours.

The day before we went into the clinic Edith said, 'Come on, let's enjoy ourselves.' We went out and bought baby's under-wear, nappies, panties, bonnets, little shoes, even a christening robe. Everything came in duplicate, blue and pink, since we could not be sure if it would be a girl or a boy.

The future father took us to the Belvédère clinic at Boulogne, and as he left Edith clung to his arm, saying, 'After the operation you'll be able to give me my baby.' We were all very touched and drank a bottle of champagne.

When the nurse saw us unpack our layette, she thought we were out of our minds. 'But, Madame, you're not expecting a baby.'

'Not today,' replied Edith, 'but it's to help me believe in it. And I'll be sure that when the child is born it won't want for anything.'

She was not joking.

'I once had a little girl when I was flat broke. I couldn't buy her anything, we had to rely on charity. Now I have the bread I want the best of everything.'

The nurse seemed dreadfully confused, but she was nearer to tears than to laughter.

As I placed the layette in the closet Edith called out, 'Leave the door open so that I can see all the little clothes from my bed. It makes me brave for tomorrow.'

The clinic was not altogether familiar with Edith's methods of preparing for an operation; they had a different system, but we had brought along our own supplies. To put her in the right frame of mind, we drank toasts to each other, to the future child, and to Henri – we owed him that at least. We had brought along the phonograph and some records to make us feel at home, but the clinic was no place for popular music. A nurse came to tell us to shut up and gave us tranquillizers.

Depressed at being deprived of music, we got up and tripped into the corridor in our nightgowns, a bottle in each hand. We kicked up quite a racket and finally they got us to bed by force.

In the morning the day nurse found us snoring like a couple of angels after our night on the tiles.

When the doctor saw Edith in that state he promptly threw us out. Apparently they had no way of sobering us up; so we had to leave with our bags and baggage, at a time of day when we were usually sound asleep.

So Edith did not have Henri's child. But it had planted an idea in her mind. With each new lover she would make an appraisal, 'This one would be good at making babies,' or 'This one would be hopeless.' The criterion was : 'Is he worthy of babies?' Those who were she kept longer, but they never knew why.

The Contet period lasted a bit more than a year, and when Edith and Henri were no longer in love she still kept him on as a songwriter and a friend. She had a good time with him, he was out of the ordinary, he was a good mixer; and he had friends everywhere. Some of them were to be very useful to us.

Rue Anatole-de-la-Forge was not conducive to love; it was antipathetic to Edith's way of life. Nor did she pay her rent regularly. When the concierge used to come round at the end of the month, Edith would say, in a saccharine sweet voice, 'Put it down there. Simone, give madame a drink, I'm going to drink her health.'

Then she would slip her a good-sized tip. For several months after that, the rent-bills would always be 'put down there'.

Edith was perpetually in debt. If she did not pay for something at the time she bought it, it could wait. Poor Andrée had such trouble with the creditors. She had to put up with the complaints that poured in from all sides. You could not discuss money with Edith. She earned it and that was enough. She did not want to know if her expenses were higher than her income.

Now we were in a sorry state. The Contet affair was over. They had turned off the central heating in our apartment; the stove smoked and we had to let it go out; we had forgotten to stock up on black market coal. Edith, who hated the cold, was bundled up from head to foot in woollies, and that put her in a bad mood. We were not too upset when the landlord finally threw us out. The old vulture had a long list of our misdoings : we disturbed the peace at night; we were drunkards; and, on

top of everything else, despite all her drinks and tips, the concierge had told him that we behaved like whores, and men came
and went at all hours of the day and night. In short, in a respect-
able house these carryings-on simply would not do.

When Edith told Henri, 'We're going to leave because we're
whores according to the landlord,' he said, 'That's a coincidence,
ma petite, because I'm going to set you up in a brothel.'

'A real one?'

'Not exactly. It's a sort of exclusive club in a nice neighbourhood, rue de Villejust [now rue Paul Valéry]. You'll be living
on the top floor, it's very quiet. You'll have all the room service
at your disposal. There are lots of classy customers. You'll be as
snug as two bugs in there.'

'That's all very well for you . . .' said Edith.

'Listen, it's bound to work; the owners will like you, it'll be
fun, you'll be warm 'cause the customers in places like that hate
draughts. And, in addition, you'll be rid of all your hangers-
on, and you'll be able to get back some of the money you've
lost.'

When Edith and I arrived at the brothel with Madame Bigeard,
the owner and his wife threw themselves on our necks and
greeted us like long-lost friends. We called them the Fredis; they
must have had another name, but I never knew it. He was an
Italian; she was a fat, dull, bleached blonde who wandered
around all the time in her nightdress that uncovered her shoulders and exposed her sagging bosom. She called her girls 'Darling'
and 'Sweetheart', but she always kept her eye on them. Nothing
got by her: 'Darling, you weren't up to the mark today. M.
Robert wasn't satisfied,' or 'Sweetheart, do something about
your undies, you put the same ones on too often. M. Emile told
me he didn't like it. You mustn't disappoint your customers, it's
bad for our reputation.'

It was a discreet whore-house, we only knew the customers by
their first names.

Things went well with both Fredis from the start. As soon as
we arrived, Edith informed them, 'I don't have any money.'
They extended us credit but, when we did have money, they got
it back – and with interest. Too, they kept us warm in the middle

of the Occupation, and we had as much to eat as we needed. And we were not alone; it was as though we belonged to a family.

We had a bedroom and bathroom, and so did Madame Bigeard (even though we were living in a cathouse, we still needed our secretary).

We made masses of friends. The young ladies' 'offices' were on the floors beneath ours, their 'reception room' on the ground floor.

The Fredis were on the ball, their brothel functioned on two levels. During the day they ran a call-girl service. In the evening it was more like the classical luxury brothels we had known before the war, like 'One-two-two', 'Sphinx', or 'Chabanais'. We had lunch and dinner in the living-room. There was a resident pianist. Everything was pleasant and comfortable. Edith would close her eyes and say, 'Let me listen to my memories. The pianist, the smell of perfumed women; they aren't the same tunes or the same perfumes, but it smells of the whore-house I was in when I was blind. It's nearly seventeen years ago, and I almost feel that I'm going to hear Grandma's voice saying, "Edith, that's enough music. Go to bed." '

There was an unusual atmosphere in the brothel. It was lively and the girls were nothing like the hookers from the streets and cheap bars. They could talk about books, music, the theatre. They had to, they entertained only the bigwigs: 'county types', black market traffickers, and collaborators. The Jerries you met there were mostly generals and colonels, discreet or 'correct' as they said, never in uniform; first-class muscle-men, the heavies from the Gestapo, both French and German. The rue Lauriston, where these German bastards worked, was close by. Between interrogations or torture sessions they came to soothe their frayed nerves. No one liked them, but the Fredis were too scared to turn them away. And – I've kept the best till last – we also got clients from the Resistance. Naturally they came incognito, and it was only much later that we found out that Fredi had a foot in each camp. I must say he made the best of it.

Henri Contet was as happy as a sandboy there. He loved the parade that came and went; he observed it in the most minute detail, and listened to the B.B.C. broadcasts in Edith's room while, on the floor below, General Von Whatever frolicked with his little French miss.

Edith had all kinds of visitors. Even our faithful and favourite old pimp, Riri, came by with a beautiful bouquet of flowers. 'How are things going?' Edith asked him. 'What are you up to now?'

'I still have my tarts, good hard-working girls. But that's not what's bringing in all the bread, I've gone into business.'

He gave us news of our old friends.

'Some of them sold out and started to work for the Gestapo; others ended up in jail for black marketing. Fat Fréhel has had her troubles too. She was singing in Hamburg during the bombing. The phosphorus ran down the streets, people were burning like torches. Houses collapsed. The flames lit everything up so you could have read a newspaper. The whole town was screaming. They were dying like flies everywhere, and there was this overpowering smell of roast pig. Fréhel's hair, eyelashes, and legs were burned. When she talks about it, it makes you shudder. You know how sensitive I am, it made me sick to my stomach. After a coup like that I started to believe that the Jerries won't win the war after all. You have to really crack down on them before they start hurting.'

When he left he said, 'Children, I'm happy to leave you here, it's warm and pleasant.'

Guite came from time to time. She would arrive on her Mobylette motor-bike (everyone was on two wheels those days), with a scarf round her head so as not to upset her hair. Scarves were all the rage, we even made turbans out of them, but Guite still looked as if she had ridden through a wind-tunnel.

She was so absent-minded, that one day she arrived on someone else's Mobylette! 'Children, I'm terribly upset, I've just realized that I took a Mobylette that doesn't belong to me.'

'Well, give it back.'

'Who to?'

'Take it back where you got it from.'

'But I don't remember where it was.'

Guite did not quite realize we were living in a brothel. One day she said, 'There's lots of coming and going here, but it's nice and warm. They're nice people downstairs.' She had taken the Fredis for the concierges!

Edith was at home to a lot of people. She had little to do with singers, she preferred actors and they came in droves. Her closest friend was Michel Simon. An extraordinary man, ugly in such a nice way that it did not matter. Listening to him, I could have fallen in love with him for his mind alone, but I wasn't his type. He was carried away by the tarts from the rue Saint-Denis whom he adored.

Michel did not talk much about his career, but about his life. So much had happened to him. He talked, too, about his monkey, whom he loved like a wife. He told marvellous stories, and his voice added a strong, mournful quality to what he was saying. He could not stand his looks; his ugliness obsessed him. 'With a face like mine no one but tarts (and they're nice girls, don't misunderstand me) and animals will have anything to do with me. My monkey thinks I'm good-looking, and she's right, she would never find a monkey as good-looking as I am. And anyway, it's better to look awful than to have no looks at all.'

That made Edith laugh, but it wrenched my heart. Michel Simon thought that Edith's face was not unlike his, that she was to women what he was to men. It reassured him, he felt he was no longer alone. 'You see, Edith, we don't have to be good-looking to succeed.'

What was amazing was that after a few moments I began to see Edith through Michel's eyes. I had always thought that she was pretty, but now I thought to myself there was something abnormal about her; her narrow shoulders, big forehead, tiny face. She looked better in real life than she did on stage, though; she lost the suffering look, and you could see that she had plump hips and good legs.

She and Michel told each other about their lives. They also loved making up stories, and they drank a lot together. While I would be sipping my first Cinzano, she and Michel were already on their tenth. Michel would say, 'We may be ugly, but we're not small-time.'

Jean Chévrier came, too, with Marie Bell of the Comédie Française. She was very much a woman of the world. We would received them in the salon, then she and Jean would go discreetly upstairs. They were not yet married at that time.

There was also Marie Marquet. When the two Maries met they were always a bit acid, for they did not like each other very much. But Edith appreciated Marie Marquet. She was a great lady whichever way you chose to look at it – both in her height (when she held out her arms, we could walk under them) and in her talent. Edith listened to her with respect. 'Marie, I learn a lot when I listen to you. A poem is just a song without music, it presents the same difficulties.'

It was very funny to see this well-brought-up woman not at all shocked by our whore-house. She would tell us extraordinary stories about Edmond Rostand's plays, *Cyrano de Bergerac, L'Aiglon, Chantecler*. She talked about the house called Arnaga near to Cambo in the Basque country where Edmond Rostand had lived. She and the poet had been very much in love. Edith was enchanted.

We also had our regulars, like Madeleine Robinson and Mona Goya.

Madeleine Robinson was Edith's best friend. They shared two passions – men and the bottle. The binges they went on together are still famous. But the most extraordinary and instructive thing was to listen to them talking about men. One picked up a lot of worthwhile information.

Mona Goya was a real nut, constantly laughing. She was chic and pretty, a real heart-breaker. She and Edith invented an amusing game. During the black-out they would leave their curtains open and the light on, the cop on his beat would blow his whistle, and finally have to come upstairs. If he was good-looking they would give him a drink for his pains, and entertain him.

But life was not all roses.

One day in 1943 Edith was called to the police station on her mother's account. It was not the first time, but it would be the last. Since Edith had become famous, her mother created one scandal after another. More than once we had to fetch her from Fresnes after she had been picked up in the street, dead drunk and high on drugs, a real tramp. We would rescue her, give her a whole new set of clothes, and not long after it would start all over again.

When Edith was at the A.B.C. in 1938, a woman dressed like a beggar clung to the door of our cab. She had hair in her face, she was high, and screamed in a terrible, raucous, drunken voice, 'That's my daughter, that's my daughter!'

She went everywhere complaining, 'Edith Piaf's my daughter, she's rolling in money and she leaves me to fend for myself.' She threatened Edith that she would expose her in the newspapers, and, in fact, in 1941 she went to ask help from the social services offered by the *Paris-Soir*. They did not take her seriously, and, by 1943, we were used to her getting into trouble with the police. This time when I went to the police station the cops told me that she was dead.

She had been living in Pigalle with a young man; their drug habit had brought them together, a poor little petty thief and an old derelict. One evening the boy got up from their flea-ridden mattress to fetch some cocaine. When he left he glanced at Edith's mother. She was snoring. When he returned she was in the same position, but when he touched her she was cold. Terrified, his mind addled by alcohol and drugs, he took the body downstairs and dumped it in the gutter.

And there in the gutter, as Dad had foretold, she died.

Henri took care of everything with me. Edith had her mother buried at Thiais. She did not go to the funeral, and she never visited the grave.

'As far as I'm concerned my mother has been dead for a long time,' she said. 'She abandoned me a month after my birth; she was a mother in name only.'

Edith worked hard, though her contacts with the Germans did not always go smoothly. Unlike her namesake Edith Cavell she was no heroine. But she was too much of a free spirit, too much a child of the streets to be able to tolerate any tampering with her freedom.

In 1942 she had an engagement at the A.B.C. On the first night every section of the occupying forces was represented – the green of the Wehrmacht, the black of the SS and Gestapo, the grey of the Luftwaffe, the blue of the Kriegsmarine – and the place was jumping with Parisians from all walks of life. At the end of her act, Edith did 'Où sont-ils tous mes p'tits copains?' complete with her tricolour light show. The place went mad.

The Germans did not take long to counterattack. On the following day Edith was summoned to appear before the Occupation Authority.

'Take that song out of your act,' they ordered.

Edith was shaking with fright but she replied, 'No, I won't.'

'Then I shall forbid you to sing it.'

'Forbid me, but all Paris will hold you responsible.'

In the end they compromised – they insisted on the tricolour flag being removed.

The Germans loved her voice. They invited her to tour the big German cities at least twenty times, but she refused. But she was always ready to sing in the prison-camps, and she never accepted the fee; she handed it over to the prisoners. She came back from these trips very upset. All those soldiers, those prisoners, were men she had always loved. They welcomed her like a princess.

Andrée Bigeard had asked if she could go on these trips in my place.

'Do you like the Jerries so much?'

'I like travelling.'

'She's lying,' Edith said to me.

We had not been too drunk to notice that Andrée Bigeard took a lot of men to her room. At first Edith was amused, 'Good lord, the place has gone to Andrée's head. She has an awful lot of men, I'd never have thought it of her.'

Later we learned that she was using her place in the heart of enemy territory to do Resistance work, and that the 'clients' who came to see her were 'terrorists', as the Germans called them

The journeys across the Rhine were very useful to Andrée, but not very restful. One day when Edith was singing in a camp, a high-up officer said, 'I hope that you're enjoying yourself, Madame, and that you appreciate the hospitality of the Third Reich. What do you think of Germany?'

'Since you brought it up,' replied Edith, 'the room is freezing, the windows are broken, the food is uneatable, and there isn't even any wine. Germany is disgusting.'

The Kraut turned bright red. He seized his telephone and started screaming into it in German. 'This time,' Edith told herself, 'I've gone too far.' An hour later, however, she was installed in the best hotel and they were feeding her a decent meal with a bottle of good French Bordeaux.

Another time Edith learned that the French prisoners had put new words to the Hitlerian anthem, the words went as follows:

> *Dans le cul, dans le cul,*
> *Ils auront la victoire.*
> *Ils ont perdu,*
> *Toute espérance de gloire.*
> *Ils sont foutus,*
> *Et le monde en allégresse,*
> *Répète avec joie, sans cesse:*
> *Ils l'ont dans l'cul,*
> *Dans le cul!*

[Up your arse, up your arse,/We shall win./They have lost/all hope of glory./They're screwed/and the world rejoices,/Say it with joy over and over/Up their arse, up their arse . . .]

At the end of her act Edith said, 'To thank all these gentlemen and officers I'm going to sing a German song for you, but since I don't know the words, I shall hum it.'

And she started off as loudly as possible. With much shuffling of boots, all the Germans stood to attention and listened to Edith who was actually humming 'up your arse'.

The atmosphere was excellent, and Madame Bigeard said to Edith, 'Ask permission to be photographed in a group with the prisoners.'

After having drunk to the Camp Commandant, to Stalingrad, to Victory, and to anything they wanted, Edith said, 'Colonel, I have a favour to ask you.'

'Granted,' replied the other clicking his heels.

'I should like to have a souvenir of this lovely day. Could I have my photograph taken with all of you and with the prisoners?'

The Germans agreed and, when they got back to Paris, Edith gave the photograph to Andrée. She had it enlarged, and the heads of the French soldiers were cut out and stuck on false identity cards and 'voluntary worker in Germany' passes. Edith then got permission to go back to the stalag. This gave Andrée the chance to smuggle the false papers into the camp in the false bottom of her make-up case, and pass them over to the prisoners. Those who were able to escape were very much helped by the papers. Several even survived because of them. Edith and Madame Bigeard performed this trick whenever possible. 'No, I wasn't in the Resistance, but I did help my soldiers,' Edith would say.

We were all set to stay in our luxury brothel right up to the end of the war. Unfortunately, the Fredis had overdone it; too much black market. Towards the end, the Germans became 'virtuous' and, to set an example, they got rid of the black marketeers. Some of the girls had robbed their customers, among them a German officer. The Gestapo bastards didn't come for their own pleasure any more, but to make trouble. One morning, in the spring of 1944, Henri came to say, '*Mes petites*, this place stinks of cops, let's get going.'

So 'We're going back to the Hôtel Alsina,' Edith decided, as rapidly as ever.

We left the Fredis with two million francs. That was what we still owed them, despite all the money we had already paid. When I said they were expensive, I was not wrong. They had taken so much money from us with their credit deals that we were almost left without a franc.

The day after we left, the house on the rue de Villejust was closed down and the owners put in jail.

The good life was at an end.

9

YVES MONTAND

We soon took up our old ways at the Hôtel Alsina, although we were pretty miserable at the beginning. The war was going badly for the Germans. Black-bordered posters carried the names of hostages, some of whom could have been our neighbours. It took away our appetite for pleasure. We were all terrorists to the Germans, even the old girl who sold papers on the corner. There was no more free zone. The fate of the Jews was sealed, they were mown down like corn. The 'correct' German, who had set out to seduce the population during the early days of the Occupation, was gone. Now the streets started to stink of fear.

We were depressed. We had no more money, no more Tchang, we had parted from Madame Bigeard in tears. Counting pennies put Edith in a bad temper. She had lived like a madwoman at the rue de Villejust. Since we were always in debt to the Fredis we had not even bought any clothes. Now we were living in our old cast-offs, and they weren't much to look at.

No money, no men, no more good times for Edith. You'd think it would teach her a lesson, but not at all; when, later, she was in the money again nothing had changed, she still spent it all. Edith went on tour to another stalag taking along Madame Bigeard, who was part of the deal. She kept crying, 'This is the last time,' and we were all sure that it was.

I remember how the Gare de l'Est was that night. It stank of greasy, sweaty leather. The smell of boots was the smell of the German army. I stood a long way off from the train, imagining the misery of the men who were leaving for the slaughter-house on the Russian front. Passes, girls, fatherland, all were finished for them. Even though they had invaded our country they were men, and my heart went out to them

When I got back to the Alsina, the doorman said to me,

'Madame Piaf's father's servant just called. He asked you to call back immediately.'

There was quite a history behind this servant. Edith had not forgotten Dad. One day he said to her, 'Now that you've made it, I'd like a servant of my own. It'll impress my mates.' We laughed a lot, but since it was the kind of thing Edith was capable of dreaming up herself, she put an ad in the paper. Dad refused to give up his shabby, dilapidated, uncomfortable old hotel, it was unthinkable that he should have a servant there, but he did. This time I was worried when Dad called us, he usually went to the café on the corner; since it involved money he did it himself. I called the servant. He must have been waiting. 'I wanted to tell Madame her father is dead,' was all he said.

I did not realize there were tears streaming down my cheeks. I had loved the old man. A whole part of my life would be buried with him in that hole. I called Henri Contet and we went along to the rue Rébeval together. We could not contact Edith, but she came back in time for the funeral.

At Dad's hotel we were greeted by a whole group of relatives whom we had never seen before. They all wanted souvenirs. When Dad was alive he would not have given them the time of day. Edith gave the servant his beautiful gold watch. 'Give the others his pipes,' she said to me. I passed out the filthy, chewed-up old pipes that he had loved so much.

They buried him at Père-Lachaise. The girls from the brothel in Normandy were at the funeral. They were crying but they did not dare embrace Edith, since Henri was with us. Dad had been buried alongside the other men from the family. Edith squeezed my hand very tightly. We understood each other; they were burying our childhood and youth.

Everything was going wrong. When Henri came to see us he appeared grey and lifeless. He hadn't the heart to write songs. Everyone stayed at home. Even Guite did not come round, she had mislaid her last Mobylette and we had no piano at the hotel, and Guite could not talk without her hands on a keyboard.

Perhaps it was not the right moment for Henri to suggest to Edith that she join the Society for Authors, Composers, and Music Publishers (S.A.C.E.M.). 'It'll give you something to do.

You've already written some songs, but you aren't allowed to sign them, so you don't get what you're entitled to. Enroll at the S.A.C.E.M., and when you're a member you'll be able to claim your royalties.'

'You're nuts, Henri. I could never pass an exam.'

I nagged Edith until she agreed to go along, even though she was very reluctant.

'I put in my request, Momone. They don't believe in fooling about. You have to take your birth certificate and a photograph along to the exam. And you have to pass some kind of test. Off the top of your head you're expected to write a song on a subject that they set. I'm scared stiff.'

It was the beginning of 1944 when Edith was called to take her exam.

'I can't do it, I've never passed an exam in my life. I know I'll fail. Think of all those men with beards who are going to judge me.' (To Edith all judges and professors wore beards and she loathed them.)

An hour before the exam she was terrified; she downed a few drinks to give herself courage. Then she went down to the S.A.C.E.M. on the rue Ballu.

Sitting all alone in a little office with the paper in front of her, she lost control. Her subject was 'Rue de la Gare'.

'The piece of paper was jumping up and down, and the words 'Rue de la Gare' kept jumping all over it like a fly's feet. It didn't mean anything to me. I can't tell you what a damn nuisance that street is. All I could think of were things like, "On the rue de la gare / The girl strayed far / She had lost her heart / To him . . ." Really dumb things. I couldn't write a word. And I didn't think about spelling mistakes. My head was spinning. I came out of it without knowing what I'd written, my heart was broken, and I had a splitting headache. I'm through. I shouldn't have had that drink. You know I can't think when I'm pissed.'

She had failed.

If there was ever a man who came into Edith's life at the right moment it was Lou Barrier, and he stayed beside her right to the end. He was a marvellous person. Even the way in which he came to us was charming. The doorman telephoned Edith to say, 'There's a M. Louis Barrier down here who would like to see you.' We did not have many visitors. We clattered downstairs and found a nice-looking blond boy, quietly standing with a bicycle at the entrance to the hotel. He was still wearing his bicycle clips.

'Madame Piaf, I have come to see you because I'm an agent.'

We looked at each other and burst out laughing. The agent we had been awaiting for more than ten years, with his Rolls and a fat cigar in his mouth, had arrived with his bike and clips! It was so funny that it had to work. He had no references except his honesty and frankness. Straightaway Edith heard her famous 'click'. She liked Louis.

'I'd like to represent you. I know you don't have anyone: it's a good time, so here I am.'

It took someone with flair and good timing to be able to say that to us, just when we felt ourselves slipping right back to the streets.

'Okay,' Edith said to him. 'I like you.'

They signed no contract, not the tiniest scrap of paper; it wasn't necessary between them, Edith had complete confidence in Barrier. That very evening she decided to sleep with him.

'You only really know a man when you've been to bed with him,' was Edith's philosophy. 'You learn more about a man after one night in the sack than you do in months of conversation. When they talk they can fool you as much as they want, but they can't kid you in bed. It's trial by fire. At the moment they think themselves the master, you really have them. Men have often given me a good time; but not always in the way they imagined.'

Louis (she called him Loulou) asked nothing more than to be put through this trial.

Edith had agreed when Loulou asked her to visit his flat. I would not have even remembered their departure for that night of love if Edith had not returned so promptly. I never laughed so much; she was scarlet with rage.

'Give me a drink, I'm suffocating.'

'Didn't he give you one?'

'Shut up. Don't ever mention that clot to me again. He may be a good agent but he doesn't have what it takes for anything else. We went to his little apartment, two rooms, not badly furnished. He'd laid on everything, champagne, food, flowers. It started off well enough. We drank a couple of glasses of champagne. He took me in his arms, started whispering sweet nothings, I felt myself beginning to melt . . . this was it. Then he gets up, "I'm going to set the mood," he says. He puts on a record and guess what? He made me listen to a song by that bitch of Henri's. After everything I'd been through with Henri because of her! It was worse than a slap in the face. But I held myself back. "That's pretty," I said. "Who's singing it?" And the idiot happily supplied her name.

'Then he treated me to a second helping of her limited talent. I leapt up and gave it to him straight. "If you've got her already as a client you don't need me. You'll be able to get her so many contracts that in a year you won't even have enough money to buy bicycle clips." Then I left.'

The next day Loulou discovered his gaffe, and he came over, absolutely shattered. 'Edith, please forgive me, I had no idea.'

She roared with laughter. 'Don't look so upset. I'd forgotten all about it an hour later.' (Not strictly true.) 'Don't worry, I'll keep you on, but you'd better look after me properly.'

Barrier looked after her marvellously. A wash-out as a lover, he was very efficient as an agent, and we saw results immediately; it was a difficult time, and yet he got her a two-week contract at the Moulin Rouge, one of the great music halls of the time.

Work fever overtook Edith again, but we still had time to chat. Sitting in the bathroom, I listened to her steering a course around the shipwrecks of her love affairs. She loved talking about her men. 'Do you remember José, the little Spaniard? He only lasted one evening, but I'll never forget him. He came between Jeannot the sailor boy and Riri the Legionnaire.'

'No, no, it was long before them.'

'Do you think so? That's funny, I'm getting them a bit mixed up.'

You would have had to label Edith's lovers to keep them in the right order. Even she got confused. And she always finished her individual recollections by saying, 'He really loved me,' some-times adding, 'And I loved him so much.' She made little dis-tinction between them. Except for the 'stars', all the beads on her rosary of love were the same size.

'I've had an idea,' she declared; 'so that we'll remember when they came along, we'll label them by period. "The street", "the sailors and the colonials", "the pimps", "madness" – do you re-member that time, after Leplée?'

Did I remember? Then she would take refuge in anyone's arms. '... Asso and Meurisse will be the "professors period", Contet the "brothel period", and, and ...'

Even with categories we couldn't sort them out, but the period which was now about to begin would last a long time. Edith called it her 'factory period', because she started to fashion a series of singers. She kicked off with Yves Montand.

'They can't force a second star on you any more,' Loulou had said to Edith. 'It's up to you to choose your own now. They suggest Yves Montand for the Moulin Rouge.'

'I don't know him. I want Roger Dann, he's a friend of mine.'

But Roger was not in Paris, and there was no hope of bringing him in from the provinces. It was July, a little more than a month away from the Liberation.

'Okay,' said Edith, 'let's audition your Yves Montand.'

Sitting in the back of the auditorium at the Moulin Rouge, Edith saw a dark, Italian-looking character come on to the stage. He was handsome, but horribly dressed in a garish check jacket and a little Trenet-type hat. And, with all that, he sang old American stuff, phony songs from Texas. He was copying Georges Ulmer and Charles Trenet. It was dreadful. After three songs he came to the front of the stage and said peevishly, 'Shall I go on or is that enough?'

'That's enough,' shouted Edith. 'Wait there.'

Edith knew he was furious at being auditioned by her; he had already referred to her as a 'sob sister', 'a raw street singer', and 'a pain in the arse'! She walked over to where he stood up on the stage, so small that her nose just about came up to his ankles. 'If you want to learn to sing, come to my place at the Hôtel Alsina in an hour.'

Yves was struck dumb. He went quite pale with anger. All the same, an hour later at the Hôtel Alsina, he had lost his defences.

Edith didn't pussyfoot around, 'We'll start with your plusses, we'll get through them faster. You've got a good face, good presence, expressive hands, a good, warm, serious voice which'll set the women off. You look like you want it, and you look intelligent. For the rest, nothing! Your clothes are fit for a circus ring, they're ridiculous. That Marseilles accent is dreadful, your o's are interminable, and you move like a puppet. Your repertoire isn't worth tuppence, the songs are vulgar, and your American mannerisms are laughable.'

'I've had quite a lot of success,' he managed to say.

'In Marseilles perhaps. They haven't seen anything else for four years. And here the audience likes anyone who gives the Germans a hard time. They're not applauding you, it's the Americans, and when they get here you'll look like an idiot beside them. You're already out of date.' By now Yves was boiling over with anger; I could hear him grinding his teeth. Edith was enjoying herself.

'Thank you, Madame Piaf. I quite understand. I'm not your type.'

'You're wrong. You *are* my type and I don't want to stop you making a living, but two weeks with me will be over quickly.'

Almost choking with anger, he was about to walk out of the door without even opening it when Edith stopped him. 'Listen, I haven't finished yet. I'm sure you're a singer, a real one. I'm ready to give you work. If you want to listen to me and obey me, trust me, I'll make you the greatest.'

He replied, 'Thanks a lot.' And left, slamming the door behind him.

I was amazed. It had not lasted more than fifteen minutes, but in this quarter of an hour I had seen a woman I did not know existed. I had no idea she had it in her.

The way in which she had reduced the man – he was like a peapod that she had opened and, having selected the best pea, discarded the rest. She had seen through everything that was ridiculous, false, or bad. I was completely bowled over. Edith had always amazed me, but never the way she did that day.

She was sitting on the bed watching the door. 'Not my type! How stupid men can be. He's fantastic-looking, the nut. He could revolutionize singing. They're waiting for him. He's the new type, the post-war model.'

'Do you think he'll take your lessons?' I ventured.

'Oh yes,' she replied confidently.

I was less sure. Yves was proud. And he was Italian, and they don't like being bossed around by women.

The next day at rehearsal he had taken off his jacket and was singing in shirt-sleeves. It was Edith's turn next and, as they stood in the wings, she fired at him, 'Have you ever heard me sing?'

'No, Madame Piaf.'

'So how do you know that I'm a sob sister? Call me Edith, and now listen. Then you'll be able to judge for yourself.'

He stayed until the end, then disappeared without a word. But Edith waited for him, and she was right again; he came back to the Alsina.

'Okay, Edith. If the offer's still good, I'll take you up on it.'

'You don't like taking orders from women, do you?'

'I don't mind. I listened to you sing, and you know everything I don't.'

We had a drink, toasted everyone, and then they got down to work.

'Have you thought about your clothes?'

'Yes, but ...'

'But you don't have any dough. So what? We're still rationed, you're not going to dress in anything fancy ... just a shirt and pants. But not a white shirt, it'd cut you in two. The shirt should be the same colour as your trousers. You're tall and thin, and you move gracefully, you should show it off.'

I could not get over Edith's authority. 'And that Marseilles accent must go; leave it to those who have nothing more to offer. I'll teach you an actor's trick. Put a pencil between your teeth. You're going to talk and recite your songs like that. And I've written out a list of words full of o's, for you to read off to me several times a day.'

'What am I going to look like with a pencil in my mouth?'

'Nothing looks stupid when you're working. Get on with it.'

Yves drooled and swore, and Edith giggled at the sight of that damn pencil stuck in his lovely, manly mouth.

When Yves was with us there was no space left in our room; he seemed to take up every spare inch with his six-foot frame and one hundred and eighty pounds. I was charmed to see him standing there, docile and eager, and I liked him for it.

Yves and I had become good friends straightaway. He was quite a change from the types we had had up to that time; like a breath of fresh air; a young wolf with all his life before him, full of strength. His smile was direct, frank, and honest, and he laughed all the time as if the sun were always shining.

After the lesson he and I left together and walked side by side down the avenue Junot. With a kick from his enormous foot (he must have taken size twelve at least), he sent a pebble flying into the air. Suddenly, he stopped, both hands jammed into his pockets. Soberly he said, 'I think I have confidence in her. I'm going to work hard.' And he got down to it right away. In two weeks, Yves had made extraordinary progress, even though he still sang the same damn songs. The lessons now took place on his home ground, because in that period he had become the new master and Edith was madly in love with him. Once more I admired her good taste. She knew how to choose her men. When Yves walked into a room at the age of twenty-two, you felt he'd brought the sun in with him. Love did not slow down the learning process, however. They worked twice as hard. Edith didn't let a thing get by her. She had decided that he would have an early success, and she would not allow herself to be wrong. She was a tireless worker and the sessions would last for hours. The room was too small. Edith hated open windows. In half an hour, Yves had drained off all the available oxygen with his athlete's lungs and it was getting difficult to breathe. But there was no thought of his going out alone, so I went with him. Edith was not suspicious, but she took precautions. 'He's too full of life, that guy, too full of health. We can't let him loose outside.'

When they were working, they attacked each other like two wildcats. Yves wanted to be told everything all at once. He had a good solid jaw and no patience. Before he was anywhere near ready, he asked, 'Okay, Edith, I need a new repertoire. Where are you going to find my songs?'

'Don't worry, my love, it'll work out.'

'How? With whom? I have a right to know.'

Yves was not very easy to handle. They both had strong personalities, and each was as tough as the other. When Edith had had enough argument, she would cut it short with, 'Do you trust me or not?'

I knew that she had not yet looked for a single song. 'You see, I don't know anything about his life. You only sing well when you're singing about something that's close to you, something that's hurt you, or something you dream about. He thought he was a cowboy, but that's just the fantasy of a kid who goes to the movies a lot. His head's stuffed with old Westerns. Honestly, he thinks he's Zorro. So he has to talk to me. He has to tell me about the time he worked with his hands, or when he was growing up. What did he think about? A little girl? Sunday? Women? Yves is a man of today. Everyone will see themselves in him. But to achieve that he must have the same dreams as them. Not many people over twelve are still longing for an old hack and a ranch in the Mid-West. I can just about make out his style, but I must be sure of it.'

Listening to Edith, I thought of how Raymond Asso had put her through her paces in the little room in Pigalle.

For several evenings I went to the theatre to listen to Yves. I enjoyed it, he told a good tale. His movements on stage were nothing, but in real life, he was, without any doubt, perfection.

'I'm an Italian, you know, a spaghetti eater. I was born in a little village thirty-six miles from Florence on 13 October 1921. The priest baptized me Yvo, and my family name is Livi. I was two when my father came to France with the whole family. He didn't like Fascism. He was worried that his sons would be forced into the Balillas (Fascist Youth Movement). "My boys will never wear the mourning shirts of Italy," he used to say and he was right; Italy in black shirts was ready in advance for its sons and wives.

'We settled in Marseilles. It was supposed to be a temporary stop on the way to America. To the Italians, America is the land of promise. You tease me because I copy the Americans, but I've always heard America spoken of as paradise. When things were going badly my father would say, "You'll see, life will be different in America ..." and the whole family would start to daydream.'

Neither Edith nor I could understand Yves's life. He had been a properly brought-up child, the kind we had never met. It got on Edith's nerves. 'You never played in the street!' she insisted. 'Marseilles must be like a carnival, full of sounds, of colours and smells. It must grab you, intoxicate you. I wouldn't have been able to resist it.'

'I got caught up in it later, when I'd left school,' said Yves. 'My father had too much to do. He had three kids and a wife to feed, it wasn't easy. So at fifteen I started to work. I did a lot of things, I was a waiter, an apprentice barman, I worked in a factory where they made pasta (paradise for an Italian!), and since my sister was a hairdresser, I even tried my hand at being a ladies' hairdresser. Can you imagine it?'

'You don't sing about all that very often.'

'I didn't only work for bread; I worked because I wanted to be free, to be able to do what I wanted. All my money went into Maurice Chevalier and Charles Trenet records. I was dying to be like them. Then one day I managed to get an engagement in some shabby place in the suburbs but, as far as I was concerned, I was singing at the Alcazar. It was because of that date that I changed my name. "Yvo Livi isn't right," the boss said. "It's too foreign and it doesn't have a proper ring to it."

'So I worked on a new name. When I was a kid, my mother didn't like me to hang around in the street in front of our house. She spoke bad French and would shout, "Yvo monta, Yvo monta." [Yvo, come upstairs.] That came back to me, so I frenchified my christian name, Yves, and monta became Montand. The war didn't help anything. I became a sander in a metalworks. It's very bad for the lungs, I was supposed to drink five pints of milk a day. Then I worked in the docks. Then I chucked everything and came to Paris, and in February 1944 I had my stroke of luck – I went to the A.B.C. After that I worked in any cinemas I could find, and roughed it.'

Yves opened his big hands – a Piaf-like gesture, 'You see, it hasn't been roses all the way.'

For the time being Yves seemed fairly gentle. He loved Edith, and he expected everything of her. Yves had thought Edith would ask him questions about his women, his conquests. But she did not care, and that annoyed him, he wanted her to know that he was a lady-killer.

He was an unknown quantity to Edith. She had discovered a talent in herself that she never knew existed; the ability to 'make' a star. It was stronger than alcohol, and more heady. After several days, she decided that she knew enough about him. 'You have to sing about everything you've told me. Show me your hands.' He opened them.

'Those are a docker's hands. You've had blisters, don't forget it. They're the hands of the people, too, so *they* must know it. Now we have to find the right people to write for you and it won't be easy. You need songs which tell a story, which allow you to create a personality, which you can bring to life on stage. But in order to really get underneath that personality, you have to be at ease in there. I want you to sing love songs, you're made for them.'

'No,' shouted Yves. 'I'm a man! Bleating about love is woman's work, I'm not a Piaf.'

I thought Edith would strangle him. She started to scream and it echoed through the whole hotel. It was the first time Yves had seen her in a temper and he stood gaping at her like an idiot. In the end he burst out laughing, 'Well, you *do* have a lot of wind!'

'Don't you understand that you can't get by without singing love songs? That's what the audience wants. You'll stand out against all those clowns who bay to the moon. They're waiting for a real man who can sing about love, they're clamouring for one. Listen, do you trust me or not?'

Yves was as jealous as a crusader; he would have liked to lock Edith into a chastity belt. Thus he took an immediate dislike to the first song-writer we thought of which was Henri Contet.

'If you ask him to write a song for me, I'll never forgive you.'

That wasn't going to make life much easier! It was the beginning of August 1944; Henri was all we had left.

The day started badly. The telephone rang. I saw Edith put her hand over the receiver and whisper something. I was very close to her, I heard, 'Yes, five-thirty. Okay? Here, come upstairs.' Yves was looking out of the window. 'Who was that?' he asked.

'None of your business!'

'Yes, it is.'

'It's Loulou Barrier.'

Around five o'clock Yves told Edith, 'I'm going out for a while.'

'Come back quickly, my love.'

'Of course.'

Edith was waiting for Henri. He had been in our room no more than a minute when Edith looked at me, we had heard a tiny noise in the room next door – mine. She started to smile and I saw the light I knew so well come into her eye; the practical joker, the revengeful one. She raised her voice to say to Henri, 'I asked you to come, Henri dear, because I want you to write me some songs.'

'The way things are at the moment I don't feel very inspired.'

'But you're the only one who can do it. I need strong songs, man's songs, for a singer with a lot of talent: Yves Montand.'

Henri was amused. 'You make me laugh. So it's true what they're saying; you're looking after that phony cowboy.'

'He's given up that style.'

'Listen, Edith, I'm going to be frank with you. He's worthless; he's a nothing. He has no presence, he's vulgar, his accent is unspeakable. He moves like a singer of forty years ago. It's out of the question.'

Instead of flying into a rage, Edith replied smoothly, 'Do you think so?'

'I'm certain. Sleep with him if you want, but that won't give him what it takes to become a singer.'

'You're right, Henri, perhaps I did make a mistake.'

On the doorstep as he left, she added, 'I'm glad I saw you, Henri, you've made me see reason.'

'Yes, that Yves of yours will never fill an auditorium.'

He had hardly left when Edith opened the communicating door. There stood Yves, white with rage.

'That'll teach you to listen behind doors,' Edith chortled.

Yves held the fragments of a glass in his hand; he had squeezed it until it broke, and he was bleeding. His voice was flat and hoarse. 'Don't you ever do that again, ever, do you understand? I wanted to kill you.'

For several days we had other things to do besides singing. It was 20 August 1944. Since the Normandy invasion in June, the allied troops had been pressing on towards Paris, and the town was in a fever awaiting the arrival of General Leclerc at the head of his Second Army division.

The German army was in retreat. What confusion! The Parisians named it the 'green Diarrhoea'. Everyone wore the tricolour armbands of the F.F.I. (French Forces of the Interior). The smell of gunpowder was intoxicating. At last it smelt of victory. Paris put out her flags.

Edith awaited General Leclerc's arrival like a kid waiting for the Bastille Day procession. To her he was the liberator. She was not interested in De Gaulle. 'He's a politician, not a real general, he doesn't march at the head of his troops!'

But on the day that De Gaulle went from the Arc de Triomphe to Notre Dame to hear the 'Te Deum', Edith could not be kept at home. What a lovely day, we were friends with everyone.

We couldn't see anything at the Arc de Triomphe, we could barely see General de Gaulle's head. There was no sign of Leclerc.

Like all the other girls we kissed the soldiers and sailors, the red berets, black berets, everyone. They did not know they were kissing Edith Piaf but they liked her just the same.

Like all singers who sang during the Occupation, Edith went before the *Comité d'épuration* (Committee to eliminate collaborators). But they did not give her a hard time and life went on as before, except that now we could breathe freely.

Yves and Edith became increasingly jealous of each other. Auntie Zizi gave me my orders, 'Momone, I'm relying on you. Don't let him out of your sight. He'll find a way of picking up a girl under your nose without your realizing it. Don't go into the bistros, they're full of the wrong type of people. Make him walk, it'll do him good.'

It was easy to say. I took three steps to Yves's one; he chuckled, 'Look, to shake you off all I have to do is this . . .' and he increased his big stride, turned round the first corner of the street and was gone.

Sometimes he sat me in a bar, saying, 'Wait for me, I'll be five minutes,' which was nearly true, I never had to wait long. I had a way of blackmailing him, 'If you stay away too long, I'll drink. And if I'm drunk, I won't answer for anything. I'll rat on you as soon as we get home.'

I never asked him what he got up to in those five minutes. I didn't want to know. When he came back he had a gleam in his eye; we had a last drink together because of Edith. She could smell the drink on us when we arrived. It didn't matter that we'd had a drink, but if I'd been the only one to smell of alcohol there'd have been hell to pay.

Work picked up. Edith made dates with Henri on the outside. The broken-glass episode had taught her a lesson, but she had not given in. Nothing would budge her once she had made up her mind. 'There's trouble with Henri. He doesn't want to work for Yves. It's too stupid, it's a long time since we broke up but he's still jealous. That's all I need.'

Finally he gave in.

'We've made it, Momone, I have some songs. Henri did them with Jean Guigo. "Battling Joe" is the story of an unlucky boxer who goes blind and "Gilet rayé" is about a bellhop who ends up in prison. And I've also got "Ce monsieur-là" about a timid little man who can't escape from himself without committing suicide. And "Luna Park", the story of a workman from Puteaux who finds happiness at Luna Park.' Yves, who was napping quietly in the room next door, came in.

'Listen to this, Yves.'

She hummed all the songs through to him without stopping.

'That's great. It'll be marvellous to sing them. Who wrote them?'

'Jean Guigo and Henri Contet.'

Yves took a deep breath, then he muttered, 'You win' in a bitter voice.

'Let's get down to work now, my love.'

And they did. He had lost his accent on stage, but it soon came back when he was careless. Edith would say to him, 'Watch out, Yves, I can smell the garlic again.'

He knew how to sing, and from that point of view things were all right. His voice was well pitched and very beautiful. All that remained was to stage his songs and do something about his gestures; he had some bad habits. She rehearsed him for hours on end, until the sweat broke out on his face, but he kept going. He was the only person who could match Edith's ability for hard work. They would bat for fifteen hours at a stretch. No one else could see straight any more, the pianist was like a puppet, but they pressed on.

'No, Yves, the beginning isn't right. You don't have to keep on hitting the air to prove you're a boxer, one punch is enough to make the audience imagine the whole match. If you stand on guard, they obviously aren't going to think you're a fisherman. There's no need to move all over the place. Now start again at *C'est un nom.*'

> *C'est un nom maintenant oublié,*
> *Une pauvre silhouette qui penche,*
> *Appuyée sur un' canne blanche ...*

'That's terrible, you look like an old fruit. A blind man doesn't look like that. Battling Joe's still a man. He's finished simply because he can't see any more. That's what you have to get across. Work on your movements, your people are just caricatures.'

'You're getting on my nerves,' moaned Yves.

The next day he worked on his movements in front of a mirror. Edith hated this practice, it went against all her principles, but Yves could not do without it; that is how he finally learnt. It was very funny because he could not see the whole of himself in the mirror on top of the dresser, the room was too small; he had to stand sideways to the bathroom door. Since he never saw himself face on, Yves would practise his movements slyly as he went past mirrors in the stores when we were out walking.

To complete Yves's act, Edith had written him two songs. 'You see, I've written my first love songs for you, "Elle a des yeux":

> *Elle a des yeux*
> *C'est merveilleux*
> *Et puis des mains*
> *Pour mes matins.*
> *Elle a des rires*
> *Pour me séduire*
> *Et des chansons*
> *La la la la . . .*
> *Elle a, elle a*
> *Des tas de choses*
> *Toutes en rose*
> *Rien que pour moi*
> *Enfin, je l'crois . . .*

. . . and "Mais qu'est-ce que j'ai?"

> *Mais qu'est-ce que j'ai?*
> *A tant l'aimer*
> *Que ça m'en donne envie de crier*
> *Sur tous les toits:*
> *Elle est à moi!*
> *J'aurais l'air fin si j'faisais ça,*
> *C'est pas normal*
> *Me direz-vous*
> *D'aimer comme ça; faut être fou . . .*

Yves had his repertoire at last. The most important thing had been accomplished, but not the most difficult. 'Now, Yves, you've got to try all this on the audience. Don't be too scared. You're ready. And don't forget there are men and women in the audience. The men must think you're handsome, everything that they'd like to be. And with a face like yours, the women'll be a pushover; they'll be making love to you while you're on stage. But hold the sentimentality until the end. That's when the guy takes his girl's hand. They'll be happy. He's the one who gets her, not you. And they'll applaud you together. You'll find out how great it is to be on stage when an audience shows talent too!'

It was September. In two months Edith had made a new

Montand. I was as affected by him as she was. His movements were touching. In his dark brown slacks and shirt he was Everyman. You believed in him. He came straight at you, and you listened to him and shouted 'Encore!'

You have to be in show business to understand the work these two did. I admired them both.

Edith had made Loulou Barrier get Yves a place in her French tour.

'Give him star billing.'

'Edith, be reasonable, he's not ready for that yet.'

'That's where Yves belongs. I won't accept anything for myself unless they take him too.'

'Don't you think it would be better to try him out alone first? I could set up a tour in the Midi, they know his name there.'

'You're out of your mind. If you suggest that to him you and I are through. There'd be girls all over him on a tour like that. Get this, this guy is mine; I made him; he'll stay with me. He's not a stop-gap, he's a star. He'll share the bill with me and that's a good start.'

Loulou shut up, the boss had spoken. But Barrier was not wrong, to go on stage before Edith with a very similar repertoire to hers was not easy to do.

The first town of the tour was Orléans. Edith had told me to go out into the auditorium during Yves's act and tell her everything about it. An agreeable task!

The curtain went up, Yves came on stage. His appearance was in his favour. He stood so straight, he looked so strong, as if he could reach right up to the sky and join the stars. Strength is always attractive. They liked him but nothing more. I could feel that something was missing, but what? He was only a mild success. Seeing him in the same show as Edith, the audience realized right away that Yves was her student. He had her tendency to roll his r's. His lighting was similar to hers. Above all, he used some movements which were pure Piaf. I had had an inkling of this during the rehearsals, but on stage it really hit you hard. He was in a very ugly mood that night, so was Edith.

'Edith, it didn't work; I could see that. How did we screw it up?'

'One town isn't the whole of France.'

'Don't make me laugh. I've toured all over the South, I even went up to Lyons. I was a terrific success everywhere.'

'And in Paris you fell flat on your face. If you don't like it, give up.'

Montand had an uneven reception. 'Don't worry,' said Edith. 'This is his crisis.'

In Lyons we came close to catastrophe. Before he went on stage, Yves managed to summon his smile again, 'I've always gone down well here. This is my audience. This is my night for revenge, you'll see.'

Poor Yves was so nearly laughed off stage that my mouth was dry, and Edith was white with fear. During his act, Edith directed things from the wings. She controlled the lights and curtains. If she had ordered the usual false curtain after the fifth song that evening he would have been lost, it would never have gone up again. When he came off stage he was dazed, like a boxer down for the count. As soon as I got to our dressing-room, Yves started talking; he had recovered his wits. 'I'm nuts to have thought they'd like me, that they'd understand what I'm doing, I don't give a shit. I'll show them yet.'

He tore off his shirt, his naked torso gleaming with sweat. 'Give me a clean shirt, I'm going to change and then listen to Edith. I want her to know I'm there close to her, that I'm not scared of them.'

I had been so scared myself that I wanted to laugh with relief. Yves realized it. He put his big hands on my shoulders and smiled at me in the way he did when we had been accomplices out on a spree. 'You see, Simone, there's no sense in losing my temper. They drove me mad this evening. You heard them asking for my old songs. They want shit, but they won't get it. It's over. I'll never sing those songs again; what I do now is good, I can feel it, and they'll have to learn to like it.'

The fight was on, and Yves would not give up.

In Marseilles we were booked at the Variétés. During the re-hearsal Edith made Yves work in a sort of frenzy, and he was as tough with her.

That night she came to the back of the auditorium with me.

She squeezed my hand. We were in more of a sweat than he was. When he came on stage the audience applauded. But that did not mean anything, the applause was for the local boy come home. In fact, they would be harder on him because of it. Edith's nails started digging into me during the first song. We realized he would not go down well here either. Here they had known and liked him for his American songs. They did not understand this new Montand. We were lucky they did not boo him, but it was almost worse, the audience remained absolutely cold

Yves was waiting for us in his dressing-room, sitting on a wobbly old chair. 'You saw them, Edith. And it was here I once had my greatest success.'

When he saw our tragic faces he burst into his big giant laugh. 'I don't give a damn, darling. I'll get them yet, the next time I come back they'll go wild. Meanwhile I've got a surprise for you; we're going to have dinner with my family.'

The Livis' little kitchen, filled with all the sounds of Marseilles, was delightful, and his family was so nice. When Yves introduced Edith as 'my fiancée' she had tears in her eyes, how lucky he was to have this family.

The following day Edith said something which shook me, 'Momone, yesterday evening when I looked at Yves, I wanted to be a virgin all over again.' She wanted to be completely un-touched just for him. She had never felt that way for any other man.

Yves had marriage on the brain; he never stopped saying, 'Edith, let's get married. I want you to be my wife.' In my opinion they didn't get married because Yves never got the timing right. He never asked her at the right moment; he always thought of it when they were surrounded by people, or eating, or when Edith was drinking and looking forward to having a good time. It made him sentimental, which she hated. Fifteen minutes' sweet talk and a little bunch of flowers was enough sentiment for Edith. She had no time for a man with tears in his eyes. She loved Yves's strength, his taste for a fight, his youth. There wasn't much of an age difference between them, but she had lived so much and he so little.

She was less kind and indulgent towards her own body.

She'd look at herself critically in the mirror and sigh philosophi-
cally, 'I'm no Venus. But you can't expect too much of it, it's
seen a lot of service. My breasts are sagging, my arse and thighs
are flabby. They're not new any more; but I'm still a bargain '

And she would go off to bed happy. She laughed as she did
everything else, more extravagantly and better than anyone else.

When we got back from the tour Edith had a booking at the
Alhambra, with Yves sharing the bill. Paris wasn't the provinces.
It could be better, or worse.

Loulou Barrier, Edith, and I did not look upon the days before
the opening as a picnic. Perhaps that would come after the
premiere, but before it we needed a stiff drink. Edith was in the
auditorium as she had been in Marseilles. When Yves came on
stage and smiled, he was a show-stopper.

'He's not the same,' sighed Edith. 'Do you remember how he
used to be? Look at him now. I'll never be able to keep him.'

Yves Montand was the eye-opener of the evening, and he had
the headlines next day. He rushed around our room at the Alsina
like a hurricane. We would have liked to hide in our kennels like
dogs, but he wouldn't leave us alone. 'Read this, Edith,' he
exulted. "Yves Montand, a name to remember." Momone, look,
"A star is born." Edith, I've made it. "A revolution in song." You
were right, Edith, I am, "This is the singer we have been waiting
for." Are you happy?'

'Yes,' said Edith, irritated by his ceaseless chatter.

'I know, you've been through it all before. But they're certainly less dumb here than in the provinces.'

'Don't be stupid, Yves. You're launched in Paris, but it's in
the provinces that you're made.'

'You can't upset me now, I'm too happy,' he cried.

That evening he looked up at the marquee in front of the
Alhambra. 'You should have asked them to make my name
bigger.'

'After your "triumph" in Marseilles, it was easy! It stood out
all on its own,' she replied drily.

Yves had an enormous appetite for life, but Edith did not like
to be devoured.

We had to put up with Yves's jealousy. Keep away! Edith was

his property. Game Preserve! He stood guard, a rifle in his hand, watching "his woman". He wasn't about to let any poachers in.

He would wake her up at night. 'Who were you dreaming about? One of your old lovers?' She told him to go to hell, but next day she would say to me gleefully, 'He really must love me a lot.'

It was okay once or twice, but not all the time. If she so much as looked at another man, let him sniff around her or flirt a little, Yves would go into a cold fury. 'Can't you see that he's a shabby, downtrodden tramp? He doesn't give a damn about you.'

She'd tell him brutally to shove it, and the ensuing quarrel would last for hours. Then for a whole day and night they would adore each other. I loved them both, but they were beginning to wear me out.

Life got more hectic than ever. After the Alhambra they went on to the Etoile which, since the Liberation, had become the smartest and most fashionable music hall. A few days before the premiere, they were floating on a cloud of happiness, and I was recharging my batteries. I needed to; between the morning bath-room sessions and the afternoon strolls with Yves, I had had about as much as I could take of their confidences and their spying. But as far as work was concerned, things were going like clockwork. Yves's name was now nearly as big as Edith's, despite Loulou Barrier's warning: 'Take care, Edith. He's becom-ing dangerous on the same programme as you. Don't give him too much.'

'Don't worry, the Monsieur Piaf who can make mincemeat out of me hasn't been born yet. The Etoile will be the highlight of my firework display, I want him to succeed. Then, who knows?'

She put everything into it. In the course of several days she had made more than a hundred telephone calls to her friends, to journalists, to the most important people in show business. Edith always did things thoroughly. Yves made money fast. He knew the value of it and didn't throw it around. He was never on Edith's payroll, he was too proud for that, but she did give him the usual suits, crocodile shoes, and the set of trophies for the perfect 'Piaf man' – lighter, watch, watch chain, and cuff-links. As always Edith spent without thinking, so much so that the day before the premiere at the Etoile, she had barely three thousand francs left. The two weeks at the Alhambra had not refilled our coffers.

'I want to be beautiful for Yves tomorrow evening. Come on, I'm going to choose some clothes,' she announced. We had not been able to buy anything since we had been at the Alsina and, as we had very little in the first place, our wardrobes weren't exactly crammed full. We had hardly reached the door when Yves appeared and asked, 'Where are you going?'

'I'm going to buy myself a dress, some gloves, and a hat.' She had never worn a hat, but she felt that the occasion called for one. It would look smart, she thought.

'That's ridiculous. You don't need anything. I forbid you to spend any money. You'll have nothing left' (which was true).

'Balls,' retorted Edith.

We left on our shopping spree without giving him a second thought; he was furious.

When we got back we were cleaned out. Edith jubilantly spread a pair of gloves out on the bed. To get to the stores we had had to pass about fifteen bars and Edith, determined that each should share her happiness, had bought rounds in all of them. Yves was in a furious temper when we got back, like a husband who's been fleeced by his wife. Which was hardly the case, but Yves had principles; a woman should obey her man.

'You're up to your eyes in debts, and you carry right on throwing money out of the window. You'll end up a beggar.'

'What difference does that make to you since you won't be there?'

'I forbade you to go, that should be enough.'

They yelled at each other at the tops of their voices and in the end Yves gave her a tremendous double slap, enough to knock her head off. She started to cry. He went out slamming the door – but in a moment he was back and they fell into each other's arms. What a circus! 'It's a good way to relieve our tensions before the premiere,' they said. An hour before curtain time they were gargling furiously over the sink; they had shouted themselves hoarse.

That evening standing in the front of the stage, Edith intro-

1. Edith at Bernay
(*Photo Séruzier*)

3. Rehearsal of 'Le Bel Indifférent': Jean Cocteau, Paul Meurisse, Edith Piaf, and André Brûlé, the theatre manager (*Photo Serge Lido*)

2. 1938: Edith Piaf and Raymond Asso (*Photo Séruzier*)

4. Edith and Paul Meurisse in one of the most famous scenes (*Studio Lipnitzki*)

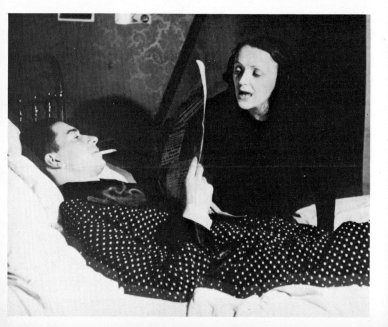

6. Edith and Marlene Dietrich at the Versailles in New York in 1948 (*Author's collection*)

7. (*below*) Piaf and Constantine in 1951 (*Photo Agence France Presse*)

8. Edith and Jacques Pills
returning from the United States
in September 1952 after their
wedding (*Photo Interpress*)

9. Edith, just after she was
awarded the Grand Prix du
Disque in 1952; Edouard Herriot
kisses her, watched by Colette
(*Author's collection*)

10 Edith during the 'suicide tour'
in 1960 (*Agence France Presse*)

11. Her last love: Theo Sarapo
(*Photo Bégoin*)

duced Yves Montand to the audience. It was the first time she had done it. When Yves came on, the fashionable house was electrified.

As usual Edith called the shots from the wings. You would never have thought she herself was due to go on straight afterwards. Each time Yves made a false exit, Edith wiped off his brow and gave him a glass of water. By the final curtain, there had been thirteen curtain calls. 'That's a good sign,' she murmured. 'It'll bring him luck.' She breathed a sigh of relief; at last her champion had made it, she was delivered.

What a pity there are mornings-after. We were treated to a repetition of the morning after the Alhambra performance, only more so. Yves was like a cock after a victory. He would not stop crowing. The press was delirious, and so was he.

It was too much for Edith to go through again. However, she had wanted it this way. Sitting back in her pillows, she followed him with her eyes. I could tell from her smile that she was going to say something deflating, 'I'm glad you're so happy. You needed this, my love. But you still have a few things to learn. You shouldn't sweat on stage, it makes you look like a docker. You . . .'

'You were the one who made me sweat,' Yves broke in, enraged. 'I made my success yesterday, me and no one else.'

Despite this squabble, Yves was bursting with pride in his new dinner jacket at the dinner party Edith held that evening. No one could get a word in edgeways. He was as puffed up as a little boy who had just won a race; I found it funny, but Edith didn't.

'You know how many curtain calls I took? Thirteen! Simone counted, didn't you, Simone?'

Edith cut him short. 'You and your curtain calls are becoming a bore.'

A breath of cold air blew through the room. It was a painful lesson for a boy of twenty-two. Yves learned it, but he needed time to digest it.

At home nothing seemed to have changed, but I did not like the way that Edith looked at him. She was watching him very closely, and I had never seen that mood before; something was cooking.

Yves was nervous. 'Simone, what's going on? Things aren't the same between Edith and me, but why?'

I knew, but how could I tell him? He had become a big star too quickly. He had escaped from the fragile hands that had made him. Song had brought them together and now song was breaking up that love which I had thought so strong. He couldn't resist the praise. I wanted to cry out to him, 'Your career is destroying your happiness.' But it was no longer possible. Yves had also become great. There was nothing for it but to let love die of its own accord.

One morning Edith burst out, 'This can't go on. I'm not going to stand around and listen to Yves reminiscing on his successes like an old trouper. In a year all I'll be good for is to shine his majesty's shoes.'

'It won't last for ever, Edith. He'll understand. Give him time. He's drunk with success.'

'Maybe so, but I don't like men who can't hold their drink. I'll sort him out, and quickly too. When I take a lover I want him to talk to me about love, not his career; I can do that all on my own.'

That very day she informed Loulou Barrier, 'I don't want any more joint contracts with Yves.'

'It's about time,' Loulou replied. 'It was getting difficult for managers to hire you both together.'

When Edith fell in love, it was always the first time, for life, and unlike anything that had gone before. Only the men changed, the pattern stayed the same. Her love could be read like a temperature chart. It started off like an arrow, rushed up to a hundred and seven degrees and broke the thermometer. Then the fever started to go up and down like the teeth of a saw – I called this the switchback period. Then there was the decline, subnormal temperatures. Once she got below ninety-five degrees, her heart was cold, and she started to look for someone new to warm it up.

The last big fever with Montand had been at the Etoile. Yves had a very naïve side. He believed his success would make him even more important in Edith's eyes. He was mistaken. If he wanted to continue their affair, she must go on being the boss.

He kept protesting his love but he was roaming all over the place and Edith knew it. I had seen her crying too often. I knew how the end would come, I had seen it all before. It was sad and it was a brawl. When Edith got nervous, she drank. In the middle of the night (really in the middle of the morning), she would telephone me to come over, or shake me if I was sleeping near her. She would start, 'Do you have any idea what he did to me?' After an hour, she would say, 'Oh, you poor thing, you're dead tired, go to bed.' Ten minutes later she'd be back and it began all over again.

One evening Yves came in looking too pleased with himself. Edith did not miss it. 'You might have asked your girl-friend to brush you off before you left.' His jacket was covered in powder and rouge. 'I don't like someone else's cast-offs. I've had it up to here with you. Show-offs make me laugh. You're laying down the law to me in my own house. If you've had enough, get out, I'm not keeping you. Go back to your girl-friends, they'll look after you.'

Yves took a quick step backwards. He laughed too hard, so it didn't sound right, then took her in his arms. He certainly had a way with him. 'Edith darling, you know you're the only one I care about. Anyone who tells you I've been unfaithful to you is jealous of our happiness. You're everything to me. Do you believe me?'

She smiled a heavenly smile, and breathed 'yes' like a sigh of pleasure. Unfortunately he went on, 'When they see our two names married on the billboard, they'll understand that this is for keeps.'

She struggled out of his arms. He had hit a chord. With her sad little waif-like smile, she replied, 'You should know by now, nothing's for keeps with me. And as for seeing our two names on the same billboard, that's out from now on. I've given Loulou my orders.'

You have to be six-foot tall and built like a truck driver to withstand a withering fire like that.

But we had still not seen the last of their names on the same billboard. During the Occupation Marcel Blistène had had an idea for a movie with Edith, and in December 1944 he turned up with it again. It was simple, tailor-made for Edith : a great singer takes a boy into her life, loves him, makes something of him, then goes on alone.

When she read it, Edith laughed, 'Marcel, you've guessed right this time. You even predicted the future. Okay, we'll do your film, only I want Yves Montand to be in it.'

Marçel Blistène agreed, but the backer didn't. The name meant nothing to him. A movie starring Yves Montand and Edith Piaf did not sound like box office.

When Edith wanted something, however, she knew how to get it. On 15 January 1945, on the boulevard Saint-Michel, Edith gave a cocktail party for the backer at the Mayfair, where Yves sang each night. Blistène asked Edith if she wouldn't be good enough to sing one of her songs (it had been arranged in advance). 'Okay,' she said, 'just one, and just for you.' She sang, and the backer was bowled over. 'That woman's a genius,' he said to Marcel, 'and the boy's very good-looking. We'll go ahead with them.'

That is how the filming of *Etoile sans lumière* [*Star without Light*] was conceived. Besides Edith, the cast consisted of Marcel Herrand, Jules Berry, and two new actors, Serge Reggiani and Yves Montand.

Some years later when Yves said, 'I owe everything to Edith,' he wasn't exaggerating.

On the day of the screen-tests Yves was pale with anxiety.

'Don't worry. You're made for the part, you're a born actor, it'll go fine,' Edith told him, and once more she was right. The movie went along without a hitch, until the very end. *Etoile sans lumière* finishes with a scene right out of Chaplin, when the great star leaves the studio all alone, and you see her little silhouette from behind getting smaller and smaller on the horizon.

For once in my life I too became the 'great star'. This is how it happened.

Edith was a bit drunk the day they shot the final scene. She started off well enough but after travelling about six feet she lost her balance.

'Walk straight,' Marcel shouted.

Edith giggled, 'I can't, I'm too unhappy.'

'You look as if you're too drunk.'

'Oh, leave me alone – get Momone to do it.'

Marcel looked at me and said, 'Put on her clothes. We'll do your hair like hers and from the back there'll be no difference.'

Yves talked a lot about the film. He worked hard at it, and in the end it proved more important for him than it was for Edith. We were still at the Alsina, and things seemed to be going smoothly between them, but I knew that Edith was living 'beside' him, not 'with' him.

With the Liberation, Marguerite Monnot came back into our lives. She adored Yves. When Edith talked about her love life Guite was always fascinated. It would not have taken much for her to set it to music!

One day Edith said to her, 'Listen, I hardly dare say this to you, but when I think of words for a song, I hear the music to go with them. You see, I hear everything at the same time, and ... I think I could try to write a little tune.'

It took someone like Guite not to make fun of Edith for her presumption. She did not even know her scales. To suggest a tune to a composer like Marguerite Monnot you had to have a lot of nerve.

'Try, Edith, I'll help you.'

'You won't make fun of me, will you? I have this little snippet of melody inside me. Can I go on?'

'Go on.'

Edith played straight off, without hesitation, the first line of music that was to become 'La Vie en rose'.

'I don't get it,' said Guite.

'Don't you like it?'

'What about the words?'

'I don't have any, it was just a little tune that was running through my head.'

One of Edith's friends, a singer called Marianne Michel, had just come up from Marseilles. Her lover owned a cabaret on the Champs-Elysées and things were beginning to look up for her But like all beginners she had no repertoire. Edith would have a drink with her now and then, and she would go on about how hard things were. 'I can't find any good songs,' Marianne complained. 'I need one hit to make me. Can't you find me one, Edith?'

'There's a tune running through my head, it's your type of thing, listen,' and she hummed the tune that she had played to Guite.

'It's marvellous. What about the words?'

'Wait, I think they're coming to me.' And suddenly Edith started to write:

> Quand il me prend dans ses bras
> Quand il me parle tout bas
> Je vois les choses en rose . . .

Marianne wasn't wild about it. 'Do you like it? What about putting "vie" [life] instead of "choses" [things].'

'That's a great idea. And the title can be "La Vie en rose".'

The following day the song was finished but, since Edith was still not a member of the S.A.C.E.M., she could not sign it. We went over to Guite's. 'Look, I've put words to the tune I tried the other day. Listen.'

'You can't sing anything as stupid as that,' Guite exploded.

'It's not for me, it's for Marianne Michel. I wondered if you could write out the music.'

'No, I really can't get the feel of it.'

We drew a complete blank, but the more people turned her down, the more adamant Edith became. But we had a little friend, a talented boy and a good composer, who was usually broke. His name was Louiguy. Edith asked him to come over, and he promptly turned her little snatch of tune into 'La Vie en rose'. He never regretted it.

Marianne Michel made 'La Vie en rose', and it became an unparalleled world-wide success. It was translated into twelve languages. Great American singers like Bing Crosby and Louis Armstrong put it in their repertoires, and they were not usually keen on French songs. It was the theme song for *Sabrina*, the movie with Audrey Hepburn, Humphrey Bogart, and William

Holden. They sold more than three million records in one year alone, and it's still selling today. A night club on Broadway was even named La Vie en rose. The song became such a success that Edith grumbled, 'I'm mad not to have sung it myself.' She did, but not until two years later.

At home – to us the place where we currently lived was always home – the love affair continued to deteriorate, but on the other hand we were riding on the crest of the wave as far as work was concerned.

'You're putting too much faith in movies,' Edith told Yves. 'You say that they'll take you to America. Maybe, but you could just as well go as a singer. You're built to succeed in both worlds. One solo concert at the Etoile would make all the difference.' She wanted to be sure that she had a solid success on her hands. Yves was her work, and she never confused her personal feelings with her work.

Before his recital at the Etoile, Yves stopped behaving like the cock of the roost. He rehearsed until his legs were jelly and his voice hoarse. When he was absolutely exhausted he would cry out, 'Edith, it's not right, is it?'

'Yes, sure it is, don't stop. Do the whole act for me.'

In the end Yves collapsed, 'I can't see straight. I don't know where I am any more.'

What she loved about him was his determination and his ability to work hard. And at night she snuggled up to him, trying to rekindle the flame of their love, a flame born of the fever of work.

It seemed madness in 1945 to dare to give a solo recital at the Etoile; two whole hours with only one man on stage. Even Edith herself had not done it. I think that before Yves's name appeared alone on the marquee of the Étoile, the only other person to have done it was Maurice Chevalier. In spite of our apparent confidence, we were scared. Henri Contet had written him two new songs, 'La Grande Ville' and 'Il fait des . . .'

On the morning of the premiere, Yves said, 'Listen Edith, I'd like to ask you something. Would you light a candle for me?'

'Idiot, I'd already made up my mind to do it. I'm going up

there with Momone.' We went up to the Sacré Coeur, and lit a candle before little St Theresa's statue. It had become a habit.

Edith stayed in the wings all the time during the performance. She never left him. I was sitting close to the Livi family, who had come up from Marseilles, and I watched them almost bursting out of their seats with pride and happiness.

During the interval I ran up to Yves's dressing-room. The door was locked, but not to me. If I live to be a hundred, I shall never forget the look he gave me.

'Well?'

'It's fine.'

'No one's left! They aren't bored?'

'They're riveted to their seats. Keep going.'

And he did keep going, right up to the end. The second part was the more difficult; I stayed in the wings. An audience could suddenly lose interest, feel they had seen too much of the same artist. We were shaking with nerves.

When Yves sang,

> *Mais qu'est-ce que j'ai?*
> *A tant l'aimer*
> *Que ça m'en donne envie de crier . . .*

[But why do I love her so much / That it makes me want to cry out], he turned his head towards Edith for a second. This cry from the heart was addressed directly to her. I saw big tears falling down Edith's cheeks.

At the end, the auditorium, chock-a-bloc with high society and show business types who had come to watch this upstart eat humble pie, gave him a standing ovation.

When he left the stage after the last curtain, Yves took Edith in his arms and said, 'Thank you; I owe you everything.'

In his dressing-room, as we watched the crowd filing by, she said to me, 'Now it's finished. He doesn't need me any more.'

Those words chilled us, with their undertones of aching loneliness.

But though he did not need Edith any more, she helped him once more prepare for his future. Marcel Carné often came to the bar at the Alsina. He enjoyed chatting with Edith. He had been at the Etoile and they talked about it. 'Montand has a great physique and exceptional stage presence,' said Carné.

'Don't forget his name,' countered Edith. 'He's not just a singer, he's a great actor. He's made for the movies.'

One year later, Yves took the lead role with Nathalie Nattier in *Les Portes de la nuit* [*The Gates of Night*], directed by Marcel Carné. Neither star had been scheduled for the roles – the original cast was to have been Jean Gabin and Marlene Dietrich.

Edith worked hard. Loulou would not let her idle away her time. Yves was still jealous, he didn't want to leave her side, but that was impossible because he had engagements too. Music, which had brought them together, was now separating them more and more.

On Christmas Eve, Edith was singing, and Yves and I were waiting for her. I don't know why, but I felt a bit depressed. Edith and I had never enjoyed the Christmas holidays. You need to have good childhood memories to appreciate them. And we didn't. As children we could only watch other people enjoying themselves.

The three of us spent a quiet evening together. Edith seemed to be very much in love still. Everything was going well when Yves said clumsily, 'I shall be in Marseilles with my family for the New Year.' That was all, but next day Edith was fuming, 'He goes on and on telling me how much he loves me, but I come after his family.' So on New Year's Day we were all alone, like a couple of old maids. After Edith's act we went down to the Club des Cinq in Montmartre. The 'cinq' had met each other in General Leclerc's Second Division and together they had founded a very smart private club. Each evening they would invite a different star to perform. They had often asked Edith, but she had never had the time.

We were completely alone. There wasn't much of a crowd, and we didn't know a soul. To make it even worse, everyone was throwing confetti and streamers. They stuck paper hats on our heads. Edith had a blue soldier's cap, and I had something that looked as if it had been left over from the Revolution. We were so down at heart that we didn't even get drunk. But at midnight we hugged each other; the holiday was over, a new year had just begun.

Three days after Yves got back they had a terrific fight – their last. Edith was rehearsing before going on tour and, as usual, she was immersed in her work. No make-up, hair all over the place, an old sweater and skirt just thrown on, she was completely wrapped up in her singing. Suddenly Yves's voice cut the air like a knife, 'Stop, that's not right.' And Edith, like a docile little puppet, stopped singing.

'What's the matter?'

'That doesn't sound any good. It's too contrived, too tricksy, too show business. It's coming from here not here' (he tapped his head and stomach).

'Would you mind repeating that?' She had her hands on her hips and pulling herself up to her full height of four foot nine, she stared at him, not believing her ears. 'Repeat it, I said! My ears must be deceiving me.'

'It doesn't sound right, I would . . .'

'You wouldn't do anything at all. You know what you can do with your advice. It stinks. The day I decide to take lessons from any Tom, Dick, or Harry I'll ring you. Now get out, I've seen more of you than I can stand.'

Five years later she might have been able to take Yves's advice, but not then.

They had no time to make up. Edith was leaving for a tour of Alsace. She was sharing the first half of her programme with a group of nine called *Les Compagnons de la Chanson*, whom she had met once or twice. We had heard them sing during the Occupation at a show organized by Marie Bell for the Comédie Française, and Edith had immediately baptized them 'The Boy Scouts of Song'. Their act was quite nice, it never does any harm to see nine attractive men singing with all their heart. Their songs were fairly ordinary and undemanding, sometimes quite refreshing, but nothing very exciting. When I found out that she was going to be with them in Alsace, I didn't think anything of it. To hear the 'click' for nine of them all at once would have been quite a feat. 'What will she bring back next?' I wondered.

I had not gone on tour with her. She wanted to leave the Alsina, and decided I should stay home to see the new house that Loulou was looking for. I was astonished when he told me, 'Edith called from Alsace and asked me to find an apartment with lots of rooms. Well I've found something for her, 26 rue de Berri, come and see it.'

The house looked simple enough, but I didn't doubt that it was in for an eventful time if Edith took it. You had to cross a courtyard, and in the back was this little house with a small garden and a couple of lonely trees. To cheer them up, we bought them a couple of chickens when we moved in, a cock called Pupuce and his hen, Nénette. But that didn't help; the trees went on looking dejected and homesick, not knowing why they had been born in the city. I felt very close to them; I didn't know what the hell I was doing there either.

You climbed three steps to go into the house. It was all on one floor. I cannot remember how many rooms there were, but it was big, not badly furnished, and fairly expensive. Loulou asked me if I liked it. I wasn't wild about it. 'It's not bad, it's big,' I said. 'She can't be intending to put up all those boy scouts.'

We laughed, but without confidence about that. I went to meet her at the station. As usual when we had been apart she sounded like a worried mother who thinks her daughter has taken advantage of her absence to get laid, 'You don't look well. I hope you haven't been doing anything stupid.' Once we were in the cab she said to the driver, '26 rue de Berri.' I was out of luck. We weren't going back to the Alsina. Timidly I asked her, 'Aren't we going to get Yves?'

'That's finished. I've made up my mind. He doesn't need me any more. He can be the captain of his own ship from now on. I'm full of ideas. I'm going to develop the *Compagnons*. I'm going to make them into a very strong act. People will have seen nothing like it. It'll be something new.'

'How do they feel about it?'

'They don't know yet. I only decided it on the train. But they'll go along with me.'

'You know, Edith, nine at a time is a lot of work. They'll smother you. Nine boys at that age have a terrific appetite.'

'Don't worry about it. One has to keep changing, that's the secret of youth.' She seemed to like the new house, but mostly she wanted to talk about her choral society. The boss was certainly ambitious; she could no longer make do with one, she needed nine!

'They don't even sing in tune. It'll be hard going, but I'm going to change that.'

I was waiting for her to single one out, to mention *the* name. But nothing happened. Perhaps she was planning to try them all before picking *the* one. It wouldn't have surprised me.

'We must find Tchang and take him on again. And I'll need a secretary.'

There was no mistake, she was going into the wholesale business. I didn't dare mention Yves again, yet I thought about him. He knew she was coming home today and no doubt Loulou would give him the rue de Berri address. What would he do? I soon found out. This break-up was easily one of the worst I went through.

That night, when he realized Edith was not coming back to the Alsina, Yves headed for the rue de Berri. He rang the doorbell, timidly at first.

'If it's Yves, don't open it,' Edith said to me.

My heart was thumping. Through the closed blinds I watched him. He was ringing like mad now. Then he started hammering with both fists. The wood echoed ominously. Then he stopped banging, and begged through the door, 'Edith, open up; don't leave me, Edith.'

He finished by shouting her name in a kind of frenzy, the despairing cry of a man who is pleading for help. I watched him collapse into sobs like a child.

I went to Edith's room. She had put plugs in her ears and her head was under the pillow. 'I don't want to hear him, Momone,' she sobbed. 'I don't want to start with him again. Make him go away.'

She still loved him, but she didn't want anything more to do with him. I would have loved to fling the door open and watch them hug each other happily and desperately – ready to start fighting all over again.

I don't know how long it lasted. I watched the sun come up.
Edith had fallen asleep like a child.

Yves was finished.

The 'boy scouts affair' was about to begin.

10

THE CONQUEST OF
AMERICA

The *Compagnons* were next in the factory period. That phase was by no means exhausted yet; there would be other candidates, good and bad.

Nine boys take up a lot of room. It's very tiring, especially since you can't multiply the pleasure; you only get that from one at a time.

I was not overjoyed to see the whole troop descending on us with their suitcases. Fortunately they stayed with us without really living there. They had a communal place on the rue de l'Université, but they came and went, and, as usual, those who wanted to stay slept over.

The new secretary was a refined little thing called Yvonne. She was completely astonished by us, and her eyes were constantly wide with surprise. She had never come across a household like this before. She wanted to see and understand everything, but she never succeeded.

Tchang brought his Chinese wisdom to bear on the situation, 'If Missy likes it, Tchang likes it.'

Edith certainly liked it. She glowed as though she were in love.

In the evening it was like being round a campfire. They sat in a circle round Edith, and there was no mistaking it, she was the fire! 'Listen to them carefully,' she said to me. 'You'll see they all have something to talk about. I'm not sure yet what I'm going to do with them. I have to get to know them first.' A well-tried technique.

I did listen to them, and I learned that Fred, the soloist, was a teacher at Annonay. From the same village came René, a painter who was a tenor. Jo was also from that area; his parents were in the paper-making business. Red-haired Albert, from Pessac in the Gironde, had been an acrobat and was now a tenor. Marc, from Strasbourg, had studied harmony at the Conservatoire.

Guy's father was the director of a bank; Jean-Louis (Jaubert) Colmarien had been at the Business School and wanted to become a professional footballer. And finally there were the two from Lyons, Gérard and Hubert, who had been destined to become businessmen.

It did not take Edith long to classify them in her usual way, to her they became Big Jo, Guy the wicked one, Paul the new one, freckled Albert, Gérard the joker, Marc the pianist, Fred the soloist, handsome Hubert, and Jean-Louis the manager.

One thing continued to bother me: who was the future master? We could not keep nine well-built, normal, healthy guys around the house without one emerging from the ranks to slip between Edith's sheets.

The little pow-wows round the campfire, the good, clean boy-scout fun, the joy of kids allowed to run wild outdoors, all this had its fountain-of-youth side, which was not unpleasant. And we enjoyed it because when you go to school in the streets you grow up too quickly, you miss a lot of your childhood; our Mother Goose rhymes were more likely to be vulgar street songs than Little Bo Peep.

Then Edith started to talk shop with them which was what they were there for. 'First off, your repertoire isn't up to much. With stuff like that you aren't going to get further than the country towns where they still have a taste for oldies. I've nothing against your old French songs, "Perrine était servante" is very sweet. But it's not the kind of thing you hear delivery boys whistling on their rounds. And without that you don't rate very high.'

Jean-Louis Jaubert, the manager, didn't let her go on. 'Listen, Edith, current hits aren't right for us. We aren't one singer, we're a chorus. We need things that have been written for a vocal orchestra. And that's exactly why we don't need someone to go around whistling our songs in the street. People come to listen to us the way they'd go to a concert.'

'You're absolutely wrong. Have you ever thought about making records? If you could find a thousand old-age pensioners in the whole of France to buy yours you'd be lucky. Either you sing for a limited public, or you sing for the public – period. You have to choose.'

'We've made our decision. We've found audiences ready to listen to us, we aren't looking beyond that.'

'Then you're mad.'

I could feel the night air growing a little cooler. Edith had decided to overhaul them. She had to succeed.

'I can't imagine anyone being so short-sighted,' Edith commented. 'They're absolute dumbells.' (And she gave one of her Piaf-like shouts of laughter.) 'That's it. That's what they'll do, they're going to sing "Les Trois Cloches" ["The Three Bells" otherwise called "Jimmy Brown's Song" in America].'

Edith had put this song by Gilles on one side for herself. She had not sung it yet. She liked it but felt nothing for it. Within ten minutes she had gathered all her 'scouts' together. 'I've found a song for you. Listen:

> *Une cloche sonne, sonne,*
> *Sa voix d'écho en écho,*
> *Dit au monde qui s'étonne:*
> *'C'est pour Jean-François Nicot!*
> *C'est pour accueillir une âme*
> *Une fleur qui s'ouvre au jour,*
> *A peine, à peine une flamme,*
> *Encore faible qui réclame*
> *Protection, tendresse, amour!*

'Well?'

They were all silent, looking at Jean-Louis.

'No, Edith, never; it's nonsense.'

'And what if we work on it together, and I sing it with you?'

'That's different.'

They would be riding on Edith's coat-tails. I could see, too, that Jean-Louis was going to be the new master. She talked about him all the time. The 'chosen one' was the leader. I should have realized it straightaway.

Each time we were alone, she would start up again, 'He's not like the others. He's untainted. You do understand, don't you?

He doesn't have a past, he hasn't wandered all over the map. He has principles about his music.'

Edith put an extraordinary amount of work into the production of 'Les Trois Cloches'. An orchestra and organs provided an astonishing background to the song. It really hit you. And there was this simple little woman standing in front of all those big singers, dressed alike in white shirts, midnight blue trousers and cummerbunds. She joined her suffering woman's voice to their youthful music. It was a hit.

Once more Jean Cocteau intervened and changed Edith's life. First he told them the song was very good. The boys were delighted. Better still, he wrote in an article, 'What a pleasure it is to hear them mingling their voices with hers, like an agate stream flowing through their bronze and gold bell.'

Suddenly everything changed. The *Compagnons* decided to listen to Edith, to follow her advice. 'Les Trois Cloches' became a world-wide success. The sale of the record in France was more than a million; in America, where Jean-François Nicot was called Jimmy Brown, the first impression of sixty thousand was sold out in three weeks.

They no longer doubted Edith's judgement. She held the key to success. They had confidence in her and their songs were changed.

Edith found them a number by André Grassi: 'T'en fais pas, la Marie'.

Then 'Moulin-Rouge' by Jacques Larue and Georges Auric, and 'Le Petit Coquelicot' by Raymond Asso and Valéry, 'C'était mon copain' by Louis Amade and Gilbert Bécaud, 'Quand un soldat' by Francis Lemarque, and 'La Prière' by Francis Jammes and Georges Brassens.

To these they added a few old songs, and they were ready to tour France or anywhere else.

When the 'Three Bells' began to peal with all their might to celebrate the joy of their success, they rang my death-knell at the same time.

Having succeeded in winning Edith's heart, Jean-Louis Jaubert was awarded the usual trophies – chain, watch, and all the trappings.

Surrounded by all these songsters who more or less had the run of the house, I felt like a country cousin, and neither pity nor charity have ever suited me.

I would do anything for Edith, but I refused to grovel in front of these companions. When Jean-Louis coldly said, 'I don't want her around,' I didn't make a fuss. He could live in a *ménage à neuf*, but not a *ménage à trois*. He was quite right, I was in his way, and he didn't like me; so I pulled myself together and got out.

A little more than a year later, when we got back together, Edith told me how it had all ended. Edith was a good story-teller, she filled in the details; it was as though I had been there myself.

'Those boys were like my own orchestra. Not an orchestra that accompanied me, but one that I conducted. Their voices were like instruments. It was wonderful. At first I had a good time at home with them. We got on well. It was like having heaps of brothers to look after me. I'd never lived with boys in that way.

'Just for fun we made a movie called *Neuf garçons ... un coeur* [*Nine Boys, One Heart*]. There was Lucien Nat, Marcel Vallé, and Lucien Baroux. It wasn't very good. Very simple, you know the kind. It was shown in the local cinemas, that's all. The boys were a bit disappointed. I only made it to please them, so I didn't care.'

Edith made Loulou take on the *Compagnons* and put them on the same programme as her, just as she had done with Yves. They did their act in the first half. Then she sang 'Les Trois Cloches' with them, then she went on alone.

Edith had never had such enthusiastic notices. The Great Piaf Years had begun.

Pierre Loiselet, very 'in' with the French Radio at the time, said, 'A big head that emerges from the gloom, a voice that you feel has been washed in all the waters of the gutter.' ('He's mad,' said Edith, 'I don't have a big head.')

She comes on stage in a simple little dress, her forehead like a doll's with the wig badly glued on, long fingers, downcast eyes, the eyes of a poor woman, haunted eyes which protect her from the cheers that rain upon her. A little girl lost in a wood with a sweet, anxious face.

Léon-Paul Fargue wrote:

She sings because the song is part of her, because the drama is part of her, because her throat is full of tragedy. Whether she has to relive for us the triumph of love, the hardness of fate, the halting sadness of trains, the joy of light or the fatality of the heart, she rises to the final, vibrant notes in a clear, pure voice, as though it has escaped from the divine palette, or the mournful stories of a Goya, a Délacroix, or a Forain...

And Charles Trenet called her, 'A white dove from the slums.'

'After that I worked a bit with the *Compagnons*, and sometimes alone. You know Loulou. I give the orders but that doesn't stop him from doing what he wants.'

She told of her tour in Greece.

'You must see that country some day. It's unique. When I saw all those old stones piled one upon the other in Athens, and that thing with columns reaching up to the sky called the Acropolis, I realized that there is more in the world than just the Sacré-Coeur. It really does something to you; especially as I was with a companion as handsome as a god.

'It was the kind of thing that I love. I had been singing for three days, and each evening I found a bouquet in my dressing-room – no name, no message, nothing. I thought to myself, "It's some old stick too ugly to dare show himself." The fourth evening I saw him arrive – curly-haired, dark eyes, built like one of their statues, and proud as a lord. He was called Takis Ménélas. An actor.

' "I dared to send you these flowers," he said. "I wanted them to talk to you before me. I should like you to know my country."

'I asked nothing better than to get to know it with him. That same evening he took me to the foot of the Acropolis by moonlight. We climbed up by a little path. It was perfumed with warm smells. The sounds from the town below us were like an orchestra, like music which rose with us. He explained to me that his ancestors used to wander around these immense columns. I could almost see them. Then he kissed me. Greece is a marvellous country.

'You have no idea how much I loved him . . . for fifteen whole days. That was as long as I could stay. A few days before I left he wrenched my heart, begging me, "Stay, don't go. I'll never see you again. You're my life. We'll get married. My country is made for goddesses, and you are one. You are Love itself to me."

'He made such an impression on me that I wondered if that wasn't what life is about after all – to give up everything for one man.

'The next day I got a cable from Loulou which brought me back to my senses: AMERICAN TOUR: ACCEPTED BOSTON, PHILADELPHIA, NEW YORK, WITH COMPAGNONS NOVEMBER 47.

'I cried a lot when I left. I've never had anyone handsomer or better than he. I was sure that I was leaving him for ever. But I saw him again in New York. He had just turned down a very good contract to go back to his country. He was as good-looking as ever.'

Several years later, when Edith was so ill and all the papers said she was broke, Takis sent her back the gold good-luck charm she had given him, with the words: 'For you. You have more need of it than I.' It had a terrific effect on Edith, 'I must really have been in the presence of true love that time.'

When she got back from Greece she began to prepare for her trip to the United States.

'My first view of America was a disappointment. I had expected to be overwhelmed by the Statue of Liberty. But it isn't any more impressive than if it were parked here in Paris on the pont Mirabeau. It seems small because there's so much space around it.

'But the buildings are amazing. It's just as Jean Cocteau wrote: "New York is an upright town!"

'Loulou had got me a suite in the Ambassador Hotel. Let me think, yes, it was November 1947 when I got there. I stood all alone in the middle of my suitcases, and I wanted to howl.

'I thought it was time to brush up on my English. I had a book called *English Without Tears*. What a laugh! First you have the word *the* which is impossible to say. You have to stick your tongue between your teeth, and push, and even then it doesn't work.

'My American agent, Clifford Fischer, he's a bit like Loulou, he organized a press conference. Lots of men and girls all ready to write down anything I said. The first question they asked me was: "Miss Idiss" (Americans can't say Edith, which is pronounced Aydeet in French), "you have just arrived in the United States, who is the first person you would like to meet?"

' "Einstein," I said, "and I'm counting on you to give me his telephone number." '

The man responsible for the meeting with Einstein was Jacques Bourgeat, our Jacquot from the Leplée time. We were still friends. He came and went in Edith's life. When she needed real advice she would either ask Jean Cocteau or Jacques Bourgeat, depending on the circumstances. He was an old gentleman by now, but he was the only person who could make difficult things penetrate Edith's mind. Thanks to him, on her bedside table beside the framed picture of St Theresa, there was a Bible, Plato, and a book on relativity.

'I'd made a good beginning. But believe me, that evening at the Playhouse on 48th Street and Broadway, I wasn't feeling so confident. The *Compagnons* did their piece; it went over quite well. But the audience started to whistle after "Les Trois Cloches" and I was almost sobbing with despair, no one had told me that in the United States that's one better than clapping!

'I kept on my little dress for my act. That was the Yanks' first disappointment.

'Later I realized they think all Parisians go to Antonio to have their hair done, to Jean d'Estrées for their make-up, and wear two-hundred-and-fifty-thousand-franc dresses!

'I'm telling you all this so you'll get the picture. The *Compagnons* are voices, whether you understand them or not is unimportant. They listened, it sounded good, that was enough.

'Then I come on in my short black dress, my hair all over the place and an undistinguished colour that doesn't even catch the light, my pale face. From a distance I was black and white. Their music hall is enormous. Four times round the stage is easily four hundred metres.

'If I'd planned to surprise them, I couldn't have done better. You could have heard a fly sneeze. I'd had two songs translated into English and I learnt them by heart. But it wasn't an unqualified success; someone said to me afterwards, "I really liked those two songs you sang in Italian."

'I'd been through so much that I could hardly stand. I didn't want any more to do with them. We weren't the same race. We couldn't understand one another. When an American goes out in the evening, he's looking for a good time; he's been fighting all day, he doesn't want to go to the music hall to listen to someone singing about poverty and sadness. He leaves his worries in the foyer. He's a romantic through and through. So if some little Frenchwoman forces him to remember that there are people in the world who suffer, who have good reason to be unhappy, she doesn't go over too well. It applies to those who understand what I say, and to the others who can hear it in my voice. And my music has nothing to do with theirs. I don't have any syrupy, easy-on-the-ear melodies, and I don't have any jazz. So what was I?

'That's what the few journalists who did write about me asked themselves. They wrote things like, "This plump little lady has eyes heavily ringed with mascara, and a mouth big enough to swallow a quart of tomato juice in one go." That's not the kind of thing that does any good, it doesn't make people rush to the box office.

'I was desperate, but Jaubert was like a dog with two tails. He could have made over some of his good notices to me without even noticing it. The "French Boys" had made it. They stood for a healthy France, they were the friends of the GIs who had liberated us. You can see it from here, a happy marriage of the "Marseillaise" and the "Stars and Stripes Forever".

'I went on for several evenings like that, without any hope. Then I said to the *Compagnons*, "I'm getting out, boys. You can't be stubborn in our business. I'm not a success. Finish the tour without me. It's going well for you, stick with it and good luck. I'm going back to the ship."

'My cabin was already reserved. Besides, they didn't exactly try to stop me. But believe me, I was sad. It hurt. That bitch success! You know I've suffered for love, but no man's ever given me as much pain as failure.

'Then suddenly everything changed, and I had my chance. A drama critic, Virgil Thompson, who never wrote about music-hall artists as a rule, devoted two columns on the front page of one of the biggest New York dailies entirely to me. He explained me to the Americans. Everything that would help people understand me was said there. He felt everything about me was musical – my voice, my movements, my body. He finished his article by saying, "If we allow her to leave on this undeserved note, the American public will have given proof of its incompetence and stupidity." He really must have rolled up his sleeves to write something like that.

'I had hardly finished having it translated when my American agent, Clifford Fischer, burst into my room with the paper under his arm and his hat on the back of his head. He has all the good American qualities, direct, straightforward, quick-thinking, and a good poker player. You'll soon see why I'm telling you all this. It's the truth, but I only found it out later.

'He tapped the paper and chewed on his stinking cigar and shouted, "Idiss, this is good for you. This article is worth thousands of dollars. Don't leave. We respect courage here. It always wins. I'm going to go to the smartest and snobbiest cabaret in Manhattan, the Versailles at 151 East 50th Street. They'll give you a contract. Order us two Bourbons to celebrate this review and I'll tell you what I'm going to do to sell you at a very high price."

'In one fell swoop Clifford and Thompson had raised my spirits. I would have swallowed twelve Bourbons for them, although I don't much like the stuff. I'd have climbed to the highest floor of the Empire State Building.

' "Look, Edith, you've got to be alone. The journalists said when you appeared in the middle of the *Compagnons* you were just a voice in a choir. In this country when a woman comes on stage with the boys she dances and sings and does more than they do. They're there to serve her. But it's just the opposite with you and the boys. It's not right. And when they go off stage, you look so forlorn all alone. Americans hate anything like that. Let the *Compagnons* go on tour. I'll tell the Versailles, 'When people get used to her little black dress, when they've understood that not all Parisian girls wear feathers in their hair, they'll be battering down the doors to hear her sing.' I'll go even farther, I'll say, 'If you lose money on her, I'll make up the difference at the end of the run.' "

'He went all the way with this poker game. He actually did more than he'd told me – he gave money to the owner of the Versailles so that he would take me on. Fischer played to win. When he got my contract he worked me like a slave every day for two weeks. I took American lessons. I worked at my two translated songs with a professor.

'The first time that I rehearsed at the Versailles, I was amazed. I thought Clifford had gone mad. Me! Perform in a room like that! It was crazy. Imagine the Palace at Versailles designed by a Hollywood set artist for a musical comedy in technicolor. It was stuffed with statues, trimmed trees, mirrors, doors, and windows. Everything done in pink and white plaster. I don't exactly stand out on a stage with the most simple hangings. I would completely disappear in the middle of all this crap.

'Fischer told me I was being naïve, it was a very French décor (the only one the Americans know, along with the Moulin-Rouge and Eiffel Tower), it suited me down to the ground.

'So I kept quiet, I wasn't going to contradict the one man who wanted to save me. I wasn't ready for another flop.

'Fischer and I agreed to do away with the MC. That was something, at least, but not enough to convince me. "Don't worry," he said, "everything'll be okay. It's in the bag. The audience knows who you are now. You have to warm Americans up before you surprise them. They have to know what they're expected to think, then everything's fine and they're ready to swallow anything."

'I was in a cold sweat. In the newspapers I was announced as "the singer the GIs had discovered in Paris" – though I don't think many of them ever heard me – and (don't laugh) as "the Sarah Bernhardt of song". They sure went to town!

'Among the guests at the first night were Marlene Dietrich and Charles Boyer and all the big shots in town. Some French people, the Craddocks and Jean Sablon came, too, to give me moral support. I needed it.

'And this time I really was a hit. They shouted Bravo, Vive la France, Paris, anything that came to mind. A lot of them could not even have seen me, I was so little in that vast place. The next day they made the rostrum higher.

'Marlene came to kiss me in my dressing-room. That's how we became friends. She launched one of her publicity campaigns for me – she was marvellous.

'After the flop at the Playhouse, I needed this success at the Versailles. They had signed me on for eight days and I stayed for twenty-one weeks. Can you imagine that?

'But the hotel was impossible. They guard your room as if you're a nun under a vow of chastity. Irène de Trébert, my friend from Paris, had two little rooms on Park Avenue which she let me use, and plenty of friends came to visit me, but I was still lonely. The nights were so long!

'Jean-Louis had finished the tour we were meant to do together and went back to Paris with the "boy scouts". That's how I divorced the *Compagnons* without any hard feelings.

'Luckily all my friends who were passing through came to see me. The one I was most pleased to see was Michel Emer. I was so pleased when he arrived at the Versailles, looking like a startled owl. And I gave him a hard time! He rushed over to kiss me and I pushed him away, saying, "Have you brought me a song, little soldier?" "No," he said, looking like a guilty child. "When you've written a song for me I'll greet you, and not before." And I left him standing there while I went off to sing. You've no idea how funny it was. He was livid. He listened to me from my dressing-room; it started the motor running again and on the corner of my make-up table he began to write "Bal dans ma rue":

> *Ce soir il y a bal dans ma rue*
> *Et dans le p'tit bistrot*
> *Où la joie coule à flot*
> *Des musiciens sur un tréteau*
> *Jouent pour les amoureux*
> *Qui tournent deux par deux*
> *Le rire aux lèvres et les yeux dans les yeux.*

'When I got back he held it out to me; "Here's your song, now you can kiss me." All he needed was to hear me sing.'

It was true. Michel used to say to her, 'If I can't see you, if you're far away, I can't write for you.' He would come to our house; 'Edith, talk to me. Sing something, anything you like.' And the next day he brought back a new song. In that way he wrote her more than thirty songs.

'The next day we had lunch together at my house, and started to work. I liked "Bal dans ma rue", but I wanted another. I wanted something sad, a story with someone dying at the end. I explained my idea to Michel, and in one sitting he wrote me "Monsieur Lenoble":

> *Monsieur Lenoble se mouche*
> *Met sa chemise de nuit*
> *Ouvre le gaz et se couche*
> *Demain tout sera fini.*

'He'd been in New York for twelve hours and he'd turned out two songs.'

That didn't surprise me, Edith had an extraordinary power over people and she made them give her the best they had in them. She was always asking for more, and they always gave it to her. I was the same as the others. You wanted to please her, to have her love you and for that there was only one recipe – to bring her something. Not money; she did not care about that, she gave it away. What was important to her, what she needed above all else, was to be able to admire those she loved.

The Americans could not understand her. Her personality was too new to them. They appreciated her talent only after Fischer's masterful poker game.

But when she went home to Park Avenue, she was dreadfully

alone again. When she gave a party, the people came to see the star. The two rooms were filled to bursting. But when the last visitor had zigzagged his way out of the apartment it was over. She had nothing to do but fall into bed and sleep.

She became close friends with Marlene Dietrich. 'I've never met a woman more intelligent than Marlene. And beautiful! Better than in the movies. Each time I saw her I thought of the Blue Angel.

'We often ate together. At first I would fool around, I was scared she would think I was dumb, but she gave me confidence in myself. One day she said, "Let yourself go, Edith, you're Paris to me; better still, you're everything Paris means to me. You remind me of Jean Gabin. You behave like him at table, you speak like him. You look fragile, but you give me the same feeling of strength that he does."

'That really knocked me out, because you can't find a greater talent or a more virile man than Jean Gabin. It was probably on an evening that I particularly reminded her of her Gabin that she took off the gold cross with emeralds that she was wearing and put it round my neck. "Take it, Edith, I want it to bring you luck as it did me. It will go round Paris with you as it did with me." She brought tears to my eyes.'

Edith wore the cross for a long time; after Marcel Cerdan's death she took it off. She decided those little green stones had brought her bad luck.

Though the friendship with Marlene had filled her life, Edith's heart was empty. She confided to me her amorous exploits in America.

'You can't imagine how hygienically they make love. It's like an army exercise, in out, in out, quick and clumsy, and then they fall asleep. And you run into perverts who think that just because you're Parisian you should do things you don't want to do, and when you turn them down they don't come back again. Or you get the ones that act like children and pretend you're their "mommy". They cuddle up in your arms, crying because they're so pissed. But that doesn't make them any better in bed.

'The funniest thing that happened to me was with a movie

actor. He was really handsome, the way that only Americans can be – tall, muscular, well-dressed; he seemed a bit languid, a bit of a show-off, but I thought to myself, "That'll all disappear when he's in bed. He'll have other things to do and think about."

'I invited him over with several friends. We laughed and drank, but not too much: I wasn't drunk, I wanted to keep my wits about me. I liked him too much to blow it at that point. Then everyone left: but where was John? "He's very tactful," I thought, "he's being discreet." I was sure that he would be waiting for me somewhere in the house. I could already imagine his smile, feel his arms around me. I was very excited, the very idea of sleeping with him made me feel better. But there was no one in the living-room. I went into the bedroom – and there was my would-be lover, lying completely naked between my sheets, smoking a cigarette.

' "Come on, I'm waiting for you," he said. I picked up his discarded clothes and threw them at him. "But ... but ..." he stuttered, "isn't this what you wanted?" and I started shrieking, "Fuck off, fuck off! What do you think I am, a whore?"

'He shot out of the apartment, leaving me to cry myself to sleep in my empty bed.'

Edith would not have to put up with that kind of insult again. A young boxer called Marcel Cerdan had just arrived in New York.

II

MARCEL CERDAN:
'LA VIE EN ROSE'

I was in Casablanca at the invitation of my future husband. I was pleased about the engagement – a new husband is always a pleasant prospect. All the same I felt lonely because the future, in spite of the matrimonial outlook, meant nothing to me really. I did not care about it. You only have one true love in your life, and I had had mine. The man I loved was killed in the war when I was twenty. You never get over a thing like that.

I had been in Morocco for nearly six months, and had had as much as I could stand of the sun. When I was in Paris I had not really believed the stories the Foreign Legionnaires told; now I was beginning to understand them, how they got depressed; why and how they went out of their minds; and also why so many drank themselves to death.

It is not easy to forget Paris when it's in your blood, but I knew that if I were to remain sane I had to put Edith, her infectious laugh, and her songs out of my mind. Yet I had nothing to hold on to. I gave up the future husband idea; he was already a thing of the past.

I could have gone to Fontenay-aux-Roses or to Bobigny, but from there I would have telephoned Edith; we would have made a date secretly like lost lovers as we did during Asso's time. That I could not do again. This time it must be out in the open or not at all, so it was not at all.

Through the papers I learned that she was doing very well. I filled in the details for myself. I was sick of thinking about it all.

In a seaside town you cannot escape the ocean; you always find yourself beside the water; it draws you to it. I felt like throwing myself into the sea; it sang too loud, banging its head against the rocks. That too-loud music had become Edith to me; Edith on stage at the A.B.C., or somewhere else accompanied by a large orchestra. I could hear her voice singing:

> *Avec ce soleil qui trouait la peau,*
> *Avec ce soleil ...*

The words resounded in my head and my heart, I was drifting with them.

One night, as I lay on the sand looking at the sky, I searched for the Great Bear. The Legionnaires had told me it did not exist in this country, that it had been replaced by the Southern Cross. There seemed to be too many stars in the sky; they twinkled so much that I lost my way and could find nothing at all. My mind was lost too. Then came a cool wind, refreshing my head and heart. I was beginning to feel better. I was alone; my mind had found a home with the stars.

Suddenly I heard the sand crunching. Someone was passing by. No, someone was coming towards me – perhaps to ask the time. I saw him. He was not Apollo, he was better than that. He looked pale in the light of the moon. His eyes glowed. The Southern Cross I had been looking for was there in his eyes. I was romantic then, and had a fertile imagination.

Without a word he lay down beside me. It was strange, he wanted to talk about his life and I about mine. It started very simply.

'What are you doing here?' he asked.

'I'm on holiday.'

Why did he seem so intimate with that first sentence? I felt as if I'd known him for ages.

'And you? Are you from around here?' I asked him.

'Yes.'

'What do you do?'

'I'm a boxer.'

He said it with a strange accent. There was no mistaking it, he certainly was from round there. He stretched out his elbow in the sand, his head resting on a hand that was so white I could hardly believe that it had anything to do with boxing. Then he announced, 'My name is Marcel Cerdan.'

He was like a kid, so proud of his name, of what it meant, of the effect it would have on me. He was a male Edith. Boxing was his life, even though at that time the newspaper pieces about him were no longer than a paragraph. Show business, singing, that was my field. But sport! If need be I could get interested in the Tour de France, but beyond that I knew nothing about sport.

He was flabbergasted by my silence. He had been so sure that I would know who he was. But all I could think was, 'If he were a singer, that name would look good on the billboard, and if the names were listed alphabetically his would be among the first.'

In that way, because of a night on the sand, we became friends, without saying anything to anyone, and no one ever knew about it. We used to meet in little bars for a mint tea or a coffee. Marcel did not drink. He was so serious. He was in training, and would not allow anything to distract him. He was a home-loving man, he had a wife, Marinette, and kids, Marcel and René. I think I was his only slip. I brought him a breath of Parisian air. He had already come under its spell, and he wanted more.

I talked to him for hours. I had never met such a gentle man, nor one with so much patience. He seemed to feel awkward in his chair, he tried to make himself smaller. Out of the ring, he always seemed a bit surprised by his own strength. He never seemed to get impatient or ill-tempered. If you had stepped on his toes *he* would have apologized.

One day I said to him, 'When one gets to know you, it's hard to believe that you earn your living by slugging other people.'

He laughed. 'But I don't hit them to hurt them, I fight clean.'

I wanted to apologize. When I watched him training he looked like a huge animal. His legs moved so fast he was like a dancer.

His work was to hit hard, but he was always afraid of going too far. 'Are you okay, kid,' he'd ask his sparring partner, who was gasping for breath.

'Yes, Marcel. You can punch, come on.'

The funny thing was that Marcel could not stand anyone hurting him, he always believed that it had been done on purpose.

I had never felt about any man as I did about Marcel. He knew everything about me . . . everything except Edith. How was I to know that this boxer from Casablanca would finally bring me back to her?

Even as I sat eating my heart out in that wretched town thinking that Edith was still with Jaubert, she was actually meeting
Marcel! While I thought I had been abandoned, she was chattering away to Marcel about me, her sister.

Later on they were both to tell me, from their separate points
of view, how they met. Edith was very proud of her Marcel. She
was obsessed with him. Sometimes I was a nuisance about her
men. When I did not like them, I made no bones about saying so.
I could tell at a glance what they were after, and I did not waste
too much time on those I considered unworthy of her.

But her Marcel was not like the others. From the beginning
Edith was dying to introduce him to me. She told him all about
her unhappy early life.

'Look, I'll give you an example,' she said. 'One day, when I
was with Momone (my sister) I said, "I do have a mother at least,
let's go visit her." We asked Dad for her address. I was just a kid
of fifteen, singing in the street. So we went to my mother's place.
She looked at us both; not a smile, not a kiss. "Oh," she said, "it's
you; and who's that?"

' "That's Momone."

' "Well come in, you're filthy."

'She touched our hair with the tips of her fingers. "You've got
fleas." We didn't care; we were used to them. She sent us to the
chemists to buy some Marie-Rose which spelt a perfumed death
to the fleas. She rubbed it well into our heads, kept us locked in
for two days, and wouldn't let us go out. Then we washed our
hair.

' "Now you can go," she said. "Here's something to eat with,"
she added, and gave us a few centimes.

'Not a kind word. Nothing. Not even a kiss.

'But don't worry, Marcel, we got even later. In 1932 or 1933,
my mother was singing in the Boule Noire, and I went along
there. She hadn't changed. "Oh, it's you again, and her," she said.

'This time she wasn't alone. She had a young girl-friend living
with her, called Jeannette. She was a really nice kid who tried to
clean us up and help us. She was devoted to my mother. She did
some street-walking on bad days – there were plenty of them
when my mother was around, more than good days. The poor

kid died of TB. So you see I didn't really have a mother. Momone is all I've got.'

After all that, what could Marcel do? 'You must make your sister come back,' he said, and Edith would have loved to, but she had no idea where I was.

When I returned from Casablanca I got work in the suburbs as a garage attendant. One evening the boss sent me to pick up a copy of *France-Soir*. On the front page was a picture of Cerdan, Edith Piaf, and a Miss Cotton, an American, stepping off their plane.

At that point I did not make the connection. I didn't really give it any thought but if I had I would probably have imagined that Marcel was with Miss Cotton. I saw only one thing – Edith had come back and there was no sign of Jaubert in the photograph.

I found out that she was staying in the Hôtel Claridge, where I had gone when I was a little girl. So I called her.

'Come over at once,' she said.

I was crying with happiness.

The hotel desk announced, 'Madame's sister is here.' It was like a vaudeville act, but I didn't feel like laughing.

In the corridor of this palace, standing outside her door, I had to put my hand over my heart to stop it from jumping out! Then I got scared. Things did not always go smoothly when we were back again and it had been a long time since I'd seen Edith.

When I knocked, I heard her voice call, 'Come in.'

She had her back to me. She was standing in front of the window, one hand clutched the drapes. It was like a movie still. She turned towards me, 'You see, Momone, I'm still waiting.'

It was true, she had spent her whole life waiting.

I stood there like a dummy. I looked at her, I felt uncomfortable, it had all happened too fast. An hour earlier I had been at my gas pump, my hands covered in grease, now I was standing facing Edith. I had changed. I was sadder – there were plenty of reasons for that. She looked beautiful and contented, surrounded by all her brand-new happiness.

There were only a few yards of carpet between us and yet I felt we were separated by thousands of miles. But in a few seconds I was in her arms. She was crying with joy, kissing me. 'Momone,' she cried, 'you don't know how happy I am. I'm in love with the most wonderful man on earth, and he's in love with me, and now you're here too. It's awful, I feel as if I'm going to die of happiness.'

Happiness is unlike unhappiness; you recover from it.

She looked me over from head to toe. I was not at my best. She opened her closet; it was full of dresses, which was unusual, it meant no one was helping himself to her funds. In a detached tone she told me to choose the dress I liked best. She did not waste much time, 'Listen, Momone, I'm really in love this time.'

I understood exactly what that meant – I had better not look down my nose at him or criticize him; this was serious. Naturally I was dying to see this superman, and after two endless hours he arrived. He knocked and Edith called joyfully, 'Come in.'

I felt the earth had opened under me, as I heard her say, 'Marcel Cerdan, this is Momone.'

He came towards me with his angelic smile, holding out his hand. Edith looked at us anxiously, to see if we were going to like each other. What courage it took for me to look her straight in the eye and say, 'You're right. He is marvellous.'

Neither Marcel nor I mentioned the past. We could not have done, she was standing there like a child.

No one moved, it was like a waxwork exhibition. And Edith was dying to tell me all about this new love while it was still hot. Fortunately he had the sense to leave and we were alone. She asked, 'What have you been doing all this time?'

'I'll tell you later.'

That was all she was waiting for, so she dived in. 'First I must tell you about the break with Jaubert – it was too funny. Marcel was in my New York apartment when Jaubert called. I was out and Jaubert hears a man's voice answering the phone. Very coldly he asks, "Who are you?"

' "I'm Marcel Cerdan," replied Marcel with his little accent.

' "What're you doing there?"

' "I can't tell you *what* I'm doing here, but you'd better not come back." Then he hung up and went to bed.

'When I got in I found a piece of paper on my pillow that said "Jaubert called and then ... It'll take too long to explain, wake me up." '

'Don't you think that's marvellous?'

I certainly did. Without knowing it Marcel had revenged me on Jaubert, and my pleasure lasted a long time.

Edith went on singing with the *Compagnons* in a cabaret, but Jaubert no longer came to our house. 'I swaggered around and really gave him a hard time. As we left the cabaret each evening, I never missed the opportunity of saying, "Good night, Jean-Louis, we're going home early because I have to look after Marcel tomorrow morning." It made him furious.'

For once we were not in the bathroom. Edith was sitting on a sort of couch, curled up in the corner. She was wearing a long sweater and skirt, and looked just as she had in our early days, except that this skirt and sweater were expensive. Her hair was shorter. With one snip of the scissors all the way round she had cut it herself one night in New York. It had been a very hot night and she had no hairdresser – she hated going to them, anyway. This new style bared her neck, which was a little short, so she kept her hair long on top and it fell forward on to her forehead. She never changed this hair-style, devised accidentally in a fit of impatience.

She was now a calm, contented woman. She was such a tiny little thing, her hands were still, but her eyes were lit up, they shone; they were beautiful.

'I first met Marcel ...'

I bit my tongue so as not to interrupt her.

'... one evening in the Club des Cinq, at the end of 1946. They said, "This is the Moroccan Bomber." That's what destiny is – a clenched fist held up for the whole world to see.'

Their first meeting was touching. Marcel was shy. He was being introduced to the Great Edith Piaf; that was how he saw her, and how he was always to see her. He had little idea of his own importance, though in his own field he was as famous as she – he was the Great Marcel Cerdan.

'Momone, I thought to myself then, "His eyes aren't like the others." And then – you know I never lie to you – I didn't give him another thought. There was not much chance of our meeting again, since our paths didn't cross. But America did it all. I was at the Versailles. Marcel's manager, Lucien Roupp, had lined up some fights for him at Madison Square Garden. I was feeling pretty low after the John Glendale business. One night the telephone rang; it was Marcel. I asked him to repeat his name, "Marcel *who*?"

' "Cerdan, the boxer. Don't you remember, we met at the Club des Cinq in Paris? I'm here."

'I thought it was terribly funny.

' "Of course," I said. "I haven't forgotten you."

' "Well, neither have I." Then he laughed so hard he'd obviously got over his nervousness. "How about dinner this evening? I'll come and get you."

'You can imagine, I didn't turn him down. I did a tremendous make-up job. I put on my smartest dress; very simple and expensive. I had hardly finished when he arrived.

' "Come on," he said. "I'm starving," and we started walking.

' "Don't you have a car or a taxi?"

' "It's very near."

'I had to take three steps to his one to keep up with him. At this speed I wouldn't last. He should have been a cross-country walker. But he didn't realize it; he was as thick as a wall.

'We went into a flea-bitten old drugstore, and he hoisted me up on to a stool. After all that walking, now he fancied some mountaineering! And I found myself face to face with a plate of pastrami – a sort of dried-up boiled beef that you wouldn't offer a tramp in Paris. The mustard was tickling my nose. Then they chucked a mint ice-cream soda at me and everything was washed down with a glass of beer. It was enough to make a dog throw up. He got the bill and left forty cents. No manners and a cheap-skate on top of it!

'Marcel gave me a big smile, he had no idea what I was thinking.

' "Shall we go?"

' "Was that the aperitif?" I asked. "It didn't cost much, did it? Is that what you call taking a lady out?"

'He went all red. He took my arm, without hurting me, but holding it all the same so there was no risk of me running off. "I'm sorry, I didn't realize. That's how I have dinner, but you're right, it can't be the same thing for you."

'We took a taxi, and we didn't exchange a word during the entire ride, he even avoided looking at me. Then we arrived at Le Pavillon, the smartest restaurant in New York. So I had two dinners on my first date with Marcel!'

It was marvellous for Edith to have a man who adored her, who did everything she wanted, not because he needed her or was scared of her temper but simply because he loved her.

Marcel was as famous as she. He had his public, she had hers, and when they went out together they shared the applause.

'When he fell in love with me, nothing else counted,' Edith recalled. 'Marcel is very faithful. Marinette, his wife, gave him two sons, and she is sacred. But I'm the one he loves. She must hate me. If I was her I'd have made a terrific scene ages ago, but she knows that she would lose Marcel if she did. He doesn't talk about her, but he thinks about her a lot. Do you understand?'

Edith could not know just how well I did understand. I already knew that Marcel was an honest and good man, not used to lying. And I knew my Edith. She was not one to hide her love; when she loved a man she had to show it. 'You know me, Momone, I can't hide my feelings,' she would say.

'One evening Marcel had a great idea, "Come on," he said, "we're going to a carnival." It was after midnight.

' "You're nuts. There aren't any carnivals around here."

' "Yes, there are. There's one at Coney Island."

'No one had ever told me about it; he had to be the one to break the news. Coney Island is acres of funfair. Those American merry-go-rounds aren't kid's stuff. When you slow down after a ride you go on turning inside. Your head's in one place, your stomach in another. We ate hot dogs, some kind of waffles, and ice cream. That evening I felt I didn't ever want to stop singing and spinning around and laughing.

'Marcel made me go on the Scenic Railway; it's like finding a Russian mountain range replanted in America. Marcel was shouting for joy; I was clinging to him. Nothing could happen to me in his arms; I was safe. Shouting was part of the fun. When we got down the crowds started shouting, "It's Cerdan." Then they recognized me and started singing our song, "La Vie en rose". I sang along with them, Momone, as I used to sing in the streets. I could smell the fair, the frying, the sugar, the sweat, you could hear all the different tunes mixing together. You don't know how wonderful it was.

'Another evening I went to see Marcel fight. He wanted me to. "I don't want to go, Marcel," I pleaded, "I'm scared."

' "So am I when you sing, but I come and listen. Perhaps that's when you're at your most beautiful. Boxing is my job. You have to watch a man do his job, until you've done that you don't really know him."

'His reasons were so simple that it was impossible to resist. At first I kept my eyes closed. I could hear blows falling on flesh and I was scared that he was getting them all. The audience was yelling and whistling. The place was full of smoke; people were eating popcorn and peanuts. It was awful. Finally I opened my eyes, and I ended up shouting, "Go on, Marcel!"

'His eyes didn't leave his opponent. It was a look that he'd never had for me, hard, squinting, alive. He won but he had a gash in his cheek and a black eye. I could have cried. I rushed over to console him, like a mother who sees her child coming home bloodied. He pushed me away gently, "No, Edith, it's nothing. That's part of my job too."

'Wasn't that a beautiful answer? He's a darling. If only you knew how darling he is.'

Indeed I knew.

'The journalists made a big thing out of us. One day Marcel agreed to give a press conference. Two French celebrities in love in New York – it was the journalists' bread and butter. They were all there, chewing their gum and smoking.

'Marcel didn't beat around the bush; he went straight to the point. You should have heard how he gave it to them. He had said to me, "There's nothing for you to say. I'd rather you stayed away." But I didn't want to, I wanted to listen. I stationed myself behind an exit.

' "Well," said Marcel to the pressmen, "there's only one thing on your minds, so let's not lose any time. You want to know if I love Edith Piaf? Yes. And if she's my mistress? If she is, it's because I'm already married. If I weren't married and didn't have any children, I would make her my wife.

' "And now anyone here who hasn't cheated on his wife put up his hand"

'The journalists were thunderstruck.

' "Now ask me all the questions you want, but I've said everything I'm going to say on this subject. Tomorrow I shall see if you're gentlemen."

'The conference was over, and the next day there wasn't a single word about us in the papers. I received a basket of flowers high as a skyscraper with a card, "To the best-loved woman, from the 'gentlemen'."

'Momone,' Edith said, 'you won't know me. Marcel has changed me. He is so pure that when he looks at me I feel as if my sins have been washed away. I feel clean with him. With the others I always wanted to go back to the beginning.'

There was another important change – when Marcel was around she never paid. He was always the one who took out his wallet and picked up the bills. 'You know, it isn't easy to make him accept a gift, but I've found a way, when he gives me a present, I give him one.

'Look, Momone, he bought me my first mink. Isn't it beautiful?' As Edith proudly displayed the coat it was heart-warming to see her hand stroking the fur, snuggling into it, taking fistfuls of it. She didn't care about the quality or the price; Edith did not need anyone to buy minks for her. It was Marcel's love that she was caressing.

'Straightaway I went to Cartier's and bought him the most beautiful pair of diamond cuff-links they had, and a watch and chain, everything that I saw. There was nothing too good for him. When I gave them to him he laughed like a child. He took me in his hands, lifted me into the air, and whirled me around like a doll.

'I'm crazy about him, Momone; he's made me completely nuts. The worst thing is that we're not together enough. Our careers keep us apart, and then there's Marinette. I keep telling myself that he's right not to leave her, but it's killing me.

'Tomorrow we're getting up early and going to the tailor. Marcel doesn't know anything about clothes, he has absolutely no taste; he's a real bumpkin. I have to teach him. So we're going to have him outfitted.'

It was the same old story. 'We're going to dress him.' How many times had I heard that sentence? Edith adored dressing her men and they all had to go through it.

One day Marcel went to the Palais des Sports in a grey suit with stripes as thick as his little finger. Edith had a suit made for me out of the same material, but I never wore it, it was quite ghastly. I still have it. Marcel wore a purple shirt and some dreadful sort of tie with orange in it. The kindly man, who was sweetness itself, merely said, 'Darling, you really think I can wear that?'

And Edith replied, 'You have absolutely no taste. Listen, Marcel, you just don't understand.' Then she turned towards me, 'How does he look?'

It was an impossible situation, and to spare Edith's feelings and to avoid a scene I replied with a cowardly, 'Marvellous, really handsome'.

But Marcel was unhappy. He suffered. Others had suffered, but not like him. He was sure Edith was his intellectual superior. He relied on her to complete his education, to teach him how to behave.

And he was all admiration for her singing; standing in the wings, this powerful man would make himself as small as possible and watch her, listen to her adoringly.

What amazed Marcel most was Edith's voice. When he heard her sing he would say to me, 'Can you imagine, she weighs a third of what I do. There's nothing to her, I could knock her flat with one breath. Such a tiny little woman with such a big voice. I can't get over it.'

Each evening when Edith sang we had to take along every-thing but the kitchen sink; her glass, her nose drops, her handkerchiefs, her make-up removers, aspirins, pencils, notebooks, English books, and so on. She would not leave a thing in her dressing-room. We took it all home with us afterwards and the next day brought it back again. When Marcel was there he would check, 'Momone, you haven't forgotten all her stuff, you do have her dress, don't you?'

I never knew why Edith only had one stage dress – a dress she would never part with. I was in charge of it. She would not allow it to be left hanging in the dressing-room. I would clean and iron it each day at home and take it back with me in the evening.

Once when we were in New York there was a real panic: Edith, in a slip, made up and with her hair already done, was bending down to put on her shoes, and 'My dress!' she called in her booming voice. I looked around and went cold all over. No dress! I had left it in Park Avenue.

To make matters worse the stage manager was calling, 'Five minutes, Miss Piaf.'

I rushed out in a frenzy without saying a word. I took a cab to get the dress, and I expected Edith would be shrieking by the time I returned to the dressing-room. But when she saw my crestfallen expression, she kissed me, took my hand, and went off to sing. God, what a relief!

Edith could best show her love for a man by looking after him. She had decided she would make Marcel read. At the beginning of their affair, she had found him reading comic books – the kid's stuff looked pretty strange in his big boxer's hands.

'Aren't you ashamed, Marcel, at your age?'

He replied pitifully, 'They're funny; you should read them.'

So Edith forced her dear Marcel to read books like 'Via Mala', 'Sarn', 'La Grange Meute', 'La Recherche de la Vérité' – not exactly light entertainment!

'Why are you making me read all this when it's such a lovely day and I want to go out for a walk?' he would ask.

'That's how I learnt, Marcel,' she replied.

He persevered bravely because he was sure she was right; could she ever be wrong? He had doubts only about her taste in suits.

We were not living at the Claridge any more. Edith had rented a little house on the rue Leconte de Lisle. It was the first time that she had her own furniture; for us that was a big step forward.

'A hotel, even a palace,' Edith pronounced, 'is no good when you have a man like him in your life.'

She wanted the best of everything for Marcel, the most beautiful, the most, well, everything – and one evening it really was.

Edith was appearing at the A.B.C. Princess Elizabeth and the Duke of Edinburgh were in Paris and Princess Elizabeth, who had never heard Edith sing, asked if she would come to Carrère where she was holding an evening of private entertainment. So it was virtually a command from the future Queen of England when, one morning, a gentleman rang up from the Quai d'Orsay. We didn't know what the Quai d'Orsay was. 'Never heard of it,' said Edith, shaking her head at Madame Bigeard, who quickly explained what it was, holding her hand over the receiver.

When Edith hung up she was bursting with joy. 'Princess Elizabeth wants to see me.'

It was Sunday. Edith had matinee and evening shows, but she went ahead as usual. Then we were driven down the boulevards and the rue Pierre-Charron in the Embassy car. Edith was very excited; the streets of Paris are a strange school, they teach you not to give anything a second look – but you don't meet queens in them.

Before going on stage at Carrère, Edith crossed herself, touched wood, all the usual business. 'I have to be at my best. I'm representing France, and the future Queen of England has gone out of her way to see me.'

For us, the people of Paris, Elizabeth was already Queen.

Edith sang that night from the bottom of her patriotic heart. When she got back to her dressing-room the Chief of Protocol was waiting for her. That man really had style. In a flowery, unfamiliar language he explained that 'Princess Elizabeth desires to entertain you at her table . . .'

The way he said it, it sounded as if Edith was doing *her* the honour. That's royal politeness.

Edith said 'Yes', in a voice that sounded like a condemned man's last wish. She looked at me, and told the Equerry, 'I can't go all alone, it's impossible; I can't go without my sister.' And since I was part of the family there were no difficulties. The Chief of Protocol gave us a few minutes to pull ourselves together. I felt as wobbly as a jelly.

'Momone, how do you curtsy? How do you talk to a queen? Oh, what the hell, she's a woman like any other.' But she didn't believe it.

Elizabeth held out her hand with a lovely smile. Edith made a quick little movement, rather like a genuflection; it must have been a new one for the Chief of Protocol.

The Princess made Edith sit beside her, and I found myself facing Elizabeth and Philip. I dared not drink, neither did Edith. It was one of the weirdest conversations we'd ever had, and I heard it all through a fog.

'You know,' said Edith, 'I was not as good as I would like to have been for you, because I did two matinees today, and an evening show. Forty-two songs between three o'clock and midnight is a bit draining. It tires the voice.'

The Princess smiled graciously and reassured Edith – in better French than we had ever spoken – saying something like, 'It was perfect. Please don't be anxious. You were wonderful.' Only it sounded better coming from her.

In a daze I heard Edith say again, 'Yes, but if you could hear me when I haven't been through two matinees, you would really be surprised.'

Elizabeth, who had a ravishing smile, very English, but very pretty, said to Edith, 'I do understand.' But it could hardly have been true. What had we in common with a young woman who was destined to be a queen from the day she was born? The Princess told Edith that her father, George VI, wished to include Edith's records in his collection. She didn't say it because she wanted Edith to give them to her; it was a nice way of letting Edith know that the King knew – and liked – Edith Piaf.

And Edith replied with her customary candour, 'Fine, I'll send them over tomorrow. Where are you staying?'

Finally it was over. It had all passed like a dream. We had no idea how long it lasted, time had stood still at that table. Later, when we had both recovered, Edith said to me, 'He's really nice-looking, isn't he, that man of hers?'

'I had a drink with the Princess and her Duke,' she kept repeating. 'It's a pity that Marcel didn't see me, he'd have been so proud. I was a bit of a bore, wasn't I, Momone? But I must have looked good from a distance.'

The famous Cerdan–Tony Zale fight was drawing closer. Marcel was training conscientiously, and so were we. Edith was taking it seriously; and when she took something seriously everything else was put aside.

Lucien Roupp was a pain in the arse. 'If you love your champion, go easy on the love-making,' he warned Edith. 'It slows him up, and Zale's very quick on his feet.'

He really watched over Marcel. His advice rained on us like a tropical storm. 'When he eats with you, watch his diet. And he absolutely must not be kept up late; he has to sleep like a child, ten hours a night.'

'Your friend's a pain,' Edith told Marcel, but he just laughed.

We led a strange life when Marcel was in Paris. He went to bed at sundown. Edith was working, so she went to bed at four in the morning; so did I, but I got up at eight o'clock to prepare Marcel's fruit juice. He would leap out of bed, completely refreshed, and, still half asleep, I had to stumble along behind him in a blue tracksuit bearing the words 'French Team', just like his. It must have been quite a sight to see me trailing behind the champion on his morning jog.

At home the fever was mounting. Edith, who knew nothing about sport and cared less, would ask people, 'Do you like boxing?'

If they replied, 'No', she would protest, 'I can't understand why some people don't like boxing. They must be so dull. You have to try to understand everything in life. But I guess there are people who don't care about anything.'

'What are Marcel's chances?' she would ask of others. As long as they gave her a list of things in Marcel's favour, she was happy. If anyone said they supported Cerdan they could ask anything of Edith, and they did.

She spent a lot of time waiting patiently at the rue Leconte-de-Lisle for Marcel, who divided his time between Casablanca, Paris, and his training. That was probably the time when she did most of her knitting. She made sweaters for her boxer. They were unbelievably ugly. Although she knitted well, she chose colours which she liked and felt were gay, but they were gay enough to stop the traffic. So Marcel would wear his sweaters during his training to sweat into. He was so kind: he always said, 'If I fight well, Edith, it will be because of your sweaters;' he might be having a little laugh on the side, but Edith was happy. 'Quick, get the needles and wool and I'll make another,' she would cry.

No one can appreciate how thoughtful Marcel was. He had no education, but he always knew what to do to avoid causing unhappiness. He had endless tact. I never heard him boast, either; everything he did was done without any trumpet-blowing.

His world was no more saintly than ours; there were as many dirty tricks, hits below the belt, sordid stories, and crooked deals, yet Marcel passed through without being tainted. Not because he was unaware of it; he saw everything. When Edith got annoyed with the hangers-on he would say, 'Leave them alone, they're so trivial. You don't have to waste your strength crushing anything so feeble.'

'I discovered the real Marcel not in bed but in the street,' Edith told me. 'On the day I met him with a childhood Arab friend who was three-quarters blind. Each morning Marcel would lead him to the oculist. He had been a boxer in Casablanca, and Marcel had brought him over, paid for everything, the hotel, the travel expenses, and finally the cure.

'You know how jealous I am. I had noticed that Marcel often left me. He would look at his watch and say, "I'll be back in an hour, I have a meeting." In the end I got so sick of it, I wanted to know what was going on. When I said just now that I met him it wasn't true; I had followed him. I didn't dare tell Marcel, he wouldn't have understood. He thought I had run into him by accident, so he told me everything. He had kept it even from me, but he had not lied to me, it *was* a meeting he went to. He was visiting his friend every day, in addition to the treatment, so that he wouldn't feel abandoned. I know how long a day can be when it's night all the time. I cried with happiness. I never believed a man like Marcel could exist. And when I think there are idiots who say boxers are all brutes, I wish I had Marcel's fists so I could smash them in the face.'

I loved Marcel, too, as much as Edith did; differently, perhaps, but as much. He was my friend.

I rarely had any pocket money. Edith never gave me any, she wanted to buy everything for me, so I never had two pennies to rub together. I was treated like a child, 'You always do something stupid when you have money. You don't need any when you're with me. It runs through your fingers like water.' That was great, coming from her! She didn't even know what she did with her money. She was incapable of saving for herself, but she paid money into my savings bank. So I never had enough to buy a paper, a packet of cigarettes, or a drink. Marcel was sorry for me, and he'd slip me a little dough from time to time. Not a lot, but often. He had a formula; 'Don't you have any cigarettes?' and depending on whether I answered yes or no, he would fork out what was needed.

Edith got a contract for seven thousand dollars a week at the Versailles in New York at the time of the Zale fight. Because of his training programme, Marcel had to leave early and Edith wanted to go with him, but Lucien Roupp opposed the idea. 'None of that, you can't arrive together. The sporting world would be against it, and the papers would be full of it.'

Lou Barrier agreed. 'It's not good for you, Edith. To the Americans Marcel is married, but not to you. You can live the kind of love story that will make the stenographers weep, but you can't arrive together like an official couple.'

'Okay,' said Edith. But that evening she insisted that I go over with Marcel to watch over him.

'Momone, he's in your charge, look after him well, he can't do a thing for himself. He may be terrific in the ring but he's just a kid.'

'But, Edith,' he protested, 'I've already been abroad on my own before.'

'Let me take care of all this,' she answered. 'Who will lay out your shirts, your shoes, your suits ? I don't want another woman, even a chambermaid, touching your things.' So I left with Marcel. I set him up safely in his room, and then went back to Paris to fetch Edith.

Naturally, when Edith and I arrived three days later, Lucien Roupp started laying down the law. 'Edith, I'm counting on you. This is going to be the fight of Marcel's life. He mustn't lose it.'

'Don't be an idiot,' Edith replied. 'No one knows I'm here. My contract starts in ten days. I've come to see Marcel, and I shall see him.'

'Now look, Marcel is a hundred miles from New York, near the training camp at Loch Sheldrake. Before he goes there he's spending some time at the Evans Hotel. I've found you a little guest-house near by.'

'Why not in the same hotel ?'

'Come on, Edith, you know America. It's out of the question for a man and a woman who aren't married to sleep in the same room. You'll ruin Marcel's career with ideas like that. You'll spend two days up there, incognito, and when Marcel goes to the training camp, you'll come back to New York and wait quietly for him.'

'If that's the way you want it,' Edith said treacherously, 'I'll go along.'

When Lucien had said to us, 'I've arranged this, or organized that,' there was not a word of truth in it. It was Marcel who had organized it, and his first thought had been to find us a lodging close to him. Lucien was just the messenger. At the guest-house everyone thought we were two sisters on a trip.

We were about to unpack when the dinner bell rang and we rushed down. It was the first time Edith had ever been on time for dinner. She had never been anywhere like this before, and neither had I. A shabby hotel or a palace, yes, but not a genteel guest-house. At table introductions were made, no one knew each other; it was not a very relaxed atmosphere.

During the meal Edith didn't touch a thing, she shoved everything on to my plate and made me eat so as not to upset the landlady, 'Be polite, we're in a foreign country.'

At last dinner was over. Or so we thought. But it was the

birthday of one of the landlady's sons, and since we were all in the family, they brought on a monstrous one hundred per cent American birthday cake – Chantilly cream, coconut, chocolate, currants, almonds, peanut butter, maple syrup, sponge cake – I would never have believed all that could be crammed together. It was enormous. A slice appeared on my plate, completely covering it. I looked at Edith's plate; she had a similar piece. 'She can't possibly want me to eat both,' I thought, but that was exactly what she figured.

'Momone, take it away, it's making me sick to my stomach. And eat it; it's a birthday cake. What would they think if we left it?' That night I thought I was going to die, each time I closed my eyes I saw the monster cake rising before me, but Edith just laughed like hell and kept singing 'Happy Birthday'.

With difficulty, Lucien and Marcel had laid a false trail for the journalists, and found somewhere we could meet. In spite of her happiness in seeing Marcel again, Edith started a row with Lucien. 'Where's our room?' she asked him, a little too smoothly to sound sincere.

Lucien said, 'I told you it's out of the question, he's in training. Discipline . . .'

'I've had enough of you,' she cut in. 'When I ring for you, you can answer and not before. You're not my husband, or my lover, or even my agent. So shut up and fast. I'm not going to ruin your champion, but our bed is a matter to be decided between us. Get lost, I'm sick to death of you.'

And Lucien, thoroughly squashed, shut up.

In a very sweet voice Marcel explained to Edith the importance of the training and the necessity to respect the sporting rules of the country and, since she adored him, she calmed down.

'If you think it's necessary, Marcel, for your own good, I accept, but I shall never last without seeing you.'

'Trust me, Edith, everything will be settled this evening.'

And this shy giant, so respectful of rules and regulations, carried out a daring and dangerous plan. He had decided to take us into his training quarters, where he was permitted to see only his manager and sparring partner. If it had become known that Marcel Cerdan had hidden two women in his camp, he would have been disqualified immediately, and the scandal would have ruined his career. The following morning we said good-bye to the maker of birthday cakes, and left by taxi. It was a real movie scene. The taxi-driver was a bit surprised when we told him to drop us off near a crossroad. He asked curiously, 'Are you planning to walk back, or were you going to hitch-hike?'

'No,' we said, 'Buffalo Bill's coming to get us on horseback,' and he roared with laughter.

A few minutes later Marcel arrived, without Lucien, and in a back road he locked us both into the boot of the car.

'If anyone asks me to open the trunk, I'll tell them I've lost the key.'

Thank God American cars have boots like the hold of a ship!

In the Loch Sheldrake camp each boxer had his own bungalow. Marcel had found one set apart from the others, but I realize on looking back what guts it must have taken to smuggle us in. We were at the mercy of anyone who chose to come by to do the housework or check the plumbing. We were all quite mad. 'You see,' Marcel explained to Edith, laughing, 'screwing's supposed to be very bad for boxers in training. It makes them slow on their feet, takes away their wind, and generally louses them up.'

He himself disproved this theory. He spent every night with Edith and he was never in better shape for a fight! We stayed in the bungalow the whole time. The water was cold, and since no one had known it would be lived in there was nothing to eat. In the evenings Marcel brought us sandwiches hidden in his shirt. And since love-making gives you an appetite, he ate his fair share too, so by the next day we had none left.

There was nothing to drink but tap-water, and we were lucky it had not been turned off. Each time she took a drink Edith was surprised at herself, 'Can you imagine how much I must love Marcel to be drinking this stuff. It'll probably kill me.'

She went on, 'There are millions of microbes and all that crap in there. Have you ever seen a drop of water under a microscope?'

'No, have you?'

'No, but I know all the same. An army doctor once explained

it all to me. He had come back from the colonies, so there you are.'

'Well, we aren't in the colonies, this is America.'

'That's even worse, they chuck so much disinfectant in the water that it wears away your stomach lining. You see where love leads you to. To suicide!'

And we laughed, but not too loudly or we would have been overheard.

This water cure was hard for Edith, who drank alcohol every day; sometimes more, sometimes less, but every day. She didn't drink enough to pass out, because she held it well, but she often got pretty high all the same.

We lived only at night, or almost. During the day the blinds were drawn, at night we could not turn on the electricity, and we dared not speak loudly at any time.

Marcel would arrive each evening beside himself with happiness. Once or twice he succeeded in bringing some beer, and when he could not make that, he brought milk, which made Edith laugh. 'Now he thinks we're a couple of cows.'

He lifted her up in his arms and made her dance in the air while Edith sang to him.

She was singing for herself, but not for me. I did not have Marcel in my bed as compensation, and I was sick to death of this training camp vacation. After ten days behind bars, I felt I couldn't go on any longer. It had become intolerable. Edith was happy enough at night, but during the day she made a terrific fuss too.

At the end of two weeks we got our reward. The world championship for Marcel; freedom for us. And so Marcel smuggled us out of the camp in the same way we had come in, in the boot of a big car. Now it was Edith's official arrival date. The Americans never did understand how she got in without going through La Guardia Airport.

When we arrived we found two furnished suites had been booked, one above the other. It was convenient and in conformity with the national customs.

Marcel was being carefully watched by the Federation of Sports, who couldn't allow any fooling around. They called it 'protecting him'. The hotel was alive with cops who all looked like Al Capone in those movies about prohibition.

Towards the end we got scared. Marcel had received threatening letters and telephone calls, saying things like, 'There's no need to train, you aren't going to get a chance to climb into the ring,' or 'We'll get you before you've even touched Tony.'

It made Marcel laugh, but Lucien was nervous, and Edith even more so. 'They're all gangsters here. This isn't Paris, Marcel, you must take precautions.'

Edith had decided that they could easily poison Marcel but she had a solution – I was to be the official food-taster. Edith would order a steak, then command me to eat half of it. The rest was for Marcel if I survived!

She did the same with vegetables, or a pear, 'Cut it in half and eat it.' When they saw that there were no ill effects Marcel ate the other half. And so it went on all the time preceding the fight. I wouldn't have done it for any of the other men she knew.

You have to live through a world championship even in New York to know what it is really like. It goes to everyone's head.

The sports-writers did not hesitate to drag Edith's name into their coverage of the big fight. 'Marcel Cerdan is not leading the ascetic life of a champion! He will pay for it.' 'The title is not in his pocket.' 'This affair will affect his training.'

Edith was horrified. She was afraid that she might be held responsible. So she prayed to St Theresa. She made vows, but she would not tell me what they were in case she had to modify them later! She was in such a state she walked around in a daze, and so did I! Then we discovered a church which had a statue of St Theresa, and there we lit more candles in one day than she'd had in a year.

The day before the fight and the day itself we did not see much of Marcel. It was no longer possible, the guard had become too strict. Lucien was on tenterhooks. The tension was terrific, none of us could have stood it much longer.

The Americans were neither kind nor generous. We went in a car with Marcel to New Jersey's Roosevelt Stadium, where the fight was to take place. He was driving it himself, while Tony Zale arrived in style with flash bulbs popping and cheers and shouts from the crowd. The damn Yanks were very sure of themselves. The parking-lot attendant said, 'Don't bother to park your car. The fight with the Frenchman won't take long. He'll last about two minutes.' He had not recognized Marcel, who turned calmly to Edith and said, 'You see, I'll be home soon.'

Then he kissed her and left us at his usual leisurely pace. When his large back had disappeared into the door of the lobby, Lucien showed us to our seats.

I thought the ringside was pretty disgusting, like a theatre with the show taking place in a ring, but they don't care too much about the spectators' comfort. Sporting types are tough, they don't have sensitive skins.

In the middle of all the shouts and whistles the two champions came on, and the shouting and stamping reached such a crescendo that the place was shaking.

Edith had a pinched expression; she was all white and strained. She had taken my hand, as she always did when things were serious. I was trying to put a good face on it, but I didn't feel any better. If I close my eyes now I can still hear that gong resounding through my head and body. We had to sit and listen to everyone's opinion – they all seemed to be experts. Fortunately we did not understand very much, if we had we probably would not have been able to stand it. There were ladies in fur coats and their escorts in dinner jackets. There were men with hats screwed to their heads, smoking stinking cigars, sucking cigarettes, chewing gum, and spitting anywhere they chose.

There was plenty of atmosphere, and everything was lost in the darkness and the smoke, except the ring which was lit like an operating table with big white lamps.

'Momone,' said Edith, 'I'm going to keep my eyes closed. When it's over you can tell me.' But she couldn't keep them closed for more than a second. With each blow that Marcel took, her nails dug a little farther into my skin, yet I didn't feel a thing; I was as agonized as she.

At the end of the first round we could see Marcel struggling to breathe, his stomach swelled.

'Do you think he's winded?'

'No. No. He's recuperating.'

A spectator who understood French said to us, 'He'll be okay.'

The second and third rounds went by; in the fourth round Tony Zale got nasty and Edith got mad. Zale tossed Marcel into the air; the Americans were delirious. Edith begged St Theresa to come to her help, and injure Tony. She was hitting the guy in front of her on the head, and he didn't say a thing; he did not even notice it.

Then Zale was against the ropes. Marcel started towards his corner. As he reached the middle of the ring he turned and saw Zale collapsing like a piece of warm wax. Then Marcel went on to his seconds. The referee came to fetch him, took him back to the middle of the ring and lifted his arm, shouting, 'Marcel Cerdan, World Champion'.

It was a wonderful moment. The French flags were unfurled. The Marseillaise began to play. Everyone was on his feet. Edith, dead white, couldn't say a word. She clutched me, her hand as limp as a rag. I looked at her.

We were alone in the midst of all these laughing, shouting Americans – many of them had recognized Edith – and we were French. But they were very sporting, all for fair play. They lifted us up in their arms shouting, 'French girls', we could not understand the rest, it went too fast. We no longer knew where we were. We were drunk with relief, and exhaustion. Edith looked as if she had won the world championship herself.

I thought to myself, poor Marinette, she's the one that ought to be here, not Edith. But as Edith remarked, 'That's life!' And this was hardly the moment to think of it.

We had no time to fetch Marcel, the place was jammed like the Metro at rush hour, and Edith was due at the Versailles.

That night there was a burst of applause when Edith went on stage at the Versailles. There were big tears in her eyes; she wiped them away, saying, 'Please excuse me but I'm so happy.'

During her act the cheers suddenly broke out again when Marcel came in. He was embarrassed. He sat down at a table very quietly and later we joined him for a drink. I think everyone in the Versailles would have liked to have changed places with us. We were so proud of him. Our very own champion!

On the evening of his world championship triumph Marcel

did nothing out of the ordinary. Hundreds of people would have given anything to entertain him. Everyone was crazy about him. But he turned them all down, and went home quietly with Edith, walking through the streets of New York, holding her little hand in the big paw that had just knocked out another champion.

It was like a second honeymoon for them. I don't think they had ever loved each other so much.

Marcel had to go back to France, where they were waiting to give him a hero's welcome. Edith finished her contract, and they were soon back to their usual routine, although often apart.

When Marcel was in Casablanca, Edith had found an efficient, if expensive and tiring, way to keep in touch with him. She wrote him letters and I took them to him by aeroplane, brought his reply back the same way. I must have done it three times a week. The airline people got to know me pretty well.

'I don't want strangers to touch our letters,' Edith explained. 'And anyway, I don't trust other people. Postmen are no better than anyone else, they might lose my letters.' Life with Edith was very tiring for everyone who came within her orbit.

If only we could have led a normal life it would perhaps have been easier, but she had no fixed times of getting up or going to sleep. When she decided she was tired, I put her to bed. I had to tuck her in, and give her the ear-plugs and the sleeping mask – they were indispensable, she could not bear the least ray of light. Then she would say, 'Go to bed, Momone.'

But I had always to be awake before Edith woke up. If she did not want to go to bed, I had to stay up with her. Nothing could make her sleep; she resisted the strongest sleeping pills. Once when she was quite exhausted and keyed up, a friend of ours who was a doctor gave her a dose of sleeping pills that would have knocked a horse out for forty-eight hours. But she went on talking and laughing, ignoring our drooping expressions. Finally he gave her an injection. She closed her eyes, we put her to bed and tiptoed out. Ten minutes later we were all fast asleep when that terrible voice woke us, 'What's the matter with you? You're all fast asleep, lousy company you are. Come on, Momone, when are you going to make some coffee for this pack of party-poopers?'

It was six in the morning.

Once, while Marcel was preparing for a fight, Edith wanted him to be so strong that out of love for him she gave up her night life and tried to live a normal existence. But it was impossible; it was more than a sacrifice, it ran contrary to her nature. She had always come alive at night.

But when Marcel was away she took up her old ways, and when he came back she dragged him along with her. 'Marcel, you aren't going to bed? You aren't going to leave me? What can I do without you? I see so little of you anyway. While you're here let's make the best of it at least. You owe me all your time, it's mine. You've proved you're the strongest. You can train when you're not with me.'

Once she complained: 'You're making me unhappy. This is no life for us. I never see you and when you are here you leave me to sleep.'

And Marcel loved her so much that he gave in.

People were beginning to say that Marcel was becoming a playboy; that La Motta, against whom he would be defending his title, could perhaps teach our champion a lesson. Lucien would fly into terrible rages. But Marcel's and Edith's love was their own business, it had nothing to do with anyone else.

One evening Edith really diced with Marcel's future. He was in Paris, training seriously at last. The fight with La Motta in New York was due shortly. Edith had become almost reasonable again. Life at home ran like clockwork.

The date for his departure had been set. Marcel had said good-bye to all his friends, who were ours too – Monsieur and Madame Lévitan, Madame Breton and her husband, and all the other regulars.

We were still living in the rue Leconte-de-Lisle. The back of the dining-room was lit, and a huge aquarium took up a large part of the wall. On the other side was a corridor.

On the evening Marcel was supposed to have left, Edith gave a dinner party for everyone who had said good-bye to him on the previous day. She was in a very good mood; she had prepared a practical joke for her guests, it was something she always adored.

The dinner was very gay, Madame Breton talked about Marcel, about his departure, we had seen photos of it in the evening papers. 'At this very moment Marcel must be arriving at La Guardia,' she said. 'He'd be having a better time here with us.'

'Well, I'm going to knock three times, and I'll make Marcel appear before you,' said Edith. 'Look at the aquarium.'

We expected to see a photo of Marcel appear, but she ceremoniously knocked three times and Marcel appeared behind the aquarium. It was quite a shock. My flesh began to crawl. In that ghostly green light, with the waving water plants, and the fish swimming across his face, Marcel looked like a drowned man.

Two months later he was dead.

Marcel left for New York the next day. The fight took place and he lost the title. He was not the same when he returned to Paris. It was clear that he blamed himself. He was a conscientious man, and he knew that champagne and sleepless nights are not the best recipe for victory.

To make matters worse a huge headline in the paper the next day proclaimed: EDITH PIAF BROUGHT CERDAN BAD LUCK. There were other articles and they all blamed Edith. Gentle as ever, Marcel tried to comfort her. 'Don't listen to them. It's true I wasn't on form but it happens to all boxers at some point. I'll have my revenge. We'll do everything we can to beat them, won't we, Edith?'

'You know,' he explained to me, 'it's not Edith's fault, it's mine. I should have been stronger,' which did not sound right coming from Marcel.

The set-back had upset Edith. 'I don't like this house,' she decided. 'It brings bad luck.'

She was always very superstitious, and had invented hundreds of little touchstones of her own. Thursday is a lucky day, Sunday unlucky. When she saw a flock of sheep she would say, 'That brings money. Clench your fist to keep it!' (That one wasn't much use!) So we moved to Boulogne, to a town house at 5 rue Gambetta, for which Edith paid nineteen million francs. She didn't care about the cost because the living-room was large enough to be turned into a gymnasium for Marcel, and that was the only reason she bought it. 'He'll be able to train here; he won't leave me.'

We lived with the workmen for weeks. The decorator had promised to finish it during our next trip to the United States.

America had adopted Edith. In October 1949 she had a new engagement for several weeks at the Versailles. She went alone, telling me to follow Marcel, who was on a tour of France giving exhibition fights for boxers who were down on their luck. It was my task to watch over him.

'I'm relying on you. Look after him. I know he doesn't run around much, but all men have it in them, so watch out,' Edith instructed me.

When the tour was finished Marcel and I planned to join Edith in New York. The date of our departure was fixed. We were going to take the boat because Edith, who hopped on and off planes the way most people take taxis, was always scared when someone else went by plane.

Twenty-four hours before we were due to leave, Edith called Marcel. 'My darling, please come over right away. I can't go on waiting for you. Take the plane this time, the boat takes too long. And hurry.'

'Okay,' replied Marcel. 'I'll be with you tomorrow. I love you.'

And those were the last words the lovers ever spoke to each other.

Why did Edith decide that Marcel must fly over on that day? I never found out. Was she bored? Was she afraid of doing something she would regret? Of cheating on him? Anything was possible with her.

I was faced with two problems: to find two seats on a plane, and to get my U.S. visa renewed. I had already put in the request, but they were taking their time about it as usual.

After a lot of wire-pulling we were finally able to find a seat for him on a plane. 'See you soon,' I said to him as I left him at the airport.

It was all over. When I woke up next morning all the newspapers carried the news that Marcel Cerdan was dead. They had identified him because he was wearing a watch on each wrist. His plane had crashed. I left as soon as my visa had arrived;

Edith needed me. The Bretons were waiting for me at La Guardia Airport. They were very kind, and through them I heard what had happened.

Loulou Barrier was in New York and had decided to pick up Marcel at the airport because he was arriving too early in the morning for Edith to go. It was 28 October 1949. When he got to the airport Loulou learned that the Paris–New York flight had crashed in the Azores. He knew that Marcel Cerdan was on the death-roll.

When Edith saw Loulou come back alone she let out a cry, 'Something's happened to Marcel. He's dead.'

Normally Marcel would have woken her. When I was not there, the man she was currently in love with woke her up; no one else was allowed to do it. As soon as she saw Loulou in her room, she had understood.

Barrier could not reply; words would not come. He just looked at her and his silence told all. During that day the telegrams started coming, people called her from everywhere. She had wired Jacques Bourgeat, 'Write me quickly, I need you. Edith,' and although he was quite old by then, and not at all well off, he came over. Madame Bigeard sent such a heart-felt wire that Edith sent for her.

Edith's distress upset everyone. She saw nothing, heard nothing. She cried all the time; not loudly, but all the time.

But when Loulou said to her, 'I've arranged everything, you don't have to sing this evening,' she put aside her grief and answered, 'I'm going to sing this evening.'

She was so drained that they had to give her a stimulant.

The Versailles was packed and when she came on stage looking smaller and more lost than ever in the spotlight, the whole room rose to its feet and applauded her.

Then she told her audience, 'No, there must be no applause for me this evening. I'm singing for Marcel Cerdan, and for him alone.'

That night Loulou slept in her room, he did not dare leave her alone, and in the morning when I arrived she threw herself into my arms crying, 'Momone, I killed him, it's my fault.'

It was unbearable.

12

LOVE CONQUERS ALL

Edith was convinced that it was her fault that Marcel had died in this terrible way. He was the greatest love of her life, and it was probably because of his untimely end that he remained so.

Poor Edith was inconsolable. She would not eat. She really wanted to die. She had to be given a stimulant every evening so that she could sing. She was like a crazed animal that had lost its master and was pining for him.

Then came an idea, born of this unhappiness and despair. Marcel had been dead no more than two days when Edith said to me, 'Listen, Momone, go and get me a round table with three feet. We're going to make it turn. We're going to try to make Marcel come to us. I'm sure he will. He's bound to hear me. Go quickly.'

So I set off. I went to a big store on Lexington Avenue, and I found a round pedestal table with three feet. Coming out of the store, I clutched the table to me with the feeling that it was going to be my salvation. I didn't know how, but I was sure of it.

After the Versailles performance that evening, we went home. The curtains were tightly drawn, we turned out the lights, put our hands on the table ... and waited all night. Suddenly Edith broke the silence, 'It's creaking, Momone, he's here. I can feel it. He's close to me.'

But nothing happened. The table remained firmly fixed to the floor.

We could see the dawn breaking through the curtains; it was getting lighter.

'You know, Edith, they never come in the daytime,' I explained.

'Don't they? But they do come at night, don't they?' She sounded like a child asking if Santa Claus exists.

'Of course, it's been proved.'

'I wasn't making it up last night. He *was* there; he brushed by me. Why didn't he speak?'

'It takes time. Perhaps it's too early, perhaps they can't speak straightaway. We'll try again tonight.'

I was saying the first thing that came into my mind. She was so tense, she believed in it so devoutly that she had almost communicated her belief to me. I began to think that perhaps he would come.

The next night was the same: nothing. Edith's face became more pinched and drawn with sadness. I was heartbroken. She still refused to eat but insisted on singing every evening. It could not last, she must collapse, she had already fainted between songs.

Sitting alone before the table I resolved, 'It must work, I'll make it work.'

Edith was living only for the moment when she could put her hands on the table each night. That evening I said to her, 'Don't worry, I feel he's going to come tonight. There's a new moon.'

'Why should he, Momone? I should never have called him. He won't come, he's abandoned me.'

I had had enough. I couldn't go on like this, either. 'It's impossible,' I thought. 'She'll go mad, and so will I. This damn table has got to move.' And so I raised it gently as we sat there.

Edith clung to it, sobbing with happiness. 'Is that you, Marcel? Stay. Come back, Marcel, my darling.'

I realized I had found a way to put the table to real use. First it would make Edith eat, then it would calm her down.

'Eat,' the table ordered her.

Edith didn't understand. 'Go and eat,' the table repeated.

Edith turned to me, astonished. 'Do you think that Marcel wants me to eat?'

'Of course; you'd better hurry.'

Edith rushed to the kitchen, opened the fridge and began to eat, just to please Marcel. I could have wept. I watched her as one watches a sick dog lapping up his milk. My scheme was working!

Two weeks later we arrived in Paris with Madame Bigeard and the table.

We spent some strange times during those first months in Boulogne. Edith was immersed in the spirit world. It was more than superstition; she was completely influenced by her dreams and her intuitions.

Predictably she had decided to get rid of the house. She did not like it any longer, though Marcel had spent little time there. In the meantime we had to go on living there, there was nothing else we could do. We couldn't just palm it off on someone. 'Get rid of it for me,' she had said to Loulou, but it was easier said than done. No one wanted it. She sold it three years later, and lost more than nine million francs on the deal.

Edith could never look at or touch the gifts that Marcel had given her. She ended up by giving them to the people who had been at that famous aquarium party. She was convinced that the joke had brought Marcel bad luck. She kept nothing for herself. Everything went, the ear-rings, the pin, all the jewellery Marcel had given her, all his things, even the trunks he wore in his fight against La Motta, still stained with the champion's blood.

She gave me the thing that meant most to her; the dress she was wearing when Marcel took her in his arms straight after the championship fight.

I still have it.

Edith thought only of the table. Every evening we clung to it. It was impossible to stop her, and it was still useful to me, for I used it to induce her to stop drinking. Marcel had always hated to see her drunk. So when she had been drinking the table kept silent. Not a word. She begged it to speak, but it was obviously angry with her.

It didn't only occupy her in the evening; it obsessed her during the day too. She was both suspicious and credulous. She mentioned it to Jacques Bourgeat, who replied guardedly, 'The world is full of strange manifestations whose cause we do not know.'

That helped Edith a lot.

Then she turned to me again, 'Do you believe in it?'

'I believe in everything I see.'

'All the same I need proof. I know what I'll do, I'll ask Marcel to write me a song.'

If one can pale inside, my insides must have lost their colour then. I knew at once that Marcel would not be writing that song; it would be me.

'You know, Edith,' I hesitatingly interjected, 'Marcel wasn't up to song-writing while he was alive.'

She gave me a withering look, and replied, 'Everything is possible where he is now.'

I couldn't get out of it; I was lost. All day I juggled words around and around in my head. Nothing came to me; I was as dry as the bottom of a saucepan hanging on the kitchen wall.

But that evening Edith demanded of the table, 'Marcel, write me a song.'

And the table replied, 'Yes'. From the beginning of our seances the table had an answer for everything. The table knew everything. As far as Edith was concerned nothing was impossible on the other side. Unfortunately, however, I was on this side.

Clutching the table, I summoned the first two lines:

> *Je vais te faire une chanson bleue*
> *Pour que tu aies des rêves d'enfant.*

Luckily for me the table's feet didn't move too fast. It took time to spell out the words and each evening I invented a couple more lines.

Then, at last, the table announced, 'That's the end.'

Although we saw Marguerite Monnot every day, Edith couldn't wait until next day to tell her the news. She called Marguerite on the telephone; 'Guite, come over right away. I have something for you.'

It was nearer to dawn than midnight, but Marguerite had no sense of day and night anyway; she came, with her hair all over the place and a coat thrown over her nightdress.

'Listen to this Guite, listen carefully,' Edith said. And she read to her, as though she was already singing it, 'La Chanson bleue.'

'Did you write that?'

'No, Marcel did.'

'When?'

'He just finished it a moment ago – on the table.'

'Don't say things like that, you give me the creeps. Shut up.'

Guite had always refused to come to our seances, but she knew about them. She sat down and murmured, 'We'll just have violins.'

To her violins were the music of the angels. Marguerite could already hear them, and so could Edith. My heart was beating wildly. I was overcome. I wondered if I was actually living this moment, or if it was indeed a part of the supernatural. Was I really responsible for it after all?

But as I watched those two women, face to face, sharing a moment of ecstasy, I had no regrets.

'La Chanson bleue' caused tears on more than one occasion.

For more than a year Edith had a weekly requiem mass sung for Marcel at the church at Auteuil. We all attended; there was no question of being excused, and besides I didn't want to be. One day, just before her concert at Pleyel, at the very end of the mass, the choir began to sing 'La Chanson bleue'.

We were speechless. Guite and I didn't dare swallow for fear of breaking down. Edith turned towards the choir; the tears were rolling down her cheeks. 'Do you hear that, Marcel?' she murmured, 'It's for you.'

After 'La Chanson bleue' episode, I hoped to put the table aside. If I could make it work for good ends there were others cruel enough to do it for profit. It was too tempting with Edith. Paris was not like New York, we were never alone. The house in Boulogne was like the one in the rue Anatole-de-la-Forge, if a little less so. It was something of a brothel, and there was no shortage of profiteers. Everyone who ran aground there was invited to the seances – when Edith got involved in something, all her 'friends' had to share her enthusiasms, they had to think like her.

The table had done a lot of talking, Marcel had been beside her every evening. Now Edith got the idea that she owed him something, 'Marcel's given me a song but I haven't given him anything. I'm sure he's waiting. He's too good to ask for it, but until I've given him something he won't be happy.'

And what about the rest of us?

She did it. That evening in our bathroom she sang a line from a song to me. Edith was really something – she often sang out of key (Michel Emer once said, 'Maurice Chevalier and Edith are the only people who can sing off key and still fall on their feet'), but she had a musician's ear, and she knew what sounded right.

'What do you think of my little tune? The title's going to be "L'Hymne à l'amour". I know I can write this song. It's singing in my head already, my heart's dancing with it. It's for Marcel. It's a pity I only have the title at the moment. I'm too dry. I can't think of the rest, nothing comes to me.' Suddenly I said: 'Listen Edith, I've got an idea; a few lines just came into my head.

> Si un jour, la vie t'arrache à moi.
> Si tu meurs, que tu sois lion de moi
> Peu m'importe si tu m'aimes
> Car moi je mourrai aussi
> Nous aurons pour nous l'éternité
> Dans le bleu de toute l'immensité
> Dans le ciel plus de problèmes
> Dieu réunit ceux qui s'aiment.

'Do you like it?'

'Did you do that yourself, straight off the top of your head?'

I said yes, but I was lying. Those lines had been running around in my head for some days; I hadn't known what to do with them and I couldn't think of an ending.

She rushed around finding the essentials, paper and pencils, and quickly the song progressed. That was how 'L'Hymne à l'amour' was born.

Edith had good ideas, and had always dreamed up pretty metaphors. Even in her early letters to Jacques Bourgeat she could write, 'So good-bye, my tame ray of sunshine.' But she had no patience, everything had to work out right away. She had to think up the story and the rhymes before she grew bored. I was patient and so I helped her. Edith had learned a lot, and I had followed in her wake. It was not exactly culture, but we were no longer ignorant. We had even read people like Baudelaire.

When she felt the words had been more or less licked into shape, Edith would call Guite.

'Hello, Guite, it's Edith, I must see you right away.'

Guite never said no. We would get half dressed and, as Edith's ideas always came to her while she was setting her hair, she threw a scarf over her curlers and out we went.

When we got to Marguerite's, Edith read her the latest. Guite listened, her hands already on her piano. And out would come one of her inimitable tunes, the kind that gets under your skin.

The night the music for 'L'Hymne à l'amour' was finished, Edith sat down at the table and said to Marcel, 'I've written a song for you. I want you to be the first to hear it.' And she sang it to him. It was very touching.

Then she said, 'I'm going to give a concert at Pleyel. I want you to tell me which order I should put the songs in, so that everything comes from you.'

You have to be in show business to understand what a heavy responsibility this is. The whole success of an act, and even more so of a concert, depends partly on the way the songs follow each other. The most difficult thing is to place those which have never been heard before.

I had never tried anything like this before. I couldn't sleep that night. The next day I made my list, tore it up and made it again. That evening I altered it according to Edith's reactions.

'You're not dumb, Marcel, you're a real genius. Do you really think that's right? I wonder if that isn't a mistake; I'd have it this way round instead. You think I'm right?'

When the list was completed, she decided he should also detail the lighting and false curtains. On that evening in January 1950, I, who never sweat, was soaking wet. You have to be pretty sure of yourself to give a solo concert in the Salle Pleyel. It was the first time that anyone had dared bring street songs into this temple of classical music.

For two days Loulou had been saying, 'There isn't a seat to be had, girls; standing room only.'

Florists and telegraph boys poured in and out of Edith's dressing-room. I had taken along some money for tips, but it was soon spent.

'Edith, I don't have any more change.'

'Give them bills, then.'

So I passed out bills as one would give out train tickets. For a fleeting moment I thought of our life of poverty in the streets of Paris.

I left the wings before Edith came on stage. I wanted to see the curtain rise on her. The auditorium was packed. All those people, breathing around me like a warm wind, their chatter sounding like the sea, deep and solemn.

The house lights went out and there was silence. The red velvet curtain rose. Behind it they had put another in autumnal colours to make the stage seem smaller. It was still too big for Edith. She looked so little that I was afraid we wouldn't be able to hear her. Yet her voice was so powerful that she filled the immense auditorium like a mighty organ. She sang 'Une Chanson à trois temps' without moving, standing straight with her hands behind her back. She was just a voice.

She sang 'Ses mains', 'Le Petit Homme', 'Je m'en fous pas mal', 'Escale', 'Un Monsieur me suit dans la rue', 'La Chanson bleue', 'L'Hymne à l'amour', 'L'Accordéoniste'. I knew them all, but I felt I had never heard them before. It went on for more than two hours.

During the interval I threaded my way through the middle of this dense crowd; 'Amazing', they murmured, 'Fantastic', 'Never heard anything like it', 'The greatest'. The words filled my ears and buzzed around in my head. I rushed to tell Edith; I poured out the words of praise like a bouquet of flowers. I think I was on the verge of tears. But she just laughed, looking at me as though we were back to our old bathroom routine: 'Calm down, Momone, it's me that's singing, not you.'

Mistinguett said, 'After the first song you go Ah!, after the second Oh!, after the third you really want to leave; after the fourth you find yourself weeping; and suddenly you've reached the twentieth without noticing it.'

Coming from Mistinguett that was praise indeed.

When the dressing-room was empty, Edith looked at me. 'I've never had such a triumph, but Marcel isn't here to share it. This evening there'll just be a table to murmur sweet nothings to me.'

I could no longer contain myself and I burst into tears.

Singing was Edith's life. It gave her everything, yet it made her more lonely than anyone. It was the solitude that great people like her so often feel, the solitude that clutches at your throat like a hand or comes at you like a punch in the stomach, the solitude that greets you when the applause is over; it is reserved exclusively for performers.

She once said, 'The audience is so warm down there in that black hole. It's as though all those people are taking you in their arms, opening their hearts to you and taking you in. You overflow with their love, and they overflow with love for you. They want you to give yourself to them. You sing, you shout, you scream your pleasure, you're beside yourself with happiness.

'Then the lights are turned off and the last of the crowd has left. But you're still in your dressing-room, still glowing. They're still in you. There are no more thrills but you're satisfied. You go out into the street. It's dark, and your heart contracts, you're alone.

'The people waiting for you at the stage door aren't the same as they were inside. They want something. Their hands aren't caressing you, they're asking for something. Their eyes assess you. "She looked better on stage," they say. Those aren't smiles on their lips; they're grimaces getting ready to bite. The actors and the public should never meet. Once the curtain has come down the artist should fly away like a magician's dove.'

I felt it too. The crowd claimed her and acclaimed her; and then, when we had passed the corner of the street and climbed into a cab, Edith took my hand, 'You see, now we have to finish the night alone.' And it was true. We went home alone and ate a solitary dinner. It was not always like that, but since Marcel's death we had spent some painful moments at Boulogne, with many lonely evenings because people no longer had such a good time at our house.

Once the curiosity and the table-rapping (which had amused some and profited others) were over, we found ourselves alone, like two shabby old spinsters in a beautiful town house.

I was not responsible for the last knocks on the table. They spelled out, 'News coming on 28 February.'

'Good news?' asked Edith.

'Yes'. We did not get any farther that evening. The next day the table started again. 'A surprise on 28 February.' 'Marcel, you've already told me that.' '28 February.'

'I understand, but what will happen?'

Edith clung to the table, shouted at it, begged it, but it maintained a wooden silence.

It was exactly four months to the day since Marcel's death. Who was using the table? What had that date got to do with it, and why?

Later I found out that it was Madame Bigeard.

I couldn't sleep on the night of the 27th. I wanted to be the first to know what was going on, so I could protect Edith. At eight o'clock in the morning the doorbell rang. There was a telegram for Edith. I opened it, as usual. She was scared of telegrams, she never opened them except on first nights.

It said: 'Come, I'm waiting for you, Marinette.'

So that was it. For months Edith had wanted to meet Marinette and get to know Cerdan's sons, but she felt it was impossible; yet today here was Marcel's wife actually summoning her.

I didn't hesitate to wake her up and read her the wire. I didn't even know if she was in a state to understand it or not. Edith leapt out of bed, threw on a coat, brushed her teeth, and in no time we were on a plane bound for Casablanca.

Marinette made us very welcome. They cried together, and hugged each other. The man who had kept them apart now brought them together. At the end of twenty-four hours the three boys, Marcel, René, and Paul, were calling Edith 'Auntie Zizi'.

We brought Marinette, her sister Hélène, and the three boys back to Boulogne. There was plenty of room. I found the friendship strange, but I was not surprised. I was used to that kind of thing with Edith. She never behaved like other people. She followed her heart and, when it commanded, she obeyed. Edith ran around after her heart all her life.

She wanted Marinette to look beautiful. She had a dress made for her by Jacques Fath, and gave her a white fox cape to wear with it. She was delighted by the result; 'Look, Momone, isn't she lovely?'

It was true, she was. It was one of the few occasions I ever saw Edith indulging another woman.

'Momone,' she confided to me, 'Marcel must be so happy. I'll ask him this evening.'

Marinette never dared come to the seances, and Edith preferred not to invite her. She wanted to keep the spirit of Marcel completely to herself.

We lugged that darn table around with us for three years; it had become a bit shaky with all the foot tapping, we must have had it stuck together at least two hundred times. We had a cover made for it. It was the first thing to leave with our luggage. At the theatre it waited for Edith in her dressing-room; sometimes she would even drag it into the wings with her, especially on first nights. It had become a good luck symbol. When Edith touched wood, she touched the table. Edith had believed in miracles since her childhood. She was right to do so. Right up until the end, her life was just that – a miracle. She had a child's spirit, and she loved to be told a good story. When you told her one, she would open her eyes wide, fold her hands in her lap, and listen enchanted. Then she would say, 'It's not true, it can't happen; but it's lovely.' The table was a bit like that. It was nice to have Marcel around each evening, to ask him questions. At the end she believed in it, without really believing. Yet she could not give it up. Nearly every evening for three years, as long as I was there, Edith would not go to bed without hearing the words Marcel had whispered to her when they were alone, and which I was the only one to know. She marvelled in it.

Then one evening the table abandoned her. Marcel had really gone over to the other side. 'This evening is the last time,' he said. 'Perhaps I'll come back later.'

I did not like Boulogne. We were not comfortable there. It was not that we lacked space; rather we had too much.

Our relationship with the house had started well. Edith had been happy when she bought it. 'Imagine, Momone,' she had said, 'a period house. Even the flagstones in the courtyard date back hundreds of years, and we have stables. And for the first time we live within our own four walls. They're mine. I could blow them up if I wanted to. I'm not a beggar any more, I'm living like a capitalist, a landowner.'

The interior decorator had obviously been carried away. The bedroom was princely. The walls were covered in lavender blue watered silk, and the cherrywood furniture was authentic.

For Edith and me it was like having our own castle right here in the Bois de Boulogne; our enthusiasm was understandable. Edith would take her visitors on guided tours. 'This is my room, the walls are covered in watered silk. Isn't it beautiful?' But her *pièce de résistance* was the bathroom, which was done in black and pink mosaic. To get into the bath you had to go down two steps. 'I don't give a damn about it myself, I never take baths, but I've got a swimming pool for my goldfish.' And she had. She put goldfish in because she thought they looked pretty against the black. But they did not stay long, once she decided that fish bring a house bad luck.

Edith's efforts had stopped after the bedroom, bathroom, and kitchen. In our absence, and in the absence of money, the decorator had refused to go any farther. And when we got back from New York, Edith didn't have the heart to continue with it – or anything else. So in the famous living-room that was meant to be Marcel's training-room there was never more than a grand piano and two linen-covered chaises-longues.

Edith had bought divans and stuck them just about everywhere so she could put her friends up.

At the entrance to our house there was a concierge's lodge. Edith furnished it very nicely with a sofa, a table, and armchairs. 'Since I'm a house-owner now, I should have some old stick around to answer the door when I ring. That way I'll never need keys. But I want her to feel comfortable.'

Luckily we never found our concierge, but Edith lived in the lodge herself; she felt at home there. For a long time the three-footed table was parked there in the middle of all the walnut furniture.

We had no tableware, no glasses, no silver, just a few odd

plates of various patterns, and some mugs that looked like mustard jars. We didn't care. We nibbled in the kitchen, under Tchang's eye. He was still around, and when he needed some peace and quiet he took refuge in the pantry. Much later, when Edith decided to give a formal dinner party, she hired everything from a store, chairs and waiters into the bargain.

The bathroom continued to be our 'living-room'. I don't know if it was the table's influence, but Edith had begun to believe in reincarnation. Now, as I put her hair in curlers, she would tell me about her past lives. I had Jacquot (Jacques Bourgeat) to thank for that. That man knew everything. When Edith wanted to know something, she called him. One day she asked him, 'Jacquot, do you believe in reincarnation?' He replied neither yes nor no. But since he had not denounced it to Edith as idiotic she believed in it. She was convinced she had been Marie Antoinette in a previous life, and I was Madame de Lamballe!

'I've gone into this very carefully. I can't have been anyone but Marie Antoinette. That woman had my character absolutely. I'd have thrown cake around like that too. They complained because she spent so much. Well, so what? It's not worth being a queen if you have to count your pennies like everyone else. And Fersen, I'm sure he had blue eyes; all those men from the North do. And if I was Marie Antoinette, you must have been Madame de Lamballe!'

She was absolutely positive about it. 'There's no doubt at all. Those are the only women in the world we can be compared to. Can you think of any others?'

I could only think of one thing – poor Madame de Lamballe, whose head was presented to her friend on the end of a pole. It made me go cold all over. I also knew that Edith's ancestors and mine had been peasants; they didn't have any boots, they blew their noses with their fingers, and they sang the revolutionary song 'La Carmagnole'. I couldn't understand why, if we had once been on the more attractive side of the fence, we had not stayed there.

'There's no connection, Momone,' Edith explained. 'You can

come back as anyone. Jacquot told me that it's a question of sins. If you've been very bad, you make up for it in your next life.'

'Well, we must really have been pretty bad then!'

When Edith made *Si Versailles m'était conté*, she sang 'Ça ira', which I thought was very funny, but it was less than complimentary to Marie Antoinette. Edith replied as only she could, 'If Marie Antoinette had done as I do and sung about it, she would have kept her head on her shoulders.'

All this helped us pass the time, but Edith still hated to be alone. Whenever there was no man in her life, things went badly.

In spite of the table's steadying influence, she really went off the rails for a few weeks. Some evenings she would be seized by an unnatural rage. We would go out to Pigalle. She loved to go back to her old haunts. We'd take a few rides on the carousel, buy pastry pigs and call them Edith and Simone, and end up at Lulu's in Montmartre. We always found men-friends whom we could invite to come home with us. I can't remember any names now; in fact we forgot them by the next day. We must have got through ten or fifteen, perhaps more, in a month.

Sometimes, when we didn't have a man, we'd go to the Lido, order champagne and ask some of the dancers to join in. They were flattered to be at Edith Piaf's table. 'Come home and make us some *frites*,' Edith would say, and they'd laugh, not believing her; but she was serious. She would ship them all off to the house and the girls would very sweetly make us chips. We drank a lot to help them down. Then we'd give some money to the dancers to make up what they'd lost out on their evening. We all had a good time, and so went to bed.

The next day Edith would say, 'Momone, I made a fool of myself again last night. But I can't come back to this barracks all alone at night.'

We felt so forsaken that Edith even went back to singing in the street. 'Come on, let's put on some old clothes. I'm feeling so low, I must do a street again.' She threw herself back into the street as others throw themselves into their mothers' arms. The extraordinary thing is that no one recognized her. Nobody could believe that this was the great Edith Piaf. We would hear remarks like, 'She sounds like Piaf, but you can easily tell it's not. What a difference!'

It made us laugh, but we never met a Louis Leplée to give us a contract. Finally we went to live at the Claridge for a week and there we really gave them a run for their money.

Edith got more drunk that week than she had ever done before. Even the table, which we had dragged along with us, was power-less over her. She would swear never to drink again, but she always found a good reason to evade her oath. Once when I saw her looking at a bottle I said, 'Don't forget your promise.'

'I know, but actually I meant I'd never drink again in the living-room, not in the bathroom.'

And she proceeded to get drunk in the bathroom. When she had used up all her excuses, she cried, 'But, Momone, I never said I wouldn't drink in Belgium.' And we took the train to go and drink in Brussels!

Each morning around six or seven we would crawl home, more or less on all fours. Once there was a man washing down the foyer. Edith made a sign and we both jumped into the bucket of water. I've never understood how we both managed to get in without upsetting it, but it certainly cooled off our feet. Edith got out of the water first, and said in English, 'I am a dog.' I repeated, 'I am a dog.' And since we were little boy dogs, we lifted our legs gaily against the wall. All this took place in front of the lift boy, the night porter, the receptionist, and the clean-ing woman.

Finally we landed in our room, and my dear Auntie Zizi chose that moment to have a nervous breakdown. She needed people around her, no matter who, just people. She grabbed the sheets and tore them to shreds. I was so scared that first time that I sobered up enough to say, 'She's going to die, she's gone mad.' I rang all the bells at once. I picked up the telephone and shouted, "Madame Piaf is dying.' That gave them a shock, fancy having the audacity to die in their hotel, their smart hotel! They all rushed in and soon Edith was surrounded by people.

They called the doctor. He found her lying on the bed, very pale. She opened her eyes and winked at me. The doctor ordered piles of stuff and the bellboy left for the chemist's at a gallop.

When the doctor had gone, Edith ordered champagne and invited all the staff for a drink.

She enjoyed that trick so much that she repeated it several times.

Edith Piaf left the Claridge some vivid memories. Perhaps she didn't always behave *comme il faut* on those nights, but I at least understood why. Edith was desperate for love. Who would fill the gap that Marcel had left in her life?

PUBLISHER'S NOTE

Edith Piaf is about to enter the second part of her life and we witness her downfall – drugs, alcohol, madness, accidents, illness, operations – it is a grim honours list of pain and the struggle to overcome it. One wishes to shout 'Enough!' One is overwhelmed by horror and pity. But while others might have foundered without protest in the depths of despair, Piaf retained her amazing courage. Her art was in effect purified. So frail, yet so strong, we must forgive her everything.

This child-woman, born on the pavement, raised in a brothel, and taught in the streets, captivated a man no less than Jean Cocteau. At the time of his first heart attack, when he was close to death, he wrote a touching note to his friend Edith.

This too is part of the Piaf miracle!

Book Two

25 May 1963

My Edith

I don't really know how I escaped death, it's a habit of ours. I embrace you because you are one of the seven or eight people I think about lovingly each day.

— JEAN COCTEAU

Book Two

13

SOJOURN IN BOULOGNE

Life in Boulogne was the time of comings and goings. Nothing had any solidity; nothing was really good. I don't know why, but the men we met in those days were either married – perhaps because they were old enough – or they only interested Edith for the talent she recognized in them, like Charles Aznavour and Robert Lamoureux.

Robert was one of the people that Edith called her 'meteors'. For a few moments they glittered in her sky, filling it with light, then they fell back to earth, like a cold stone, never to be mentioned again.

That is how we watched Robert Lamoureux's fortunes rise and fall. It started out as a business meeting. One day he turned up at our house, with his good earthy face, his big body balanced on outsize feet. He was wearing a check jacket even worse than the one Yves wore at the Moulin-Rouge.

He came, like many others, with a bunch of songs to sell. They all began like that. It was easy. If you wanted to see Edith, you didn't need a reference, you just had to say you had a song under your arm.

Edith liked him right away. 'That guy's got talent, he's got a career ahead of him. I'm going to give him a push.' And several months later she did.

Robert would have liked to have got off this professional footing into something more intimate, and I would have been pleased. He was nice, and good-looking into the bargain; when he smiled his whole face seemed to crack open, it made you want to go for a ride on a merry-go-round with him; he was made to take girls to carnivals.

Robert took a real fancy to Edith. And if nothing happened between them it was not for want of ... let's say wooing. But only his talent interested Edith; the rest didn't appeal to her.

It was the same with Charles Aznavour. Their relationship was strictly professional.

One day Edith overheard someone say, 'I've found a great new place, Le Petit Club on the rue Ponthieu. There's a bunch of musicians there, jamming, and fooling around. They sing and play the piano. It's a lot of fun.'

'Let's go,' said Edith. When she got something into her head, she could not wait five minutes.

It was true, it was a nice place, very friendly; you felt as if you were sitting in your own home. We met Francis Blanche there – thin as a rake, he quickly became a good friend and later wrote Edith a marvellous song, 'Le Prisonnier de la tour'; Robert Pierre and Jean-Marc Thibault; Darry Cowl, who was an excellent pianist – the difficulty with him wasn't to get him to sit down in front of the piano, but to dislodge him later; and the Roche–Aznavour duo.

'What do you think of those two?' Edith asked me.

'Not too bad.'

'You're wrong. The little dark one with the ugly nose is a natural. He's got what it takes.'

Ten minutes later, when Charles Aznavour was chatting with Edith, she came straight out with 'Your nose looks terrible on stage, you'll have to change it.'

'It's not a tyre, I don't have a spare!'

'Come to America with me, I'll make them fix it for you.'

We were, at most, six months away from our next trip. Charles was flabbergasted. So was I, though I should have been used to Edith's whims by now. She had not known him for an hour and already she was talking about taking him to America. I'd better get a closer look at this character. At first glance he didn't look like one of Piaf's men; he didn't even have blue eyes. What had he got, then? I found out pretty fast.

'You write songs, don't you? The one you just sang, "Paris au mois de mai", was that one of yours? You've got talent.'

That was it. Edith spotted anyone who could write songs for her.

She immediately set him straight about his duet. 'It's old-fashioned. Pierre Roche isn't bad, but he drowns you. Less of your personality comes through, and his isn't enough to over-power you completely. You're not going to get far that way.'

Charles was annoyed. He liked Pierre, and was always very faithful to his friends.

'You must split up.'

'I can't do that. Later, perhaps. He's going to Canada for a while. We'll see about it when he comes back.'

'Come and see me when he's gone,' advised Edith.

Within a week Charles was installed in the Boulogne abode on a little divan that would have cramped a thirteen-year-old. Edith made him comfortable. 'You're like me, you don't take up much room.'

That set the style for their relationship. Charles brought out the 'Auntie Zizi' in Edith; she would not let him get away with anything. He endured the special treatment, like me; I was the maid-of-all-work, he was the man-of-all-work.

Before he had even had time to settle in properly he was driving the car, carrying her suitcase, accompanying Edith when-ever she wanted him. From morning to night you heard her, 'Charles, do this. Charles, do that. Charles, did you call so and so? Charles, have you written any songs?'

To get some peace, Charles had to hide himself in places where she could not see him writing. He was never satisfied with what he did, and threw away little snatches of songs all over the house. I gathered them up, and I still have them.

Charles did try to write for Edith. He put all his talent into it, and all his heart, but it didn't work out. Edith's songs were like her men, either they clicked, or they didn't. She sang only a few of his compositions – 'Il pleut', 'Il y avait', 'Un Enfant', and 'Plus bleu que tes yeux'.

One evening Charles handed her 'Je hais les dimanches' – it was one of her bad days. 'Is that for me? Do you honestly think I'm going to sing that shit?'

'You don't want it, then,' Charles mildly replied. 'Can I do what I want with it?'

'You can stick it up your . . .'

So Charles quietly took it to Juliette Greco, who immediately put it in her repertoire. When Edith found out she really went off the deep end. 'Are you giving *my* songs to Greco?'

'But, Edith, you told me you didn't want it.'

'I told you that? Do you think I'm an idiot? Did you tell me you were going to take it to Greco?'

'No.'

'So you think you can double-cross me? You haven't heard the end of this...'

Edith's dishonesty was quite overwhelming.

Charles had started off on the wrong foot with Edith. He said yes to her all the time, and that was a mistake. You never agreed with everything she said, only then would she respect you. You also had to know how to cheat on her sometimes, unless you wanted to be devoured entirely. But Charles couldn't; he was too honest, too clean, too pure. He admired her so much that when she abused him, he simply said, 'Edith is the greatest, so she can do what she wants.'

Like a carrot dangled in front of a donkey's nose, she kept the image of America dangling before him. 'It'll do you good to go there. They really know what show business is about.' Charles would raise his eyebrows, his eyes would grow round; looking like a dog dreaming of a bone, he sat and listened to Edith talk about her travels and experiences.

If Charles had become Monsieur Piaf, everything would have changed. He didn't turn Edith on physically, and I thought to myself that if I pushed them together a bit, perhaps they would finally make out.

One evening when Edith had had a bit to drink, and Charles had too, some friends and I decided to undress Aznavour and put him in Edith's bed. While they were taking care of him, I fussed around the 'bride'.

'Do your hair better than that. Put some perfume on. Put on your prettiest nightdress, the one with...'

'What's the matter with you this evening? You're running around in circles.'

'I want you to look beautiful.'

'I can't imagine what for.'

'You never know.'

'You think someone's going to come down the chimney?'

I went into her room with her, but the bed was empty. We had failed.

Charles would never let himself be coerced into it. I think he loved Edith too much, and he was too good.

Luckily for us all, Edith's bed would not remain empty much longer.

She was doing a show at the Baccara. One evening a strapping great fellow with massive shoulders strode in to see her. In pidgin Franco–American slang he told her that he had written an English version of 'L'Hymne à l'amour'. It wasn't a bad idea. Edith was still singing the song.

He had a good face, although pitted with scars and pockmarks which added to his masculinity. He had a nice smile and a far-away look in his eye. Right away I thought, 'Now there's one man who might stand a chance.' The trouble was that we only picked up about three words in ten. Perhaps conversation can be dispensed with during an affair, but it does help at the beginning.

'Listen,' Edith said to him, 'that's a very good idea.'

'For you?'

'No. Not for me.'

'I'm very sorry.'

'Don't be, we'll work something out. Call me.'

Very much the tough American, he waved two fingers in the general direction of his hat and said, 'Okay. Tomorrow.'

As soon as he had gone Edith started to roar with laughter. It was months since I had heard her laugh like that, the laugh that Henri Contet described so well in an article:

Suddenly an enormous, magnificent, pure laugh breaks out, gushes into the room and fills it with joy. Edith Piaf comes towards me, clings to me, and laughs and laughs until she can't breathe any more, until you think she is going to suffocate right there on the spot. I see her extraordinary face close to mine, with the expressions shifting, and changing colour. I see her eyes like a deep sea, her curved forehead, and that monumental laugh which possesses her, and pushes out through her lips as if it is glad to be bitten by those little animal teeth.

It was good to hear it again. We were coming out of the doldrums. I could have kissed that fellow.

'Well, at least we won't get into any deep discussions with him. What's his name, Momone?'

'I couldn't understand what he said.'

'Don't worry, we'll have plenty of time to find out.'

The next day someone called up, and I said to Edith, 'There's an Eddie Constantine on the phone, he wants to speak to you.'

'Don't know him. What's he want?'

'To show you his songs.'

'Tell him to come over.'

Two minutes later we had forgotten all about him, until that afternoon when the bell rang.

'Charles, open the door,' shouted Edith.

It took us a moment to realize that the visitor was Eddie Constantine. He had been afraid to call us himself because he felt we would not understand his accent, so he had got a friend to do it for him.

That was how Eddie came into Edith's life.

Under his toughness, there was a very tender heart. He seemed to know instinctively how to handle Edith.

'He's really gentle, Momone. He told me that he had a very special feeling for me. Isn't that nice?'

'And you understand him?'

'I'm getting there. You know, his songs and the translation of 'L'Hymne à l'amour' were just an excuse to meet me. What do you see in him that's different?'

She liked me to admire her men, and to discover their unusual qualities. My mind went quickly to work, like an ant in the heat of summer. I wanted to say I was pleased she had found a new man at last. That was essential. Physically he was certainly okay, but for the rest she would have to take her chances. So I pulled out the most impressive sentence I could come up with, 'Edith, he's got a heart.'

A heart! We hadn't had one of those yet! She was happy.

In any case, he did have the one thing Edith needed – two arms to hold her tight.

And, inevitably, he became the new boss.

The handing over of power never presented much difficulty. Edith had a man. He sat in bed like a pasha while she said to the chambermaid or cleaning woman – depending on which she had – 'This is your new boss.'

The affair had to be at least two weeks old before this happened. The boss wore a chain and medallion around his neck (usually it was St Theresa of Lisieux, but if he was not a Catholic he could wear his sign of the zodiac). Beside the bed lay the cuff-links, watch, and lighter from Cartier's. The suit, draped over a chair, would be of good quality, but in some unbelievably lurid colour, unspeakable to look at and even worse to wear. The tie would go with it, if you noticed it at all next to the suit; we bought several dozen at a time.

Blue was Edith's favourite colour for men, because of their eyes! It was too bad if they had brown eyes; as far as she was concerned they were still blue.

Charles Aznavour always tells this story. 'There was never any difficulty in recognizing Edith's man of the moment. Whenever he went out with her he wore a blue suit. One evening she in-invited several of her old flames over together. They all wore blue to please her. There were eight of them, looking like a troop of scouts. Edith leant towards me and said, "I'm not in the least bit annoyed, you know."'

She also had a passion for shoes. She always chose them in crocodile, but unfortunately more than one of her men suffered as a result of Edith's rather simple opinions about feet. 'People who have big feet are stupid.'

Only Cerdan and Montand resisted her. All the rest wore their crocodile shoes one size too small. She really made her men suffer!

She was tyrannical, impossible, difficult to live with, but only in little things; for the rest, she allowed herself to be led. Edith sometimes paid dearly for her dreams where men were concerned. She was not always taken in, though. 'What upsets me is that it's not me they love. Not old Gassion's daughter. They wouldn't give her a second glance. They're not in love with me, but with my name and what I can do for them.'

In the meanwhile we had a new one. I warmed to Eddie the first time he slept over. I found him in the bathroom washing out his nylon shirt. He had only one. Fortunately, that didn't last long. In our house they were bought by the dozen.

Eddie was nice, but apart from his tough looks, his appearance was against him. He believed in Paris, but Paris did not believe in him yet.

He was of Austrian origin, born in Los Angeles in October 1915 into a family of opera singers. His father, grandfather, cousin, and nephew all sang. He had no difficulty in choosing a career. His ambition was to 'make great music', and he won a prize at the Vienna Music Conservatory as a bass.

He returned to California with a swollen head, and it wasn't until he had sold newspapers, delivered milk, and been a parking attendant that he finally succeeded in getting a spot on the radio – seventeen times a day he extolled the virtues of a brand of cigarettes. That made him. They gave him Coca-Cola, chewing gum, and a funeral home. Then, still singing, he furthered President Roosevelt's electoral campaign on the radio; and while he was at it, he switched sides and did Dewey's too.

Singing advertising copy does not allow for much creativity. You're a bit like a talking clock. You say the same thing over and over, there are no surprises. So Eddie, who wanted a few surprises in life, left his wife Helen – without too much difficulty, they were already on the verge of a break-up – and his daughter, Tania, and came to Paris to try his luck. He thought that after the war an American would go down pretty well in Paris. Since his face, his build, and his accent gave him away, he didn't have to drape himself in the stars and stripes to make his nationality known.

After an amateur try-out at the Paris-Inter, Lucienne Boyer engaged him for the Club de l'Opéra. He did a little act with Léo Marjane and Suzy Solidor. It was better than singing the praises of chewing gum, and with his build he could take care of himself. But it wasn't El Dorado.

Edith gave him his break, as she did so many others. She had an amazing flair. She sensed talent where no one had yet seen it. Appearances did not bother her. She visualized what the people who approached her would be in five or six years' time, and that was what she was thinking about as she was helping them.

Edith always enjoyed men who wanted success; who were obsessed with it. Constantine was no Yves Montand, but he was a personality all the same. Edith started off by making him learn French. It was becoming an urgent need for a number of reasons: conversations were not over-long, and Edith had never enjoyed saying the same thing twice. You had to understand quickly and have your reply ready.

Even in his tortured French Eddie had been able to tell Edith all about his life. He didn't keep a thing from her. She knew he was married and separated from his wife, and that he adored his daughter Tania. One thing was certain: his marriage with Helen was over, he never gave her a moment's thought. 'I'm glad that he broke with her well before he met me,' Edith said to me. 'This time they won't be able to accuse me of breaking up the marriage. At least he's free. And it's easy to get a divorce in America.'

She always gave herself to her men in this way, swallowing whatever line they chose to hand her. The tall stories slipped down like sweet liqueurs, very sticky, very sugary, with just enough alcohol at the bottom.

One afternoon a boy called Leclerc came for an audition. Constantine was there, so he listened in. Leclerc sang nothing but love songs, floods of love songs. You could have drowned in the waves of sentiment.

In the middle of the act, Constantine got up, his eyes full of tears, and went out. Edith dropped everything and rushed out into the street after him. She was sure that Eddie had left like a fool because he had finally understood that she loved him. The tears in his eyes proved it.

'I caught up with him, Momone, and asked, "What's the matter, darling?" And do you know what he replied? "I'm thinking of Helen."'

Edith was quite pale when she got back. 'It's nothing, it only lasts a couple of seconds, a couple of words. But they're long seconds, and you have to recover from them afterwards.'

She received more than one blow like that, and each one hurt.

That was what you were paying for when you had to go along with her crazy fads. When we were in a restaurant she would pick up the menu and order authoritatively for everyone. There were times when it helped her get her own back on someone. Several days after the love songs had made Eddie weep for his ex-Helen, several of us went to a restaurant.

Edith ordered ten *jambons persillés*. It was her latest gastronomical discovery, and each evening we were expected to stuff ourselves with it, and no complaints. Constantine asked for sausage. We were kicking up quite a row, and no one noticed. When Edith saw that Eddie was quite calmly about to eat something other than the sacred dish, she started shouting, 'You really must be mad, eating sausages!' and grabbed his plate. 'Here, taste this,' she said to the others. Everyone tasted a little bit and said, 'It's awful.' When the plate found its way back to Eddie it was empty. He was not given anything else.

We no longer had to go to the Lido to fetch dancers so that we had some company; our house was mobbed. It was carnival time. Everyone was getting ready for the next show. Edith was preparing for her fourth trip to America and a two-month tour through France.

Pierre Roche had not come back from Canada, and she had decided to take Charles on tour with her before going to the United States. 'I want to see how you do alone on the stage. It'll do you good.' Naturally Constantine was included in the celebrations.

The house on the rue Gambetta was like a factory, with Edith, Constantine, and – when he had the time – Aznavour, rehearsing like crazy.

In addition there were the musicians and friends, Léo Ferré and his wife Madeleine, Guite, Robert Lamoureux, who came to pay his respects whenever he passed by – he had not given up entirely and he was right – and others, people I had never seen before who always used the same old trick, 'Madame Piaf will know me, I'm a friend.' It used to make me laugh because Edith would tell me to throw them out.

In the middle of it all I made coffee and chips, lugged bottles of wine around and cut up sandwiches at all hours of the night. It was fun. It would have been even more fun if I hadn't had worries of my own! Before long they were bound to be noticed. I was pregnant. Luckily Edith hadn't realized it yet.

It had been planned, in fact, but I didn't dare admit that to Edith. Then one morning I decided to take the plunge, 'Edith, I'm going to have a child.' She wasn't angry, worse than that. 'Momone, it's not true. You can't do that to me.' Just what a real mother would have said!

Naturally she told Constantine straightaway. He was very sweet about it. 'But, Edith, that's marvellous. *Très* marvellous. God sends little children. *C'est* very happy. It'll bring the house good luck. *C'est beau* for a woman to have a little life growing inside her. It's very touching.'

Edith had not looked at it that way. As far as she was concerned I had betrayed her. Wouldn't I love this child more than her?

Two minutes before, she had not even wanted to set eyes on my future child; three minutes afterwards she was ready to bawl me out for not having given birth already!

'I feel as though it's my own child, Momone. So you better not do anything stupid. You make the baby good and strong while it's inside you. You mustn't look at anything ugly or he won't be handsome. And I'm going to look after your diet myself.'

She would not leave me alone. When we were at the movies she took my hand, and if she felt that the picture was improper – bad for the baby – she would squeeze it, 'Momone, don't look.'

It was like that all the time. 'You must drink beer, it's good for your milk.' I wondered how I was expected to feed the baby myself; my breast would have disappeared completely into his little mouth.

Ever since Henri Contet, Edith was always putting on an act about the baby she wanted to have; and when she assessed a man she asked herself if he would be a good sire. But it wasn't completely an act. It still broke her heart to think that her little girl had died in poverty and that now when she had some cash she could not have any children.

It was a heaven-sent opportunity to trot out the turning table, too, and find out if my baby would be a girl or a boy. And the good old table replied, 'A boy, and you must call him Marcel.'

Now Edith loaded Charles with a new job – being my nurse-maid. 'Charles, go with Momone. I'm putting her in your care. You are responsible for her and the baby.'

And at all the clubs we went to, as my stomach grew larger and larger, Charles would offer me my chair, hold my handbag, watch my drinks. 'No alcohol, it's bad for her,' Edith had ordered. It must have made poor Charles really mad, having to parade around with a woman who was pregnant up to her eye-brows. But he did it all the same.

If Charles forgot to take my arm in the street when Edith was there, she would shout 'Charles' so loudly in that famous voice that all the passersby turned round.

Charles carried his cross without complaint right up until the last moment when I went into labour, though he was even more impatient than I for the whole thing to be over.

Several days before the baby was born, Edith got nervous, 'It mustn't happen while I'm away. If you're sure of the date, you're due very soon. It can come on you very suddenly. I'm going to tell Charles to take your suitcase around with him.'

So not only did he have to hold me up with one arm, but now he had to drag my suitcase around with the other.

'You should be pleased,' Edith said to him. 'It's something to have a pregnant woman on your arm.'

I shall never forget Charles's kindness.

The approaching birth had not changed anything in our life. Edith still took me everywhere with her. At seven o'clock one morning we were dashing gaily out to a cabaret with the rest of the gang, when I stopped short on the pavement.

'This is it, the pains are starting.'

'Let's go,' ordered Edith.

We set off. I was clinging to Charles's arm for dear life, Edith followed with Eddie and our friends, and soon we all arrived at the nursing home. It was very funny, in spite of the pain in my stomach. The nurse kept calling Charles, 'Monsieur', and he didn't dare say, 'But you're wrong, Mademoiselle, I'm not the father.'

No maternity ward has ever seen an entry like ours. We swept in like a boozy wedding party, and Edith regally told the nurse, 'We're the family.' The poor girl had obviously never met a family like this.

Once I had been put to bed, my 'family' crowded into the room. 'We're not going to abandon you, Momone,' Edith said charitably. 'So hurry up, because I'm tired.'

Hurry up! There was nothing I wanted more. I was not seeing very clearly by then.

'While we're waiting for you, we'll go off and have some champagne.'

The hospital was spared an occupation by Edith and her forces because they didn't happen to serve champagne. So they left, Charles promising to call them as soon as there was any news.

I was pretty fast. By ten that morning I'd brought a fat baby boy into the world; we baptized him Marcel, and of course Edith was the godmother.

That damn table was right again.

When I got home, Edith went on tour with Eddie, who was included on her programme, and Aznavour. She wanted me to go, too, but I preferred to look after my son. Still, I joined them for a couple of days whenever I could.

That tour was a real trial for poor Charles. I began to wonder if maybe he was enjoying being a martyr.

Constantine still had a dreadful accent, and he wasn't exactly a raving success in the provinces. That drove Edith crazy, and Charles got the worst of it. She gave him all the jobs to do; he took care of Edith's luggage, looked after the props, and saw that the stage was properly set up. And on top of that, he had to go on before the others.

'Charles, you'll go first. We'll need you backstage during the show.'

And Charles, under-rehearsed and barely dressed, would rush

with all the ceremony he could muster on to the stage to do his little turn for an audience which couldn't have cared less.

He was really whistling in the dark, but it seemed to please Edith. And if things went better for him one evening, the next day Edith would command, 'Tonight you can take the second and fourth verses out of your song. Don't sing them.'

'But, Edith, it won't mean anything,' Charles would protest.

'I know what's best for you. There's no point in you staying on stage too long, they don't like you.'

And Charles obediently would make the cuts. The song meant absolutely nothing. As he was trying to pull himself together after a miserable performance, Edith would say delightedly, 'You see, I was right. Even like that your song's hopeless.'

Charles laughed, a bit sourly as he explained to me, 'It doesn't matter. It's teaching me my job.' And he plugged on in spite of everything. He was fed, housed, his laundry was done, and he was writing songs. No more scrappy meals. This was what he wanted. He was getting ready for his future.

One evening after they had gone back to Paris, Charles came in dressed from head to toe in black. He had a new suit, and he was pretty pleased with himself, reckoned he looked very smart. Edith soon put a stop to that, 'Are you copying me now?' she demanded.

'But, Edith . . .'

'Shut up. I've just ordered a suit like that for Eddie. I'm not going out surrounded by men in black. It'll look as if I've hired a couple of undertakers. Go upstairs and take it off.'

And he did.

Of course she had not ordered a suit like that for Eddie, but she realized that when Charles wore black he had a quality like her own, and she couldn't stand it. His singing got on her nerves, too: 'The Piaf style's okay for me, but it's not right for a man.'

She was being unfair. In all the men she moulded from Montand to Sarapo, you could see Piaf-like gestures, and hear her intonations. But not in Charles. Yet he was more like her than the others, and that was what angered her. She knew very well that if anyone was going to move an audience like her, to get them in the heart and in the guts, it would be Charles.

I liked Charles a lot. He was a real friend and one of the few people who were completely honest with Edith.

It was getting near the time to leave for America. We were living at fever pitch. Eddie let the storms roll over him. Charles ran around in all directions. It made him laugh. 'I only need the coolie hat,' he told me, 'and bells on my feet to look like a one-man band.'

Edith worked, sang, shouted, shook up Guite, Michel Emer, Henri Contet, and Raymond Asso, in fact all the composers who came to hand. She took English lessons, rehearsed the songs that had been translated, and learned little introductory speeches off by heart. In between times she gave performances in night clubs and music halls, and dragged me along to Jacques Heim and Jacques Fath. She certainly wasn't going to arrive bare-arsed this time. She had twenty-seven dresses, coats, and all the accessories, plus seventeen pairs of shoes. And she had decided that I must match her grandeur. 'I'm not going to have you looking like a tramp. I'm going to take you to Jacques Fath. Do you remember, Momone, when I used to tell you I'd buy you dresses from the great couturiers?'

I was the mother of a family, but to Edith I was still a teen-ager. She made me wear a net over my hair and no make-up. 'You're like me, simplicity gives you class. You have the face of a virgin.' There was nothing better, of course, than to look like her.

Jacques Fath and Jacques Heim made dresses for Madame Piaf which cost millions of francs, and which she never wore. I have seen her spend three million francs on dresses in half an hour. When they were delivered she rushed to try them on. But as soon as she was no longer surrounded by clucking saleswomen she decided they were ugly.

We had hardly got through the door of Fath's saloon when the circus started.

'Quickly, get Madame Piaf's dresser. Go and warn Monsieur Fath.'

'I'm not going to try anything on today, it's for my sister. She's coming to New York with me. We'll have people to see, parties . . .'

'Of course, Madame Piaf,' said the vendeuse. 'I understand, I am Madame Hortense.'

'I'm going to leave her with you,' Edith said regally to Hortense, 'do the same as you would if I were here. I have complete confidence in you.'

Her confidence was well placed! They chose for me, and I was not allowed to say a word. 'That's absolutely you,' they cooed. But they must have been giggling inside because, as the whole world could see, they'd turned me into a performing dog.

Before we left for the United States, Edith decided to give some dinner parties. 'It's essential, I'm going away for two months. This way they won't forget me.' And indeed, no one who came to one of those dinners was likely to forget the occasion.

She decided to invite Michèle Morgan. This was really because she wanted to see Henri Vidal, with whom she had had a little fling when they shared the bill at Montmartre-sur-Seine, when Vidal was not yet married to Michèle Morgan.

The furniture, the table, the chairs, the silverware, the plates, the tablecloth, and the waiters were all hired.

'I'm starting with Michèle Morgan,' Edith explained, 'because she's high-class but not affected.'

Michèle certainly was well brought up, and it was just as well. When the waiter started by throwing the lobster Thermidor down the front of her dress she roared with laughter, much to our relief; throwing the lobster down her front was going a bit far.

Everything was carried out in defiance of the normal routine. We couldn't all have coffee because we did not have enough coffee cups of our own, and we had forgotten to hire more. So before Michèle Morgan arrived Edith had decreed who should have coffee, and who should not – Charles and I were to go without. Naturally Charles was very tense, and when he was offered coffee he said yes. Immediately Edith thundered down the table, 'Not for Charles, it keeps him awake!'

I discovered that evening that Michèle Morgan was an exceptional woman. After dinner I had a telephone call from

Marcel's nurse, telling me my little boy was sick. Since he was quite far away in the suburbs, I telephoned every hour to know how he was. And Michèle Morgan, whom I had met that evening for the first time in my life, stayed behind when the others left for a night club, and sat up with me all night. I was nervous about my son, but in the midst of my anxiety I thought about Edith; I was afraid she was planning to get off with Henri Vidal.

When Edith got back with Henri at dawn, Michèle appeared to find it quite natural, and I thought that perhaps after all I had a dirty mind.

When they left, Edith said to me, 'You know, Momone, I really respect that woman.' Believe me, respect was not a sentiment that came easily to Edith.

We had just a few days to go before we left for New York, but they did not pass as I expected.

First of all, and for the first time in my life, I refused point-blank to go with Edith. She started to bawl me out, but I had expected it.

'I will not stay away from my son for two months.'

Constantine, trying to smooth things over, suggested I join them later.

'If she doesn't leave with us now she won't be joining us anywhere.'

Then Charles chimed in, 'Look Edith, she's right. Her son's still a baby. But that's a good idea of Eddie's. Simone would join us later.'

That was a mistake. 'What's it got to do with you? You aren't coming either. I'm going to Canada first and there's nothing for you to do there.'

The storm was at its height; the lightning struck all around. For the first time Charles stuck to his guns, 'I don't care, Edith, I'll join you in New York.'

'Like hell you will.'

But she didn't know Charles as well as she thought. She had not been in Canada a week when she received a cable: AM BEING HELD AT ELLIS ISLAND. SEND FIVE HUNDRED-DOLLAR BOND. AZNAVOUR.

Charles had kept his word and gone to America. But the trip went badly. He was travelling steerage like an emigrant, and since he had no contract and no money, the Emigration Control had welcomed him to the camp at Ellis Island.

Edith was delighted. It was the kind of thing she enjoyed. 'Little Charles isn't as stupid as he looks. He managed to get across.' And, naturally, she paid the bond.

I had taken a stand, but it couldn't last. Marcel was well looked after by his nurse, and I was dying to join Edith. 'The bitch,' I thought to myself, 'she's quite capable of letting me rot here.' When he left, Eddie had said to me, 'Don't worry, you'll come.' He had had time to forget, but nevertheless he sent me my ticket for New York. It was kind, but I suspected he had another reason.

I hadn't been there more than three days when Eddie started to look really depressed. It was a bad sign. It could not go on much longer.

'What's the matter with you? Why are you sulking?' asked Edith.

'I'm not sulking, Edith. It's just that it'll be Christmas soon and I can't see my daughter in California.'

'Why not?'

'My wife won't let me.'

He wasn't so stupid; he knew how to handle her. Edith flew into a rage, heaped insults on his wife and ordered him to go and see his child at once.

On the morning that he left Eddie whistled while he shaved. As she was putting him into the taxi, Edith said a little drily, 'Don't forget to come back.'

'There's no danger of that.'

Before the taxi had even turned the corner she shrugged her shoulders, 'Momone, I think I've been had.'

'No, he's going to see his daughter.'

Everything went very well. He called to say that Tania, his daughter, was beside herself with joy at having her daddy home, etc., etc., etc. I thought he was rather overdoing it, and I could see Edith was not swallowing the story either.

Charles pestered Edith to let him go and join Roche in Canada, but she wouldn't hear of it. 'No, you'll never get anywhere with that friend of yours. Leave him alone.'

As always, Edith was right. But Charles was an honest and faithful friend, and he was stubborn.

'I can't do that to Pierre. We've been through too much together.'

'Look, there's nothing for you to do here, you aren't helping me. I promised you I'd have your nose fixed. It'll give you time to think things over, straighten out your ideas. When you have a new face, you'll think differently ... And while you're in the hospital, you can adapt "Jezebel" for me.'

This was an American song, sung by Frankie Laine, which Edith was very fond of. Charles did adapt it, and turned it into one of the greatest successes of the time.

Once again we were without a man. But Edith had her own idea on the subject and the idea this time was called John Garfield.

She could fall in love with someone at the drop of a hat just by seeing him in a film or on stage. One evening she took me along to the theatre to see *Hamlet*.

She said, 'There's a man in this I really like. I noticed him before. I must get a closer look at him.'

And so every evening before going on to the Versailles, we went to look at and listen to John Garfield in Shakespeare. And worst of all, I did not understand a single word, and Edith was hardly any better off. The only person I understood was Edith saying, 'Oh, Momone, he's so handsome, so handsome.'

I don't know how many times we sat through that damn play. After ten I stopped counting. Charles was already up and about with his new nose in plaster, but we continued to go to the bloody theatre.

'I'm studying him,' Edith said to me in all seriousness. 'This way he won't be able to escape me.'

He didn't escape her. She got what she wanted – to be in his arms.

Afterwards she said to me, 'We made it, but that was the most difficult one of the lot.' And I could not disagree.

The morning after her happy night with him Edith waited for

John to call. Nothing. No one came that evening, either. The next day and the day after there was still silence. She was furious. A month later, as we were preparing to leave New York, the telephone rang. A man's voice asked, 'Hello, who's this?'

'This is Edith.'

'This is John.'

'Oh, is it? You've got a nerve calling me now!'

'See you tonight,' he said, and hung up.

But it didn't work. Eddie had been back for some time, and Edith had lost interest in John. So that evening when John swept in as if he owned the place, he found me instead of Edith. He figured she was angry, but he never could understand why.

When Eddie got back from the bosom of his family he looked to me like someone who had been playing around, pleased with himself and guilty at the same time. Since Edith herself was not above reproach after her night with John Garfield, she did not ask him too many questions. Charles's new nose was the main subject of conversation.

'Do you like the way you look?' Edith asked him.

'Well, it's different. When I catch a glimpse of myself in the mirror I think, "There's someone I know," but it takes me a second to realize it's me.'

'What do you think of him, Momone?'

'Wonderful.'

'And you, Eddie?'

'He's a new man, marvellous.'

But Charles said, 'I wonder if they'll notice the change in Paris?'

Before we left there Edith had a nice surprise: she met General Eisenhower. He had come to hear her at the Versailles, and, like Princess Elizabeth had done in Paris, he invited Edith and Eddie to his table. Eddie was very proud to meet the man who a few months later was to become the President of his country.

It was all very friendly. Edith was flattered but not out of her element. A general was not to be compared with a princess. The General asked Edith to sing his favourite song, 'Autumn Leaves'.

She had never sung it before, and I was scared she'd muck it up, but it went off very well.

The General knew a lot of French songs and he kept asking, 'Do you know this one? What about this one?' enjoying himself thoroughly and singing along with her.

We were getting ready to leave. Eddie and Charles were both coming with us. Everything had been worked out painlessly with Pierre Roche; he had married a Canadian girl, Aglae, and she didn't want to leave her log cabin, so Charles and Pierre were able to separate without any ill-feeling.

Edith was delighted. At last he belonged to her alone. 'Charles, trust me, you'll see I'm right.'

We did see. Edith was driving him to despair; she was no longer worried that he would leave her, therefore she could do what she wanted with him.

As soon as we got back to France, Edith slipped across to Casablanca to see Marinette and kiss the three boys, Marcel, René, and Popaul. She couldn't spend much time there though, because *La P'tite Lili* was waiting for her, back in Paris.

There was quite a story behind that musical comedy. It had been in the works for two years, and when it was finally performed *La P'tite Lili* was a personal triumph of will-power for Edith.

Everyone involved in the show was dragging his feet. None of them wanted to work with the others. Mitty Goldin, the all-powerful director of the A.B.C., had ordered Marcel Achard to write a musical comedy, *La P'tite Lili*. Marcel Achard told us about it. It was tailor-made for Edith. She wanted Raymond Rouleau to produce it. Raymond Rouleau declared that he would never set foot in a show that belonged to Mitty Goldin, and nor would he ever work with a text by Achard. The author insisted that Lila de Nobili design the sets, but Goldin would have nothing to do with her. Marguerite Monnot was the only person they all agreed on.

'Momone, they're driving me mad. I've decided to do *La P'tite Lili* at the A.B.C. with Raymond Rouleau, on a set designed by Lila de Nobili, and I shall do it. They talk big, but I'll show them who can shout loudest!'

I didn't believe she could do it. I had sat through one or two of their abortive meetings, and they were so violent and vindictive about each other I was sure they would never be able to work together.

But I was wrong. It was just an act. They finally agreed when Edith said, 'I'm bankrolling the show, and I'm giving the orders.' But what a business!

When casting started everything broke down again. Edith had decided that Eddie should play Spencer, the gangster. Physically he had what it took, but otherwise it wasn't so good. Mitty wouldn't have anything to do with him. 'He walks like a dancing bear and his accent is terrible.' That was pretty funny, considering that after thirty years in Paris Mitty's accent still left plenty to be desired.

Raymond Rouleau finally persuaded Mitty, saying, 'We'll cut the part down. Gangsters don't talk, they act!'

The song-writer Pierre Destailles was supposed to play Mario, the lead. But the whole thing had dragged on so long that he was no longer available, so Edith proposed they hire an unknown singer called Robert Lamoureux. On this point at least the others were all in agreement – unanimously they did not want him.

But when Edith had discovered someone with talent, she did not forget him. Mitty and Raymond tore their hair. 'Two newcomers on the billboard, I'm ruined!' cried Mitty, who had very little at stake anyway. 'I'll never make it,' said Rouleau.

The situation already promised to be amusing – but Marcel Achard had kept the best bit till the end. For two years they had been arguing about an unwritten play. We knew only the title, *La P'tite Lili*, and the songs. Marcel Achard had thoroughly enjoyed writing them, and at least Marguerite had been able to compose the music.

'The music and songs are all that count in a musical comedy – the rest's just filling,' said Edith, who hated having to learn her lines.

Marcel Achard was delighted that she understood him so well. Only Rouleau's nose was out of joint; he reckoned that he really didn't have enough to work on.

On the day of the first rehearsal Marcel strolled in very much at ease, his eyes flashing wickedly behind diver's goggles – he wore enormous spectacles. He had brought a few sheets of paper, and these he handed round.

'Here we are, children, this is the first scene.'

'But I need the whole play if I am to direct it at all,' cried Rouleau.

'Don't get upset, it's all in my head.'

Ten days later Marcel Achard had been brought to bed with a fine healthy *P'tite Lili*.

I never missed a single rehearsal, and for good reason – Edith had given me a part in the play. I was one of the dressmakers, and in the first act I had an exchange with Edith; I had to say, 'You're not going to make us believe you're a virgin!' Each time I said it, we became helpless with laughter.

When Achard arrived each morning, followed by his wife Juliette – an extraordinary girl – with the sheets of paper in his hand, everyone crowded round him, showering him with questions.

'Am I the murderer?' asked Eddie.

'Do I marry *La P'tite Lili*?' Lamoureux wanted to know.

And Marcel Achard replied laughing, 'You'll find out at the end, children, just like the audience.'

Rouleau used the delay to turn Spencer (Eddie's part) into a non-speaking one.

Despite a new onslaught of lessons, and the best will in the world, Eddie still had a terrible accent. Rouleau, undaunted, would say, 'Say *terrible* again. You can't say it? It doesn't matter, old boy, we'll take it out.' And he crossed out the entire exchange, which was not at all to Edith's liking.

'Now don't worry about Spencer,' said Raymond very calmly. 'It's all in his biceps, the way he wears his hat and uses his face and fists. The play will be a success, and Constantine won't lose anything.'

Then Mitty threw in his two cents' worth, 'There's no sense in him singing, it slows up the action.'

That did it. The scene that then erupted in Mitty's office shook the seats in the A.B.C. with its vibration, you could have heard Edith's voice on the boulevard Poissonière.

'Do you think I'm a complete fool? You bastards! Your bull-shitting makes me sick. Because Eddie doesn't understand French very well you're trying to cut his part down to nothing. He will act and he will sing or you can forget about the play. I'm ready to pay the penalty.'

She went on and on, longer and louder than before. Finally they gave in to her. Rouleau shrugged his shoulders, and Mitty said, 'I shall never set foot in that theatre again. It doesn't belong to me any more.' For a week he refused to come into the audi-torium or to speak to Edith.

Perhaps Edith would not have stuck up for Constantine if she had known about the surprise he had in store for her. We were in the middle of rehearsals when, one morning, Eddie took the breakfast tray out of my hands. 'Let me do it, I'll take Edith her breakfast.'

It was the first time he had ever done that. Usually it was Eddie who had his breakfast brought to him.

He felt that what he had to say to Edith could not wait, but he was no psychologist. If you planned to wake Edith up with bad news, it was advisable to carry a shield.

'Edith, I, er, think I should ... at least ... that's to say ... er ... I've sent for my wife. She's coming to Paris.'

The words were hardly out of his mouth when he received the tray, coffee, sugar, and all, full in his face.

She attacked him in true Piaf style, as only she knew how.

'That was why you wanted to see your daughter, was it? You bastard! You cheated on me with your wife, you shit, you low-down ... no-good ...'

I shall cut her off here. When he had visited his daughter in California, naturally Eddie saw his wife too and they had decided to give it another try.

Edith did not want to admit it, but she was hurt, though it was only for a moment, since she had forgotten about it by the next day. Unfortunately she did not have time to refill the ranks. We were too close to the premiere of *La P'tite Lili* to find a replacement.

After he had left Boulogne, sure that all was forgiven, Eddie told Edith he would like to introduce her to his wife.

'Of course,' she replied. 'Bring her along to the rehearsal tomorrow.'

Edith went to great lengths with her appearance that day. 'I don't want to look plain beside his American.'

Judging by what we had heard from Eddie, we expected her to be one of those dream creatures that only the United States can produce.

When we got to the theatre, I saw a marvellous-looking girl standing in the shadow close to Eddie; she was blonde and as elegant as a model. There could be no doubt, it was her. Edith hung back. Constantine turned around. On his other side stood a homely little woman, with a plain hat on her head and her hair done in coils over her ears. This was the one he introduced to Edith. The other was Praline, one of the most beautiful girls in Paris.

It gave Edith such a laugh that Constantine was completely forgotten as a lover, although they remained good friends.

On the first night of *La P'tite Lili*, Edith was very nervous for him. Her worries were not entirely unfounded. Physically he was perfect, his shoulders were exactly right. But by the time his lines reached the audience, they were a bit moth-eaten, full of gaps. The audience made out as best it could. But Constantine's triumph came when he sang.

If I had been his wife, I would not have been completely happy about it. He held Edith too close and too naturally as he sang:

> *Petite si jolie*
> *Avec tes yeux d'enfant*
> *Tu boul'verses ma vie*
> *Et me donn' des tourments.*
> *Je suis un égoïste*

> *Voilà jolie petite*
> *Il ne faut pas pleurer*
> *Le chagrin va si vite*
> *Laisse-moi m'en aller.*

He was cheered and gave an encore. It was a success. I, who knew the truth, thought that those words fitted Edith like a glove.

The final song was Edith's big success. She adored it. On the first day she heard it, she said to Achard, 'That's the story of my life, Marcel, though it's a bit too optimistic. If I ever write my autobiography, I shall put your song at the beginning of the book:

> *Demain il fera jour*
> *C'est quand tout est perdu que tout commence*
> *Demain il fera jour*
> *Après l'amour un autre amour commence*
> *Un petit gars viendra en sifflotant*
> *Demain*
> *Il aura les bras chargés de printemps*
> *Demain*
> *Les cloches sonneront dans votre ciel*
> *Demain*
> *Tu verras briller la lune de miel*
> *Demain*
> *Tu vas sourire encore*
> *Aimer encor', souffrir encor', toujours*
> *Demain il fera jour*
> *Demain*

The reviews were excellent. *La P'tite Lili* ran for seven months. And it would have run much longer if Edith had not had her first accident, which heralded the beginning of her dark days.

There was one curious thing about *La P'tite Lili*: someone who had already seen it could return a week later and see a different play.

Edith had no memory for her lines. They bored her. A story which spread itself out over three acts was too long. When she forgot a bit she simply threw in the first thing that came into her head.

Eddie, for his part, had difficulty in remembering all the French words, so he either translated them into English or he abridged them.

Robert Lamoureux, who was a great joker, would answer them in his own way – but he had to keep his wits about him.

It was very *commedia dell' arte*, terrifically lively. Everyone enjoyed it, and it is thanks to Marcel Achard's musical comedy that Robert Lamoureux and Eddie Constantine got started. But they had Edith to thank for putting them in the play in the first place, and Eddie, who was a good guy, did so. He wrote in his memoirs:

Edith Piaf taught me everything – me and several others – about how a singer should behave on stage. She gave me confidence in my-self, and I had not had any self-confidence until then. She made me want to fight, and I had never wanted to fight. On the contrary, I had drifted along. In order to turn me into someone, she had to make me believe I was someone. She had a sort of affirmative genius in hammering home a personality. She would repeat endlessly, 'You've got class, Eddie. You're a future star.' Coming from her, a star of the first order, that affirmation galvanized me.

What Constantine never did know was that Edith not only gave him confidence, she also gave him money. When Mitty hired Constantine, he paid him two thousand francs, while Eddie thought he was making five. Edith made up the difference, and he never knew it. She had done the same thing at concerts and on tour. She was happy to be able to say to him, in good faith, 'Your fees are going up. That's good, sweetheart, it means you're getting more important.'

That secret way of giving and helping someone in whom she believed – that was Edith.

14

A TIME OF DARKNESS

For the first time, Edith had been taken unawares. A replacement for Constantine was not far off, but he was not there yet. He was not yet installed.

When André Pousse arrived with Loulou, I liked him straightaway. He had the sensitive-hooligan good looks of someone like Belmondo, and a good firm handshake. He was solidly built; he almost seemed to be formed out of concrete with a heart inside. He had a nice smile, and his first words told us he was a Parisian.

He was a well-known bicycle racer, now retired. In that profession, unfortunately, your legs give out faster than in others. He wanted to try his hand at show business. With Edith he jumped into it head first. He couldn't have found a better partner.

André had come to see Edith at the A.B.C. during *La P'tite Lili*. He had the right kind of shape, and Edith took a good look at him – and then burst out laughing: 'I know you!'

'Yes, we met in New York in 1948. I was the champion cyclist then, I was racing at Madison Square Garden. I came to hear you at the Versailles with my team-mate Francis Grauss. I needed a breath of Paris. It was great, listening to you. Then I shouted out "L'Accordéoniste", and you laughed, and said, "There's a Frenchman in here..."'

'That's right, and afterwards we all four, you and your friend and Loulou and I went to a French restaurant for steak and French fries.'

Charles and I took bets on André's chances. They seemed pretty good. But we did not see Pousse again after the meeting in her dressing-room, and Edith did not mention him, which was a bad sign. And, as always, when she was in the trough of a wave, there were a lot of one-night stands. Charles and I would have been delighted if she had stopped partnering all-comers in her frenzied, lonely dance. She lived each day as if it were her last. Even little things, little pleasures, were sucked dry by her single-minded passion. When we were all sated and nauseous, she went on with all the enthusiasm of her first mouthful.

Marguerite Monnot had taught her to like classical music. One day Edith happened to hear Beethoven's Ninth Symphony on the radio, while Guite was there. Edith looked at us all accusingly, 'Guite, why didn't you make me listen to this earlier? Charles, have you heard it before?'

'Yes.'

'So I suppose you think it's too beautiful for me to listen to? Go out and buy me the record immediately.'

She looked at us as if we had betrayed her, we all felt guilty, even I, who knew nothing about it.

Naturally, we listened to the Ninth Symphony for weeks. The minute someone got to the house, she would say, 'I'm going to let you hear a marvellous piece of music.' And so that he would appreciate it to its fullest extent, she played it two or three times in succession. She turned the gramophone up so high we all had earache.

It was the same with books. We all had to read the ones she liked and talk to her about them for hours. In addition, she would read aloud the passages to which she felt particularly drawn. I still know whole pages of them by heart – *Via Mala*, *La Grande Meute* [*The Great Chase*], *The Old Man and the Sea*, and *The Sound and the Fury*.

One book struck her particularly, a complicated thing about relativity, atoms, and neutrons, a real treasure trove! It was more difficult than *Madame Bovary*, but Edith liked it. 'You see, this stuff's difficult to understand. When you read it you realize that who you are and what you do amounts to absolutely nothing at all. But at the same time, just because you are so unimportant, you become big, as big as the world. Do you understand what I mean?'

I said yes, but only to please her. I did, however, share her opinion when she said, 'That Gide is really something.'

It went on for days. Luckily for us she did not read very

much. Her eyes tired easily and her work took up a lot of her time. It was not only rehearsals, she never stopped working – when she was in the street, or in a restaurant, she looked around her and listened, she got her ideas out of everything.

She never went to art galleries, but Jacques Bourgeat had somehow succeeded in familiarizing her with the great masters. Edith's enthusiasm knew no bounds.

Edith adored the cinema. When she liked a film, she would buy a whole row of seats and take all her friends. Charles and I were used to it. The others dropped out along the way, but she still dragged us along. We saw *The Third Man* nineteen times.

Our only bit of luck was that she had taste. But we weren't allowed to cheat, we had to arrive at the beginning of the movie. 'You see, Momone, the beginning prepares me for *my* part.' She only went to a film for the part that carried her away. 'In *The Third Man* there's a moment when Orson Welles raises his eyes. Don't miss it.' It turned out to be the last shot in the film.

When there was a man in her life, we at least had time to breathe while she was busy with him.

I knew that Charles would not last much longer. He was staying on with Edith out of an enormous bond of friendship; however, quietly but effectively he was beginning to cut loose. He spent all his evenings at Carrol's, he was not particularly well paid – two thousand francs – but he was having quite a success. That did not stop Edith from giving him advice, 'Charles, when you face an audience, you're shy. You've got what it takes, but you'll have a beard down to your toes before you've got together enough money to buy a Rolls.'

Perhaps, but while we were waiting for that to happen it was her good fortune that he had been saving money. Someone came to turn off the gas, and we hadn't a penny in the house. We all went through our pockets – nothing. The maid had had more than she could take. Madame owed her too much. Edith borrowed money from her at the end of every month. Then, without a word, Charles bounded up the stairs, four at a time, to the comfortable little room on the second floor where he had wound up, and came downstairs again covered in glory, bearing three one-thousand-franc notes.

Edith was touched; since Cerdan no man had dipped into his pocket for her. She didn't give a damn about the cash, it was the love that mattered. If the electricity and gas were turned off, what fun! she would move into the Claridge.

This sort of story seems hard to credit especially when you remember that Edith was already earning between three and five hundred thousand francs an evening. But it's true, and it was that way right till the end, when she was earning a million and a quarter francs an evening.

Loulou was tearing his hair in desperation. One day he came in looking completely beaten and fell into an armchair. 'Listen, Edith, you can't go on like this – you'll ruin yourself.' Edith laughed. 'But I am and I don't care either – you should do the same, just laugh about it.'

'I can't, Edith. But what do you do with your money?'

'I don't know,' replied Edith. 'Do you, Momone?'

It wasn't any good asking me, I was as bad as she was. I never took any notice. I think we took so little care because even during our most poverty-stricken days we had always found money somehow. We had always scraped up enough to eat, drink, and laugh together. We knew how to make it, and we saw how it went away; what we did not know was how to save it, and above all *why* it should be saved.

'Look, Edith, perhaps one day you'll need your savings to fall back on.'

'Are you joking? or are you pulling my leg? I shall always sing, on the day I stop singing I shall die. Understand that, Loulou? I want to make you happy, but I'll never save money. I'm not a housewife. I don't have to give a damn about the future, it'll take care of itself.'

Loulou tried to believe her, but he was doubtful. Then he had a bright idea, and brought it to Edith while it was still hot.

'Edith, why not have two bank accounts? Each time that you deposit money, you put half in each account; but you'll only draw money for your expenses out of one of them. You'll behave as if the other one didn't exist.'

'That's not a bad idea at all; that way I'll have a bit of money on the side to spend when I want to,' mused Edith.

The deposit side worked impeccably. Madame Bigeard handled it very well. Edith was radiant. Old Bigeard kept her accounts carefully. 'This system of Monsieur Barrier's is very good,' she said to Edith. 'By now we should have already saved three million francs.' Edith roared with laughter. There wasn't a penny in either account, she had used it all up. Instead of drawing on only one account, she had used both.

In Edith's hands money was like water or sand, it just poured through. It was impossible to keep a check on the money she spent in a day. There were always at least ten of us in the restaurant we went to every evening after the A.B.C. The same gang also visited several night clubs, and in each one we had a bottle of champagne each. If Edith was on form she bought a round for the whole club. That's where it went. And the gifts, the professional expenses, the friends, the cars, and the rest, all that cost a lot of money. And finally, the taxes were no small burden.

Some friends suggested she bought a farm just outside Paris, it would be amusing and nice to have somewhere to go 'en weekend'.

'Paris poisons you,' she explained. 'Some country air would do me good.'

The very idea of Edith on a farm in the middle of all those cows, pigs, and chickens was worth the expense. She bought a farm for fifteen million francs at Hallier, near Dreux. To make it habitable she poured in an additional ten million.

She spent no more than three weekends there in the five years she owned it. When she finally sold it, she got six million for it.

It was nearly a month since she had seen Pousse. Then one day she asked me in the bathroom, 'Momone, what do you think of that Pousse?'

The reply came out all on its own, 'He's a real man.'

'He is, isn't he?' said Edith, in seventh heaven, getting ready once again to clamber on to the merry-go-round of love. 'I'm going to invite him for the weekend.'

The weekend bit was new, she had never done it before. But apart from that, everything went as it usually did. When they came back from the country, Pousse came home with Edith to Boulogne, and he stayed for a year. Some weekend!

I liked Pousse a lot. He was very honest, and always thought of Edith's interests, and not his own. Like Loulou he did not want her to throw her money around, he even scolded her for the gifts she bought him. 'You're absolutely nuts. I can't wear more than one suit at a time. I'd understand if you waited for an anniversary or a birthday or something, an excuse for giving presents but you throw them around . . .'

'If it pleases you, isn't that a good enough reason? Stop complaining, I promise you that the others didn't make such a fuss.'

But André had brains under all the muscles. He was quite right when he said to me, 'Edith pretends she's in a movie all the time; she has to believe in love, she can't live without it, so she kids herself that she's *in* love. But it isn't often true. That's why she does such crazy things.'

Crazy things! He was right there, and this led to some serious quarrels. Edith never gave him any peace until he had slapped her. André wasn't a brute; he was very gentle, but some things are too much for a man to swallow.

We would set off to spend an entire afternoon together with some other fellow, and come back feeling pretty pleased with ourselves. André was not. 'I will not be treated like a fool!' he shouted. He was no sophisticated intellectual; no amount of sweet talk could pacify him. He was straightforward, and he saw only one thing, Edith had cheated on him. He would throw real temper tantrums in the middle of the night, and chuck all Edith's presents out of the window. I had to go out with a friend and pick it all up by the light of passing cars – jewellery, watch, clothes, he threw out everything that came to hand.

Afterwards when they had calmed down, they would both go quietly to bed, while I was still down on all fours on our antique flagstones, recovering the loot.

Edith was always switching moods, and that upset André; he found it difficult to follow her. One day we brought back about fifty red balloons, all bearing the inscription, 'André, the shoe maker who knows his business' [André le chausseur sachant chausser].

'Where'd you get all those?'

'Go and look in the car,' replied Edith.

It was full of patent pumps.

'You see, André, when I was a kid I never had any balloons of my own. I saw the other kids showing theirs off as they pranced around. Their shoes were as round, as clean, and as shiny as their red balloons, and I was doing the streets with my old man. I was dirty and scruffy; to them I was a bum. Today they were giving away a balloon with each pair of pumps. I bought enough to fill the house.'

All evening she played with them under Pousse's moist and kindly gaze. He was a sentimentalist, but he did not know it.

Edith left and I stayed at Boulogne. Pousse wanted to be alone with her, and I wasn't sorry to be left in peace. I waited quietly for their return and, because it was Edith, we called each other several times a day.

On 24 July, she called me earlier than usual. We chatted for a while, then she finally said, 'I've got something funny to tell you: with a little less luck I'd have been calling you from heaven. This morning I was sleeping in the back of the Citroën, Charles was taking the turn at the Cerisiers when we went off the road, flew into the air, and ended up in an apple tree. Isn't that funny?'

I tried to catch my breath so that I could summon enough to laugh.

'Don't worry, Momone. I'm fine, nothing happened at all, I'm not even bruised. If you could have seen what Charles and I looked like, lying side by side with our noses buried in the grass! We didn't dare look at each other; we got the shakes when we saw little pieces of car scattered all over the place. Honestly, you should see it. There's nothing left at all. It's hanging to the tree like a piece of scrap iron. But you know, as long as St Theresa's on my side nothing can happen to me.'

I was much less sure than she was. It was the first time that Edith had been in an accident. Now, every time that damn telephone rang I leapt into the air. Three weeks later she called again; she sounded strange and far away, 'Momone, guess what? They've just built a little plaster house for my arm. Now don't worry, everything's okay. But I'm coming home, I can't sing with my arm in a cast.

'André was driving. He isn't hurt. We were close to Tarascon. Charles and I were fast asleep in the back of the car, we didn't see a thing. We skidded on a turn, and there we were! See you tomorrow.'

I was dreadfully worried, waiting for her to come home. I would have been even more so if I had known that these two consecutive accidents meant Edith's luck had run out.

When I saw her emerging from an ambulance, her face all white and strained, her eyes full of fever, I realized she had lied to me. As well as the broken arm, she had two ribs in plaster which hindered her breathing.

'I have to go to the hospital, Momone, come with me.'

She was in great pain. She, who was hardened to all suffering, lay groaning for hours. The pain ceased only when they gave her the injection. 'Those injections are doing me good. Thank God for them, I couldn't live without them,' she said later.

What Edith did not tell me was that she was starting to develop a taste for the drug. She did not talk about it. She was so sure it would not last that, once the pain had gone, she would not need them any more.

We had not been at the hospital more than two days when she said, 'The food here is disgusting, ask Tchang to make me something to eat.'

So every evening I went to fetch her meals from the house. She would not let anyone else do it.

One evening when I got to the hospital, André Pousse was waiting for me in the corridor. 'Listen, Simone, this can't go on. I should be by Edith's side, not you.'

'Okay. I'll take her these books and say good-bye.'

'No, you shouldn't see Edith. If you say good-bye, she won't let you go. Let me take care of it all alone. If you love her you should leave now.'

I decided that maybe he was right; I gave him my books and left. The thing that got me was that each time one of her men wanted me to make myself scarce, he arranged it in such a way that it looked as if I had walked out on her. I knew that I would see Edith again because she always called me back. Poor Pousse, he would have done better to keep me, he did not last long after I left, not even a few weeks.

Every day one of his friends, 'Toto' Gérardin, another cycle racer, went to the clinic to see Edith, on the pretext of distracting her, but actually he was quietly double-crossing his friend.

Of course I found out about all this when Edith got back to Boulogne. She had given André the push and had asked me to come back.

It was a familiar tune; a bit too familiar. I was no longer alone, I had my own life, a child. It did not stop me from loving Edith, but it made me think. I needed to breathe and most of all I needed my freedom.

It was annoying that André was no longer there. He was strong; he might have stopped her from sliding backwards. The business with the injections was beginning to worry me. While she was in the hospital, I could be sure that they would not give in to her.

Her arm was still in a cast; she was breathing better, but not well enough to be able to sing, and when Edith was not singing she was capable of making all sorts of trouble. As long as she had a private nurse at home things did not go too badly, but she didn't keep her for long.

'Why don't you have a nurse any more? Who'll give you your injections?'

'Don't worry, Momone, there are a lot of people around me, and I can give myself the injections.'

I could not know that all the new friends I saw prowling around her were the kind of people who charged a high price for a little capsule.

Toto came to see her every day, as he had done at the hospital. He was handsome and slim, with a kind of cold look in his eye and strong cyclist's legs. He was much better looking than Pousse, but not as straightforward and uncomplicated. And he didn't stand up to Edith; he was weak.

He told her that he couldn't live without her, that before he had met her he had never been in love. He was no shrinking violet, he went to great lengths to protest his love. He was pedalling hard, he moved along fast and achieved his goal – he came to live at Boulogne.

Edith, now out of her plaster, was better, and looked as if she was ready to make a new start.

This illusion did not last long.

There was a Madame Alice Gérardin who was not at all happy with the way things stood. In December she accused Edith of being her husband's accomplice. Her husband, she said, had left their conjugal home, taking with him several items which belonged to her. A charming list followed, read by an unsmiling Police Chief. Edith listened, torn between rage and raucous laughter: 'Championship trophies in precious metals, bracelets, necklaces, pendants, rings, pins, a porcelain vase, a mink coat, eighteen kilos of gold ingots, the contents of the family safe . . .' There can be no theft between husband and wife, but Edith was accused of being an accessory and a receiver, no less.

Edith told me what happened.

'The cops went into Madame Bigeard's room, rummaged through her closets, messed up all her papers. She always avoided having any trouble with the Gestapo, but she got her ration of it from our own cops. She was white with rage. They were beginning to get on my nerves, so I took them straight to the room where that idiot [Toto] kept his stuff. There were also several bronze busts of my cyclist. He was so proud of them he couldn't wait to bring them to me. The chief said to me, very seriously, "I'm not looking for proof of adultery, but of receiving." So I let them romp through all the rooms. They left empty-handed and not very happy. It would have been a field day for the cops if they had finally been able to get their own back at Piaf after fifteen years.'

Perhaps I was not in a very good humour, I found it hard to laugh at this.

The affair with Toto dragged on for another few weeks. Alice Gérardin had hired a private eye to follow Edith; she was amused at first but, when the novelty wore off, got angry. Besides, ever since the days when she sang in the streets, Edith had been able to smell a cop fifty yards away.

Once more she was alone.

Poor Edith, those lonely nights passed slowly in her beautiful town house. Charles was no longer there, Madame Bigeard and Tchang had left too. This was the time when the new friends drove out the old.

Edith could not bear to be alone. Silence scared her. 'I tell you, Momone, at night in this damn house I can hear the minutes falling; a terrible noise. It tears my heart.'

She used to go into the streets and wander into bars, just so that she could have people near her; and she started to drink.

And now she, who loved life so much, wanted to die.

I had been there since morning; Edith was depressed. She had started talking to me about her mother, about Dad, then about Marcelle. I did not like that at all, it was a subject we were usually too ashamed to discuss.

'How old would my baby, my Marcelle, be now? Do you remember how she used to look at me, and how she laughed?'

It hurt me to listen to her. She went on and on about her baby. At lunch she did not eat a thing, and hardly drank. And that day she really would have needed it. I hated to hear her talk about the baby. I had always taken the parts that she wanted me to play, but that evening I could not replace her little girl.

She told me that Guite and Francis Blanche were going to stop by. I waited impatiently for them, I felt uncomfortable alone with her.

At last they arrived, practically at the same time. They had hardly been there ten minutes when Edith left the room.

'What's the matter with her?' Francis asked me.

'I don't know, she's got the blues.'

'We mustn't leave her alone,' said Marguerite.

Coming from our vague Marguerite, that was serious. We went to look for Edith, and found her hiding in an empty room on the third floor.

When she saw us she rushed out on to the balcony. 'Why are you spying on me? I'm hot, I'm going to get some air.'

The three of us exchanged glances. We did not like the balcony idea, but no one dared say anything to her.

Suddenly she started to scream, 'Fuck off, leave me alone, I'm sick of you all spying on me, you make me sick.'

Francis and Marguerite murmured to me, 'Has she been drinking?'

'No,' I replied. 'Not much.'

Edith clung to the edge of the balcony, staring into space. She did not seem drunk; she was quite steady and her speech was clear. There was something like hope in her eyes.

We stayed there, waiting to see what would happen. This depression was not like the others. Suddenly Marguerite leapt to her feet, yelling, 'She's mad, she's going to do it.'

Edith was already astride the balcony, half hanging out in space. Marguerite grabbed her arms and tried to hold her. Francis went up to them. I was chilled with fright. I went closer but Edith cried, 'Leave me with Marguerite. Go away.'

Each time we drew near she started to struggle and Marguerite had difficulty holding her. We went out. Half an hour later, Guite had finally managed to bring her to her room, and between us we put her to bed.

That night I stayed at her side. I talked about songs, show business, her career, I don't know if she heard me. Then she started to make plans, and I realized that it was over.

Before she fell asleep she said, like a child, 'Forgive me, you know I didn't mean it.'

When she said that, I knew that she *had* meant it; but why? If I had known that morphine was the reason I would have stayed with her, but Edith had said, 'It's all over, I've stopped taking the drug. I'm not in pain any more so I don't need it.' And I was stupid enough to believe her.

15

THE LOVE FEAST

Car tout était miraculeux,
L'églis' chantait rien que pour eux,
Et mêm' le pauvre était heureux!
C'est l'amour qui f'sait sa tournée,
Et de là-haut, à tout' volée,
Les cloches criaient: Viv' la mariée!

When Henri Contet wrote 'Mariage' for her, he had captured everything that marriage meant to Edith. She had always said to me, 'A wedding is a church and pealing bells, it's a love feast.'

But she had not mentioned it for a long time, because she no longer believed in it. Things often came into Edith's life just at the moment she had decided there was no hope, that they would never happen.

While she was grappling with drink, with drugs, and with fear; lying to her friends, to Guite, to Michel Emer, Loulou, Charles, me, and several others aboard the *Ile de France*, in the middle of the ocean, two men were talking about her – Eddie Lewis, the American agent who had replaced our friend Clifford Fischer when he died, and Jacques Pills.

They were standing at the bar, the boat was headed for France. Jacques hummed a song. 'What do you think of it, Eddie?'

'Great. Is it yours?'

'Yes. Who do you think I could offer it to?'

'To Edith, of course.'

'It's a good job you said that, because I wrote it for her; but it's a long time since I saw her, I don't know if I would dare.'

'Why not? When we get to Paris, I'll set up a meeting with her.'

Edith had met Jacques Pills in 1930, just hello and good-bye, nothing more. He was the great Jacques Pills of Pills and Tabet, the most famous of the duet acts. Edith had just done her show at the A.B.C. and it did not amount to much beside his. He was also Lucienne Boyer's husband. They led a very stable life; it just wasn't up our street.

In 1941, on a tour in the unoccupied part of France, we bumped into Jacques again. Things went a bit better this time. He was a handsome man, very classy and loaded with talent – a real dreamboat.

We were touring with Paul Meurisse in *Le Bel Indifférent*. Henri Contet was the next in line, and Edith was not short of love, but that did not stop her from fancying Jacques.

'He's nice, Momone. You can see *he* wasn't born in the gutter.'

True enough, he was the son of an officer who had been stationed in Landes. He had studied to be a pharmacist but the provincial chemists' shops did not appeal to him. He gave everything up to become the office boy at the Casino de Paris, and from there he went on to form his duo. Lucienne gave him a daughter, Jacqueline, and they were later divorced.

When Pills and Lewis arrived in Paris, Lewis kept his word; he called Edith and said, 'I have a song you're going to like. It's written by a very talented boy, and he wrote it with you in mind. It's very, very good.'

'What's his name?'

'Jacques Pills.'

'Come on over.'

She hung up and ran to the bathroom. A quick fix to put her in shape – 'just one more'. That's how far she was hooked.

'Oh, Momone, when I saw myself in the mirror and remembered how I looked when Pills had met me in Nice, I was ready to break down and cry. I was all swollen. My face was lumpy, I looked like an old drunk. My hair was disgusting, all tangled. I looked ten years older. I couldn't see them like that, I had to pull myself together. So I called and delayed the meeting. "I'll come to your hotel." It was the sickness – you do understand that, Momone, don't you?'

She arrived late, laughing too loudly. The two men were waiting for her quietly, smiling, very relaxed.

'Jacques hadn't changed at all. He was as handsome as ever;

he seemed happy to see me. We had two or three drinks, and I felt a bit better. Then Jacques said, "Look, Edith, I've written a song for you. I did it during my tour of South America."

' "I didn't know you wrote songs. Do you compose the music too?"

' "No, that's Gilbert Bécaud, my accompanist. He's fantastically talented. Do you want to hear it?"

'This Gilbert was a tough-looking guy from the south with Spanish eyes. He sat down at the piano, and Jacques sang:

> *Je t'ai dans la peau*
> *Y'a rien à faire*
> *Obstinément, tu es là*
> *J'ai beau chercher à m'en défaire*
> *Tu es toujours près de moi*
> *Je t'ai dans la peau*
> *Y'a rien à faire*
> *Tu es partout dans mon corps*
> *J'ai froid, j'ai chaud*
> *Après tout je m'en fous*
> *De c'qu'on peut penser,*
> *J' peux pas m'empêcher de crier:*
> *Tu es tout pour moi*
> *J'suis un intoxiqué*
> *Et je t'aime, je t'adore à en crever*
> *Je t'ai dans la peau*
> *Y'a rien à faire*
> *Je sens tes lèvres sur ma peau*
> *Y'a rien à faire*
> *Je t'ai dans la peau!*

This was more than a good beginning, it was love at first sight. Edith was off. She liked everything, the song, the man, the music. She could already see herself escaping from the nightmare syringe. With a man like that around she would not need it any more.

An hour later they were having dinner at her house. In the bathroom she took a quick fix. That was the last one; she would never do it again!

There was not a minute to lose. The next day Jacques came

back to work on 'Je t'ai dans la peau', and every day after that. Jacques was in her heart; but the drug was in her blood, and she was ashamed.

She held out for hours, with the moral support of her favourite saint, to whom she had promised a whole forest of candles, an altar fashioned in gold (it would have been less expensive than the habit). But when Jacques saw her, she looked so tense that he said. 'You're sick, shall I call a doctor?'

'No, no, it's nothing, it'll pass. It's my rheumatism. I'll take my medicine.' And she went off to take another shot.

One evening she called me, 'Come over quickly, I absolutely must see you.' I rushed over. She threw herself into my arms like a child. 'If only you knew, I'm sick with happiness – I'm going to marry Jacques.'

We looked at each other with big tears in our eyes.

'Are you surprised that I'm getting married?'

'Yes, a bit.'

But that was to please her. It was the future husband that surprised me. I could not see him being much help; he was not the solid type. He had a lovely smile, the spoilt good looks of a pleasure-seeker. He was gay, and Edith needed to laugh again, to have a man around the house, giving orders, chasing away the parasites, the bloodsuckers, who scurried into the corners like cockroaches when I arrived. They would be more impressed by a husband than a lover.

'And he's free, Momone, he was divorced a long time before we met. No one can call me a home-wrecker or a man-eater. This time my lover is my fiancé. At least I shall have had one!'

The idea of getting married drove her into ecstasies. She told everyone, even people she hardly knew.

Edith, who had been through so much, still had a convent girl's ideas about marriage. Her husband would be like no other man, he would take care of her, protect her, help her. Husbands can be cheated, but not left. That was what she needed. She had heard that marriage changed people, and she wanted to know if it was true.

She kept on repeating dizzily, 'This is my first marriage, so I really must love him.'

What worried her most was the wedding dress. She wanted to have one. 'But it would be ridiculous if I got married in white. That would be going a bit far. I can't wear a veil either, can I? You know, that was something I always wanted. I never celebrated my First Communion with the dress and the gown and all the rest of the stuff. First communicants look like little brides. I used to be jealous of them.'

This woman, befuddled with drink, her body already corroded by drugs, was dreaming like a ten-year-old kid about her first communion dress.

Then she had an idea. 'I've been thinking about it. The virgin's colours are blue and white. There's nothing purer than Our Lady; I'll get married in sky blue. I'll have a little violet tulle hat instead of the veil. It'll look white in the photos.'

She was transformed, happy. Physically she looked ill, but she was less tense. What I didn't know was that she had found the solution – she had stopped rationing the drugs. She wanted to be well for the wedding; afterwards ... *on verra*.

On 29 July 1952, in the Town Hall of the sixteenth arrondissement of Paris, René Victor Eugène Ducos, stage name Jacques Pills, aged forty-six, married Edith Giovanna Gassion, aged thirty-seven.

'I didn't like that wedding in the Town Hall. It didn't mean anything. They galloped through it. It wasn't a real wedding at all. But I'm going to make up for it. We're going to go through it again in New York, in style, in a church. I won't feel married until I've stood in front of a priest. You can't cheat God. Look, I'm not wearing my wedding ring; I didn't even want to see it until it had been blessed.'

Selling off the house in Boulogne occupied her for a month before they left for the United States.

'I can't stay there any more; just going into it gives me the creeps. I've been through too much here. It's full to bursting with bad memories. There were so few good ones. There were nights when I was so lonely, if I'd been a dog I'd have howled myself to death. I would have gone mad if I'd stayed there any longer. Loulou's found me a place at 67 boulevard Lannes, a ground-floor apartment with a separate entrance, a tiny garden and nine rooms. It's very nice. I'm going to move in, so when I get back from America with my husband, we'll be in new surroundings.'

It was her fifth journey to the United States and on 20 September 1952, in the church of St-Vincent-de-Paul in New York, Edith had the wedding of her dreams. That morning in her suite at the Waldorf Astoria, Marlene Dietrich helped her to dress. Edith was trembling with happiness. She was still a bit puffy, but it was not noticeable. She had had a shot; she couldn't have kept going otherwise. Loulou Barrier and Marlene were the witnesses at the ceremony. Edith's expression melted their hearts. It contained everything, her joy, her fear, her hope. 'It can't be true,' she said to them. 'I'm dreaming.'

It was true. She came into the church on Loulou's arm, dressed in sky blue from head to toe. The bells rang, the organ pealed, all was so beautiful. Behind her stood Jacques in a navy blue suit with a white carnation in his buttonhole. Edith was walking on air. Her simple heart had been repaid for all its suffering, she was getting married as she had dreamed she would, when she was a little girl.

The priest blessed the rings. Edith slipped one on to her husband's finger. Her hand was trembling from emotion – and from alcohol and drugs. As she came out of the church the Wedding March was played and outside, in the American style, friends and well-wishers scattered rice over the couple for luck.

Nothing was too good for her. Two receptions had been arranged, a cocktail party given by the director of the Versailles and a luncheon in the most famous restaurant in New York, Le Pavillon. It was very gay. The champagne was French. And Edith laughed and laughed and laughed – she was drugged.

Then the guests left one by one, Marlene Dietrich the last of all, kissing Edith and wishing her good luck.

Several hours later Edith went to the Versailles, and Jacques to La Vie en Rose where he sang, 'Ca gueule ça Madame', and a song that he had just written for her, 'Formidable'.

For several weeks it was the smart thing in New York to go to hear Edith at the Versailles, and Monsieur Piaf at La Vie en Rose. In the American newspaper indexes under 'Peals (Jacques)' it said 'see Piaf (Edith)'. The Americans had anglicized Jacques's name to Peals.

Their wedding trip seemed mouthwatering – Hollywood, San Francisco, Las Vegas, Miami – but to them it was also work.

The first evening in Hollywood she collapsed in front of her make-up mirror. It was a drug. Her make-up wouldn't go on, the powder flaked off, her skin rejected it. Her hair was dead-looking. Only her eyes shone, but they shone too brightly.

Edith flew into a rage such as she usually reserved for other people. Then there was a knock at the door. Angrily she shouted, 'Come in,' and it was the director of the club, who said:

'Edith, Charlie Chaplin's in the audience; he's come to listen to you. He never usually goes to night clubs, this is a real coup.'

Edith was ecstatic.

'In my book Charlie Chaplin's the greatest. There are girls like us in his films, Momone. He understands how hard life can be, I felt close to him. But his genius – it was like a ravine between us. I was scared stiff. I didn't think I'd be able to open my mouth.

'I sang for him. I gave it everything I had, and he must have realized it. He invited me to his table and he said things that I've never forgotten, about how he almost never went to listen to a singer; that he was never impressed by them; that I represented not only the misery of the towns but their lights and their poetry too. He said the stories I sang had no barriers, they were universal, because they were about men and love; and that I, Edith Piaf, had made him cry.

'I was speechless. I must have looked completely dumb sitting there beside him saying, "Thank you, oh yes, I am very happy." I even blushed.

'I've had enough compliments to fill a library, but coming from him it was different.'

The next day Charlie Chaplin rang up and invited her to his house in Beverley Hills. Telling about this visit, Edith said:

'If you could only see his house. It's wonderful. I hardly dared touch a thing there. It's like the set for a technicolor movie, it looks as if they give it a fresh coat of paint every day.

'Chaplin has beautiful blue eyes, thick eyelashes, silver hair; his smile opens you right up. His voice is gentle and steady. He hardly makes any gestures. Everything he says, everything he does, is simple, and right.

'He told me stories about the time when he was part of Fred Karno's comedy act. Then he played the violin, tunes that he had composed himself. He's good, but his music isn't like his films, it's a little too sugary.

'When I left he promised to write me a song – words and music. Perhaps he'll forget. But I'll never forget that house. It must be marvellous to live in a place like that. But I shall never know, I don't have that kind of talent.'

When Edith got back to her new apartment on the boulevard Lannes in Paris, she made a lot of promises. She even went up to our old Sacré Coeur and prayed to St Theresa. She begged her with all her strength to give her the courage to kick the drugs which were tearing her apart. Then she went home and collapsed on her bed in her beautiful new Louis XV room.

The room looked on to a courtyard. It was dark and quiet, just what she needed. The living-room was as big as a ballroom; there was no furniture, only the grand piano and heaps of equipment – radios, tape recorder, record player – and records were piled high on the rug that Loulou had given her. If someone wanted to sit down, they dragged in one of the armchairs from the little sitting-room next door; it was furnished in a very ordinary way, nothing stylish, just comfortable.

The kitchen was charming. It came right out of *Good Housekeeping* magazine. It was just as well because we all ate there together *en famille* much more than we had in Boulogne.

She entertained all her friends after midnight, rarely before. You would always find Jacques there, her pianist Robert Chauvigny, her accordionist Marc Bonel and his wife Danièle (who was not yet playing a leading role but would eventually become Edith's secretary), Michel Emer, Guite, Loulou, and the rest, the small fry who came and went with the changing tides.

Edith's four-year nightmare had begun.

When I saw her after she came back from the States I was horrified. This time it was serious. Gone was the waif-like Edith of the street corners – pale, like any little Parisian urchin, but sturdy; slim but in good health.

'It's fatigue, Momone, I'm dead tired. Look, I've brought you something.'

It was a rose from her wedding bouquet, to bring me luck. Then she told me about the wedding and tour.

'Are you happy?'

'Oh yes, Jacques is marvellous.'

But I could sense that she wasn't happy. She wasn't with me any more. Where was she? I had heard the rumours circulating about her. 'The boss is on drugs,' they were saying, but I did not want to believe it. Edith had always pursued good, wholesome vices, nothing artificial, nothing complicated.

'Is your rheumatism playing up again?'

She had had an attack of crippling rheumatism in 1949, but it hadn't lasted long. She leapt at the excuse as a drowning man reaches for a life-belt. 'Yes, that's it. You see, the cortisone tires me so.'

She was not lying; the rheumatic attacks had started again. Edith was always frightened of pain; now she could not stand it. The minute she felt it was going to start up again she filled herself up with cortisone injections. The doctor had ordered two a day; she took four. Since she could not get it without a prescription, some bastard or other easily got it for her. She paid outrageously for a dose of cortisone – as much as she paid for the morphine.

If she had been some poor old beggar she could have been screaming with pain as far as the pushers were concerned. But Edith Piaf could have what she wanted; she had the wherewithal to pay for it. Success and money can kill you quicker than poverty.

As I was not living with her, I had no idea of what was going on. I should have known her better, but I swallowed everything she told me. She could make me believe anything she wanted. She would look me straight in the eyes, take my hand, and say, 'You know I miss you, you're all I have. You know what I'm going to say even before I say it.' That was not strictly true any more. I must have been blind.

The accident was really the cause of it all. Without it she would never have touched that poison. Edith was not depraved, she did not even know what the word meant. Before those dreadful times began, she used to drink for pleasure. When we got pissed together, it wasn't merely to get drunk, but rather so we could get up to some silly game or other.

She used to dress badly, with a scarf over her head. We would go into a night club full of people and she would walk up to a table, saying, 'I'm Edith Piaf,' which made people laugh; no one believed her. She'd turn to me : 'These idiots will pay money to see me and when they can have me for free, they don't want to know me. They'll see if I'm Edith Piaf or not.'

And then she'd start to sing. She could parody herself extremely well, and everyone thought it was very funny, but they were even less prepared to accept her as the real thing.

When she went out she was laughing and happy. 'When they get home they'll say, "There's some crackpot going around saying she's Edith Piaf. As if we'd be taken in. Poor fool." '

Other times we would go to the theatre and Edith would buy heaps of ice creams and sweets and hand them around. 'Here, this is to thank you for coming, it's from the Association of Grateful Actors.'

Sometimes she would give them away to apologize for having caused a disturbance during the play, and anyone who did not accept got bawled out.

Men were not vital to her, but love was. She had to believe in it, without it she could not have gone on living or singing. That is why she was so easy to deceive. 'It's hard never to be able to forget that I'm Edith Piaf. It's hard to be exploited all the time, to realize that no one cares about me personally; even the man in bed with me is just thinking EDITH PIAF in capital letters.'

This became an obsession with her; she talked of nothing else. If someone made fun of her she often did not notice until several days later when she would say, 'God, that son of a bitch made a real fool of me!'

I have seen her give money to people who didn't give a damn for her. The next day, as we sat in the bathroom, she would remember and say, 'But he doesn't care about me. Well, I'll never give him another penny.' But when he came back, she had forgotten her vow, and she left again with his money.

I could not understand why she had become so bitter. I did not like the look in her eyes; they were cloudy like dirty water, or they were too shiny; she seemed to avoid looking directly at you. She spent more and more time in bed. She had always enjoyed being in bed, but this was abnormal. She lay simply stretched out like an old heap of rags. She spent whole days there, dirty, uncombed, vacant.

Then one morning I telephoned and was told: 'Monsieur Barrier and Monsieur have taken Madame Piaf to Meudon; she is going into a clinic.'

Jacques had been fully aware before their marriage that Edith was on the needle. At first he thought it was only cortisone, and she had spun him the same yarns as I got. When he realized she was also using morphine she explained, 'It's for the pain, but don't worry, there's no danger of me getting addicted.'

In America only the syringe had held her together. There was no question of her taking the cure there, the publicity would have been disastrous, and they had to fulfil their contracts. When they got back to Paris she cheated herself. She swore that she would only take two injections a day – two injections after the two allowed by the doctor, which, after all, did not count! Since she wanted to fight it, she waited as long as possible to take her dose. By the time she finally gave in, she was so on edge that she did not even have time to boil the syringe and the needle, or even swab them in alcohol; she would stick the needle straight into her arm or leg, even through her dress or her stocking. When she got to that stage she was finished.

Her double contracts with Jacques were going badly, but she did not want to be separated from him, so she decided they should do *Le Bel Indifférent* together. In the first half of the show they would sing their songs, in the second they would do the play.

As she could not do it in her present state she agreed to take the cure. So, clinging to Loulou's and Jacques's arms, she went into the clinic. She was scared but happy.

'It was a little like going to prison,' she recalled, except it was cleaner than most prisons. There were bars at the window, and the nurse who took charge of me looked like a prison screw; she could have licked Bourreau de Béthune [a famous French wrestler]. I saw her through a fog, the way I saw everything, even the little men who used to come and sell me my stuff at fifty or sixty thousand francs a throw. She frisked me like a customs man when he thinks you're hiding a twenty-pound ingot in your undies. Apparently we drug addicts are very crafty!

'She scrubbed me in a bath, tucked me into bed, and gave me my fix. That first day was heaven.'

Edith was at first entitled to five injections a day. Day by day the dose was diminished until the day arrived when there was none.

'I thought I was going mad. Terrible pains cut through me, tearing at my muscles. My limbs jerked about all on their own. I was all knotted up like an old vine root, then suddenly I would uncoil like a spring. Above me there were blurred white figures. Little bits of faces appeared and disappeared. They opened their mouths like fish, but no words came out. I was strapped down. I had become a slobbering animal, senseless. I couldn't rest, I couldn't think clearly. They told me it only lasted twenty-four hours; it felt like a thousand years.'

After twenty days the doctor told her that the cure was finished, but that she was not yet recovered; she might go into a nervous depression. She didn't care, she wanted to go home.

There was no longer any question of performing *Le Bel Indifférent* or of singing. Edith would slump exhausted in a chair, or lay limply in the corner of a divan or on her bed. She had no interest in eating, or moving, or living. She watched Jacques and Loulou come in and go out; they did not even know if she could hear them. She refused to listen to music, noises hurt her. She gazed at her hands as though she did not recognize them.

Then one day she started to talk again; she came back to life. But it was no miracle – she had simply gone back to the needle on the sly.

The new production of *Le Bel Indifférent* was the most

miserable failure of her career, and the worst economic disaster. No one wanted to produce it, so Edith said, 'Too bad, I'll do it myself.'

We were all horrified. She leased the Théâtre Marigny, decided to direct the play herself, and to do the production between two bouts of singing, hers and Pills. 'This is marvellous,' she said, 'I'm living again.'

The bill was colossal. The scenery cost a million francs, the musicians five thousand a day. On a 'friend's' advice she sent for two mandolinists from Florence, and she paid them three thousand francs each per evening. She shelled out seven hundred thousand in overtime to the stage hands. Everything was like that. She would ask for a rehearsal and turn up several hours late, give herself a fix, in the wings, to get through it, and work all night.

But Pills was kind. Sure, he loved Edith, but he didn't carry enough weight, either in their own life, or on stage. The Americans called him 'Mr Charm'. Edith had decided to take all the strong songs out of her act so that her voice would not drown his out. The light ones that remained would give the audience, and her, time to rest. Butchered in this way, her act was worth nothing. This lackadaisical, syrupy Piaf was a disappointment. If this was what had become of Edith Piaf, obviously she was through.

That was the only time in her whole career that Edith alarmed me. *Le Bel Indifférent* was quite dreadful, and it was her fault. The part that Paul Meurisse had created was worthless when performed by Jacques Pills. He was all smiles, all seduction, but seemed quite out of his element when he was expected to brood and keep quiet; he succeeded in merely looking bored. Edith's little capsules of ersatz happiness had riddled her memory with holes so she cut her part considerably. The first night was painful, and the critics barely polite. The two singing acts only emphasized the fact that *Le Bel Indifférent* was a flop. The show ran for a month to save face, and Edith paid.

After this unfortunate episode Edith and Pills went on a tour. Through her personal fog, through the marshes in which she was floundering, she clung on to him.

'I can't leave him, he's all I have. If only you knew how kind and patient he is with me; he's never lost his temper with me, and I've given him plenty of reasons.'

I said nothing, but I thought to myself that it might be better if he did lose his temper, even if he gave her a few hearty slaps.

She drank to try to keep herself off the drugs. When it came to drinking, Jacques was more of a companion than a bodyguard. He figured that as long as she was holding a glass, she could not be sticking a needle into herself.

During that tour they went on a series of sensational drinking sessions. One night in Lyons they entered a bistro at half past midnight to have a beer. At eight o'clock the next morning they were still there, roaring drunk. Everyone around them was asleep. They went to Valence for breakfast, staggered into the café and ordered two fried eggs and a bottle of white wine.

They were now wide awake, and on top of the world. Edith looked at Jacques with admiration, at last she had found a guy who could match her glass for glass, she thought. Suddenly Jacques exclaimed with his drunken, seductive smile, 'Hey, I wonder who drove us here.'

He himself had been driving!

She had to make an appearance at the Casino de Royat, and it was there that the drug/alcohol mixture finally gave Edith a scare. She could not find her way on to the stage from the wings, she bumped blindly into bits of scenery mumbling to herself, 'The bastards, they've closed off the stage entrance. They've pulled down the curtain, we can't go on.' They had to push her on stage. Loulou was wet with perspiration. On stage it was terrible.

'I thought I was singing,' she confessed, 'but I was saying words that didn't mean anything at all. I thought they were pretty. Some people started hooting at me, then shouting, like they did during the Leplée scandal. That sobered me up enough to get to the end somehow.'

At that point the drug took over again.

'I don't know how I finished the tour. I would get to my dressing-room in a complete daze, take my fix, and sing. When I came off stage Loulou took me in his arms, otherwise I'd have

collapsed. I held on, I didn't want to take more than three injections a day, but soon I was taking four and more. When I
looked at myself I wanted to throw up; I was disgusted. One
evening I said, "No! I'll hold out, I'm going to cure myself," and
I didn't take the fix.

'I got on stage somehow. The spotlights spat full in my face,
their light was like a fire full of red stars. I couldn't hear the
musicians any more, I waited for them to play before I began. I
could feel a disgusting, sticky sweat running down my face,
taking my make-up off with it. I started to fall, grabbed the
microphone and clung on to it for dear life. It was pitching
around like a mast in a storm. I started, then stopped dead, nothing would come out, not a word. Way off in the distance I heard
the audience laughing – loud, vulgar laughter. Words came to my
lips like bubbles and exploded in my head and my ears. I started
to weep. I called out to Marcel – I don't know whether I meant
my child or Cerdan. Then I cried to the audience, "Forgive me,
please forgive me, it isn't my fault." '

They rang down the curtain. It was the first time that Edith
had failed to sing, even badly. They had to refund money to the
audience. Next day the papers referred to Madame Piaf's 'indisposition' on stage, but that did not help her much.

It was very serious. Back in Paris Edith had no choice, she had
to go back to the clinic. It was 1954, barely two years since her
beautiful wedding. Jacques did what he could, but he was not
often there.

This time Edith didn't last four days in hospital. Before she
had been taken off the drug she ran away.

'My head was like little bits of cracked mirror, and parts of it
were digging into my brain. Someone was hammering in my
skull. They had taken all my clothes. I didn't care; I left in my
dressing-gown. I crawled by the gate-keeper's lodge. Then I took
a taxi home. I went to my loose board straightaway. The morphine was still there, everything could go on as before.

'Being hooked on drugs is like being at a carnival in hell, with
carousels and slides. You go up, you plunge down again, up
again, down again. Everything is alike, it's always the same;
monotonous, grey, dirty. But you don't notice it, you just go on.

'When the needle dug into my flesh I gasped, not with pleasure, but with relief. It comes quickly, as soon as you do it; not because it makes you feel good, but because you don't hurt any more. But the more you take, the more you suffer; then you have to take more still to suffer less. Reasoning stops, you see everything through a fog.'

In this state Edith decided to leave on a ninety-day tour with the Super Circus. No one could stop her, she kept insisting, 'If I stop singing I shall die.' What she didn't say was that she needed money so that she could go on poisoning herself. She was spending everything she earned.

Every day Loulou expected her to collapse and he could then take her back to the clinic for the third time. He knew that she would never go back of her own free will.

She lost all self-awareness. Her arms and legs were swollen with edema, covered with scabs and sores. Others had to make her up, dress her, and push her on stage. Nothing meant anything, all she was waiting for was the moment when her 'connection' brought her more magic capsules.

The tour was a nightmare for everyone. Edith's friends trembled for her. The journalists who had found out that she was sick ran after her, waiting for her to collapse. They had to be tricked so that Edith could be kept from them at the end of each show when she was carried out of the theatre. She was unconscious for hours on end.

Recalling it all, Edith said, 'Apparently the circus went to a new town every day. I don't know, I didn't see, I don't remember anything. It's all blank. I vaguely remember being pushed into a car ... then into a hotel bed ... then towards the stage ... before that I had had my fix. Then I sang. It went on for days and days. I didn't care, nothing mattered ...

'The circus finished up at Cholet. Loulou wrapped me in a big blanket and carried me to a waiting car. We drove for hours, I don't know how long and then I found myself back in the clinic. The doctor said, "Oh, it's you, is it?" And everything started all over again. It was hell.'

This time the cure started off with ten shots a day, which will give some idea of just how hooked she was. When she was down to four, Edith started to throw fits. She got out of bed, broke up everything around her, screamed and shouted obscenities, her hair matted over her face. She hurt herself and had to be strapped down.

I telephoned every day and I also went to the clinic for the news. The head nurse was a lovely girl, very strict but kind, too. She explained that drug 'withdrawal' was always like this, but that it went away; I must not get upset, Edith was no worse than the others. But would she be the same as she used to be when it was all over, would she stop completely?

'Sure. There are always relapses, but plenty of people get cured completely.'

No one was allowed at her bedside, and the corridor in front of her door was empty too. Sometimes I saw Loulou's solid shadow, but that was just about all. The day that the injections stopped I went to the clinic. I didn't realize I'd chosen the worst day. I went up to her floor as usual. From below I could hear someone screaming in pain. When I got out of the lift I thought I recognized Edith's voice. I stood there transfixed at the door to her room. Someone came out, and I caught a glimpse of a screaming thing strapped down to the bed, the veins on its forehead ready to burst, glistening with sweat. Around her men and women in white were looking on dispassionately – as though they were studying an inanimate object – at that foaming, slobbering figure. I couldn't even cry. All I could say was, 'It can't be her. It can't be her.'

The head nurse took my arm. 'Come away, don't stay here. It's very hard on the family, but it's really nothing. Tomorrow it will be all over.'

'But she's in pain.'

'Terribly, but it's necessary, there's no other way.'

Edith screamed for twelve hours on end, and for days I heard that animal sound echoing in my head.

Then she was out of it.

'I screamed, Momone, I couldn't do anything else,' she told me, 'but I wanted to get better. And I think I've made it this time. The doctors were frank with me; they said I have to take care because I'll start wanting it again after three, six, twelve, and eighteen months.'

For eight months Edith lived at boulevard Lannes in terror that 'it' would come back; she stayed shut up in her room in the darkness, refusing to see anyone. But this did not stop the peddlers. They overcame every obstacle to force their shit on her. They murmured sweet messages : 'Why don't you try cocaine, Madame Piaf; it's not like morphine, it isn't habit-forming.' And others blackmailed her. 'If you don't pay us, we'll go to the press and tell them you're hooked.' One of her chauffeurs, who had seen a great deal, wanted a million francs to keep silent, and she gave it to him.

When Jacques was there, she was calmer. He did not hesitate to throw all the scum out. Once he even punched a fellow who demanded money. But he was not there often enough and Edith stayed alone with her servants who cared nothing for her; they were just looking after themselves.

The cure, drugs, peddlers, blackmail are expensive, and Edith was not working. She sold the farm at Hallier, some paintings that she had bought, and a handful of jewellery that she did not care much about.

'I don't look right in pearls and diamonds,' she said to me. 'On me they always look as if they were bought at Woolworths.'

Ten million francs meant nothing to her. Loulou was in despair.

Then Edith gradually started to return to the world. She could bear daylight and electric light again. When I heard that she had opened her shutters I sent her dozens of roses. She called me right away. Her voice sounded normal, almost gay. 'I'm not finished yet.'

We all breathed again. It was only just in time; Loulou turned up with a contract from the Versailles in New York.

Edith was still a bit nervous. 'Loulou, do you think I can go?'

'They're waiting for you. They don't know what's been happening. You have to go.'

And show business opened its arms once more to her. Only love had no part in the festivities. Edith did not want any men.

She was fond of Pills, though perhaps a little less than friends like Loulou, Charles Aznavour, and Guite. Jacques was good to her, but she knew her marriage was a failure.

'It's no one's fault; it was the drug that did it. Jacques is too soft; a little boy. He was meant to laugh, not deal with serious problems. He can't take part, so he stays outside it. I'm all alone, see.'

When she left for New York, Jacques went to London to rehearse a musical comedy. Edith improved all the time; America did her good. This was her audience; the Americans are reliable people. When they love you, it's the real thing. They don't constantly fall in and out of love like the French. Mind you, she hid everything from them. She wasn't at home, and she was on her best behaviour.

The reviews were still good. One critic wrote, 'Edith Piaf, the little French Isolde, goes on bravely dying of love. She dies five hundred times during dinner, and five hundred times afterwards, and always in that marvellous voice. The loudest voice coming out of the smallest body.' Every day there were articles about her; they piled up by her bed every morning; but she never forgot that one.

Back in Paris she mentioned it to me. 'That's right, you know; I die for love five hundred times in an evening. If he knew about my life, then he'd really have something to say. When I'm not dying of love, when I don't have any, I die anyway. You see, marriage doesn't change anything.'

She did not work in Paris. She waited. She did nothing for a year. She had difficulty with her breathing. I don't know if she was getting her second wind.

Then suddenly everything changed. Loulou got her a contract at Carnegie Hall – the first time a variety star had ever been invited to sing in the most celebrated concert hall in the United States.

Again she was swept up by all the attendant excitement. The whole troupe gathered at boulevard Lannes. As usual she rehearsed with all her energy, exhausting everyone around her. She laughed, she was happy and she was back on top form.

In 1956 Edith landed in New York for the seventh time. She

was received like a queen. It was freezing cold when she got off the plane; Loulou wanted her to go inside, out of the sub-zero temperatures. But Edith snuggled into the mink coat Marcel had given her (it had somehow escaped the purge) while the journalists clamoured for photographs: 'Just one more ...'

'It's okay, Loulou, leave me alone, I'm not sick any more. Let me give them what they want. I belong to them.' It was true – people had been standing in line for several days in the fifteen degrees of frost to get tickets to hear her.

Bouquets arrived non-stop at her room in the Waldorf Astoria; they overflowed into the corridor. Eddie Lewis was rushing around like an excited schoolboy. 'You're in great shape; better than last time. How's your husband? Imagine, I was practically the match-maker!'

But he did not notice that new touch of bitterness. Edith was marked, as is anyone who has been to hell and back is scarred. But that new face, and those new eyes would take Edith to even greater heights yet.

That evening she sang Pierre Delanoë's song, 'Les Grognards', for the first time:

> *Ecoute, peuple de Paris*
> *Ecoute, ces pas qui marchent dans la nuit,*
> *Regarde, peuple de Paris, ces ombres éternelles,*
> *Qui défilent en chantant sous ton ciel ...*

It was staggering. You could almost see the Parisian sky, the tricolour flag waving over the Arc de Triomphe and the Champs-Elysées. Pierre Delanoë who, like many others, had followed Edith over to hear her sing at the Carnegie Hall, made a tape recording of that performance: it is a unique record; 'Les Grognards' was followed by a storm of applause, shouts, whistles, and stamping feet which almost lasted as long as the song itself.

She sang twenty-seven songs. The audience was delirious. After the final curtain they remained on their feet for seven minutes, applauding the tiny woman alone on the enormous stage, the woman who had made them cry and shout and want to die of love for her.

'Loulou timed them. Seven minutes is a long time, you know. Time enough to think. I kept listening to them, it was so beautiful, it was so good that I ached; it was too much for me.

'During those few minutes my heart went mad with joy, and I felt that more than anything else I was married to my audience. Jacques was finished. It wasn't his fault, nor mine; just bad timing. So I've asked him for a divorce. I wasn't made for marriage. It lasted four years; that's not too bad. It's all over now, the next time the church bells ring for me will be at my funeral.'

16

'I WANT TO DIE YOUNG'

Carnegie Hall was more than just another success for Edith; it was her supreme triumph.

'I've done with all that shit at last, Momone. The Americans did me good. They don't put on airs, but when they love you they do it openly. When I got there I was scared stiff, but I'm completely better now. I'm going to do a concert at the Olympia.'

'Take care, Edith. Don't do too much at once, you're still weak.'

'Don't nag, I have enough people to do that. You know what General Eisenhower said to the doctors when they told him he had better take care of himself – "Better live than vegetate." I have a lot of time to make up for.'

The nights on boulevard Lannes started up again. Plenty of people were willing to share them with her – A. R. Chauvigny; Marc Bonel and Danièle; Robert Burlet, the chauffeur, and his wife Hélène, who was to become, for a short time, Edith's Girl Friday; Christiane, the chambermaid, with her mother Suzanne, the cook. They were her solid base, they lived in, they were Madame Piaf's employees. Then there were those who came to see Edith, lifetime friends like Loulou, Michel Emer, la Guite, Contet, Charles, and others. And there was the passing trade – old boy-friends were always welcome when they dropped in to say hello – and the people she had befriended during the day.

Anyone who had lived through a night at boulevard Lannes was guaranteed to come back for more; you just couldn't give them up. You drank rough red wine or beer, depending on Edith's taste. If one person mentioned that he liked caviar, Edith would buy it by the pound; but she took just a teaspoonful herself, she didn't care for it.

When Edith felt up to it she sang, tried out new songs, did a skit. The night lasted until eleven the next morning.

On armchairs, on day-beds, wherever they fell, the visitors lay snoring loud enough to wake the dead.

I could hardly keep my eyes open, but I managed to, it was a matter of training – and of pride. Edith would not have understood if I had abandoned her – a little soldier fights on to the bitter end!

But it wasn't the same any more. Even with me Edith was playing a role. She was often in pain. The joints in her hands were beginning to knot up. She who refused to gamble with her life began playing poker with her body. She would not accept the fact that it had the upper hand, that it could deal the trump card. Only she was entitled to have the trumps. When her tortured body screamed too loudly she silenced it with drugs so she would not have to listen to it.

The most difficult thing was to put her to bed. 'I'm not tired, I don't want to go to bed.' She had no patience. Sleep had literally to knock her out, she wasn't going to lose time waiting for it in bed. She had all sorts of sleep-inducing tricks, but they did not always work, she was too used to them.

When I did finally succeed in getting her into bed with her earplugs and her sleeping mask, I would creep out of the room on tiptoe. Too often, as I had my hand on the doorknob, would I hear her shout, 'Momone'.

She never changed her routine just because a first night was approaching, she simply piled more work on top of the pleasure. She was in the middle of preparing for her return to the Olympia. It was close to two years since Edith had sung in Paris, and this 1956 premiere was an important step for her.

Bruno Coquatrix, still suspicious because of all the evil gossip that surrounded her, had signed her on for a month. That was not too bad, at least it was in the star class – other people got two-week contracts.

On the first night we were so nervous we were jumping around like hungry fleas on a dog. If the show flopped Edith's whole career would be in danger. The tour with Pills and the Super Circus débâcle had not gone unnoticed. There had been some narrow escapes. 'Piaf is finished,' they said, 'she doesn't keep her contracts.' They were waiting for her to pack up completely. The wild animals in the auditorium were gnashing their teeth. But by the fifth song they were bleating like lambs. She sang 'Marie la Française', 'Une Dame', 'L'Homme à la moto', 'Toi qui sais', 'Les Amants d'un jour', 'Bravo pour le clown'.

That evening I experienced emotions I had never felt before. From the very first song I was stirred and shaken. She had never sung like that. Her voice came from a long way off. When the sea wind blows it sweeps up the sand and throws it in your face, your lungs burn. Edith's voice swept like that across the town, into the corners of the squares. It washed through the bistros, it was full of the love of the slums, of street corners, of chance meetings, and celebrations. It *was* the street. Rich and poor were equally moved. They didn't care about the words, she could have sung la la la, or recited names from the telephone book, as Germaine Montero said, she would have affected you just the same.

No one noticed her hair or her clothes, or if she was off key. They didn't care. If she made a mistake, or stopped for a moment, they were happy, it was more natural. This was not contrived, it was not made up, it came directly from her, and from everything inside her, love and suffering. It was as if that drug that I had cursed, which should have killed her, had scoured her insides, bringing every part of her to life. She sang with a violent love we had never heard before.

The curtain could not go down, she took twenty-two curtain calls, and sang more than ten encores. My throat was dry and my hands hurt from clapping.

Bruno cancelled all the contracts that followed Edith's and extended her run once, twice, three times. She stayed at the Olympia for twelve weeks.

The auditorium was packed every night, they had to sell folding seats in the aisles. There were record attendances; the theatre made three million francs a day. The sales of her records soared to three million, three hundred thousand of them in four months. In the first two weeks alone, the record of the Olympia concert sold twenty thousand copies. In one year her record company paid her three million francs in royalties. Her fee each evening was one and a quarter million francs. You would think she'd have been able to put plenty aside, but she didn't, not a franc.

But Edith was earning this money with her life. 'Each time you sing, you're shortening your life by a few minutes,' her doctors warned her, trying to frighten her. 'I don't care, if I stop singing I'll die even sooner.' She could throw her money away if she wanted.

In *Ma route et mes chansons* Maurice Chevalier wrote:

Piaf, that bantam-weight champion, spends herself with a single-minded passion. She seems to be no more sparing of her energy than of her earnings. Flying in the face of all opposition, she seems to be running confidently, full tilt towards the abyss that, horrified, I see looming ahead of her. She wants to take in everything, and she does. She ignores the traditional laws of caution that used to govern a star's career.

'Well,' said Edith when she read it, 'if he has enough to pay for a gold coffin, I've no doubt it'll help him on his way. When my time comes a simple pine-box will do me. And anyway, I want to die young. Growing old is awful, sickness is ugly.'

At Olympia, one of Edith's old fans re-emerged, the most important of all – Claude Figus. I had never forgotten Claude. He had been crazy about Edith from the time he was thirteen. It was an old story; we had originally met around 1947, when Edith was singing at the A.B.C. It was raining that evening and Edith had run out of Corydrane. I rushed out to get some more; even if she did not take it she needed to know it was there. Outside the stage door I bumped into a kid, standing in the rain like a little tree trying to grow. I rushed past him, and when I came back five minutes later the tree caught my sleeve.

'Mademoiselle, I've seen you with Madame Piaf, couldn't you let me in?'

I looked him over – soft eyes, brown eyes in corkscrew curls, pale, like all slum kids, cheap clothes, but nice. He looked okay.

'Where do you come from?'

'From Colombes.'

'Well, I'm from Ménilmontant, so don't start throwing your weight around and running it down.'

I looked at him out of the corner of my eye; he took me back twenty years.

'You're cute,' he said, letting go of my arm.

'Okay, come on, I'm late.' I rushed down the corridor but he kept up easily. I got to the stage just as Edith was going on.

'What have you dragged in now? You cradle-snatching?'

'What do you think? It's you he's mad about, not me.'

He gazed at Edith as if she were Joan of Arc come down from her stained-glass perch to pass the time of day with him.

'Stay if you like,' said Edith. 'But keep out of sight!'

He listened to her sing, flattened against a strut like a leaf, the stage hands could have moved them both without noticing him.

The next day he managed to get back into the wings by saying he was my friend. His devotion to her was so complete and naïve that Edith autographed a photograph for him.

'What's your name?'

'Claude Figus.'

'How old are you?'

'Thirteen, but I love you, Madame Piaf.'

Edith was delighted. 'I know age doesn't have much to do with feelings, but you'll have to wait at least ten years to marry me.'

Wherever she sang we found little Claude. On first nights he bought himself a place in the gallery, and then he would come backstage. He was really a cute kid. 'Bring your head over here, Claude, so I can touch it,' Edith used to say; 'Touching wood brings good luck.'

We got used to seeing him following us around. We did not even realize that he was getting taller, that he was growing into a man. He clung to our skirts for years, then one day he disappeared.

On the opening night of Olympia '56 (they gave them dates like good wines) I was backstage with Charles. We watched the people lining up in front of Edith's dressing-room, when I heard Coquatrix say, 'Go on, scram, you don't know anyone here.'

'Yes I do, M'sieur – Madame Simone and Monsieur Aznavour.'

I looked at the kid who had just spoken; he was a handsome boy. Charles, who had known him too, and had always been very good to him, said, 'It's little Claude.'

'But you're a man now – where have you been?'

'Doing my national service.'

'You want to see Edith, I know. Come back tomorrow when things are quieter.'

He said, 'She's bound to have forgotten me,' and I could tell he was still in love with her. Then he said, 'You live on the same street as me.'

'Why didn't you ever come and see me?'

'I didn't dare.' He looked like a man, but he still had a boy's heart.

Next day he came to see Edith. And since she always needed someone who adored her around the house, she took him back with her that very evening to boulevard Lannes, and baptized him her secretary. He stayed for nearly eight years.

His love for Edith was unchanged, he was totally devoted to her. She could have asked him for the skin off his back to make a lampshade, and he would have offered the skin from his front instead because it was better quality. She didn't spare him, he did everything she wanted. Poor little man, he was hardly as tall as her and he certainly didn't have what it took for a lover.

For months the morphine had replaced everything in her life. When it had her by the throat, choking her, Edith had thought of nothing else. Now it was different, she needed love again. But she was empty inside, there was not a hint of romance in the air and she needed one to live. Without love she would find some new and more dangerous pastime.

In the evenings there was the Olympia show. But between coming off stage and going back on, much too much time passed. So she drank. Not for fun, like the old days; she drank to knock herself out. She decided that wine was bad for her, so she got paralysed on beer.

Claude did not know that alcohol was as dangerous for her as drugs. It was all a big joke, she made him hide the bottles he bought for her in the bedroom, the bathroom, all over the house. She had found an accomplice.

Loulou and I and several other good friends tried to fight

against the drink, but we did not live with Edith and it was impossible.

Loulou tried to reason with her. She told him to shut up, or swore that it was over, that she had vowed never to drink again. She was so full of alcohol that three glasses of beer were enough to get her drunk. And poor innocent Claude told me, 'I promise you she's not drinking too much, I keep an eye on her.'

Edith was due to go on an eleven-month tour of the United States, the longest and most important of her career. The money was good : after Bing Crosby and Frank Sinatra she was now the highest paid star in the world. But Loulou was beside himself with anxiety. 'What are we going to do? She'll have even less will-power in the States than she has here. Momone, you must do something, she listens to you.'

'I wish she did, but you know damn well she hasn't listened to anyone in ages. What do you expect, she hasn't got a lover; she's like a ship without a captain. We'll have to find her a man.'

When Loulou succeeded in launching a successful bottle hunt, when every possible bottle had been ferreted out from under the Louis XV bed, from the medicine cabinet, the cupboards, the lavatories, the grand piano, anywhere a bottle could be hidden, even the wastebin, Edith would fly into a rage and start breaking things, or rush out into the night with a coat over her nightdress and get plastered in a bar.

One morning Hélène, the chauffeur's wife, had a telephone call from a barman. 'It's six o'clock and I want to close up. Come and get your boss. She won't leave and she keeps shouting, "I belong to you," but we want to go to bed. And bring her cheque-book.'

Edith's sprees were no longer a joke.

One evening when she was rehearsing for her tour she stopped suddenly in the middle of a song. 'I left something in my bathroom.'

'I'll get it for you, Edith,' said Claude.

'Okay, come with me.'

Since she had been in the clinic, Edith couldn't bear being alone, she made people go everywhere with her, especially when she was going to the bathroom – a man or a woman, she didn't care.

She came back after a moment, her eyes shining. She started to sing, burst out laughing, 'I can't, the words're all bumping aroun' in my head, they all wanna come out at the same time. Don' push, I said to them, but they don't listen. There's too many of them in my mouth, I'll have to go an' spit 'em out.'

And she went back again. When she came back, she was pale, her nostrils pinched, sweat beading her forehead.

'Aren't you well, Edith?'

'Sure, it's jus' these damn words, they're stopping me from talking. Be back in a moment.'

A few seconds later we heard a scream, followed by the sound of breaking glass. Everyone rushed towards the noise, Claude in the lead. We found Edith clambering over her bed, screaming and throwing empty and full bottles of beer into the corner of the room where they broke against the wall. The beer was trickling across the floor. And Edith, dishevelled, gasping, 'Spiders, mice, kill them, kill them! They're coming, they're coming! They're climbing all over me with their feet, they're scratching me,' and ripping off her clothes, scratching her face and arms, and shrieking in horror.

The ambulance came to take her away that night. It took two men to subdue her. She was in terrible pain. Next day she was shut up in the clinic, and a month later she came out, drained but cured.

'That stinking cure's worse than any of them,' she told me. 'I raved for days. It's like love, it always starts out well but the ending's awful.

'The first day this nurse with fat arms (that place is full of dikes) came in to take my order for the day. I picked a pretty good assortment while I was at it: white wine to start with, beer for the day, a good strong red wine for dinner, and whisky to finish up.

'All day the sister kept coming in with my order, and she watched me to make sure I swallowed it all. She didn't have to worry. I was good and pissed by the end of the day. I sang as much as I could. If I hadn't been all alone I could have had a great time.

'You know doctors always use the same methods. It's just like the drugs. They give you less each day, and at the same time they give you a medicine that makes you throw up. It's awful when you see them bringing in your glass, and you know you're going to bring it right up again. It's a horrible punishment. I didn't know where I was any more. I was like a sick dog, I lay in my bed hiccuping, and begged them to stop. Then I had more attacks. I saw disgusting oozing creatures with hundreds of feet. That bit about pink elephants isn't true, I can tell you. I didn't know anything could be so bad.

'I'd never have believed that after all those good times we had, all those parties, I'd end up in all that shit. But I swear to you, anyone who's prepared to go through with it is okay.'

She only had ten days to get her tour ready, but she was all right when she left.

Eleven months is a long time, from New York to Hollywood, from Las Vegas to Chicago, from Rio to Buenos Aires – especially when you're on milk and fruit juice. By the time she got back Edith had had a bellyful, but she was happy.

'It was a great trip, a bit too long, but really great. In 'Frisco there was a French battleship called the *Jeanne d'Arc* and the captain invited me on board. I've never said no to a sailor, so I got together some friends and some American journalists and we went along.

'The captain's launch picked me up, and when I got on board all the sailors were standing to attention as if they were expecting an admiral! What's more, on the gangway a party of them presented arms. You should have seen those Americans' faces, thinking, "Boy, they really do things in style in France."

'I missed you, you would have enjoyed me reviewing the French navy. Actually they owe it to me, really; we've made a lot of them happy, haven't we?

'The young Americans were really nice. On New Year's Day the students from Columbia University wanted to hear me sing "L'Accordéoniste" in front of the Statue of Liberty. I must have been a bit off key, singing in the cold, but it was marvellous to sing for them. They cheered like mad, enough to shake old Liberty's foundations.

'They got pretty thirsty after all that, that's the effect I have on

Americans. One journalist wrote, "Edith Piaf is the best champagne saleswoman in the United States, as soon as she starts to sing in a club your throat is parched with emotion."

'A really funny thing happened. Someone from Paris sent me a note in a large envelope. He didn't know my address, so he just wrote "Edith Piaf, U.S.A." The fellows in the post office wrote on the envelope, "The postmen of Paris send their love." That letter followed me all over the place, and everywhere it stopped the local postmen added a note of their own, like "Us too", "Love from Chicago", "Los Angeles too". There wasn't a free inch of paper when I finally got it. They must have been frightened it would get lost, because they sent someone to deliver it to me personally and, instead of knocking on my door, he whistled "La Vie en rose". Isn't that sweet?

'Still, a year is a long time to go without Paris air, without seeing my friends. I was caught up in my schedule like a fly in a spider's web, no way out. Apart from that everything went well. The Americans wanted me to start all over again; they were so good to me. I love them, but I'm not going to hurry back there.'

I watched Edith wandering round the living-room, looking critically at everything, as if someone had changed the wallpaper. I thought she looked well, less puffy, her hands almost back to normal. But I knew I would never be at peace again; I would always be worried that it would start again.

We had put the trunks from her tour in there, and Edith sat down on one, saying, 'This isn't a bad seat; I'll leave them here, we're always short of chairs in this stupid place.

'You know, I drink nothing but water till mid-day; a little glass of wine at lunch; milk for the rest of the day, though I don't much like it; and not more than two or three drinks in the evening.'

'Does it help?'

'It doesn't do any harm. But it's a bore being so sensible. Did you see the heap of manuscripts on the piano? I'm not going to be short of work.'

She pulled pages at random out of the pile, read them, tapped them out on the piano, and then rang up Guite.

'Guite, I'm back. What did you do while I was away? The

music for *Irma la Douce*? Are you pleased with it? Good. Have
you done anything for me? Yes? Then come on over here,
quickly, you should be here already! You know I can't live
without you. I missed you so much ...'

I heard that sentence several times during the day, and each
time she meant it. She missed us all.

Marguerite had hardly sat down at the piano when Edith held
out a song-sheet. 'Read this, it's called "Salle d'attente", by
Michel Rivgauche; he's great, I've asked him to come and see
me.'

Before Marguerite had finished reading the script, Edith inter-
rupted her, 'Listen to this record. I picked it up in South America,
on a tour in Peru. It's a Spanish girl singing.'

'Edith, that's beautiful,' said Guite. 'Play it again.'

'I need some words to go with it. Who'll write them for me?'

In the end Michel Rivgauche supplied them, and the song
became 'La Foule':

> Emportés par la foule
> Qui nous traîne
> Nous entraîne, l'un vers l'autre
> Nous ne formons qu'un seul corps.

Michel was Edith's latest find. He was slim, with a narrow
little moustache which made him look like the bad guy in a
silent movie, thin, slanted eyebrows and wild hair. He was
kind and intelligent, very talented, always a little behind the
times.

But boulevard Lannes had become even more hectic than the
foule, the crowd, in the song. The Great Piaf was back, and getting ready for Olympia '58.

It was one of her greatest concerts. The new songs were
written by Pierre Delanoë and Michel Rivgauche. Edith's way of
working suited Michel well, he became one of her 'night-time
friends'; Delanoë was just an operative. To him the night was
for sleeping or for work; he hated to feel he was wasting time.
He did not know that Edith had to be followed, that she only
worked when the mood was on her; but that when she did get
down to it, she outlasted everyone. Still, this did not stop him

from writing 'Les Grognards', 'Le Diable de la Bastille', and 'Toi, tu ne l'entends pas' for her.

Before the Olympia concert Edith had decided to take her act on a tour of the provinces. As usual Loulou took care of everything. 'There's a new man in your show, Félix Marten,' he told Edith. He knew his boss well.

'I'll take your word that he's okay,' Edith replied.

Tours was the first stop on their route. Edith was in her dressing-room, going through the usual blue funk that she felt before shows, never a good moment to pay her a courtesy call. She was in the middle of putting on her make-up, another thing that got her down, when there was a knock at the door.

In walked a tall, good-looking, arrogant young man. 'Good evening, Edith, I'm Félix Marten.'

Edith hadn't exactly been brought up surrounded by good manners, but this man seemed most unimpressed by the fact that she was Edith Piaf. He introduced himself as if he were Jesus Christ almighty, and she didn't like it, she was going to take care of that. But he had not finished. 'I'm very pleased to be working with you,' he added. 'Thank you.'

'Not at all,' replied Edith sarcastically.

Félix may not have had any manners, but he had a way with him. Edith listened to him sing, once, twice, three times. He was as cynical on stage as off it, but she wondered if underneath it all he did not have a kind heart. He sang 'T'as une belle cravate', 'Fais moi un chèque', 'Musique pour ...' – hardly love songs. She listened, but she could not make up her mind. All the same, he had something, a personality, and the more she looked at him, the better she liked him, and she realized that if she ever heard him say 'I love you' it would send shivers down her spine – just what she needed.

A few days later Edith called me 'This is it. I've found someone new, I'm in love.'

We were off again.

This time it was I who asked, 'What do you think of him?'

'He's a mixture. He's a bit like Montand, he's tall, and he was a docker; and a bit like Meurisse, cold and very much in control of himself; and a bit like Pousse because he looks like a hand-some thug.'

'He's not a man, Edith, he's a cocktail!'

What she liked most about Félix Marten was that she had decided to make something of him, to remake him in her own image. There was no time to lose, she told Loulou. 'Call Coqua-trix. I want Marten in my show.'

Bruno had trusted Piaf from the start. He would have hired a deaf mute to sing Tosca if she had wanted. Besides, the cheaper they came, the more he liked it; Félix Marten was hardly well known enough for him to want a lot of money. The arrange-ments were made easily enough. More worrying was that Edith had only a month and a half to put Marten to rights. She did not like him the way he was.

He had a lot to learn before he could graduate from the Piaf academy. Edith did not lose a minute, she called Marguerite, Henri Contet and Michel Rivgauche.

'Meet me tomorrow in Nevers, I've got someone new to show you. He's coming to Olympia with me and I want him to have a new repertoire.'

And the three of them found themselves on the train headed for Nevers. She had chosen well, they would never have let her down.

She set them to work that evening. Two days later they left for Paris on the point of collapse, ready to sleep round the clock. But when Edith got back from her tour she had her songs.

For about a month she was in high spirits, getting ready for her new concert, manufacturing her latest love. Félix was not the easiest guinea pig to work on, however. He had ideas of his own and they seldom coincided with hers. They had some terrible fights, they reminded me of the ones she'd had with Yves and the *Compagnons* about their work.

'You'll do some love songs.'

'No, that's not me.'

'You'll do what I tell you. Love songs are the secret of success.'

'I'm not a whore.'

'That's right. Whores don't sing about it, they just do it.'

She won in the end. Félix Marten sang 'Je t'aime mon amour'.

Félix was not really the new boss, but he was entitled to a blue suit all the same, and he entered the ranks of 'Piaf's Boys', as Charles Aznavour called them. He did not have much time to get to know Edith, though; I used to wonder if they managed to spend any time together at all.

When she got back from her tour Edith also found time to make *Les Amants de demain* [*Tomorrow's Lovers*] before going to Olympia.

Les Amants de demain is an old story. Pierre Brasseur, an old drinking friend, had had an idea for a screenplay which appealed to Edith. She talked about it to Marcel Blistène and then, as often happens with movies, nothing else was done. But when Edith returned from America Marcel called her out of the blue and said, 'Are you free? We're doing *Les Amants de demain* in two months.' The cast consisted of Michel Auclair, Armand Mestrel, Mona Goya (his old friend, whose last movie it was), Raymond Souplex, and Francis Blanche.

Not content with writing the screenplay, Pierre Brasseur also wrote a song for Edith, 'Et pourtant'.

In the beginning there had been a sort of misunderstanding between them. Pierre would have been delighted to share Edith's bed at least once, and she was not averse to the idea. But on the day he had decided to proposition her, Edith turned up with some man or other and Pierre decided that this wasn't the right time.

I liked Pierre a lot, but I was glad that he never became one of Piaf's men. It was difficult to imagine an alliance between them. We didn't have much china at home, but what there was wouldn't have lasted a week.

They could never agree about the way they met. He was sure that they had met at Louis Leplée's, but Edith always contradicted him, 'It wasn't there at all, it was in the Tourbillon dance hall. I wasn't Piaf in those days, and I was singing with an orchestra through a bullhorn. You came along one day with some sporty-looking friends, and when I came off the platform after my act, you said to me, "Oh, you're the little girl who was just singing over the bullhorn." '

Pierre had always dreamed of writing songs for her. The idea haunted him to such an extent that one day he called her and said, 'I've just written a song. I was re-reading Anouilh's *La Sauvage* last night, and one of the speeches was written for you; listen: "There will always be a lost dog somewhere to keep me from being happy." I thought it was so beautiful that I asked Anouilh if he would let me write a song using that line. He wasn't sure, but when I told him, "It's for Piaf, she'll like it," he said, "Oh, if it's for her, go ahead." '

And that is how 'Et pourtant' was written:

> *Et pourtant*
> *Il y aura toujours un pauvre chien perdu*
> *Quelque part qui m'empêchera d'être heureuse*

The nights got shorter and shorter at boulevard Lannes, as the rehearsals gathered speed. It was a madhouse, everyone rushing around getting in everyone else's way. Claude kept up as best he could. Edith shouted, laughed and sang. We knew every note of her music by heart.

And there was Marten. Not much to say about him, a puff of wind, he lasted less than four months. That wasn't long, considering he got the full Piaf treatment. Edith was bursting with ideas. It was a long time since she had been like this; but it was an Indian summer, we would never see it again.

Meanwhile we were happy, and there was nothing to make us think we were wrong to be. Life was running smoothly.

One day we were all sitting around the kitchen table. Some woman was there who seemed to think she was in Maxim's and kept her hat on all the time, Michel Rivgauche and Guite. We were talking about songs, and Edith suddenly hushed everyone, 'I've got a song on my mind,' she said, and she beat out the rhythm on the table. 'That's a great rhythm – the tune would go something like this,' and she hummed a melody.

Marten said he would write the words with her.

'You see, you're coming round to love songs after all,' said Edith.

A composer friend, J. P. Moulin, was there. Edith ordered him over to the piano immediately. She too left the table and everyone followed. Dinner was forgotten. We worked all night. Félix had had it, his tall body slumped into a chair, he was yawning his head off. Edith called him to order, 'Hey, we all work together here, we sleep later.'

'I hadn't noticed,' he said, and Edith flew into a rage. I was roaring with laughter. The good old days were back. The song was finished by the morning; it was to be Félix Marten's big success at Olympia. At dawn Edith was still fighting fit. 'Momone, make them some coffee, they're falling asleep,' she commanded.

I looked at them all, their eyes glazed. 'Listen, you'd have to wake them up to make them drink it.'

'They're weaklings. Come into the bathroom and have a chat.'

This time Bruno Coquatrix had been less cautious. Edith's contract ran for four straight months. Once again she broke all records, both in the length of her stay and in takings. More than ever she was the Great Piaf. She was happy, though it was spoiled by Félix Marten; he was not really up to scratch.

'He'll last until the contract at the Olympia runs out.'

It was not a very encouraging thought, but even then it was over-optimistic. Félix was out on his arse after two months at the Olympia, he could not keep up with her any more.

She said to me, 'He may have broad shoulders, but they aren't all that strong.' But she was being unfair. You needed more than broad shoulders, you had to love her selflessly. She was tyrannical, jealous, and exacting, though you could ask anything of her and she would give it to you. She and Félix were never madly in love, so it was understandable that he couldn't take the pressure.

Edith had never been easy to live with, and now there were times when she was frankly impossible. Success and money had added weight to her authority. Too many yes-men kept telling her how great she was, and how beautiful. Yet behind those neon lights stood a damaged woman, shot through with drugs and alcohol. Her heart bore the scars of many blows. Not one man had spared her, each had left his mark.

To keep her spirits up, she started drinking again. Not a lot, but enough to make her temper worse. At that point Marten threw in the sponge. He thought a great deal of himself; he was sharing the bill with Piaf, he wasn't her flunkey, and he was old enough to take care of himself. The contracts should flow in now. So they split up.

Her heart was not really affected, just a little scratch; but even a scratch hurts.

'He was the first one after all the loneliness and the madness. I thought he would help me climb out of the hole, but he pushed me in deeper without realizing it.'

Edith's pride was hurt. She had been jilted. She had fallen so low that a man could walk out on her without giving it a second thought. Each day for the next two months she would have to put up with Félix Marten's dressing-room being beside her own, his cold little smile when they met. But not for long.

Georges Moustaki sang at the College Inn in Montparnasse every evening. He was no fool. He held the ace; admiration was still the best card to play when Edith was around. Not two days after she had broken up with Marten, he knocked on her dressing-room door.

'When I saw him come in, Momone, something clicked. It's a long time since I felt that. He's slim, with kind eyes, and he smiles like a kid at a party. He didn't make a fuss, just said that he composed and sang songs in a club in Montparnasse, and he wanted me to come by and hear him because my opinion meant a lot to him. You know the type.

'I said to him, "Okay, I'll come over this evening." You'd have done the same thing in my place, wouldn't you?'

'Of course; what happened?'

'He's marvellous, sensational! And such a talent! You'd have died if you'd seen me coming out of the Olympia. Robert [the chauffeur] was waiting for me with the car. I told him "Not to-night" and got into Moustaki's old wreck, it's a sieve on wheels. "Are you sure this goes?" I asked him. But I'd told Robert to follow. After all, his songs could be as full of holes as his car.

'I was so pleased to think that when we bumped into old Félix he'd know that I hadn't gone home alone to cry for him, and that I hadn't had to look far to find a replacement.

'But what I really liked about him was his honesty. You know, he'd been spying on me and Marten. Every evening he used to come to the Olympia and walk round checking up on my love life. Isn't that touching?'

Edith's candour and innocence where men were concerned always amazed me.

Four days later, following the well-tried custom, Edith introduced the boulevard Lannes household to their new boss, Georges Moustaki. Nothing was too good for him, the first real boss since Eddie Constantine. The lighter was not gold but platinum, a trifle which cost four hundred thousand francs. Three days later Moustaki lost it and next day she bought him a new one, exactly the same.

Edith was sure she had found a soul-mate in Georges. He was gay, he liked staying up all night. He wasn't choosy, he didn't mind eating in the kitchen. He was ready to be friends with everyone. He led a topsy-turvy life himself, so Edith's chaos didn't bother him. And he was no missionary, his motto was live life as it comes, and as you like. He never read Edith the riot act, never said, 'Go to bed, sleep, don't drink so much, you don't need pills to put you to sleep or to make you work.'

And Edith came back to life again.

Georges wrote one of her most beautiful songs, 'Milord':

> *Allez! venez Milord*
> *Vous asseoir à ma table*
> *Il fait si froid dehors*
> *Ici c'est confortable.*
> *Laissez-vous faire, Milord*
> *Et prenez bien vos aises*
> *Vos peines sur mon coeur*
> *Je vous connais, Milord*
> *Et vos pieds sur une chaise*
> *Vous n' m'avez jamais vue,*
> *Je n' suis qu'un' fill' du port*
> *Une ombre de la rue*
> *Allez venez, Milord ...*

But there was more to him than just talent. Georges revived Edith's taste for a brawl. He was not a model of patience, and when they were on tour Edith more than once had to put on a thick base of pancake make-up; the nights left their scars and they were not always from love-bites. But it didn't matter, she always enjoyed it. When she telephoned me, she sounded happy, 'Georges and I had a fight last night. We went at it hammer and tongs. What a scene! I adore him!'

This was never a bad sign. If Edith put a man through the mill it was because she wanted to hold on to him, and when he got mad enough to slap her, it meant he wanted to keep her.

She made Georges her guitarist and decided to take him with her (on 18 September 1959) to New York for her ninth trip to America; Loulou had signed a four-season contract at the Waldorf Astoria. She was only to do one season. No more United States for her.

When Edith got back from her current French tour, she rented a house at Condé-sur-Vesgre in Seine-et-Oise, for a change of air and so that she could rest. 'You see, I need some oxygen before I leave for New York; it'll do everyone good.'

She also had to give up eating melon in port and strawberries in wine, her latest food fad – they were becoming more of a cocktail and less of a dessert by the day.

Edith had taken a great interest in Marcel's sons since his death. Her favourite was Marcel Junior, probably because he looked so like his father and wanted to be a boxer like him. She invited him to spend a month in the country with her, the whole crowd were going there. Which did not stop Edith, who could never stay in one place for any length of time, from spending most of her time in Paris.

One morning she telephoned me, 'I'm leaving for a few days in the country, you must come with me. Call Charles, if he's there he'll bring you down; it's a long time since I've seen him. I'll be coming back on Saturday. Marcel's leaving for Casablanca and I'm driving him to Orly, so you can come back with us.'

I should have said yes; but I didn't.

On 7 September Edith had her third car accident. Georges was driving Edith's DS 19. She was beside him, and Marcel Cerdan and a young girl-friend sat in the back. It was raining hard. Too late, Georges saw a big shape coming towards them. He slammed on the brake, they skidded, the car flew into the air and left the

road. Some people rushed over and helped Edith get out of the
car. Her face was covered in blood. Cerdan, stunned and also
bleeding, tottered out. Georges, who was untouched, shouted,
'She's Edith Piaf, look after her.'

Someone called an ambulance and she was taken to Ram-
bouillet, where the surgeon sewed up a four-inch wound in her
forehead, a nick in the upper lip, and two tendons that had been
severed in the right hand. Her face was covered with smaller
cuts, too.

On the whole it was not very serious, and I should have been
relieved, I tried to tell myself that she had been lucky, but I
didn't believe it.

When she got home to boulevard Lannes, she gave us all her
waif-like smile and said, 'Well, that's torn it. I can't go off to
America looking like this. The Americans will call me Miss
Frankenstein, won't they?'

An enormous raised scar ran across her forehead and curved
towards her hairline on each side. The upper lip was still deformed. I could hardly pretend she looked like Cleopatra. I said,
'It's noticeable now, but it's only superficial.'

'What sort of a fool do you think I am? It's more than noticeable, this thing on my lip stops me from singing, it's like having
a hare lip; my pronunciation's ruined. It's a disaster. The hospital
told me to try facial massages.'

No one who was there could forget those sessions. The mas-
seur started with the skin on her head, working down to the
scar on her forehead and all over her face, concentrating on the
cuts and bruises. She turned bright red, and the blood beat
visibly beneath her skin. She looked ugly and in pain.

'Shall I stop for a moment?' asked the therapist.

'Are you sure this torture will help me sing in America?'

'Absolutely.'

'Go on, then; and don't worry, I'm okay.'

The one person who escaped all this was Moustaki. Edith,
who was often unfair and bad-tempered, had extraordinary tact
and understanding too. When Georges said, 'Edith, I did this to
you, please forgive me,' she would reply, 'It's not your fault, if
someone else had been at the wheel it would have happened just

the same. It's destiny. Don't bore me with your self-reproach, being sorry is one thing, blaming yourself is another.'

A month later, she arrived in the United States, to be welcomed like the returned prodigal. The press was terrific.

Yet for the first time in her life, Edith was really tired. She loved these people and their country. They would help her pull through. But the fights with Georges were endless, and she no longer enjoyed them. They hurt her, and she was afraid of being left in the lurch again. She did not eat for several days; she drank, but the alcohol burned her. She was cut in two with pain.

On 20 February, as she stood on stage at the Waldorf Astoria, she felt the room spinning round her like a merry-go-round out of control, then it went dark and she collapsed.

They took her into the wings. She vomited blood, then she lost consciousness. They rushed her to the Presbyterian Hospital on 168th Street.

The doctors diagnosed a perforated stomach ulcer with internal haemorrhaging. When she came to they were giving her a transfusion. Edith watched the alien blood rushing into her veins; she asked for Georges. When he left her room he looked furious. Edith's musicians were waiting outside. 'Is it serious?'

'They're going to operate,' was all he would say.

Back in her room, Edith was crying. Later she told me, 'I asked him to kiss me, to tell me that he still loved me a bit, and he said, "Later, Edith, later." '

At the hospital there was no time to lose. For the first time the spectre of death stood at Edith's door. She was four hours on the operating table, and received three transfusions.

The Americans could not get over it. They had thought Edith was the toughest woman in the world. The New York newspapers carried bulletins, telegrams and good wishes poured in, and flowers blocked the way to her ward. Yet Edith had never been so alone.

When I spoke to her on the telephone, she sounded less weak than I'd expected. Finally I said, 'Is Georges there?'

She burst out, 'Don't ever mention his name to me again. I

want to forget him. When I came round after the operation he
wasn't there – he'd gone to Miami. He had the nerve to call
me and tell me that the sun was shining. I couldn't think of anything to say.

'Don't worry, though, I've been feeling better since this
morning; a complete stranger sent me an enormous bunch of
violets, it helped a lot ... Who? Oh, an American, Douglas
Davies.'

17

'NON, JE NE REGRETTE RIEN!'

When Loulou went to see Edith in the hospital and found her propped up against her pillows, her hair done, make-up on, he looked as if he'd seen a ghost.

She burst out laughing, ready to shout at him, ready to bite him, ready to live again. 'What are you gaping at? Did you think I'd had it?' Loulou couldn't find anything to say. He laughed idiotically with delight, 'You're better. I'm so happy.'

'I'm fine, but I need visitors. This place is too depressing. White's even sadder than black. I need some colours, something that can shout and sing. Do you know this fellow Douglas Davies?'

Loulou had been around Edith long enough not to waste any time. 'I'll go get him.'

'I didn't tell you to bring him here, I asked you what he was.'

'He's a young painter.'

'Obviously talented, sending me bunches of violets like that. I'd like to see what he looks like. Maybe he's boss-eyed.'

Loulou got up and headed for the door.

'Don't rush off like that, the place isn't on fire. New York isn't a village, how do you know him? Is he as famous as all that?'

'Oh no, not yet.'

Edith went out like a snuffed candle. Her self-confidence was getting a bit ragged around the edges. 'Did you tell him to send me those flowers? If you did you can kick him out, and you can go with him.'

'No, I know this boy because he came every evening when you were singing at the Waldorf. Since you've been ill he's spent two hours on the subway every day coming across town to ask the hospital how you are.'

'Poor little thing, didn't anyone ever tell him about telephones? Or doesn't he have a dime?'

'He wanted to come himself.'

'If this is a bluff, I'm going to have a relapse. And if it's true I'm getting up tomorrow. Go and get him, like you should have done hours ago. No, wait – give me my mirror. Shit, he's going to be disappointed.'

'Perhaps you will be.'

'I'd rather not wait too long to find out. Go on, Loulou. It'll do me more good than a transfusion.'

Her face was ravaged, her arms thin, her high forehead wrinkled, her cheeks hollow, her skin sickly pale, but Douglas Davies didn't care. All he could see were those violet-blue eyes looking at him and that wide mouth with its welcoming smile.

'Miss Edith, *vous êtes* marvellous,' he spluttered. 'Thank you very much.'

Edith was in seventh heaven. Everything was starting again. She asked for needles and wool and immediately knitted him one of those impossible sweaters on which she owned the exclusive rights. She had not knitted for a man since Marcel Cerdan. The signs could not be wrong, she was certain this was going to be a great new love.

When Jacques Pills was in America he went to see her and found her so radiant that he said at once, 'Is it possible? Are you in love? You look beautiful!'

And she said, 'You know, Jacques, I was so far gone, love was the only thing that could have saved me.'

Douglas came every day to see her and work on his French. She could do and say whatever she wanted. Douglas was awe-struck, he had never seen a woman like her before.

She was certain that her black period, the bad-luck time was over. On 25 March, however, when she was convalescing, and starting to go for walks on her Doug's arm, she had a relapse. This time she was not alone; Douglas followed the trolley which took Edith to the operating theatre for the second time, and when she came to he was there.

Nearly two months later, she stood at the hospital door holding Douglas's and Loulou's arms. 'When I went in there it was winter, now it's spring.'

The people waiting for her in her room at the Waldorf did

not share her optimism. The musicians who were waiting for her looked very depressed. Despite their boss's recovery, there was nothing very spring-like about them. Edith had been away for more than three months, and they had had to take work wherever they could find it, just to make ends meet. There's no shortage of musicians in the United States, and Edith's men ate hot dogs more often than *paté de foie*.

When she came in, Edith started to laugh. 'Couldn't you even put up a few flags to welcome me back?'

'Edith, the hospital cost more than three million francs. We have to pay the hotel bill, and buy our return tickets. We're broke.'

She did not hesitate. 'We can't have that. Loulou, you announce that I'm going to do a week at the Waldorf.'

'You can't do that, Edith. You won't do it. It's madness.'

'Yes, I will. It'll do me good. And that way I can leave the Americans with a good memory; I certainly owe them one.'

And sing she did. She looked more fragile, more pathetic than ever. Yet her voice held a new sound, the sound of her joy. Doug was there, his eyes never leaving her face.

She was not wrong. Edith always knew what to do where her career was concerned. They admire spirit in the United States and the reviews were ecstatic: 'Miss Courage ...' 'The brave little Frenchwoman'. 'A lion's strength is contained inside that tiny frame.' 'She never sang better.' 'Her voice still has its magic.'

But she had to take 'L'Accordéoniste' out of her act, the range was too demanding, it tired her. When she returned to France she sang it less and less, and finally she had to cut it out altogether.

For a week, dressed in black, she devoured herself nightly at the Waldorf Astoria. But she kept going. Not only did she make the money she needed, she had enough left over to get into mischief.

'Come on,' she told Douglas, 'I'm going to take you back with me.' It was a mistake, exporting this pure U.S. product. He should have been left on his home ground.

On 21 June 1960, when she got off the plane at Orly, all the reporters were waiting for her. Edith was proud of her American teddy-bear, and showed him off all round. Douglas tagged along, looking happy but obviously not really understanding – he never did.

He was no threat to the old hands at boulevard Lannes. He was an innocent, a Daniel in the Lions' den, and they saw that Edith still gave all the orders. They tapped him familiarly on the shoulder, called him Doug, and went about their business. He would have been less lonely in the Sahara.

They had their first run-in immediately on their arrival.

'Douguy darling, this is our room.'

He stared at the bed as if there was a snake on it.

'Don't you understand, I said it's our bed.'

'I'm sorry, Edith, that just won't work. I'm not used to double beds, in America we have one bed each.'

Edith slammed the door on him, scarlet with rage. No man had ever done that to her before. He was not the first American in her life, none of the others had ever dared say no to her.

'Momone, can you imagine how I felt? If I take up with a man it's because I want to have him within easy reach. If I have to traipse through the apartment or ring for him like a servant I'll have lost interest by the time he arrives.'

The next day he tucked his paintbox under his arm and quite naturally got ready to go out. Then that famous voice nailed him to the spot, 'Douguy, where do you think you're going?'

'I thought I'd go out and do some painting, look around Paris, see the Louvre.'

'You're mad, you'll get lost. You don't know Paris. When you go out Robert, the chauffeur, will take you in the car. But right now I need you; stay here, my love.'

He gave in to her, smiling, thinking that perhaps it was right to stay with her on the first day, he would go out tomorrow.

Only once did she allow him to open his paintbox, and that was to have her portrait painted. She was very proud of it. 'It's beautiful, isn't it, Momone? That's how he sees me.'

But it was not Piaf on stage, it was the image of her that the crowds carried around in their hearts.

I realized straightaway that their relationship would not last, and that reality would finally overtake Douglas's fantasy. He could only be shocked by the boulevard Lannes household, by the people who surrounded Edith, by a foreign world crawling with parasites who clung to her sick body.

Despite her courage and her will to live, Edith had over-reached herself. She had barely a week to prepare her summer tour. She plunged into the work, not wasting a second, but she found it hard to go through with it, especially without the help of drugs or liquor. The diet the American doctors had prescribed was wise, but it was not much fun – plenty of milk and broiled food, and nothing else.

'They'll kill me with this jockey's diet. I can't sing with only that inside me.'

She was taking Douguy along on the tour, of course – she had bought him a huge Chevrolet, because he did not like driving French cars. Michel Rivgauche was also in the party.

The evening before they left, Edith was in great spirits, as good as she had ever been, and Loulou said to me, 'When I see her like this I have to pinch myself to make sure I'm awake. I start wondering if that whole business was a nightmare or whether it really happened.'

At midnight Edith refused to go to bed. She had decided that she would sleep in the car. 'We're going to show our American Paris by night. The poor lamb, I haven't taken any notice of him since we've been back.'

'That guy's going to need a life-belt before long,' Loulou murmured. 'You have to rest, Edith ... remember the doctor's orders.'

'Oh shut up, I'll only be drinking milk. Fuck off and leave me alone. I haven't been so happy in ages.'

So we spent the night rushing about between Pigalle and the Champs-Elysées.

At dawn they climbed into the car to begin the tour. Edith closed her eyes. How long would this one last? She did not want to know any more. Before they left she had said to me, 'I have to buy my happiness now, like a head of lettuce, or three lemons for twenty centimes. I choose them, pay for them, wrap them up, and take them home. When I get back the lettuce is wilted and the lemons are sour. Yet while I was holding them in my hands, bringing them home, I believed in them.'

Then Douglas's attention lapsed, he closed his eyes and the brand-new Chevrolet ploughed off the road and into the guard-rail.

Robert and his wife Hélène were following them in Edith's DS. When they got to the scene of the accident, they found Douglas crying like a child over Edith. She had fainted. Michel Rivgauche was trying to pull himself together, his forehead bleeding from a huge gash.

Edith came round very quickly. She looked at them all, one after the other, as though she were making an inventory, and said, 'I don't have much luck on the road, do I?'

She was right. She had three broken ribs and bruises all over.

They bound her in a very tight plaster cast. She insisted on morphine – how could she sing without it? This time she was not doing it for herself, but to fulfil her obligations.

This time she would win, the drug would not overpower her. Before she went on stage, the doctor gave her an injection. After the tenth song she disappeared into the wings for a moment and he gave her a second. During the day she did without them, but little by little she started to drink again.

Edith stayed several days in Cannes, and the sunbathers cooking themselves on the beach were treated to a sight of the famous Piaf–Davies couple. Just a glance at him in his bathing trunks with his fine muscular body was enough to make the girls swoon. Because she was Edith Piaf they forgave her her old-fashioned bathing costume, the scarf on her head and her strained white face. Her thighs were too thin, her knees too fat. But she did not care about any of them. She had a handsome boy of twenty-three on her arm. What no one knew was that under her blouse was a tangle of bandages that pinched her and hampered her breathing. It was unbearably hot in the sun. But it did not matter, she stayed beside Douglas, she would not leave him. She hated the sun and the swarming beaches, but she thought that he would enjoy swimming, so she went with him. She was sure she had done as much for him as he could wish for.

But Douglas wanted something else. Picasso and a whole group of artists lived near Cannes. The core of the contemporary painting world was gathered within a few square miles. This was what he had dreamed of, back in the States. He had come to France, but he had seen none of the things he wanted to see. All he saw was a little woman who had touched his young heart one evening under the false lights of the stage, because she sang of a truth which bowled him over, a truth he had not understood until then. He did not know this world which had seduced him was not a gentle world at all, but a hard and discouraging one.

Edith fought her illnesses with any weapon that came to hand. She had been told that garlic is good for rheumatism, so she ate it all the time; it nauseated Douglas. She had gone back on to cortisone to overcome the pain, but it had blown her up. And to help keep her spirits up she was drinking. She was slowly killing herself.

Douglas could not keep up with her. This woman, who was held together by a doctor with injections, who lost her temper over trifles, who insisted on his constant presence and blind obedience, had worn him out. And he was not alone: not one of her entourage was left – even the leeches had run out of stamina. Edith was a tightly coiled spring unwinding. She went on with the same energy as before, but when she stopped, she would stop dead.

In Bordeaux, the next to last town on their tour before Biarritz, Douglas and Edith had a fight. They hurled a few home truths at each other, then Edith, full of barbiturates, fell asleep. Douglas took advantage of this respite to scamper off to the station. He spent the night sitting unshaven in the second-class waiting-room, with his belongings under his arm like a tramp.

When Edith emerged from her heavy sleep, she realized he had gone. Like a maniac, with her hair all over the place and a coat thrown over her nightdress, she jumped into a taxi. 'Take me to the station, quickly.'

'Which train do you want?'

'I don't know, but hurry.'

'You must understand,' she told me later, 'I couldn't afford to lose him. I simply couldn't. He was the last. I must have looked like a madwoman, the station was full of holidaymakers, but I didn't care, I had to catch him. The guy at the entrance said to me, "Ticket please," I just told him to screw off.

'I stood on the platform, it was like a scene from a bad movie, the train was drawing out. I must have looked so forlorn standing on that damned platform, it was so stupid I was laughing and crying like a lunatic.'

The rest of the tour was a disaster.

In this state she left for Stockholm, where she had an engagement at the Bernsbee, the biggest music hall in the country. She was singing 'Tu me fais tourner la tête' for five thousand people when she collapsed like a little black rag at the foot of the microphone. Everyone clapped, they thought it was part of the act. But the curtain was brought down, and she was carried off stage. Then, for the first time, she was filled with fear, 'I don't want to die in Sweden, I want to go home.'

'There's no plane.'

'Then get one. You aren't going to let me die here.'

She hired a DC4 to take her home to Paris. Her fear cost her one million, five hundred thousand francs that she could not afford.

On 22 September she went into the American hospital in Neuilly, where they performed an emergency operation for an inflammation of the pancreas. Once again she won another round against death, lying all alone in her empty, antiseptic hospital room.

I knew what all those illnesses hid though, I alone knew the truth. When they had operated on her in New York, they had discovered cancer, but too late for a cure. If she had agreed to behave reasonably she would have lived a few more years, but now she was lost. From now on her life would amount to no more than a series of visits to hospitals – and yet a year from now she was to reach a new height in her career.

When she came out of the hospital, she was to record 'Milord'. We begged her not to do it, but in vain. She came out of the hospital at eleven and by two o'clock was rehearsing. She stayed on her feet for eight hours, saying to the technicians, 'Keep going, don't give up on me. I'm not coming back to do it again.'

Loulou was angry. 'That's enough, Edith. You've got to stop.'

'Don't stop me from singing now, it's all I've got left.'

That sentence became very familiar; whenever we said no to her she would trot it out, and we would shut up.

As usual, she had overdone it. So Loulou took the opportunity to wrap her up like a baby, stick her in his car, and carry her off to his house at Richebourg, saying, 'You shan't leave here till you're better, Edith.'

He could say what he wanted, she took no notice. She only wanted one thing, to sleep and forget. The only people with her were a nurse and Claude Figus. She was so used to seeing Claude hanging around that she did not even notice him any more. But she was still his idol. He loved her enough to put up with anything.

She often introduced him as 'my secretary', but it didn't mean much, he was little more than a glorified errand-boy.

But now, for a few weeks, Claude was in luck. There was no one around to talk to Edith of love, to say the words she needed to hear. So one evening, when she was feeling better, Claude forgot himself, and emptied his heart to her; and there was a lot there, for it had been accumulating since he was thirteen. No one could resist this flow of candour and love; Edith took him in her arms and he got his reward.

It did not go much beyond that, but he didn't care. His happiness lasted through Edith's convalescence.

It took her close to a year to learn how to live again. Her crippling rheumatism had stopped her from walking. Vimbert, a chiropractor, came daily. He massaged her and patiently righted her spine, unknotting one by one the twisted muscles and tortured nerves. It was amazing to watch how docile she was in his hands as he taught her to walk, 'The right foot now, bring it forward. That's good. Now the left. Three more steps, Edith. That's enough for today.' In the end he accompanied Edith on all her trips, she could no longer live without his help.

Boulevard Lannes was about as lively as a tomb. You felt like going around on tiptoe. No music, nothing. I had never known such silence.

Edith's face was so swollen she looked as if she had stuck her head in a bee-hive. 'I look pretty awful, don't I, Momone?'

'Well, your cheeks are a good colour. They look quite healthy.'

She waved it aside. 'Can you imagine me on stage with a face like this?'

Clearly not. When Loulou called me to say she was coming back, he said, 'It's okay, she's getting better. She'll be completely over it soon and ready to go again.'

She was ready to go, but not in the direction he thought. In a short time she was back in hospital again, in a deep coma. She was ninety per cent finished, but somehow she pulled out of it, and again the newspapers shelved the obituaries.

No sooner was she back at boulevard Lannes than she was offered a tour. Loulou protested with all his might, Figus and I begged her not to go, she told us to go fly a kite.

'I've got two months to prepare for it, that's quite enough. And anyway, how am I going to eat? I've got nothing left to sell. I'm broke. So what can I do? I even called Michel Emer' (her last hope when she was down), 'he went to S.A.C.E.M. for me, but they won't give me a penny for the songs I wrote. I have to sing.'

Soon after, I arranged to meet Edith in the Bois de Boulogne. I sensed the change as soon as I saw her. I could not compare her with the way she had looked two years before, but there was a happy light sparkling in her eyes.

'You're in love.'

'Does it show already? I'm not even sure I am, yet.'

'Tell me about it anyway. We'll decide later if he's worth it.'

'You know I don't feel up to much at the moment. Michel Vaucaire [a song-writer who worked for her] called me the other day and said, "I'm sending over a man called Charles Dumont; he's absolutely right for you. You must see him. I want you to listen to the song he's bringing you. I've written the words and he did the music. The lyric's nothing special but the music's fantastic."

'I said yes, but I was bored to death by the whole idea. By the time he was supposed to come over, I had completely forgotten about him. There were two timid little rings at the door, it really annoyed me. Claude brought him in, "It's Charles Dumont, Edith, you have a meeting with him."

' "So what?" I said, and then he came in. Not my type at all, big and strong-looking but dressed like a civil servant. He stared at his shoes the whole time, hardly dared to look at me. If he'd been a travelling salesman I don't think he would have made a single sale in a year, not with God on his side.'

It started badly. Edith said brusquely, 'Seeing that you've brought me a song, you'd better sit down and play it.'

Poor Dumont was sweating profusely, but he did not even dare wipe his face.

Edith cruelly said, 'Do you want my handkerchief?'

'No, no, I have my own ... thank you.'

And he started to play, 'Non, rien de rien ...':

> Non! Rien de rien ...
> Non, je ne regrette rien!
> Ni le bien qu'on m'a fait,
> Ni le mal. Tout ça m'est bien égal!
> Non! Rien de rien ...
>
> Non, je ne regrette rien!
> C'est payé, balayé, oublié,
> Je me fous du passé!
>
> Avec mes souvenirs
> J'ai allumé le feu.
> Mes chagrins, mes plaisirs,
> Je n'ai plus besoin d'eux!
>
> Car ma vie, car mes joies
> Aujourd'hui
> Ça commence avec toi!

That changed everything, once again it was love at first sight.

'That's wonderful, unbelievable ... you're a wizard. That's absolutely me. That's just what I feel, just what I think ... it's what I believe.'

'Do you like it?' he said, still trying to pull himself together and not succeeding very well.

'It's terrific. It'll be my best song ever. I wish I were already on stage singing it.' And she sang it straight off.

Dumont was very moved. 'When you sing it it's shattering.'

Everyone who turned up that day had to listen to the song. By the fifth time she knew it by heart. By the tenth, the routine was so well worked out that Edith hardly changed a thing on stage.

Charles Dumont could not get over it. He had watched the growth of his luck reflected in Edith's face. His happiness had left him quite speechless.

'Come back tomorrow and we'll work on it,' she told him.

'You know, he's been coming for a week now, like a good little civil servant going to his office. At exactly two-thirty he sits down at the piano and we sweat over it together. I like him because he's a man, he's reliable. I'd like to hold his arm, he wouldn't faint dead away, he'd stand up straight. There's something very touching about him, he adores his mother. He's big but he's so gentle and shy.'

She stopped and looked at me.

'I know what you're thinking, Doug was the same way, but he was just a kid. It wasn't a heart he needed, it was a sense of reality. He saw me through rose-tinted glasses, like something in an American fairy story, half sister, half mother. There was no room for a woman in his picture.

'Doug's been calling me since the thing in Bordeaux. He's had an exhibition in America. He said to me that he'll come back when he's grown up a bit. But I'm too old to take on kids. I'm not young enough, and I'm not old enough. I really loved him, but he's used to his antiseptic world, and mine is crawling with germs. You need more than a vaccination to stand it.'

We chatted a long time that day, Edith seemed very well. 'It's true, I don't regret a thing, just like the song says. But all the same, that drug thing scared me, and it still does. When they give me morphine now I start shaking, I don't want to have to go through all that again. I couldn't bear it.'

As I had expected, Charles Dumont kept his distance, not at all like the others. Patient, gentle, and kind, he did not boss her around, but he did not obey her either. He was on the same level as she. It changed Edith, and it did her a lot of good. But Charles Dumont did not move into boulevard Lannes; that was a pity, for Edith was very lonely.

He wrote about thirty songs for her, some of them have remained classic Piaf: 'Les Mots d'amour', 'La Belle Histoire d'amour' (for which Edith wrote the words), 'La Ville inconnue', 'Les Amants', and 'Mon Dieu':

> *Mon Dieu, mon Dieu, mon Dieu,*
> *Laissez-le-moi, encore un peu,*
> *Mon amoureux...*
> *Un jour, deux jours, huit jours...*
> *Laissez-le-moi, encore un peu,*
> *A moi...*

She was in much better spirits, but physically she was still not entirely well. After that next tour, she was due to sing at the Olympia. It was almost a year since Edith had sung. She was nervous; fear, stronger than ever, gripped at her throat and paralysed her.

On the first day, at Rheims, when she came on stage, the audience would not stop clapping, and each time the orchestra tried to start up the first number the cheers and clapping broke out again. Finally she managed to start, but her throat was so dry that she had to stop in the middle. Everyone in the wings was shaking with fright. It was a disaster. But she began again, and when she sang 'Je ne regrette rien', there were three encores.

But she overestimated her strength. The next day she was exhausted. She sang almost mechanically, the audience could feel it, and their applause was mechanical too.

Before her Edith could see the list of towns stretching out like a snake, ready to wrap itself round her neck and throttle her. But she had to keep going, so she took stimulants. She still had enough strength to turn down the injections that they kept offering her, although this time they were for her own good.

But the theatre-owners realized that they were taking a risk that she might collapse on stage. And for the first time in her career, towns like Nancy, Metz, and Thionville cancelled Edith's contracts.

At Maubeuge there was a new crisis. They had to bring down the curtain and announce to a jeering audience that Madame Piaf had a slight indisposition, nothing serious, and would they please be patient for a few seconds.

Someone in the audience shouted out, 'They're taking her to the hospital!' Edith heard it and pulled herself together. 'Give me a shot, I'll go back.' The drugs were taking over again.

The orchestra and the stage hands protested, 'No, you've no right. It'll help her to sing, but it'll kill her too.'

'If you won't help, I'll go on alone.' She had already drawn back the curtain. The audience sat down again.

She went on stage and she kept going to the end of the tour, but the price was high. Singing was torture. Every inch of her body hurt, made her want to cry out. But she went on until the very last town, Dreux.

The journalists were there, waiting for her inevitable collapse, like vultures. She knew it, and she found the strength to yell at them, 'It won't happen tonight!'

When the curtain went up, there on the stage was a little black figure, its white face puffy with antibiotics; a circus puppet with an Edith Piaf mask. It was grotesque and tragic.

Loulou and Charles Dumont and the orchestra all begged her to stop. The manager was going to clear the theatre. Edith swallowed half a tube of her pep-pills – enough to keep a horse on its feet – and shouted at them, 'If you do that I'll kill myself. Please let me sing,' she begged them.

She clung to the piano to stop herself falling over. An icy sweat ran down her back. She cried to the audience, 'I love you, you're my whole life.' It was true, and the audience gave her a standing ovation, encouraging her like a boxer. 'Come on, Edith, you can do it. Keep going.'

It was a fight, a vile battle between a little, frail woman and her disease. She wanted to give the audience what remained of her life, and the audience, understanding her, encouraged her. In the wings everyone was in tears. It was too much, she could not go on. The eighth song KO'd her. She fell down and did not get back up again.

No one wanted their money back. The auditorium emptied in silence. They all bore the pain of a woman who had wanted right up to the end to give them the best thing she had to give, her voice ... her life.

In the black DS Loulou and Charles Dumont watched Edith, a little pile of mink, shaking with fever. They drove her straight to the hospital at Meudon.

The Olympia show was due to start in sixteen days. Loulou Barrier and Bruno Coquatrix wondered whether to cancel the contract. The doctors had said, 'She won't sing,' but Edith forbade Loulou to cancel; then she gave in to the rest cure which would allow her to sleep, at least to recoup her wavering strength, and to forget.

One of the doctors protested, 'But, Madame, to go back on stage is suicide.'

Edith looked at him and said, 'I like that kind of suicide. It's all mine.'

On 29 December 1960, the curtain went up on Olympia '61. She had not had enough time to rehearse, so the premiere was set for early January.

Edith had overcome everything, sickness, the bottle, drugs; as if, in the words of the song Dumont had written for her, they were forgotten, swept away – 'oublié, balayé'. Her final martyrdom had purified her. She would go on and on, the greatest of all time. In the middle of 'Mon vieux Lucien' she made a mistake; she stopped everything, laughed and said, 'Don't worry,' and started all over again.

On that evening Edith first sang one of the most difficult songs in her repertoire, 'Les Blouses blanches' by Marguerite Monnot and Michel Rivgauche.

She started gently, sounding as if she were far away:

> Ça fera bientôt trois années
> qu'elle est internée
> Internée avec les fous
> Avec les fous.

Then the delirium crept over her and she shouted out

> *Et chaque fois il y a des blouses blanches ...*

Through this song she saw again the man she had loved, the man she had dreamed about.

> *Et reviennent les blouses blanches*

And at the very end she screamed,

> *J'suis pas folle, j'suis pas folle ...*

You could no longer bear to listen to her wailing about her madness. You wanted it to end, you wanted her to break down, anything rather than listen to this poor little woman shaking and screaming. She had never been as great as she was at that moment.

When she finally fell silent, there were several seconds of total silence, and then the audience burst into applause.

That audience, the smartest people in Paris, applauded her as they had never done before. Women were crying; flowers were thrown on to the stage and landed at Edith's feet, and she bowed and bowed. I was in the back of the auditorium; it was too much for me, I could not stand any more; I went to the lavatory so that I could cry in peace.

Someone wrote about her: 'She has smashed all our previous ideas. She is Piaf, she is a new phenomenon.'

On 13 April she left the Olympia to go on tour once more. There was to be no more normal life for Edith, she had gone too far. On 25 May she gave in and went into the American hospital in Neuilly, to be operated on for intestinal adhesions. Once more she recovered, and Loulou took her to his house in Richebourg for more rest. Next day, on 9 June, almost cut in two by pain, she went back to the American hospital with an intestinal blockage.

For months she lived in slow motion. Charles Dumont stayed with her, his reliable affection perhaps what she needed to help her get over it.

But a man was to come who would sweep everything else

aside, and give Edith the last and most perfect love of her life. She said to me, 'I've been through a lot of lovers, but until now I only loved one man, Marcel Cerdan. All my life I've been waiting for one more: Théo Sarapo . . .'

18

A FAIRYTALE COMES TRUE

A few months before her marriage to Théo, Edith said to me, 'When I talk about Théo, I feel I should begin by saying, "Once upon a time . . ."' She was right, it *was* a fairy story. Their love was the most beautiful of all, the most pure.

Edith saw herself and others very clearly when she chose to do so. 'Marcel and I loved each other a lot, but I know that if he hadn't died he would have left me. Not because he would have fallen out of love, but because he was honest, and so was I. He had a wife and three sons, and he would have gone back to them. If I had not met Théo, I would have really missed something in life.'

Yet Théo Sarapo caused more gossip than any of her other men. She was forty-seven, she was burnt out, exhausted, famous. He was unknown, twenty-seven, and as handsome as a Greek god. They said that he was poor, but that was not true, his parents were comfortably off. Edith, whom everyone believed rich, was absolutely ruined. It was hard to imagine, especially when you heard that Loulou Barrier had chalked up a thousand million francs in contracts for her. Just the same Edith left her husband forty-five million francs' worth of debts when she died. Théo had to go and sing abroad to keep going and to make a bit of money for himself. In France his fees were attached by his debtors, and so were the ten million francs in royalties that S.A.C.E.M. levied annually on Edith's songs.

Love and money do not often go together. But once the way is clear, once you know all about it, the story of Edith and Théo can begin the way she wanted it: 'Once upon a time . . .'

The winter of 1962 was freezing, Edith felt the cold in her heart and in her bones. The days were long.

'I'm not living any more. I'm not allowed anything, I can't eat what I want, drink, go for walks, sing, crying is bad for my morale, the only thing I'm allowed to do is to laugh, and I don't feel like it. Laughing and loving can't be done to order. So what am I waiting for? I don't know.'

Charles Dumont, Loulou, and Guite discussed new plans with her to help sustain her interest in life, but month by month they were always postponed. She was surrounded by silence and emptiness. There was not much fun to be had at Piaf's place any more, she had run out of money. Going to visit Edith had become a 'good deed', a duty. Only her most faithful men still kept in touch. Yves called, Pills and Henri Contet dropped in from time to time. Charles Aznavour did too, but he hadn't much time. Raymond Asso had never forgotten her, but he was bitter. He called to criticize and complain. Raymond was the only man who had never forgiven her for leaving him. Constantine was kind, though.

The old guard remained faithful. They would pop in now and then. All her old friends, Pierre Brasseur, Robert Lamoureux, Suzanne Flon, Jean Cocteau, Jacques Bourgeat. Her musicians and her song-writers, Francis Lai, Noël Commaret, Robert Chauvigny, Michel Rivgauche, Pierre Delanoë, Michel Emer. It was quite a crowd, but it didn't mean anything.

On the days that Edith surfaced there were still parties, but the nights at boulevard Lannes were a shadow of their former selves. As soon as she felt better, Edith started to overdo it. When Loulou asked her to take care she would reply, 'But why should I be good now, for whom? I never have been, and I do so want to live a little now.'

It was on an evening like that, when she was just about on her feet, that Claude Figus brought a friend of his to see her, a tall boy dressed in black, with dark hair and dark eyes. His name Théo Lambouskas. He sat on the moquette in one corner like a beautiful racehorse, or a big black greyhound, and he didn't say a word.

He got on her nerves. 'I don't like silent people. If he was bored, he could have left. I was putting Claude through his paces for his recording, "Quand l'amour est fini", and "La Robe bleue", and this Théo just sat and listened and didn't say anything.'

He was so quiet that in the end Edith forgot he was there. But he had not forgotten her.

In February 1962 Edith went into the clinic of Ambroise-Paré, at Neuilly, with double bronchial pneumonia. She had got in the way of a draught that was looking for a customer.

'I'm beginning to feel at home in the hospital now. I know how to behave, what to say, and especially how bored one gets, so when they told me that a Théo Lambouskas had asked to see me you can imagine I said yes. What I was most pleased about was that it was someone new, someone I didn't know. But I was wrong. It was the boy who sat in the corner, Claude's friend. He didn't bring me flowers, he gave me a little doll instead. It really amazed me, he must really have given it some thought.

' "I'm a bit old for dolls, you know," I said.

'He laughed, his smile was unlike anyone else's, it lit you up, it made you want to be pretty for him. He looked like a sleek black tomcat, he made you want to do better just for him. And yet I felt so little in my hospital bed.

' "You know, Edith – do you mind if I call you Edith – this doll is different, it comes from my country, from Greece." '

They chatted about this and that in a relaxed way, then he promised, 'I'll come back tomorrow.'

By the way in which he said it, she could tell it was true. She was looking forward to tomorrow.

The next day he brought flowers. And he said, 'See you to-morrow.' Each time he brought her something, not expensive but chosen with care. Edith, who had squandered fortunes to bring pleasure to people, was finally learning that only the thought counts.

After several days Edith asked him, 'Don't you have anything else to do? How is it that you can come and see me every day?'

'I make out.'

'I really wanted him to talk about himself. But, you won't believe this, I didn't dare ask. He seemed to be keeping something from me, all locked in, like in a safe. He had a secret.'

One afternoon, in an offhand way he asked, 'Would you like me to do your hair?'

'Why? Are you a hairdresser?'

'He blushed, and I was so pleased he could blush like a virgin. That was his secret – he was a hairdresser. In a flash I wanted to be young and beautiful. My heart was hurting me. I realized that I was about to climb back on that merry-go-round. But looking the way I did, I was afraid I'd be climbing up there alone. An old hag like me with this boy, it was impossible ...'

She turned away and said, 'No.'

'Do you think I'd make a mess of it?'

It was not that. She was ashamed of the little hair she had left, it grew like moss on her head.

'Théo's hands were made for fine silky hair, not for my three shrivelled rats' tails.'

But he did not listen to her, he did her hair.

There were plenty of next days. Edith held her breath, never daring to say, 'See you tomorrow.' Don't talk about happiness, she decided, keep it to yourself. It's fragile, it can break easily. And if he had said no, her happiness would have skittered away.

As Edith improved, Théo stayed longer. He brought her books.

'Don't you read?'

'I'd like to but it tires me.'

So, patiently, he read to her.

Edith left the clinic, and things went on as before.

It took a long time for Théo to confess that he wanted to sing.

'You can't imagine how happy that made me. At last I am going to be able to do something for him. I tried him out right away, he had everything he needed – looks, a voice, sensitivity.' Now she had another reason for living – to create a new singer.

She was the boss again.

'Your name's no good. Théophanis Lambouskas, no one'll be able to get their tongue round it, and besides it's too foreign; they'll think you're going to start singing in Greek. Théo is good. But Théo what?' Then she burst out laughing. 'I know, *Sarapo*. That's what you'll be called, Théo Sarapo. And I'm the one who found it for you. *Sarapo Théo* – I love you, Théo.'

To the French *Sarapo* means 'I love you'; it was one of the few Greek words she learned during her adventure in Athens with Takis Menelas, and she had never forgotten it.

Edith had stopped caring about the way she looked a long time ago. She had made a big effort for Marcel Cerdan, but when he died she had given me all the dresses he had liked. She had gone on one of her couturier binges before her American trip, but it had not lasted. She lounged around in a sweater and skirt the way we used to do when we were kids, and occasionally in slacks. Her dresses were fifteen years old. For months she had wandered around in an old blue nightdress that a tramp wouldn't have picked up.

Théo gently told her, 'You must dress up more. You look good in trousers.' He was sensitive enough to understand that she did not want to show her body and legs any more. And for him she began to take pride in her appearance again.

For the first time in her life Edith did not rush around shouting, 'I'm in love, he loves me.' She kept it to herself, warm in her heart. But it burst through and lit her up. She was so radiant that we were able to forget how she really was.

They loved each other with a powerful love, the kind you read about in books and say to yourself, 'That's too good to be true.' He did not notice that Edith's hands had become all knotted, or that she looked as if she had lived a hundred years.

They went to Biarritz together, the town where Edith had suffered so much three years earlier, the day after her break-up with Douglas Davies. At the Hôtel du Palais, where she had stayed before, no ghosts haunted her. There would never be another ghost, Théo had chased them all away.

She had always refused to sit in the sun, go in the water, or spend time in the open air, but she gave in to Théo. She put on a swimsuit and tanned herself like all the other women. She uncovered her body beside theirs on the beach, and Théo had eyes for her alone. She had no need to say to him, 'Don't go away,' or 'Come back quickly.' He never left her side.

'When I looked at this Apollo,' Edith said, 'handsomer than anyone I'd ever known, I thought to myself how selfish I was, that I had no right to love him, no right to chain him to me; it couldn't last. I'd gone crazy again. And for the first time in my life I wanted to savour these days; not to throw the minutes, the hours, the weeks that he had given me out of the window.'

When they got back to Paris Loulou started talking about contracts again. The first one would be at Olympia, he already had a date: September.

'Okay,' said Edith. 'But with him.'

Théo had no experience, he was a beginner. Loulou wanted to say no, but he gave in. Like all of us, he gave way to them. The impossible became the possible, Edith had started to work. Théo said to her, 'The best lesson for me is to hear you sing.'

At the end of April Douglas passed through Paris, and he came to see Edith. Boulevard Lannes had come back to life, though it was not the same as before. There were fewer bottles of red wine, fewer staff, and lots of young boys, Théo's friends. Edith had said, 'I want Théo to have friends around him, boys of his own age.'

She was pleased to see Douglas again, but he seemed such a kid next to Théo. As far as she was concerned, there would never again be anyone to compare with Théo.

Doug spent several days with them, and painted Théo's portrait as a surprise for Edith. 'It's for you, Edith, to put beside your own.'

When he was ready to leave, she said to him, 'Already?'

'Oh, this was just a short visit. I'll be back.'

On 3 June 1962, Douglas Davies took off from Orly Airport. A few minutes after take-off the plane crashed.

They hid the papers from Edith. The radio and television 'broke down'. Who could tell her about this latest disaster?

But some deaths cannot be hidden, and in time Edith found out about it. Her mouth fell open, she started to scream, 'No, no, it can't be true! It's impossible! He was killed like Marcel!'

This latest blow sent her back to her room. She spent some days in darkness, coming out only to make Théo swear he would never take a plane.

Once more Edith refused to leave her bed. It was Michel Emer who got her out of it. Edith was broke, and as she had done so often in the past, she called him. 'You know why I'm calling?'

'Of course.'

'You'll have to see if you can get me an advance on my royalties. Being sick is free, but getting over it isn't.'

'Don't worry, I'll get you out of it.'

He strode like a warrior to the Society of Authors and the S.R.D.M. – the Society for the Administration of the Rights of Mechanical Reproduction of Authors, Composers, and Publishers, and he got a good stake out of them. When he told Edith the good news she asked him, 'Don't you have a song for me as well?'

'You know I can't write anything if I don't see you.'

'I look awful, but if that doesn't frighten you, you can come over.'

Michel rushed over at top speed.

'Well?' asked Edith.

'Nothing. I can't do it unless I hear you sing.'

Edith got out of her bed and sang her old songs and her new ones. Théo was delighted, he had never seen her like that.

'Well, Michel, is that what you wanted?'

'Yes. You've recharged my batteries.'

And the next day he brought Edith 'A quoi ça sert l'amour?'

A quoi ça sert l'amour?

L'amour ne s'explique pas
C'est une chose comme ça
Qui vient on ne sait d'où
Et vous prend tout à coup

A quoi ça sert d'aimer?

On 26 July 1962, Théo asked Edith, 'Will you be my wife?' He did not make any fuss about it, he asked her directly and gently as if he were afraid of frightening her.

'Oh, Théo, it's impossible.'

'Why?'

'I've led such a full life; my past weighs heavily on me. And I'm much older than you.'

'As far as I'm concerned you were born on the day I met you.'

'But what about your parents? I'm hardly the girl they'd have had in mind for you.'

'We'll find out tomorrow, they're expecting us for dinner.'

'We can't, I'm much too scared.'

She could not sleep that night.

Yves was the only man who had ever introduced her to his parents and they weren't engaged, she wasn't his prospective bride. 'Do you remember,' she said to me, 'how we used to read in our cheap little novels, "He introduced her to his parents"? And we thought that was great, it was important, it was the beginning of marriage. I don't deserve this kind of happiness, it's too beautiful.'

So she tossed and turned in her bed while Théo slept at the other end of the apartment. Since Edith had become ill, she, who had always loved sharing her bed, who was insulted if a man refused to sleep with her, could herself no longer stand it.

Her bedside lamp was on. She could not sleep. She was almost tranquil. She loved the blue walls in her room, they kept her calm. She started to daydream gently about all sorts of things ...

In the light of the lamp she saw her hands resting on the sheet. She thought about how they would look on the following evening. Were these the hands that Sacha Guitry had taken a cast of, to keep in the window of his office beside Jean Cocteau's? The hands about which so many poetic phrases had flowed. They had been called flowers, birds, delicate things with wings, things which could fly away. Did these two withered stumps with their twisted tendons and knotted veins belong to her? She could no longer open them to make the most simple movements necessary to live, to eat and drink. She needed other hands, living hands to help her. 'I'm responsible for these hands,' she thought. 'I should have foreseen today.'

As if a sparrow could foresee anything.

It was impossible, she had no right to do it. What would she look like sitting beside Théo in the middle of his family? ... an invalid! It was one of the worst nights of Edith's life. But she couldn't send him away.

She cried, 'Oh God, leave me a little longer with my love.' '*Mon Dieu, laissez-le-moi encore un peu, mon amoureux ...*'

When Théo came in the morning she did not say a word. She put on her make-up and he did her hair. She put on her blue silk dress. She always wore blue for anything she really cared about, it brought her luck.

That day Edith was not late. She got into her white Mercedes with Théo, and let herself be driven to her fate. She no longer wanted to fight, she would wait and see. Things always worked out in the end, and she always paid for them, sometimes in advance.

She was cold in her old mink coat. One hand was in Théo's, and in the other she held her good luck charm, a rabbit's foot. That was Edith – one hand being held by a virile young man, an old beat-up mink, and a furry good luck charm.

At la Frette, in the suburbs of Paris, the hairdressers had shut up early that day. Dressed up in their best clothes, *papa* and *maman* Lambouskas and Théo's two sisters, Cathy and Christine, sat waiting in their living-room, waiting for Edith Piaf, the fiancée of the son of the house.

It would not have been possible with anyone else, but Edith's lost little girl's eyes made everything possible. They liked her at once, and hugged her warmly. This Madame Piaf was so unaffected. And she was drawn to them.

The meal that she had thought would be a nightmare went off very well. By the time the dessert came everyone was laughing, and Edith discovered what it felt like to be part of a family, sitting round a table under a chandelier. She was going to have a father-in-law and a mother-in-law. Laughing, she said, 'I'll certainly be a strange daughter-in-law – and it's the first time I've called any woman Mother.' She would have two sisters-in-law, too.

'Momone, my heart was jumping all over the place with happiness, it was making so much noise I couldn't hear anything else.'

Once more, but without the family, just with Loulou, Edith celebrated her official engagement at Saint-Jean-Cap-Ferrat, where she had come to rest up before the Olympia '62 performance in September. The wedding date was set for 9 October.

Boulevard Lannes had become a whirlwind of work, though Edith moved less quickly than before. She slaved away with Théo, correcting everything, his voice, his intonation, his movements. She put her stamp on him, as a great couturier does on a dress, in the search for perfection.

Edith's last gala performance was her greatest. On 25 September 1962, two days before Olympia, she sang from the top of the Eiffel Tower for the premiere of the film *The Longest Day*.

There was a dinner in the gardens of the palais de Chaillot, and present were General Eisenhower, Winston Churchill, Lord Montgomery, Lord Louis Mountbatten, Bradley, the Shah and Begum of Iran, the King of Morocco, the Prince and Princess of Liège, Don Juan of Spain, Queen Sophia of Greece, Prince Rainier of Monaco, Elizabeth Taylor, Sophia Loren, Ava Gardner, Robert Wagner, Paul Anka, Audrey Hepburn, Mel Ferrer, Kurt Jurgens, Richard Burton, and more than two thousand seven hundred spectators, who had paid between thirty and three hundred and fifty francs each.

For them, Edith Piaf, her shadow projected on to a gigantic screen, sang with Théo Sarapo 'Non, je ne regrette rien', 'La Foule', 'Milord', 'Toi tu n'entends pas', 'Le Droit d'aimer', 'Emporte-moi', 'A quoi ça sert l'amour?'

But I who had paid nothing, who had not so much as put on an evening dress, I will never forget that evening. From my kitchen window I saw the Eiffel Tower – that kitchen had always been one of Edith's and my special places – I opened the window to the sky, the night like no other, and I heard Edith's voice soaring over Paris.

It was fine, and frightening like all things that are too big for you to handle.

On the first night of Olympia '62, once more all the smart Parisians, the show-business types, and the others were in their place. They were sharpening their teeth and their claws and their tongues, they had come to see Edith display her latest catch and future husband, Théo Sarapo, without a safety net.

When she came on stage, the auditorium went mad. I heard thousands call bravo, whistle, and shout. And then to a man the whole audience burst out, 'Hip, hip, hurrah, for Edith.' It was like a storm sweeping everything before it, and curling up docilely at her feet. This audience whom she loved so much, whom she respected, proclaimed their love for her before she had been able to give them anything. For a minute and a half she could not start. Then with a single movement of her little hand she quietened them, dominating their passion. The orchestra started to play the first song, and a church-like silence reigned in the theatre. Everyone took to his heart each word, each movement. And during the whole concert, after each song, the ovation started up again. It was their way of saying thank you.

Once more the Piaf miracle had taken place. When she sang 'A quoi ça sert l'amour?' in duet with Théo, the audience accepted their marriage, and the cheers gave them their triumph.

Edith had won.

The miracle was also that Edith was able to open her hands on stage; she planted them on her black dress in her familiar, old gesture, the one she had picked up that first evening at Leplée's because she was scared and did not know what to do with them.

That evening, as they left the Olympia in the white Mercedes, Edith clinging to Théo's arm, she was happy. 'You see, Théo, we made it.'

Théo felt that it was her victory, they looked on him as part of the bargain. He thought that it was really expecting too much of a newcomer to go straight from rehearsals at boulevard Lannes to Olympia. He understood that without her he was nothing, he had no career.

The car stopped in front of the Hôtel Georges V. It was Edith's idea.

'You see, Momone, I'm getting married. I don't want to go back to that apartment each evening. There are too many memories there. I've been through too much there. I've been beaten there too often. When I'm married it won't be the same.'

Singing every evening was killing her, but she did not want to admit it.

On the night of 4 October, Edith was racked with terrible pains in her wrists, ankles, and legs. She stuffed the sheet into her mouth to stop herself crying out loud, but she did not want to say anything to Théo. She went to see her doctor and begged him, 'Doctor, I'm getting married on the 9th, I must keep going till then.'

In two days the cortisone had got to the root of the trouble. But that was not the end of it. She caught cold, she ran a temperature of a hundred and three, she couldn't breathe. But she went on singing, just the same, and on 9 October Edith married Théo at the town hall of the sixteenth arrondissement.

'It was funny, listening to the mayor droning on. Here I was, the kid from Belleville-Ménilmontant, getting married in the poshest neighbourhood in Paris. All the same, when Théo said, "I do," and I did too, it sent shivers down my spine. I was so happy.'

For the second time in her life Edith heard the sound of wedding bells. The ceremony took place in her husband's Greek Orthodox church. In the middle of all the gold leaf and the chanting choir her 'I do' rang out even louder than it had in New York. She was happier than she had ever been.

She should have been able to slow down now, as she left the church on her husband's arm. But life had never been that easy on Edith. 'What sort of a bill must I be running up?' she asked me. 'I'd rather pay for it right now, so that when I finally start climbing that ladder to heaven I won't have any debts. I don't want them presenting me with any unpaid bills.'

That evening she sang with her husband at the Olympia. The audience was ecstatic. They cheered Théo. They wanted to know if at last she was going to be happy.

Then she went home, and a surprise awaited her – Théo had furnished all the empty rooms. The house was warm, no longer makeshift. Théo was delighted, 'You see, it isn't *your* house any more, it's a new home, *our* home.'

Théo made her happier than she would have believed possible. I always felt he was decent and kind, and that he loved Edith as no one had done before. He could expect nothing from her but sorrow and debts. Before their marriage the doctors had warned Théo. He knew the truth; he knew that Edith was finished. And he married her all the same. It was the greatest proof of his love. His feeling for Edith was very powerful, much more than physical love. Thanks to him she was able to believe right up until the end that she was a desirable woman, when she was no more than a poor scarecrow whose body was twisted with pain. Up until the final moment, he gave her the one thing she had lived for, and that was love.

At the end of January 1963, Edith thought that she was back in good health. She began to live as passionately as before, but she was using up her last reserves without realizing it. Sheer will-power kept her head above water now. We were all nervous, we knew that she could be carried away by the next strong wave, that we were helping her towards her shipwreck, without being able to offer her a lifebelt. She lived that month as she had always lived – with passion. At one and the same time she was getting ready for a show in Brussels at the Ancienne Belgique, preparing for her return to Bobino, and preparing a tour of Germany. She was confident of success.

Michel Emer and René Rouzaud had written her a very lovely song, 'J'en ai tant vu, tant vu':

> J'en ai trop cru, trop cru, trop cru,
> Des boniments de coins de rues,
> On m'en a tant dit, j'en ai tant entendu
> Des 'J' t'adore', des 'Pour la vie!'
> Tout ça pour quoi? Tout ça pour qui?
> Je croyais que j'avais tout vu,
> Tout fait, tout dit, tout entendu,
> Et je m'disais: 'On n'm'aura plus'!
>
> C'est alors qu'il est venu!

Francis Lai, Michèle Vendôme, and Florence Véran, all young people of twenty to twenty-five, wrote three songs for her, all at the same time: 'Les Gens', 'L'Homme de Berlin', and 'Margot coeur gros'.

'You see, Momone, however much the young people may like you and write for you, you're still ill, it doesn't change anything.'

At the Ancienne Belgique Edith sang 'Margot coeur gros' for the first time:

Pour fair' pleurer Margot
Margot coeur tendr',
Margot coeur gros,
Il suffit d'un refrain
Air de guitar',
Pleur d'Arlequin!

It was so well received that that night before going to sleep she telephoned Michèle Vendôme, 'Your song went off very well, I'm very happy for you. Come and see me in Brussels.'

In February 1963 Edith did a show with Théo at Bobino. Once again she watched the red curtain going up on her, she felt the stage lights warming her skin, she breathed in the warm smell of her audience, and heard their cheers. The two songs by Francis Lai and Michèle Vendôme had their début here, 'Les Gens':

Comme ils baissaient les yeux, les gens,
Quand tous deux, on s'est enlacé,
Quand on s'est embrassé
En se disant 'Je t'aime . . .'

and 'L'Homme de Berlin':

Je m'voyais déjà l'aimer pour la vie,
J'recommençais tout, j'étais avec lui,
Lui l'homme de Berlin!
Ne me parlez pas de hasard,
De ciel, ni de fatalité,
De prochains retours, ni d'espoir,
De destin, ni d'éternité . . .
Sous le ciel crasseux qui pleurait d'ennui,
Sous la petite pluie qui tombait sur lui,
Lui, l'homme de Berlin!
J' l'ai pris pour l'amour, c'était un passant,
Une éternité de quelques instants
Lui, l'homme de Berlin!

On 18 March 1963, at the Opera House in Lille, Edith sang on stage for the last time in her life.

Despite a worrying relapse, she wanted to make a working tape of 'L'Homme de Berlin' at home to send to Germany to be translated. She would sing it in German during her tour.

Everyone was against it. Singing drained what little strength she had left. But no one could stop her. On 7 April, with Noël Commaret as accompanist, and Francis Lai, Edith sang 'L'Homme de Berlin'.

That recording was made into a record and released five years after her death. It is an extraordinarily moving document. The aura is all that is left of the Great Piaf. The voice is worn out, she gasps for breath after each word. The song is neither sung nor spoken, it seems to come from far off, it is heart-rending. No one but Edith could have done it.

She asked Michèle Vendôme to come over and listen to the tape. 'My poor Vendôme,' she said. 'I'm so sorry about your song; it deserved better than that.' Generosity and honesty in the face of death – that was Piaf too.

On 10 April an oedema of the lung was diagnosed. Edith was taken to the Ambroise-Paré clinic at Neuilly. For five days she was in a coma, and was for two weeks delirious; during that time Théo never left her side. He lived in Edith's room, though she no longer recognized him, he wiped the sweat off her forehead, he straightened out her hands when they clasped an imaginary microphone. In her delirium Edith thought she was on stage, she sang, as others groan, day and night. Then she came to her senses. The first thing she said to Théo was, 'You shouldn't have been made to go through all that.'

Once again Edith left the hospital. Théo had decided to take her to convalesce on the Côte d'Azur. As if she knew that she would never return to it, Edith clung to the boulevard Lannes.

I had not been living in Paris for the last two years, but in Beauchamps in the Oise *département*. Everything kept me apart from her. Our lives were parallel, but we rarely saw each other. Fortunately, there was always the telephone.

Before she left for the coast, Edith called me. 'I don't want to go away, Ménilmontant is my turf. I can rest up perfectly well here. And besides, I don't want to miss going back to America. My friends there are waiting for me. I'm singing for John Kennedy at the White House, I can't pass that up, I'm dying to meet him – he's so handsome.'

We talked on for a little while, then she said, 'When you feel better come and see me. In any case, when I get back – if I leave at all – I'd like you to come back and live with me.'

She let herself be persuaded by Théo, in the end, and he rented the villa Serano at Cap Ferrat for two months – at a cost of five million francs. It was a mistake. The sea air was too strong for Edith, it tired her, and her nerves and lungs could not take it. So Théo took her to the near-by mountains, to Gatounière at Mougins.

In June she went into another coma and in July she had a relapse. On 20 August she went into a third coma, and they took her to Méridien Clinic at Cannes. The doctors thought she was finished. For a week death sat quietly by her bed, waiting for her.

Théo still watched over her night and day. From the time he had met her he had never left her. Nothing disgusted him, nothing drove him from her. He took care of her as though she was his mother, his child, and his wife.

When she left the clinic, Théo took her to Plascassier, in the hills above Grasse.

And in September, this woman, who could hardly function at all, who had to be taken around in a wheelchair, listened once more to 'L'Homme de Berlin' and decided to work.

She was a shadow of the woman she had once been. She weighed seventy-three pounds, her face was swollen like a blow-fish. All that remained of her were her violet eyes and that special look, the look of the Little Sparrow.

Yet intellectually and spiritually she was as whole as ever. Her character had not changed – she was as impossible as she had always been. She turned her nose up at her diet, ignored her bedtime. Every evening she wanted to see a movie. Since she could no longer go to the cinema, Théo had bought her a projector when they were still at boulevard Lannes, now he brought it to Plascassier and each night he showed her a movie. Her laugh, the famous Piaf laugh, still broke out – it had not become harsh. She did not spare what remained of her life.

One thing gave me a terrific shock; fortunately, Edith never found out about it. On 5 September 1963, I read in the papers that Claude Figus was dead, aged twenty-nine.

Like a well-trained errand boy, Claude had gone ahead to open up the gates of death for his boss, the woman he had truly loved. The newspaper reports sickened me, 'He committed suicide. Two empty bottles of nembutal were found near the body in his hotel room. On several occasions Claude Figus had confessed a desire to take his own life, which had been nothing more than a succession of deceptions.'

Poor little Claude. Even now his last record was about to be released. It was one of his own compositions, 'Les Jupons'.

'. . . On Saturday morning he tore off the medal that always hung around his neck, and gave it to some friends, crying, "I don't need it any more . . ." '

That was the medallion that Edith had given him when he became what he himself laughingly called 'The half-arsed boss'. He hadn't the build to be anything else. But for a brief moment he had been happy, he had believed in it.

Beside this report was another, headed: 'In her retreat at Plascassier, Edith Piaf is unaware of the tragic end of her ex-secretary.

' "It is imperative that she is not told, we have kept it from her. She must be prepared for it gently." These were the words that met our reporter late yesterday afternoon at L'Enclos de la Rourre at Plascassier, where Edith Piaf has retired with her husband Théo Sarapo.'

The article ended with, 'We have asked for news of Edith Piaf's health. "She is making a slow recovery," her nurse told us, "She is convalescing." '

How much time was left? She was talking of the Olympia, of going to Germany and to the United States . . .

19

'I HAVE LIVED TWICE'

I shall never forget that day. It was a grey, miserable Wednesday. Paris looked badly washed. I was terribly depressed. The news of Edith was alarming, 'She can't come to the telephone.' 'Not much change.'

It was 9 October 1963, her wedding anniversary. 'I'll call her,' I thought. 'She'll be pleased' I asked for Plascassier and by a stroke of luck Edith answered the phone straightaway. I was so sure that someone else would answer that for a moment I didn't recognize her voice. Our conversation did not last long. I was so upset that I didn't really take it in, it was only later that it struck me. 'Momone, come and see me,' she had said.

'Sure, I'll come on Monday,' I replied.

She wasn't happy with that, she always wanted things to happen right away. She used to say, 'I've done too much hanging around in this damn life to be patient now.' Now her voice was clear but toneless, the old Piaf richness was gone. 'Monday's so late. Couldn't you come before? Isn't there anything you could do to come earlier?'

'No, Edith, I really can't possibly come before Monday.'

She did not make much of a fuss. She sounded resigned. A resigned Edith simply wasn't right, in fact it was all wrong. She sounded like a sad little girl. 'Okay, I'll see you Monday; don't forget.'

I rang off. My mind was far away, but I sensed that something was wrong, something that I had not caught on to. Then it came to me; Edith had called out to me, I had to go straightaway, there was not a second to lose.

I called the travel agency. I was broke, but that had never stopped either of us from doing something once we had made up our minds. I ordered a return ticket to Nice, borrowed thirty thousand francs from my grocer and rushed to Orly, still in slacks and with no luggage but my purse.

Sitting in the plane I felt that we were not going anywhere, we were suspended in the sky. Up until the very moment when I saw Edith I felt as if there were two me's. One Simone sat back watching a movie in which the other Simone was starring, but the second Simone did not see anything at all.

It was unexpectedly cold at the Nice airport. My senses were numbed by the icy wind. Standing in the middle of the hall, all alone with the mirrors and chrome, I started to tremble.

There were very few people there – I had taken the last flight – and they looked like waxworks in the neon lights. It gave me the creeps.

I wanted to talk to someone. Edith and I had a lot of memories of this part of the world; I knew all those little lights winking in the baie des Anges. I started to reminisce. My head was so full of old images I thought it would explode, and my throat grew tighter and tighter. Our beautiful years spread out beyond the anonymous windows of the limousine.

From Nice I took a taxi to Grasse. There was no question of waiting until the next day or taking buses. Edith had said, 'Come,' and now I understood, I knew that I couldn't lose a second.

Grasse was easily reached, but no one had any idea where Plascassier was. Worse luck, the taxi-driver was no jolly Niçois, but a dumb old man who didn't know the district. That, however, didn't stop him from taking me out of my way. Finally he stopped in a village. Everything was deserted except a sort of little bistro-cum-grocer. Curtly he said, 'Go and ask them, they have a light on.'

The owner was a fat, chatty woman. 'Edith Piaf's house? But my dear lady, she won't want to see you at this time of night. She's very ill. We know her well, we deliver everything to Monsieur Théo. To tell you the truth, I don't think the poor dear will last much longer. You won't be able to see her, though, not even tomorrow; she doesn't see journalists any more.'

Then I exploded, 'I'm her sister!' It did me good to shout.

'Oh well, then. There's no need to get upset, you wouldn't

know it by looking at you. Except, yes, if you look closely there is a family resemblance. I'll call my husband, he'll go with you.'

We set off again. Her husband was very angry at being imposed upon; he spoke only to the driver, and that was to tell him to go faster.

'You can't miss Plascassier. It's in the Enclos de la Rourre park, on a sort of plateau.'

It got colder and colder, the wind was bitter. Everything looked the same in the headlights. I thought, 'We're lost.' When he'd had enough the husband told the driver, 'It's there, up that road.'

The other protested, 'I can't take the car up that road. The house is down there, you can't miss it.'

I paid him and they took off. Naturally, they were both wrong. I was knee-deep in slush. It had been raining, the moon splashed in the water, and I splashed in the puddles. I could not go on. But I was pressing on mechanically. I did not know where the end was, but I knew I had to get there. Finally I saw a derelict house, at least it looked derelict. There was a light at a window. I drew near and looked in.

It was like a scene in a movie. I saw a kitchen, I could almost feel the warmth, the cooking smells mingling together. The Bonels sat at the table. I knew them well, they had worked for Edith for more than ten years. Danièle had been a sort of secretary/Girl-Friday, the usual arrangement with Edith; Marc was her accordionist and he helped his wife out with little jobs. We had never been madly attached to each other. I had always found them, not exactly evil, but a little grasping, and they found me a nuisance. All the same, in their own way they were devoted to Edith. It was just that we did not show it in the same manner.

I knocked on the window pane. They lifted their heads, and then she signalled to her husband to open the window. He took his time about it. He said, 'What are you doing there?'

'I've come to see Edith.'

He opened the door. They were in the middle of preparing a rabbit. I hadn't eaten, but it must have been their dinner.

'We must inform Monsieur Théo,' they said formally.

Théo was with Edith.

When I saw him, framed by the door, I smiled at him quite naturally, although it had been hours since I'd smiled at anything. He looked different, almost a tiny bit like Edith; I could feel it. He was dressed all in black with a turtle-neck pullover, like a photograph against the white wall. He had beautiful, expressive hands, the kind Edith loved, and the medallion around his neck, the watch around his wrist, the wedding ring on his finger.

Edith once said to me, 'If a man has really elegant hands, he can't be ugly inside. Hands don't lie like faces. Especially when they speak.'

'You're Simone; you're her sister?'

And he smiled too, a welcoming, slightly shy smile like my own. It did us both good.

Even if she had not talked about him to me, I would have understood everything, why and how she loved him. He was like a lithe tomcat, his hands, his smile, everything said he was one of Edith's men, and above all that he was good, honest, and sincere. 'I don't think you can see Edith now, she's going to sleep.'

Behind him stood a woman in white – Simone Margantin, the nurse. She seemed neither friendly nor unfriendly. She looked smooth and a bit dry, but Edith was very fond of her, and she had been very dedicated and efficient. During Edith's last coma, Simone had been a great help to the doctors. And Théo trusted her.

She said, 'Edith's been much better today, but she needs to sleep now. I don't think you can see her, I'm going to give her her injection, you'll have to come back tomorrow.'

I could understand her, she was protecting her patient. It was difficult to get Edith off to sleep. But I had come to see her, and see her I would. I am neither tall nor imposing, but at that moment I felt as if I filled the room. She wanted me to leave. How? On foot?

Sweetly I said, 'I sent the taxi away. Perhaps you have a tent. I could camp under Edith's window. I wouldn't disturb her.'

Then, even more sweetly, I added, 'And perhaps you don't know that Edith called me this morning and asked me to come.'

Then Théo put in, in his calm way, as if he were saying, 'Perhaps you've forgotten, but I'm her husband,' 'If Edith wanted to see you, Simone, I'll go up and tell her that you're here.'

There was a silence, and la Bonel stirred her rabbit stew.

When he came back downstairs Théo's face was filled with joy. 'Go straight up, she's waiting for you.'

They were all amazed. There was no reason to be; I was not in the least bit surprised. The only difficulty had been to find a way of letting Edith know that I was there.

I no longer remember what the stairs looked like. But I looked at that door, and at Théo's hand on my wrist holding me back: there was something he wanted to tell me. In a very low voice he asked me, 'You haven't seen her for several months, have you?'

'Not since a while before your marriage. I was sick, but we've kept in touch over the telephone.'

'She's changed a lot, Simone; don't let her see it in your face.'

When he pushed open the door, I understood. She was almost bald; her face was too round, and dominated by two enormous, hungry eyes and a pinched mouth.

I smiled at her – at least, I tried to smile as I used to do during our life together when she used to say to me, 'You're a brave one, you're a little soldier.'

'Oh, Momone, I'm so happy to see you. I wasn't expecting you until Monday.'

'I have something else to do on Monday,' I pretended jauntily, 'so I came earlier.'

'I'm glad.'

Théo went out, tactful as well as everything else.

'What do you think of him? Isn't he great?'

'He's better than that, Edith.'

Was that why she had wanted me to come? Because I had known all the rest of them, and she wanted to know what I thought of this one?

'You do understand me, don't you?'

'Oh yes.'

'I've changed, haven't I? No, no, don't pretend; it's not worth it any more. It's hard, being a rag doll in someone else's hands, even the kindest hands in the world. The days and nights are long, I have time to think. I've done nothing but dumb things, all my life. I spoilt a lot of good things, including my loves and my health. I didn't deserve Théo, but I got him all the same; so I think I've been forgiven, don't you, Momone?'

It was awful, I had tears in my eyes, but thank heaven she changed the subject. She smiled at me, she was happy. I was the only person she could talk to about her youth, about our father, about her little daughter, about little Louis. I was her witness.

'Do you remember...?' Suddenly she no longer looked like a sad, sick person. She came alive. She was no longer a living corpse, compelled by the beating of her heart to stay alive. She became Edith Piaf again, as she used to be. Propped up almost to a sitting position by her pillows, her cheeks pink, her eyes glowing, she laughed again.

Only her poor crippled hands, endlessly gripping and raking the sheets, insisted that she was in the last stages of her life. I couldn't look at them.

'Having you here is so good for me. You know, my nurse has the same name as you. When I call her, sometimes I believe that you're still with me, and that you'll come instead.'

'In two seconds,' I thought to myself, 'she'll be blaming me as usual for leaving her in the lurch.'

'I know this isn't the moment to mention it – but I always wondered why you left me.'

I couldn't stop myself laughing, and Edith joined in. It was so good to hear her laugh. But it was no longer the old booming laugh, it had been cut down to size, it was pale and a little cracked.

'No more than ten minutes,' the nurse had said. They were already well past when Théo came back. He looked at Edith and then at me, and his happiness did me good.

'It's a long time since I've seen Edith like this.'

He looked at us, trying to understand what there was between us. 'May I stay a while?' he asked.

'Of course,' Edith said. 'You'd never get in the way, and if you do we'll go into the bathroom – won't we?'

'But, Edith, you can't get up,' he protested, uncomprehending.

Edith laughed. 'You can't understand. Momone, you explain to him. Tell him about our life.'

Like a faithful dog he stretched out at the foot of the bed, and that is how I shall always think of him – as a faithful dog, with living eyes which would not face up to the reality that I had sensed straightaway. This was the end. The curtain was about to come down. He was so used to her miraculous recoveries that he could not see the truth. But it had come right out and hit me immediately. Edith could stay up all night if that was what she wanted to do – it was no longer very important.

At breakneck speed she and I relived our forgotten hours. Our childhood and youthful memories were unpacked shamelessly before Théo; we had no time to censor them. We told the truth. We were the only ones who could unravel this thread, he could not follow it. Everything was there, spinning like Pigalle fair.

'Do you remember the sailors?' she said to me. 'Our pimps, the legionnaire, little Louis, Papa Leplée . . .?'

'Do you remember? . . .' That is how all our sentences began. But that night my Edith was completely honest. It no longer embarrassed her to say to me, 'I lied to you about that day,' or 'I shouldn't have done that.' She saw her life so clearly that it frightened me.

The inside of my head was like a whirlpool. The past and present were all mixed up, and my eyes never left Edith's; and in place of her invalid's face, I saw – and so, perhaps, did Théo – the marvellous features of the Great Piaf returning.

She wanted to talk, she was all pink and wide awake; she said, 'I'll never forget tonight, my dears, I'll take it with me to Heaven.'

Listening to us, Théo discovered an Edith he had never met. I was struck by the fact that she was not talking at random about her childhood, the old days, and the present; that night Edith joined the beginning of her life to the end, one to the other, solidly, for always.

She wanted to explain to Théo what our youth together had been like. He dabbed eau-de-Cologne on her face, brushed her hair, washed her hands; but he couldn't straighten out her deformed, rheumatic fingers.

It was enough to make you weep when you thought of her hands as they had brought her songs to life under the spotlight. Above all I remembered that familiar stance, with her hands flat on her hips, pushed forward, almost encircling the waist of her black dress – the hands which seemed at once to caress and to beg forgiveness. Now she was struggling once again to find that gesture which she had repeated so many thousands upon thousands of times, her hands were seeking their proper place.

She let Théo do it for her. Bit by bit she became an invalid again. She looked up at him and in her eyes I saw reflected all the joy that he gave her.

She wanted to talk about show business, about her work, but she was getting weaker.

'You know, I've made up my mind now. I've decided to get better. I'm going to prepare for my next appearance at Olympia. I mean it.' Later on Théo, and everyone else in the household, confirmed that that day, for a few hours, it really seemed as if Edith was going to recover once again.

Did she have any idea of how sick she was? Was she sure that things would turn out all right? I think not. She wanted to believe it for a few more hours – but the way she had cried out to me, to her past, was a cry of finality.

The nurse gave her an injection. Edith wanted to go on talking, to go on reliving her life, but she was already getting confused.

With her old authority she announced, 'You'll sleep downstairs in the living-room. I'll see you tomorrow.'

Then she took my hand. Like a little sparrow's claw, her fingers closed over mine. The current between us flowed strongly and warmly. When she touched you, something happened. I would have done anything to keep that current alive. I did not know then that there was nothing left to keep.

She opened her eyes, already glassing over, and said to me in a very loud voice, almost a shout, 'I can die now; I've lived twice.'

She paused for a moment and then said, as strongly as before, 'Watch out, Momone; in life, you pay for the stupid things you do.'

I knew what she meant – only too well. I kissed her and said good-bye.

I understood. I did not want to believe, but I knew it was over.

I was right. Very early the next morning she went into a semi-coma from which she never emerged.

Théo said to me, 'I must leave you here, Momone. It was good. I'm glad you came, you did her a lot of good, but I can't leave her.' And he turned back towards his wife.

I went into the kitchen to join the Bonel family and company and the smell of rabbit stew. They had made coffee to keep themselves awake. They did not say, 'Are you thirsty? Would you like a glass of something?' or even, 'Rest there, your plane leaves at noon.' Danièle raised her head, peered at me through her glasses, and asked, 'Are you leaving?'

Edith had ordered me to sleep downstairs in the living-room. But her command had not filtered down to the kitchen. Yesterday she could have demanded anything and they would have said, 'Of course, Madame Edith. Yes, what a good idea. Night's day, if you say so.' But that morning, Edith was no longer the boss. They knew that I would not disturb Théo, and that I would not go back to her.

At last one of them spoke, 'The chauffeur'll drive you back to the airport.'

It must have been five in the morning when we got to the airport.

At that time of day an airport is empty of living beings. Finally I unearthed a helpful employee and I asked him, 'I'm supposed to take the noon plane to Paris, but is there an earlier one I can take?'

'I'll try to work something out,' he said. 'Come back around seven thirty and I'll have a seat for you.'

So I took a taxi back into Nice, and wandered around. Nice doesn't rise early, it stretches and yawns for a long time. It's not easy at that hour to find a café open where you can get a cup of coffee.

My throat was tight, I couldn't swallow a thing. No one, I thought, should have to go through what we had been through. I went to look at the Boîte à Vitesses, and our Hôtel Gioffredo, the passage Negrin . . .

I got back to the airport and took the plane, I was dead tired.

When I got home I went to bed, but I simply could not get to sleep. I twisted and turned under the covers, and all that past, all those images haunted me, crashing around in my head. I was swinging back and forth . . .

I must have dropped off in the end. Next morning the young boy from downstairs came up. He was full of some important news. He was so excited it was impossible to tell from his face whether it was good news or bad. Finally he burst out, 'Your sister's dead.'

I knew it, but I didn't want to believe it. He went and got a newspaper, and it was true. Edith was dead. She had fallen asleep and never woken up again. It was unbelievable. If I had not gone to Plascassier I would never have seen her again. But she had said to me, 'Monday will be too late,' and I had dropped everything and gone. If I had been petty, if I had stopped to think, I would have said, 'She's being unreasonable,' and I would have missed her last hours.

Edith was brought back to boulevard Lannes. She had always said, 'I want to die in Paris.' She made her last journey by ambulance. Théo had taken a big bunch of mimosa from her room in Plascassier and placed it on her breast. The mimosa is still at boulevard Lannes, perfectly preserved. It's been six years now, but it has not lost one ball or leaf, it has simply turned grey; there's no more sunshine inside.

No one knew that Edith had died in the Midi. It was more convenient that she died at boulevard Lannes, so that the final good-bye could be made in Paris. People she had never even shaken hands with came and went with bowed heads . . .

But the people of Paris were there too, clutching the railings in front of the house. They had begun their long watch. The women had their shopping bags over their arms, the men were wearing their working clothes, they had not hesitated to sit for an extra hour in the Metro after work to come and say good-bye. All day, and for a good part of the night, and early the next morning, all the nameless people she had loved so much filed by. The women left modest bunches of simple flowers, the only ones

Edith liked – she always gave away the big bouquets – the simple women, apologizing to the maid, 'Tell her husband I won't be able to come to the funeral tomorrow. This isn't much, but my heart's in it.'

These women, Edith's sisters, were concerned about her man, Théo Sarapo, who had collapsed in a corner of the beautiful apartment, sobbing like a child over this fragile woman whom he had loved for little more than a year. 'I didn't think it would happen,' he kept saying. 'She had made me believe in miracles.'

In Edith's room were her old slippers, the little woollen jacket that she wore in bed was on a chair, and the brand-new leather coat that Théo had just given her (she loved it, but she never had the chance to wear it). The closets were full of her old dresses, and the famous black dress hung there too, a little dead thing that no one dared to touch. Manuscripts and musical scores were piled up on the piano. If Edith's lifeless body had not been on the bed you would have expected her to burst in, shouting, 'What the hell are you all doing here with your long faces, you poor, sad things!'

Théo's mother and sisters had gathered round him: they were Edith's last family.

On 14 October 1963, Paris wept for Edith Piaf. Forty thousand people jostled around at the Père-Lachaise cemetery. Her funeral was as crazy as her life. It was a beautiful, hot day. The mourning black disappeared in a mass of colours. There were Foreign Legionnaires in uniform, soldiers who had never seen her, all of them in love with her. Eleven carloads of flowers followed her little body, lost in its big coffin with the rabbit's foot that she had taken to her engagement party.

Everyone who had been in her life was there; everyone who had loved her; everyone she had loved. But her men were not wearing their blue uniform, they were all in black.

The women of her people, old grandmothers in headscarves, cried for Edith. She, who had had no real mother, had thousands that day. Men of all ages cried; even an old sailor in blue, holding a red rose in his hand, was not ashamed to shed a few tears.

As the coffin made its way down the narrow path, the crowd hurled themselves towards it, and knocked down the barriers. A surge of people destroyed any semblance of order, clambering over the tombstones to get to the foot of the Gassion grave, in the 97th division, cross-section number three. Marlene Dietrich in mourning, a black silk scarf over her blonde hair, very pale under her make-up, turned towards the wave of people and said, 'How they must have loved her.'

The noise of the crowd was like a stormy sea. All of a sudden it stopped, and there was silence, the detachment of legionnaires stood smartly to attention, their pennant waving in the sunshine. Father Leclerc said the Lord's Prayer.

She, who had loved God all her life, who sang for Jesus, who prayed to Saint Peter and adored Saint Theresa, who so often sought refuge in the church, was not permitted a requiem mass, Rome having declared that 'she lived in a state of public sin'. But a bishop, Monseigneur Martin, and Father Thouvenin de Villaret, went out of their way to say prayers over her tomb.

She disappeared under the flowers, and the crowd continued to file by her all day.

The next day Jean Cocteau was also buried. He died the same day as Edith, just as he was preparing to read a eulogy to his great friend Edith Piaf over the radio.

On the evening of 14 October Théo wanted to be alone. He returned to the untidy apartment where the few remaining flowers reminded him of the cemetery. On a table was a piece of wood carved in the shape of a leaf, bearing Edith's motto, 'Love conquers all'.

The papers devoted their front pages to Edith, and for days and days they served up slices of her life. At the cemetery, dominating the wilted flowers on her tomb, was a huge bouquet of purple wild flowers bound with a tricolour ribbon, 'A leur môme Piaf. La Légion'. The Foreign Legion's last tribute.

When I got home from the cemetery I threw myself on my bed. I did not cry. I was beyond tears, beyond the pains I had known. I had not simply lost my sister, I had lost the whole life we had lived together. She had always made me promise not to leave her alone. When she said to me, 'I want to die young,' I had replied, 'What about me?'

'You'll come with me.'

To her it was logical, and finally I too believed it. Yet here I was and life went on and on. It would drive me mad.

I feel she is not dead but away on tour. She will come back one day and send for me.

Quietly, for myself alone, I played the record she had made of Michel Emer's poem:

Une chanson à trois temps,
Fut sa vie, et son cours.
C'est beaucoup de chagrins,
Et pourtant, c'est pas lourd.
Toi, passant qui t'arrête,
Fais pour elle une prière,
On a beau être grand,
On finira poussière.
Pour laisser derrière soi
Une chanson de toujours,
Car l'histoire, on l'oublie,
C'est un air qu'on retient,
Une chanson à trois temps,
Voilà qui est parisien ...

INDEX